WITHDRAWN

No longer the property of the
Boston Public Library.
Sale of this material benefits the Library.

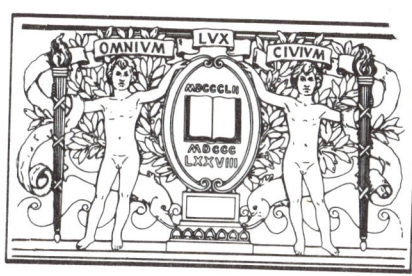

BOSTON PUBLIC LIBRARY

ISAAC BABEL

Modern Critical Views

Henry Adams
Edward Albee
A. R. Ammons
Matthew Arnold
John Ashbery
W. H. Auden
Jane Austen
James Baldwin
Charles Baudelaire
Samuel Beckett
Saul Bellow
The Bible
Elizabeth Bishop
William Blake
Jorge Luis Borges
Elizabeth Bowen
Bertolt Brecht
The Brontës
Robert Browning
Anthony Burgess
George Gordon, Lord
  Byron
Thomas Carlyle
Lewis Carroll
Willa Cather
Cervantes
Geoffrey Chaucer
Kate Chopin
Samuel Taylor Coleridge
Joseph Conrad
Contemporary Poets
Hart Crane
Stephen Crane
Dante
Charles Dickens
Emily Dickinson
John Donne & the Seven-
  teenth-Century Meta-
  physical Poets
Elizabethan Dramatists
Theodore Dreiser
John Dryden
George Eliot
T. S. Eliot
Ralph Ellison
Ralph Waldo Emerson
William Faulkner
Henry Fielding
F. Scott Fitzgerald
Gustave Flaubert
E. M. Forster
Sigmund Freud
Robert Frost

Robert Graves
Graham Greene
Thomas Hardy
Nathaniel Hawthorne
William Hazlitt
Seamus Heaney
Ernest Hemingway
Geoffrey Hill
Friedrich Hölderlin
Homer
Gerard Manley Hopkins
William Dean Howells
Zora Neale Hurston
Henry James
Samuel Johnson and
  James Boswell
Ben Jonson
James Joyce
Franz Kafka
John Keats
Rudyard Kipling
D. H. Lawrence
John Le Carré
Ursula K. Le Guin
Doris Lessing
Sinclair Lewis
Robert Lowell
Norman Mailer
Bernard Malamud
Thomas Mann
Christopher Marlowe
Carson McCullers
Herman Melville
James Merrill
Arthur Miller
John Milton
Eugenio Montale
Marianne Moore
Iris Murdoch
Vladimir Nabokov
Joyce Carol Oates
Sean O'Casey
Flannery O'Connor
Eugene O'Neill
George Orwell
Cynthia Ozick
Walter Pater
Walker Percy
Harold Pinter
Plato
Edgar Allan Poe
Poets of Sensibility & the
  Sublime

Alexander Pope
Katherine Ann Porter
Ezra Pound
Pre-Raphaelite Poets
Marcel Proust
Thomas Pynchon
Arthur Rimbaud
Theodore Roethke
Philip Roth
John Ruskin
J. D. Salinger
Gershom Scholem
William Shakespeare
  (3 vols.)
  Histories & Poems
  Comedies
  Tragedies
George Bernard Shaw
Mary Wollstonecraft
  Shelley
Percy Bysshe Shelley
Edmund Spenser
Gertrude Stein
John Steinbeck
Laurence Sterne
Wallace Stevens
Tom Stoppard
Jonathan Swift
Alfred, Lord Tennyson
William Makepeace
  Thackeray
Henry David Thoreau
Leo Tolstoi
Anthony Trollope
Mark Twain
John Updike
Gore Vidal
Virgil
Robert Penn Warren
Evelyn Waugh
Eudora Welty
Nathanael West
Edith Wharton
Walt Whitman
Oscar Wilde
Tennessee Williams
William Carlos Williams
Thomas Wolfe
Virginia Woolf
William Wordsworth
Richard Wright
William Butler Yeats

These and other titles in preparation

Modern Critical Views

ISAAC BABEL

Edited and with an introduction by
Harold Bloom
Sterling Professor of the Humanities
Yale University

CHELSEA HOUSE PUBLISHERS ◊ 1987
New York ◊ New Haven ◊ Philadelphia

© 1987 by Chelsea House Publishers,
a division of Chelsea House Educational Communications, Inc.,
  95 Madison Avenue, New York, NY 10016
  345 Whitney Avenue, New Haven, CT 06511
  5014 West Chester Pike, Edgemont, PA 19028

Introduction © 1987 by Harold Bloom

All rights reserved. No part of this publication may be reproduced or transmitted in any form or by any means without the written permission of the publisher.

Printed and bound in the United States of America

∞ The paper used in this publication meets the minimum requirements of the American National Standard for Permanence of Paper for Printed Library Materials, Z39.48-1984.

Library of Congress Cataloging-in-Publication Data

Isaac Babel.
  (Modern critical views)
  Bibliography: p.
  Includes index.
  Summary: Critical essays on the work of Isaak Babel, one of a group of poets and novelists whose works were part of a rebirth in Russian literature in the 1920s following the Communist Revolution.
  1. Babel', I. (Isaak), 1894–1941—Criticism and interpretation. [1. 1. Babel', I. (Isaak), 1894–1941—Criticism and interpretation. 2. Russian literature—History and criticism] I. Bloom, Harold. II. Series.
  PG3476.B2Z715 1987   891.73'42   87-661
  ISBN 1-55546-275-8 (alk. paper)

Contents

Editor's Note   vii

Introduction   1
  Harold Bloom

Isaac Babel: A Critical Romance   9
  Viktor Shklovsky

The Fate of Isaak Babel: A Child of the Russian Emancipation   15
  Raymond Rosenthal

The Forbidden Dialectic: Introduction to *The Collected Stories*   23
  Lionel Trilling

The Right to Write Badly   41
  Irving Howe

Isaak Babel in Retrospect   47
  Renato Poggioli

The Romanticism of Violence   57
  Frank O'Connor

The Wise Rabbi (Memoirs)   67
  Ilya Ehrenburg

Isaac Babel: Horror in a Minor Key   77
  Edward J. Brown

Isaac Babel   87
  Andrey Sinyavsky

Line and Color: The Structure of I. Babel's Short Stories in *Red Cavalry*   97
  Victor Terras

I Promise You Maupassant   113
    Konstantin Paustovsky

Red Cavalry: Art Renders Justice   123
    Patricia Carden

Babel the Dramatist   135
    Richard W. Hallet

The Odessa Tales: An Introduction   143
    James Falen

The Example of Isaac Babel   171
    Simon Markish

Yiddish Folklore Motifs in Isaak Babel''s *Konarmija*   191
    Maurice Friedberg

Fat Tuesday in Odessa: Isaac Babel's "Di Grasso"
as Testament and Manifesto   199
    Gregory Freidin

Midrash and History: A Key
to the Babelesque Imagination   215
    Efraim Sicher

Isaac Babel and Violence   231
    Peter Stine

Color and Line: Notes on the Art of Isaac Babel   249
    Victor Erlich

Chronology   257

Contributors   261

Bibliography   265

Acknowledgments   267

Index   269

Editor's Note

This book brings together the best criticism available in English on the work of Isaac Babel. The critical essays are reprinted in the chronological order of their original publication. I am grateful to Eden Quainton and Jane Sharp for their erudition and zeal as researchers.

My introduction contrasts the *Tales of Odessa* and their hero, the Jewish gangster Benya Krik, with the Cossack stories of *Red Cavalry* in order to take serious exception to Lionel Trilling's contention that Babel had any admiration for the Cossacks. My own sense of Babel as a Jewish writer is then exemplified by a reading of the fierce story, "The End of the Old Folk's Home."

The chronological sequence begins with Victor Shklovsky, who celebrates Babel's originality in a critical romance or dialectical prose lyric. Raymond Rosenthal also sees Babel as a celebrator of the lost hope of the marvelous. In the most famous essay on Babel, the great critic Lionel Trilling analyzes *Red Cavalry* in terms of Babel's fascination with Cossack vitality and violence, an analysis that I dispute in my introduction, since I believe that Trilling misreads some aspects of Babel's quite Jewish irony.

Irving Howe movingly finds in Babel the demand upon life for happiness, which is consonant with the retrospective overview of Renato Poggioli, who finds in Babel an overwhelming power to touch and move. The Irish short story writer Frank O'Connor, shrewdly apprehending Babel's sly humor, shows more distrust of Babel's overt appreciation of "the romance of violence" than Trilling did.

Ilya Ehrenburg, the Soviet Jewish writer most schooled in survival, offers his tributary memoir of Babel, as well as his later memorial speech in Babel's honor. Edward J. Brown's overview emphasizes the terrible pathos of Babel's life and work, perhaps to the exclusion of more salient qualities. The heroic Andrey Sinyavsky accurately praises Babel for his cognitive strength, a quality that helps account for Babel's extraordinary ingenuity at structuring his stories, which is analyzed by Victor Terras in his deeply informed essay.

Konstantin Paustovsky contributes a fascinating personal account of Babel, while Patricia Carden analyzes Babel's mastery of the grotesque in *Red Cavalry*. Babel's abortive career as a dramatist is sketched by R. W. Hallet, after which the *Tales of Odessa* are illuminated by James Falen's introduction to their background, an introduction that rightly emphasizes the element of fantasy in the stories. Simon Markish follows with an appreciation of the implicit stance of Jewish resistance in Babel's work.

Yiddish folklore, a deep if somewhat concealed motif in Babel, is investigated by Maurice Friedberg in the *Red Cavalry* stories. The great *Odessa* story, "Di Grasso," is read by Gregory Freidin as Babel's artistic manifesto and testament.

Efraim Sicher analyzes the ironic myths both of Babel's literary career and of his writings, after which Peter Stine gives us an exegesis of the artistic "violences" in Babel, so many of which have been weakly misread.

This book ends with a superb brief essay on Babel by the great scholar-critic of modern Russian literature, Victor Erlich, an essay that is published here for the first time. Erlich emphasizes Babel's extraordinary ability "to bring together incompatibles, to juxtapose contraries" at every level of his art. The aesthetic dignity of Babel's work receives its proper answering voice in Erlich's critical eloquence.

Introduction

I

> "If you need my life you may have it, but all make mistakes, God included. A terrible mistake has been made, Aunt Pesya. But wasn't it a mistake on the part of God to settle Jews in Russia, for them to be tormented worse than in Hell? How would it hurt if the Jews lived in Switzerland, where they would be surrounded by first-class lakes, mountain air, and nothing but Frenchies? All make mistakes, not God excepted."
> —"How It Was Done in Odessa"

Benya Krik, Babel's outrageously insouciant gangster boss of Jewish Odessa, utters this defense to the bereaved Aunt Pesya, whose wretched son has just been slain by one of Benya's hoods in an exuberant error. The Jewish presence in Russia, then and now, is one of God's exuberant errors, and is both the subject and the rhetorical stance of Babel's extraordinary art as a writer of short stories. Babel's precursors were Gogol and Guy de Maupassant (and Maupassant's literary "father," Flaubert) but repeated rereadings of Babel's best stories tend to show a very different and older tradition also at work. Babel's expressionist and economical art has unmistakably Jewish literary antecedents. The late Lionel Trilling undoubtedly was the most distinguished critic to write about Babel in English, but he underestimated the Jewish element in Babel, and perhaps introduced a perspective into Babel's stories that the stories themselves repudiate.

Babel was murdered in a Stalinist purge before he was forty-seven. His work is not officially forbidden in the Soviet Union, and he was legally cleared of all charges in 1956, fifteen years after his death. Yet there are few editions of his stories, and little Soviet criticism is devoted to them. Presumably Babel's erotic intensity does not please cultural bureaucrats, and so overtly Jewish a writer, in mode and in substance, is an uncomfortable shadow in a country where teaching Hebrew is currently a legal offence. Anyone who believes that Babel's world is wholly lost ought to wander some Friday evening through "Little Odessa," as Brighton Beach in Brooklyn is called these days. Benya Krik's descendents are alive and well, a little too well, in Little Odessa. Babel is the storyteller of Jewish Odessa, the city also of Vladimir Jabotinsky, founder of the Zionist Right, teacher and inspirer of Menachem Begin and the Irgun Zvai Leumi. The Odessa of Babel was a great center of Jewish literary culture, the city also of the Hebrew poet Bialik, and of the Yiddish writer Mendele Mocher Sforim. Like Bialik and Sforim, Babel writes out of the context of Yiddish-speaking Odessa, though Babel wrote in Russian.

Trilling ought to have had second thoughts about his characterization of Babel's self-representation in *Red Cavalry* as "a Jew riding as a Cossack and trying to come to terms with the Cossack ethos." Lyutov, Babel's surrogate, is trying to survive, but hardly at the cost of coming to terms with the Cossack ethos, terms that Tolstoy in one of his modes accepted. On the contrary, Babel's Cossacks are not Tolstoyan noble savages, but are precisely the Cossacks as the Jews saw them: subhuman and bestial, mindlessly violent. Trilling imported something of his own nostalgia for the primitive into Babel, with curious results:

> Babel's view of the Cossack was more consonant with that of Tolstoy than with the traditional view of his own people. For him the Cossack was indeed the noble savage, all too savage, not often noble, yet having in his savagery some quality that might raise strange questions in a Jewish mind.

But those questions certainly are not raised in Babel's mind, the mind of the Odessa Jew, with a perpetually glowing awareness of "how it was done in Odessa." That awareness informs his two very different ways of representing violence, ways that urgently need to be contrasted when we reflect on Babel's stories. This is one way:

> Then Benya took steps. They came in the night, nine of them, bearing long poles in their hands. The poles were wrapped about with pitch-dipped tow. Nine flaming stars flared in Eichbaum's cattle yard. Benya beat the locks from the door of the cowshed and began to lead the cows out one by one. Each was received by a lad with a knife. He would overturn the cow with one blow of the fist and plunge his knife into her heart. On the blood-flooded ground the torches bloomed like roses of fire. Shots rang out.

Introduction

> With these shots Benya scared away the dairymaids who had come hurrying to the cowshed. After him other bandits began firing in the air. (If you don't fire in the air you may kill someone.) And now, when the sixth cow had fallen, mooing her death-moo, at the feet of the King, into the courtyard in his underclothes galloped Eichbaum."
>
> ("The King")

> And meantime misfortune lurked beneath the window like a pauper at daybreak. Misfortune broke noisily into the office. And though on this occasion it bore the shape of the Jew Savka Butsis, this misfortune was as drunk as a water-carrier.
>
> "Ho-hoo-ho," cried the Jew Savka, "forgive me, Benya, I'm late." And he started stamping his feet and waving his arms about. Then he fired, and the bullet landed in Muginstein's belly.
>
> Are words necessary? A man was, and is no more. A harmless bachelor was living his life like a bird on a bough, and had to meet a nonsensical end. There came a Jew looking like a sailor and took a potshot not at some clay pipe or dolly but at a live man. Are words necessary?
>
> ("How It Was Done in Odessa")

This is the other way, the violence of the Cossack and not of the Odessa Jew:

> But I wasn't going to shoot him. I didn't owe him a shot anyway, so I only dragged him upstairs into the parlor. There in the parlor was Nadezhda Vasilyevna clean off her head, with a drawn saber in her hand, walking about and looking at herself in the glass. And when I dragged Nikitinsky into the parlor she ran and sat down in the armchair. She had a velvet crown on trimmed with feathers. She sat in the armchair very brisk and alert and saluted me with the saber. Then I stamped on my master Nikitinsky, trampled on him for an hour or maybe more. And in that time I got to know life through and through. With shooting—I'll put it this way—with shooting you only get rid of a chap. Shooting's letting him off, and too damn easy for yourself. With shooting you'll never get at the soul, to where it is in a fellow and how it shows itself. But I don't spare myself, and I've more than once trampled an enemy for over an hour. You see, I want to get to know what life really is, what life's like down our way.
>
> ("The Life and Adventures of Matthew Pavlichenko")

Notices were already posted up announcing that Divisional Commissar Vinogradov would lecture that evening on the second congress of the Comintern. Right under my window some Cossacks were trying to shoot an old silvery-bearded Jew for spying. The old man was uttering piercing screams and struggling to get away. Then Kudrya of the machine gun section took hold of his head and tucked it under his arm. The Jew stopped screaming and straddled his legs. Kudrya drew out his dagger with his right hand and carefully, without splashing himself, cut the old man's throat. Then he knocked at the closed window.

"Anyone who cares may come and fetch him," he said. "You're free to do so."

("Berestechko")

The first way is violence stylized as in a child's vision: "On the blood-flooded ground the torches bloomed like roses of fire," and "There came a Jew looking like a sailor and took a potshot." The second way is highly stylized also, but as in the vision of a historical Jewish irony: "With shooting you'll never get at the soul, to where it is in a fellow and how it shows itself," and "carefully, without splashing himself, cut the old man's throat." When Babel represents the violence of the Jewish gangs of the Moldavanka, he colors it as he renders Benya Krik's wardrobe: "He wore an orange suit, beneath his cuff gleamed a bracelet set with diamonds," and "aristocrats of the Moldavanka, they were tightly encased in raspberry waistcoats. Russet jackets clasped their shoulders, and on their fleshy feet the azure leather cracked." But Babel's representation of "the training of the famous Kniga, the headstrong Pavlichenko, and the captivating Savitsky," is quite another matter. The irony, ferociously subtle, is built up by nuances until the supposed nostalgia for the virtues of murderous barbarity becomes a kind of monstrous Jewish in-joke. General Budenny's fury, when he denounced *Red Cavalry* as a slander upon his Cossacks, was not wholly misplaced.

II

Whatever the phrase "a Jewish writer" may be taken to mean, any meaning assigned to it that excludes Babel will not be very interesting. Maurice Friedberg, the authority on Babel's relation to Yiddish folklore and literature, rather strangely remarks of him that: "A leftist, Russian, Jewish intellectual, particularly one strongly influenced by the adamant anti-clericalism of the French Left, could hardly be expected to return to the fold of organized religion." That Babel did not trust in the Covenant, in any strict sense, is palpably true, but the nuances of Jewish spirituality, at any time, are notoriously difficult to ascertain.

Babel's irony is so pervasive that sometimes it does threaten to turn into the irony of irony, and yet sometimes it barely masks Babel's true nostalgia, which is not exactly for the primitive. Gedali, Babel's "tiny, lonely visionary in a black top hat, carrying a big prayerbook under his arm," may be as ironic a figure as the "captivating" Savitsky, whose "long legs were like girls sheathed to the neck in shining riding boots," but the two ironies are as different as the two visions of violence, and can be conveyed again by a textual clash:

> We all of us seated ourselves side by side—possessed, liars, and idlers. In a corner, some broad-shouldered Jews who resembled fishermen and apostles were moaning over their prayerbooks. Gedali, in his green frock coat down to the ground, was dozing by the wall like a little bright bird. And suddenly I caught sight of a youth behind him, a youth with the face of Spinoza, with Spinoza's powerful brow and the wan face of a nun. He was smoking, shuddering like a recaptured prisoner brought back to his cell. The ragged Reb Mordecai crept up to him from behind, snatched the cigarette from his mouth, and ran away to me.
>
> "That's Elijah, the Rabbi's son," he declared hoarsely, bringing his bloodshot eyelids close to my face. "That's the cursed son, the last son, the unruly son."
>
> ("The Rabbi")

> His things were strewn about pell-mell—mandates of the propagandist and notebooks of the Jewish poet, the portraits of Lenin and Maimonides lay side by side, the knotted iron of Lenin's skull beside the dull silk of the portraits of Maimonides. A lock of woman's hair lay in a book, the Resolutions of the Party's Sixth Congress, and the margins of Communist leaflets were crowded with crooked lines of ancient Hebrew verse. They fell upon me in a mean and depressing rain—pages of the Song of Songs and revolver cartridges. The dreary rain of sunset washed the dust in my hair, and I said to the boy who was dying on a wretched mattress in the corner:
>
> "One Friday evening four months ago, Gedali the old-clothes-man took me to see your father, Rabbi Motale. But you didn't belong to the Party at that time, Bratslavsky."
>
> ("The Rabbi's Son")

And I don't mind telling you straight that I threw that female citizen down the railway embankment while the train was still going. But she, being big and broad, just sat there awhile, flapped her skirts, and started to go her vile way. And seeing that scatheless woman going along like that and Russia around her like I don't know what, and the peasant fields without an ear of corn and the outraged girls and the comrades lots of which go to the front but few return, I had a mind to jump out of the truck and put an end to my life or else put an end to hers. But the Cossacks took pity on me and said:

"Give it her with your rifle."

So I took my faithful rifle off the wall and washed away that stain from the face of the worker's land and the republic.

("Salt")

The pathos of Elijah the Rabbi's son is rendered bearable by a purely defensive irony, the irony of incommensurate juxtapositions, of Communist leaflets and the Hebrew Song of Songs. Irony in "Salt" dissolves all pathos, and defends Babel, not from his own affections and identifications, but from Cossack bestiality. It cannot be that Babel did not understand his own cultural affections. His first mode of irony is altogether biblical, and is neither the irony of saying one thing while meaning another, as in "Salt," nor the irony that contrasts expectation and fulfillment, for no expectations remain in "The Rabbi" and "The Rabbi's Son." Babel writes the irony of the Covenant, the incommensurateness of the Chooser and the chosen. That irony is no less Jewish than the allegory of "Salt," but its Jewishness is far more archaic.

III

The best of Babel's stories are neither in *Red Cavalry* nor in the *Tales of Odessa*, though those are my personal favorites. Babel's best work is in "The Story of My Dovecot," "First Love," "In the Basement," "Awakening," "Guy de Maupassant," "Di Grasso"—all tales of Odessa, but with the difference that they are tales of Babel himself, and not of Benya Krik. But if a single story has in it the center of Babel's achievement, it is the extraordinary, outrageous, and ultimately plangent "The End of the Old Folk's Home." Restraining himself from overtly celebrating the raffish inmates of the poorhouse by the Second Jewish Cemetery in Odessa, Babel nevertheless portrays this motley group of old men and women with a gusto and exuberance that make them the peers of Benya Krik the gangster. Gravediggers, cantors, washers of corpses, they live by their wits and unscrupulousness in hiring out their single oak coffin with a pall and silver tassels, recycling it through endless burials.

Alas, the Bolsheviks use the coffin to bury one Hersch Lugovoy with full military honors, pushing away the old men when they attempt to turn the coffin on its side so as to roll out the flag-draped corpse of the heroic and faithful Jewish Bolshevik. The rest of the story, an astonishing mixture of Dickensian pathos and Gogolian humor, portrays the doomed but still vital antics of the old folk in their final days before they are evicted from the poorhouse. With the expulsion itself, Babel achieves his finest conclusion:

> The tall horse bore him and the manager of the department of public welfare townwards. On their way they passed the old folk who had been evicted from the poorhouse. Limping, bowed beneath their bundles, they plodded along in silence. Bluff Red Army men were keeping them in line. The little carts of paralytics squeaked; the whistle of asthma, a humble gurgling issued from the breasts of retired cantors, jesters at weddings, cooks at circumcisions, and ancient shop-assistants.
>
> The sun stood high in the sky, and its rays scorched the rags trailing along the road. Their path lay along a cheerless, parched and stony highway, past huts of rammed clay, past stone-cluttered fields, past houses torn open by shells, past the Plague Mound. An unspeakably sorrowful road once led from the cemetery to Odessa.
>
> ("The End of the Old Folk's Home")

The troping of "road" for the unspeakably sorrowful procession itself is characteristic of Babel. As for the squeaking, whistling, and "humble gurgling," it is the funeral music by which Babel implicitly laments the loss of a desperate vitalism in the old folk, roisterers who in a sense are coffin-robbers, but never grave-robbers. These aged scamps are Babel's heroes and heroines, even as the Bolshevik bureaucrats and brutal Cossacks are not. Presumably Babel was another victim of Stalin's virulent anti-Semitism, but his best stories transcend his victimization. They give nothing away to the anti-Semites, nothing away even to Stalin himself. We hear in them finally a voice masterly in its ironies, yes, but also a voice of comic celebration eternally commemorating "the image of the stout and jovial Jews of the South, bubbling like cheap wine." Benya Krik's heroic funeral for the poor clerk killed by mistake is a superb exemplification of Babel's art at its most joyous:

And the funeral was performed the next morning. Ask the cemetery beggars about that funeral. Ask the shamessim from the synagogue of the dealers in kosher poultry about it, or the old women from the Second Almshouse. Odessa had never before seen such a funeral, the world will never see such a funeral. On that day the cops wore cotton gloves. In the synagogues, decked with greenstuff and wide open, the electric lights were burning. Black plumes swayed on the white horses harnessed to the hearse. A choir of sixty headed the cortege: a choir of boys, but they sang with the voice of women. The Elders of the synagogue of the dealers in kosher poultry helped Aunt Pesya along. Behind the elders walked members of the Association of Jewish Shop Assistants, and behind the Jewish Shop Assistants walked the lawyers, doctors of medicine, and certified midwives. On one side of Aunt Pesya were the women who trade in poultry on the Old Market, and on the other side, draped in orange shawls, were the honorary dairymaids from Bugayevka. They stamped their feet like gendarmes parading on a holiday. From their wide hips wafted the odors of the sea and of milk. And behind them all plodded Ruvim Tartakovsky's employees. There were a hundred of them, or two hundred, or two thousand. They wore black frock coats with silk lapels and new shoes that squeaked like sacked suckling-pigs.

("How It Was Done in Odessa")

Those orange-shawled "honorary dairymaids," stamping their feet like gendarmes on parade while "from their wide hips wafted the odors of the sea and of milk," are Babel's true Muses. The entire paragraph becomes a phantasmagoria, a visionary evocation of a Jewish child's delight in the muscular exuberance of the Odessa mob. Babel's pragmatic sorrow was in his political context. His joy, fantastic and infectious, was in his nostalgia for his own childhood, and for the archaic and celebratory force of the Jewish tradition that claimed him, after all, for its own.

VIKTOR SHKLOVSKY

Isaac Babel: A Critical Romance

I find myself somehow reluctant to take a close look at Babel. An author's success must be respected, and the reader should be given the opportunity to learn to like a writer before trying to figure out the reasons for his success.

I'm ashamed to take a close look at Babel. His story "The Rabbi's Son" (*Syn rabbi*) contains this passage: "The girls, planting their unpretentious bandy doe legs on the floor, stared coldly at his sexual organs, that stunted, tender, curly-haired masculinity of a wasted Semite."

So for my article on Babel I have chosen the method of lyrical distancing. Once there was old Russia, enormous, like a mountain spread wide with furrowed slopes.

Some people wrote upon her with pencils, "This mountain will be saved."

That was before the Revolution.

Some of those who had written on the mountain in pencil worked on Gorky's *Chronicle*. Gorky had just arrived. He was stooped, discontented, sick, and he wrote the article "Two Souls." A highly erroneous article.

A story by Babel appeared in one issue. It concerned two young girls who tried unsuccessfully to perform an abortion. Their father held the post of prosecutor in Kamchatka. Everyone noticed that story and remembered it. Then I met Babel himself. Average height, high forehead, huge head, a face unlike a writer's, quiet dress, entertaining conversation.

Came the Revolution, and the mountain was cleared away. There were

From *Major Soviet Writers: Essays in Criticism*, edited by Edward J. Brown. © 1973 by Oxford University Press. This essay was translated by John Pearson.

some who still ran after it with pencils in their hands. There was nothing left for them to write on.

Just then Sukhanov started to write. Seven volumes of reminiscences. They say he wrote them before the events happened, since he foresaw everything.

I arrived from the front. It was autumn. Gorky's *Novaya Zhizn* was still being published.

In it Babel wrote some comments under the heading "The New Day." He was the only one who maintained his stylistic sangfroid throughout the Revolution.

Babel's sketches dealt with such things as how plowing is done today. It was then I became better acquainted with him. He turned out to be an imperturbable man with a concerned voice, and a lover of fine feeling.

For him fine feeling was as necessary as a country house (*dacha*).

I met Babel for the third time in Petersburg in 1919. Petersburg was covered with snow in winter, as if the city itself stood snowbound in the middle of a road, only it was something like a latticed snow fence along a railroad track. In summer Petersburg was covered by a deep blue sky. There was no smoke from the chimneys, and the sun hung over the horizon; no one interfered with it. Petersburg was empty—its inhabitants were at the front. Among the cobblestones on the streets the grass in little shoots of green flame struggled up towards the sun.

Side streets were already grassed over.

In front of the Hermitage, on the wooden pavement which was resonant right at that place, children played at skittles with torn up blocks. The city was beginning to be grown over, like an abandoned military camp.

Babel lived on 25th of October Street, No. 86.

He lived alone in his furnished apartment; his visitors came and went. Maidservants saw to his needs, cleaned the rooms, emptied the buckets with bits of unfinished food floating in them.

Babel lived, contemplating at leisure the city's hungry lechery. His room was clean. He would tell me that "nowadays" women could be had only before six since the streetcars stopped running after that.

He had no feeling of alienation from life. But I had the impression that when he went to bed, Babel would sign his name to each completed day as though it were a story. The tools of the man's trade had left their mark on him.

A samovar inevitably graced Babel's table, and even sometimes bread. And that was a rarity in those days.

He was always a warm and willing host. A certain retired chemist used to visit him, a Tolstoyan and also a teller of incredible anecdotes. He was the man who, having publicly insulted the duke of Baden, appeared at his own trial in Petersburg to testify against himself. (However he was pronounced insane and punished only by having his laboratory confiscated.) He was a bad poet and an indifferent critic, that most unlikely man, Peter Storytsin. And Babel valued Storytsin.

Kondrat Yakovlev visited him, a few others, I myself, and some veterans from Odessa who were always ready to tell a tale, along with other assorted Odessites, who told all the stories that were written in them.

Babel wrote little, but steadily. It was always the same story—about two Chinamen in a brothel.

He loved that story as he loved Storytsin. The Chinamen and the women kept changing. They grew young, aged, broke windows, beat up a woman, organized this or that.

A good many stories resulted from all this, and not just one. Though he had not really finished with his Chinamen, Babel went away one sunny autumn day, leaving me his grey sweater and leather satchel. . . . There was no word at all from Babel; it was as though he'd gone to Kamchatka to talk to the prosecutor about his daughters.

Once a visiting Odessite, after having spent all night losing at cards in a well-known house, and having borrowed enough the next morning to cover his loss, offered me as a sign of gratitude the information that Babel was either translating from the French or putting together a book of stories from a book of anecdotes. Later, when I was wounded and was passing through Kharkov, I heard that Babel had been killed while with the Red Cavalry.

Fate, in its own time, worked a hundred changes in each of us.

In 1924 I again met Babel. I learned from him that he had not been killed, though he'd been beaten at great length.

He hadn't changed. He could tell even more interesting stories. From Odessa and the front he had brought with him two books. The Chinamen had been forgotten, stowed away in one particular story.

The new pieces were beautifully written. I don't think there's anyone else nowadays who writes as well as he does. He has been compared to Maupassant, because readers sense a French influence, and they are quick to name a sufficiently worthy object of comparison. But I prefer another name—Flaubert. The Flaubert of Salammbô. The Flaubert of that marvelous operatic libretto.

The shiniest jackboots, handsome as young girls, the whitest riding breeches, bright as a standard against the sky; even a fire blazing as bright as Sunday, cannot be compared with Babel's style.

A stranger from Paris—from Paris alone with no touch of London—Babel saw Russia as a French writer a century earlier, conscripted into Napoleon's Grande Armée, might have seen it.

The Chinamen were no longer needed; their place had been taken by Cossacks from French illustrations.

Connoisseurs of flattery say that its very effective if your "sweet talk" is couched in abusive language. "The peculiar force that results from the use of words whose lexical coloration [*sense*—ed.] is the opposite of their intonational effect arises from the fact that one feels the incongruity" (Yury Tynyanov, *The Problem of Poetic Language*).

Babel's principal device is to speak in the same tone of voice of the stars above and of gonorrhea.

Babel's lyrical passages are not successful.[. . .]

In his descriptions Babel adopts an elevated tone and enumerates many beautiful things. He writes:

> Here we are, you and I, walking about in this magic garden, this Finnish forest that almost baffles description. All our lives we shall never see anything more beautiful. And you can't see the pink edges of the frozen waterfall, over there by the stream! You are blind to the Japanese chiseling of the weeping willow leaning over the waterfall. The red trunks of the pines are covered by snow in which a thousand sparks are gleaming. The snow, shapeless when it fell, has draped itself along the branches, lying on their surfaces that undulate like a line drawn by Leonardo. In the snow flaming clouds are reflected. And think what you'd have to say about *Fröken* Kirsti's silk stockings; about the line of her leg, that lovely line!"

True, this passage ends with: "Get yourself some eyeglasses, Aleksandr Fyodorovich, I beseech you" ("Line and Color"—*Liniya i tsvet*).

Babel is gifted, and he is able, by the device of an irony communicated just in time, to render acceptable the highly colored objects he describes.

Without the irony it would be painful to read such things.

He even anticipates our objections and provides a designation for his tableaux: "opera":

> The scorched town—broken columns and, dug into the earth, the hooks of the little malevolent fingers of old women—seemed to me raised aloft in the air, as snug and chimerical as a dream. The crude brightness of the moon flowed down on it with inex-

haustible force. The damp mold of the ruins flowered like the marble of opera seats. And I waited, disturbed in spirit, for Romeo to appear from the clouds, a satin-clad Romeo singing of love, while a dismal electrician in the wings keeps a finger on the moon-extinguisher.

I used to compare *Red Cavalry* (*Konarmiya*) with Gogol's *Taras Bulba*. There are decided similarities in certain techniques. That "letter" telling of the murder of a father by his son is a Gogolian plot turned inside out. Babel also uses the Gogolian trick of enumerating family names, a device that may have its roots in the classical tradition.

But with Babel the enumeration is suddenly broken off. The Cossack Melnikov writes:

> For thirteen days I've been fighting with the rear guard, protecting the invincible First Cavalry, and am finding myself under hot rifle, artillery, and air fire from the enemy. Tardy has been killed, Lukhmannikov has been killed, Lykoshenko has been killed, Gulevoy has been killed, Trunov has been killed, and the white stallion is no longer under me, so, in line with the changing fortunes of war, don't count on seeing your beloved divisional commander Timoshenko, Comrade Melnikov, but we'll meet again, in—to be blunt about it—the kingdom of heaven, though rumor has it the old man in heaven hasn't a kingdom, but a regular whorehouse, and there's plenty of clap on earth already, so maybe we won't see each other after all. So long then, Comrade Melnikov.

Babel's Cossacks are all insufferably and ineffably handsome. "Ineffable" is a favorite word of Babel's. Babel makes use of two contradictions, which in his work take the place of plot: 1) His style is in contrast to the life he describes, and 2) that life is in contrast to the author himself.

He is a stranger in the army, a foreigner who has a right to be surprised. When he describes the military way of life he accentuates the "weakness and despair" of the observer.

In addition to *Red Cavalry*, Babel has written *Tales of Odessa* (*Odesskie rasskazy*). These are full of descriptions of various bandits. The atmosphere of banditry and the bandits' motley chattels Babel requires as a justification of his own style.

We recall that the divisional commander had "jackboots that looked like girls"; but consider the aristocrats of the Moldavanka district, who "were girded in crimson vests. Russet jackets covered their steely shoulders, and azure leather burst its seams around their fleshy feet" ("The King"—*Korol*).

Babel is a stranger in both worlds. He is a stranger even in Odessa. There he's told: "Forget for a time that you've spectacles on your nose, but autumn in your heart. Stop raising hell at your writing desk and stammering in public. Imagine for a moment that you raise hell on the streets and stammer on paper." Of course those remarks don't describe Babel. He isn't like that at all; he doesn't stammer. He's a brave man. I even think that "he could spend the night with a Russian woman and the Russian woman would be satisfied."

Because the Russian female loves eloquence. Babel plays the part of a foreigner because that device, like irony, facilitates his writing. And even Babel would not dare attempt high emotion without irony.

When Babel writes, he keeps the music to himself while describing the motions of the dance, yet at the same time he renders the whole piece in a high register. No doubt it was from the epic that he borrowed the device of giving answers which repeat the questions:

Benya Krik in the *Tales of Odessa* talks that way:

> Grach asked him:
> "Who are you, where do you come from and what do you fill your lungs with?"
> "Try me out, Froim," answered Benya, "and let's stop playing around."
> "Let's stop playing around," said Grach. "I'll try you out."

And the Cossacks in "The Letter" (*Pismo*) speak in the same way:

> And Senka asked Timofey Rodionych:
> "Are you doing all right, Dad, in my hands?"
> "No," Dad said ... "doing badly."
> Then Senka asked:
> "And Fedya, when you cut him up, was he doing all right?"
> "No," said Dad, "Fedya did badly."

Babel's books are excellent books. Russian literature is as grey as a siskin; it needs crimson riding breeches and boots of sky-blue leather.

It also needs the thing that Babel understood when he left his Chinamen to fend for themselves and set off with the "Red Cavalry."

Literary heroes, girls, old people and young people in all their possible situations are long since played out. Literature needs concreteness, and it must interbreed with our new way of life in order to create a new form.

RAYMOND ROSENTHAL

The Fate of Isaak Babel: A Child of the Russian Emancipation

For almost two decades, Isaak Babel maintained a place in Soviet literature as an obsolete but durable survivor of a moment of romantic *élan* that came with the revolution and quickly passed. From the perspective of the present, he merges with that group of writers which included Vladimir Mayakovsky, Boris Pilnyak, and Vsevolod Ivanov, all of whom were both created and destroyed by their fascination with the period of the Revolution's exuberant lyricism—the October overthrow and the Civil War. All of this group were either forced into conformity, disappeared mysteriously, or committed suicide. Yet Babel somehow survived. The price of his survival was tragically simple: he stopped writing for publication.

In recent years, Babel's unbroken silence became a sore point to the eulogists of Soviet literature. They were unable to resort to the customary invective in his case because Babel had never been under full official condemnation. On the contrary, it was well known that he had the friendship and support of leading figures in the Soviet government. His silence, therefore, could not be attributed to political disaffection. Instead, it seemed to be a voluntary act—an impression reinforced by the periodically hopeful announcements in Soviet literary journals that Babel was soon to publish a new and longer work. Unhappily, this new work was never published; in fact, since 1936 Babel's name itself has disappeared from all Soviet publications. More recently, the mere mention of his name produces an uncomfortable silence in Soviet circles.

Yet Isaak Babel is not a writer to be easily forgotten. Maksim Gorky,

---

From *Commentary* 3 (January-June 1947). © 1947 by the American Jewish Committee.

who published his first short stories in 1916 in his review *Letopis,* thought him the finest artist to come to maturity in the first sweep of the enthusiasm loosed by the October Revolution—an evaluation upheld by Soviet and European critics alike. Furthermore, Babel's stature as an artist was to some extent equalled by his significance as a symbol. To a whole generation of Jews in Russia and Europe in the years after the First World War, Babel had the appeal of a personal myth that had reached living realization.

Born and brought up in Odessa's noisome and lusty ghetto, the half-European, half-Asiatic Moldavanka, Babel appeared on the stage of international literature as the embodiment of that despised world of battered synagogues and festering alleyways, the sub-world of the stifled *luftmensh,* which had never before received complete citizen's rights among the reigning cultures of Europe.

He was the voice and the symbol of a new emancipation that promised the child of the Russian ghetto everything that Germany's enlightenment had offered Mendelssohn, Börne, and Heine—and infinitely more.

Moreover, Babel was not simply a Jew writing in the language of Turgenev and Dostoyevski (even under the Czar quite a few Jews had used Russian as a literary medium); he was a genius who spoke with a new inflection and expressed a folk life that had roots in the deepest soil of Russian experience.

Babel, the ghetto Jew, broke with the overwhelming tradition of psychological realism so firmly established by the nineteenth-century masters of the novel. Immediately after the publication of his first book of short stories in 1923, Russian literature recognized him as its authentic spokesman in a renaissance of the imagination which, in those early days of the new regime, seemed to be in its springtide.

What happened to that promised springtide is now quite clear—how soon it was frozen over by the hard crust of bureaucratic control and censorship. Nor is it difficult to conceive how Babel lapsed into silence under a regime of art-by-edict. Yet his fame remained so widespread that stories about him continued to filter through the Soviet blockade. They became especially persistent when Babel returned to Russia after a trip to Paris in 1934, and again in 1938 when Gorky, his acknowledged protector, died. Yet in all these rumors, there was never anything to indicate that Babel was considered politically suspect.

The latest news received by Babel's wife, who now lives in Paris, is much more serious, however, than ordinary rumor. According to her informant, Babel was jailed in 1941 because of an indiscretion that he let slip either in print or conversation while traveling in a remote province of Russia as a correspondent; and while in jail he contracted typhus and died. Since hearing this story, his wife has repeatedly approached the Soviet consulate in Paris, only to be met with impenetrable silence when her questions have become too concrete.

One factor in this story is underscored by Mrs. Babel's informant: her husband's death was *not* the result of a planned purge. It should rather be looked upon as the bad luck of a Soviet citizen treading his way through the *normal* hazards of Soviet life. Of course, professional people such as writers and journalists carry an additional risk because of their extreme public visibility. Thus, if Isaak Babel had not been at all famous, his chances of still being alive would have been much greater. The supreme irony, however, is the attitude taken by the highest levels of the Soviet bureaucracy when confronted with the unplanned death of one of their country's most important writers. Acutely embarrassed by this *faux pas* on the part of an overdutiful underling, they have done everything to quash the story. Counter-rumors have been carefully circulated through journalistic channels in Europe and America that Babel is alive and well, retired "in the country" on his accumulated royalties. But as yet the Soviet government has given no proof of these unofficial statements.

Isaak Babel was born in Odessa in 1894 and grew up in the traditional atmosphere of a lower-middle class Jewish family. In his autobiographical story "The Awakening," published in this issue of *Commentary*, he alludes to the bitterness of a childhood "nailed to the Talmud." Most accounts of his youth contain as a running theme this urge to escape from the ghetto. But this wish was hardly unique with Babel. Under the buffetings of the great social storms of the late nineteenth and early twentieth centuries in Russia, the ghetto stood in a particularly exposed position. All the fury of aroused reaction was directed at its inhabitants, as though to warn them against the social transformation for which they longed. Yet in Babel, the impulse to escape took a contradictory form. While trying to throw off the hermetic restraints of the ghetto, he was still unable to rid himself of its molding influences. Throughout his writings it is this conflict between the ineradicable imprint of his Jewish heritage and his passionate wish to rise out of its circumscribed environment that imparts a lyrical tension to his prose.

Given this understanding of Babel's background, it would be futile to draw parallels with those Jewish writers who developed their themes in a relatively peaceful ghetto. There, writers like Sholom Aleichem and I. L. Peretz found it quite natural to immerse themselves in Jewish folkways. Their stories have the intimacy of exultant ghetto-gabble: the entire community seems to participate. Isaak Babel could not join in the Jewish conversation in this way. For him, the cultural walls of Jewish life had become an obstacle to his most poignant aims. To learn how to swim, to understand nature, to write a story as elegantly as Maupassant—all these desires of a gifted fourteen-year-old were thwarted by the ghetto.

The central part played by the idea of flight in Babel's writings becomes more apparent as one tries to take in their entire range. It is useless to approach these brilliant stories with the conventional paraphernalia of literary criticism; the pattern beneath the ornamental surface of his style will never be understood in that case. Before the phenomenon of Babel's highly conscious yet strangely naive stories, the English-speaking critics of Russian literature have been able to do nothing more than almost mechanically check off a list of qualities—romanticism, ironic humor, sharp juxtaposition of the tragic and the ludicrous, accurately realistic observation blended with a poetic texture of words and images; none has even tried to find the core of meaning that informs the whole.

Babel's art, literally the product of a flight, represents the loot accumulated by a shrewd, inspired, sensuously receptive *luftmensh* catapulted by a political explosion into the attractive regions beyond the ghetto walls. We get glimpses in his autobiographical writings of these restless years; first in Petersburg as a hungry and bohemian writer living in a cellar and dodging the Czarist police because he lacks the passport required of all Jews; and later, swept along by the Revolution's tidal movement in wanderings that last through the Civil War and find him successively a soldier in Budenny's army, a Bolshevik propagandist, and a typesetter in a Tiflis print shop. Out of this seven years' flight came the intuitively brilliant stories about the revolutionary epoch. While such writers as Boris Pilnyak and Alexander Blok imagined these years in the metaphoric terms of a great natural catastrophe, their panoramas give the impression of having been composed on the periphery of, and at distance from, the turmoil. It is Babel who carries us right into the heart of the storm. Only a cultural *naif* touched with urban sophistication could have responded so adequately to the paradoxical and extravagant contrasts of a Russia leaping out of feudalism into modern history.

In Babel's epic-like chronicle of the Civil War, *Red Cavalry*, nature, seen through the new eyes of a Jew, takes on the stylized perfection of a Byzantine mosaic: rivers, plains, and trees become the richly brocaded background for the crudest deeds of war. The coarse dialect of Budenny's Cossacks, newly encrusted with the jargon invented by the Revolution, and the liturgical eloquence of the Hasidic Jews, sound to him like the words of some ancient folk song. Certainly James Joyce's dictum that genius turns its very handicaps into "the portals of discovery" is wonderfully illustrated by Babel: he converted his very rootlessness into the organizing principle of a fresh perception of reality.

Red Cavalry is undoubtedly Babel's masterpiece. So far it is the only complete book of his to have been translated into English. The book purports to be a series of disconnected sketches, but actually it is a subtly counterpointed saga. When Sherwood Anderson said that he thought "the true history of life is but a history of moments," he was describing perfectly the aesthetic approach of Babel's concentrated *nouvelles*, which depend for their impact on the flash-like capture of a passionate moment. In one of his autobiographical stories, "Guy de Maupassant," Babel also testifies to the profound influence that French writers, especially Flaubert and Maupassant, had on his sense of form. "A phrase," he says, "is born into the world both good and bad at the same time. The secret consists in a barely perceptible turn. The lever must be held and warmed in the hand, and must be turned once, and not twice."

Reason never speaks in Babel's work. Never is an attempt made at logical analysis or persuasion. Few writers have so completely depended on the immediate flow of sensible reality for their total effect. Overwhelmed by sensations, immersed in atmospheres, colors, voices, we are in contact with a universe that, grasped wholly by the senses, never requires the intervention of the reasoning intellect to explain it. Babel's mastery of the primitive and unthinkable joy of sensuous delight has secular affiliations with the Hasidic literature, but in him it is the ecstasy of experience as such, stripped of the religious logic of the Hasidim.

Equipped so bizarrely, Babel went out into the Civil War, in Heine's phrase, "like God's spy," and with great detachment recorded the brutal episodes of the Red Army's Polish campaign of 1921. At the center of his canvas stands the familiar figure of the alienated Jewish intellectual—the sceptical, ironic observer "with spectacles on his nose and autumn in his heart"—obviously Babel himself. He is in love with the Cossack's primitive directness of instinct, but he is also fascinated by the Hasidic Jew—the war is being fought on the traditional ground of the Jewish Pale—and holds him up as a counter-hero of the spirit to offset the Cossack's primitiveness. Babel identifies himself with a Cossack commander who, as he says, "looked on the world as a meadow in May—a meadow crossed by women and horses." But he is drawn to the Jews, too. Ghedali, the Jewish antique dealer, voices Babel's own discontent when he cries out: "Where is the joy-giving Revolution?" For moments, in certain of these stories, Babel's subtle shuttling back and forth between the two opposing groups of Cossacks and Jews seems designed to call up from all the disorder and bloodshed the image of a totally *new man* who would contain in himself the traits that attracted Babel in both Jew and Cossack. Not the natural savage of Rousseau, nor the Talmudic genius of ingrown religiosity, but the new and more rounded man that the social upheaval might produce, fills Babel with the longing that underlies his *Red Cavalry* stories.

The mood of elation that flares up so often in these stories reflects the dominant feeling of the Russian Jew immediately after the October insurrection. At one stroke he had been freed from the Czarist prison and had attained—so it appeared to him—the open arena of unlimited social possibility. From his own experience, the Jew knew the violent contrasts, the dizzying velocity of the transformation, more completely than anyone else in Russia. Compared with the nineteenth-century German emancipation, which had unfolded in organic fashion, permitting the Jews over a long period of years to infiltrate slowly into the bourgeois setup, the Russian liberation took place overnight. No wonder that it raised such intense hopes—above all in the Jew.

Soon after his success with *Red Cavalry,* Babel wrote the *Tales of Odessa,* a group of exotic sketches about the ghetto of his youth. Here the hero is the fabulous Jewish gangster Benia Krik. Having found his true voice in the Civil War, Babel has returned to the streets and docks of Odessa to fashion a Jewish Cossack. These stories are based to a large extent on fact; Odessa provided fertile material, being more akin to Marseilles or Naples than to the ghetto towns of the Pale.

Tales of Odessa was also the final symbolic action of Babel's creative life. His next stories are written in a pared, elegantly simple style that departs from his usual manner by going in for psychological investigation. They deal exclusively with reminiscences, not with contemporary events—as if Babel were impelled not only by a state censorship, but also by his own curiosity, to retrace the trajectory of his flight from the ghetto.

When everything about Babel is taken into account—his scrupulousness as a writer, the years lost in politics, the paralyzing effect of the bureaucracy—the fact still remains that his production was very small. Besides the volumes of short stories already mentioned, there exist a number of short pieces, two scenarios for movies that were never filmed, and a three-act play, *Sunset.* One doesn't have to search far for the cause. Babel points to it himself in his story, "Guy de Maupassant," where he describes how his artistic freedom was crippled by his Jewish conscience. Strongly attracted to sexuality, his guilt-ridden feelings inextricably mingle the dangers of eroticism with the practice of art, pervading them with the same element of delectable risk. Maupassant's death in an insane asylum after a wildly sensual life looms in the young writer's imagination as the archetype of the artist's fate.

Although Babel's attitude towards art borrows dark overtones from romantic literature, it is still an intuitively keen analysis of the roots of his own alienation. For Babel was unquestionably an alienated artist. "Guy de Maupassant" is not simply a casual story, but contains a retrospective summing-up of his whole career, a kind of parable of what happened to his art. Yet to plaster the term alienation on Babel and imagine we have dealt deeply with him would be a grave mistake. For the artist is always a special case; it is in his very nature to be detached. He transforms his aloofness from life into a valid and functioning value, a movement of the nerves prior to any rupture occasioned by society.

Thinking of the process of alienation in this special sense, Henri Bergson regarded all artists as the fortunate products of a profound detachment. "Now and then," he declares in his book *The Creative Mind*, "by a lucky accident, men arise whose senses are less adherent to life. When they look at a thing, they see it for itself, not for themselves. They do not perceive simply with a view to action; they perceive in order to perceive—for nothing, for the pleasure of doing so. In regard to a certain aspect of their nature, whether it be their consciousness or one of their senses, they are born detached."

Surely Babel was such a "lucky accident." But to "perceive for nothing, for the pleasure of doing so"—precisely this had implications that eventually led to his opposition to traditional Jewish life. Even in the semi-cosmopolitan seaport of Odessa, the ghetto remained a village, with its strict ethical system, its own customs and rituals as a protection against the alien surrounding world. Any interest in the world, in sexual love for its own sake, in the uneconomic activity of art, in pleasure, was anathema to its code. At this point, when Babel was forced to break with Jewish life in order to become an artist, the process of alienation, a process already begun in his nerves, acquires a sociological meaning. Yet one can readily see that this is a peculiar alienation which has as its chief characteristic not sickly and introverted self-regard, but an outgoing and eager interest in the world. Isaak Babel was that rare figure in Jewish-nurtured literature, a Jew who found his purpose in enjoying the world.

Always ready for the "mystic" experience that the world might offer, Babel yet suffered from a flaw inside himself, an inherited sense of the ethical. In his most ecstatic passages, one can hear its harsh undernote. Like the Hasidic rabbis of modern times, he had learned all the prayers, but the miracle of complete possession which should have accompanied them never occurred. And only the "miracle" of revolutionary events brought his art to its highest achievement in *Red Cavalry*. But this was an external event, and the artist, in the long run, depends only on his own powers.

In the end, one recalls the final story in *Red Cavalry*, the one in which Babel presents the portrait of Ilya, "the last, cursed and unruly son" of the Hasidic prince, Rabbi Motaley Bratslavsky. Using a technique that reminds one of Eisenstein's montage effects, Babel compresses the whole history of Jewish participation in the revolutionary movement into one brief sketch.

Ilya has become a Bolshevik and a Red Army soldier, and now he lies on the dirty floor of the retreating troop train dying of typhus, surrounded by the lyrical disorder of this life. In elegiac tones Babel fondly enumerates the items, the images of Ilya's torn existence: "the mandates of the propagandist and the memorandum books of the Jewish poet; the portraits of Lenin and Maimonides lay side by side; the knotted iron of Lenin's skull beside the dull silk of the portrait of Maimonides. A lock of woman's hair lay in a book, and the Resolutions of the Party's Sixth Congress, and the margins of Communist leaflets were crowded with the crooked lines of Hebrew verse. They fell in a mean and depressing rain—pages of the Song of Songs and those revolver cartridges."

And while Ilya, last prince of an aborted Hasidic destiny, waits for his death, "a monstrous and inconceivable Russia" tramps in bast shoes alongside the train. All the despair and confusion of military defeat sigh enormously over Ilya's dying body. "And I," cries Babel, "who can scarce contain the tempests of my imagination within this primeval body of mine, was there beside my brother when he died." Reading this story now, with Babel's real fate in mind, one thinks of him as he thought of Ilya—as the last of those joy-possessed Hasidic princes who rose out of the submerged but deeply spiritual ghetto world. And his lamentation for Ilya becomes his own lament for the loss of that hope of the marvelous, that perfection of joy which animated his entire life's search.

LIONEL TRILLING

The Forbidden Dialectic:
Introduction to The Collected Stories

A good many years ago in 1929, I chanced to read a book which disturbed me in a way I can still remember. The book was called *Red Cavalry;* it was a collection of stories about Soviet regiments of horse operating in Poland. I had never heard of the author, Isaac Babel—or I. Babel as he signed himself—and nobody had anything to tell me about him, and part of my disturbance was the natural shock we feel when, suddenly and without warning, we confront a new talent of great energy and boldness. But the book was disturbing for other reasons as well.

In those days one still spoke of the "Russian experiment" and one might still believe that the light of dawn glowed on the test tubes and crucibles of human destiny. And it was still possible to have very strange expectations of the new culture that would arise from the Revolution. I do not remember what my own particular expectations were, except that they involved a desire for an art that would have as little ambiguity as a proposition in logic. Why I wanted this I don't wholly understand. It was as if I had hoped that the literature of the Revolution would realize some simple, inadequate notion of the "classical" which I had picked up at college; and perhaps I was drawn to this notion of the classical because I was afraid of the literature of modern Europe, because I was scared of its terrible intensities, ironies, and ambiguities. If this is what I really felt, I can't say that I am now wholly ashamed of my cowardice. If we stop to think of the museum knowingness about art which we are likely to acquire with matu-

From *Isaac Babel: The Collected Stories*, edited and translated by Walter Morison. © 1955 by Criterion Books.

rity, of our consumer's pride in buying only the very best spiritual commodities, the ones which are sure to give satisfaction, there may possibly be a grace in those moments when we lack the courage to confront, or the strength to endure, some particular work of art or kind of art. At any rate, here was Babel's book and I found it disturbing. It was obviously the most remarkable work of fiction that had yet come out of revolutionary Russia, the only work, indeed, that I knew of as having upon it the mark of exceptional talent, even of genius. Yet for me it was all too heavily charged with the intensity, irony, and ambiguousness from which I wished to escape.

There was anomaly at the very heart of the book, for the Red cavalry of the title were Cossack regiments, and why were Cossacks fighting for the Revolution, they who were the instrument and symbol of Tsarist repression? The author, who represented himself in the stories, was a Jew; and a Jew in a Cossack regiment was more than an anomaly, it was a joke, for between Cossack and Jew there existed not merely hatred but a polar opposition. Yet here was a Jew riding as a Cossack and trying to come to terms with the Cossack ethos. At that first reading it seemed to me—although it does not now—that the stories were touched with cruelty. They were about violence of the most extreme kind, yet they were composed with a striking elegance and precision of objectivity, and also with a kind of lyric *joy*, so that one could not at once know just how the author was responding to the brutality he recorded, whether he thought it good or bad, justified or not justified. Nor was this the only thing to be in doubt about. It was not really clear how the author felt about, say, Jews; or about religion; or about the goodness of man. He had—or perhaps, for the sake of some artistic effect, he pretended to have—a secret. This alienated and disturbed me. It was impossible not to be overcome by admiration for *Red Cavalry*, but it was not at all the sort of book that I had wanted the culture of the Revolution to give me.

And, as it soon turned out, it was not at all the sort of book that the Revolution wanted to give anyone. No event in the history of Soviet culture is more significant than the career, or, rather, the end of the career, of Isaac Babel. He had been a protégé of Gorky, and he had begun his career under the aegis of Trotsky's superb contempt for the pieties of the conventional "proletarian" aesthetics. In the last years of the decade of the twenties and in the early thirties he was regarded as one of the most notable talents of Soviet literature. This judgment was, however, by no means an official one. From the beginning of his career, Babel had been under the attack of the literary bureaucracy. But in 1932 the Party abolished RAPP—the Russian Association of Proletarian Writers—and it seemed that a new period of freedom had been inaugurated. In point of fact, the reactionary elements of Soviet culture were established in full ascendancy, and the purge trials of 1937 were to demonstrate how absolute their power was. But in the five intervening years the Party chose to exercise its authority in a lenient manner. It was in this atmosphere of seeming liberality that the first Writers' Congress was held in 1934. Babel was one of the speakers at the Congress. He spoke with considerable jauntiness, yet he spoke as a penitent—the stories he had written since *Red Cavalry* had been published in a volume at the end of 1932 and since that time he had written nothing, he had disappointed expectation.

His speech was a strange performance. It undertook to be humorous; the published report is punctuated by the indication of laughter. It made the avowals of loyalty that were by then routine, yet we cannot take it for granted that Babel was insincere when he spoke of his devotion to the Revolution, to the Government, and to the State, or when he said that in a bourgeois country it would inevitably have been his fate to go without recognition and livelihood. He may have been sincere even when he praised Stalin's literary style, speaking of the sentences "forged" as if of steel, of the necessity of learning to work in language as Stalin did. Yet beneath the orthodoxy of this speech there lies some hidden intention. One feels this in the sad vestiges of the humanistic mode that wryly manifest themselves. It is as if the humor, which is often of a whimsical kind, as if the irony and the studied self-depreciation, were forlorn affirmations of freedom and selfhood; it is as if Babel were addressing his fellow-writers in a dead language, or in some slang of their student days, which a few of them might perhaps remember.

Everything, he said at one point in his speech, is given to us by the Party and the Government; we are deprived of only one right, the right to write badly. "Comrades," he said, "let us not fool ourselves: this is a very important right, and to take it away from us is no small thing." And he said, "Let us give up this right, and may God help us. And if there is no God, let us help ourselves."

The right to write badly—how precious it seems when once there has been the need to conceive of it! Upon the right to write badly depends the right to write at all. There must have been many in the audience who understood how serious and how terrible Babel's joke was. And there must have been some who had felt a chill at their hearts at another joke that Babel had made earlier in his address, when he spoke of himself as practicing a new literary genre. This was the genre of silence—he was, he said, "the master of the genre of silence."

Thus he incriminated himself for his inability to work. He made reference to the doctrine that the writer must have respect for the reader, and he said that it was a correct doctrine. He himself, he said, had a very highly developed respect for the reader; so much so, indeed, that it might be said of him that he suffered from a hypertrophy of the faculty of respect—"I have so much respect for the reader that I am dumb." But now he takes a step beyond irony; he ventures to interpret, and by his interpretation to challenge, the official doctrines of "respect for the reader." The reader, he says, asks for bread, and he must indeed be given what he asks for—but not in the way he expects it; he ought to be surprised by what he gets; he ought not be given what he can easily recognize as "a certified true copy" of life—the essence of art is unexpectedness.

The silence for which Babel apologized was not broken. In 1937 he was arrested. He died in a concentration camp in 1939 or 1940. It is not known for certain whether he was shot or died of typhus. Both accounts of the manner of his death have been given by people who were inmates of the camp at the time. Nor is it known for what specific reason he was arrested. Raymond Rosenthal, in an admirable essay on Babel published in *Commentary* in 1947, says, on good authority, that Babel did not undergo a purge but was arrested for having made a politically indiscreet remark. It has been said that he was arrested when Yagoda was purged, because he was having a love affair with Yagoda's sister. It has also been said that he was accused of Trotskyism, which does indeed seem possible, especially if we think of Trotsky as not only a political but a cultural figure.

But no reason for the last stage of the extinction of Isaac Babel is needed beyond that which is provided by his stories, by their method and style. If ever we want to remind ourselves of the nature and power of art, we have only to think of how accurate reactionary governments are in their awareness of that nature and that power. It is not merely the content of art that they fear, not merely explicit doctrine, but whatever of energy and autonomy is implied by the aesthetic qualities a work may have. Intensity, irony, and ambiguousness, for example, constitute a clear threat to the impassivity of the State. They constitute a *secret*.

Babel was not a political man except as every man of intelligence was political at the time of the Revolution. Except, too, as every man of talent or genius is political who makes his heart a battleground for conflicting tendencies of culture. In Babel's heart there was a kind of fighting—he was captivated by the vision of two ways of being, the way of violence and the way of peace, and he was torn between them. The conflict between the two ways of being was an essential element of his mode of thought. And when

Soviet culture was brought under full discipline, the fighting in Babel's heart could not be permitted to endure. It was a subversion of discipline. It implied that there was more than one way of being. It hinted that one might live in doubt, that one might live by means of a question.

It is with some surprise that we become aware of the centrality of the cultural, the moral, the *personal* issue in Babel's work, for what strikes us first is the intensity of his specifically aesthetic preoccupation. In his school days Babel was passionate in his study of French literature; for several years he wrote his youthful stories in French, his chief masters being Flaubert and Maupassant. When, in an autobiographical sketch, he means to tell us that he began his mature work in 1923, he puts it that in that year he began to express his thoughts "clearly, and not at great length." This delight in brevity became his peculiar mark. When Eisenstein spoke of what it was that literature might teach the cinema, he said that "Isaac Babel will speak of the extreme laconicism of literature's expressive means—Babel, who, perhaps, knows in practice better than anyone else that great secret, 'that there is no iron that can enter the human heart with such stupefying effect, as a period placed at just the right moment.'" Babel's love of the laconic implies certain other elements of his aesthetic, his commitment (it is sometimes excessive) to *le mot juste*, to the search for the word or phrase that will do its work with a ruthless speed, and his remarkable powers of significant distortion, the rapid foreshortening, the striking displacement of interest and shift of emphasis—in general his pulling all awry the arrangement of things as they appear in the "certified true copy."

Babel's preoccupation with form, with the aesthetic surface, is, we soon see, entirely at the service of his moral concern. James Joyce has taught us the word *epiphany*, a showing forth—Joyce had the "theory" that suddenly, almost miraculously, by a phrase or a gesture, a life would thrust itself through the veil of things and for an instant show itself forth, startling us by its existence. In itself the conception of the epiphany makes a large statement about the nature of human life; it suggests that the human fact does not dominate the scene of our existence—for something to "show forth" it must first be hidden, and the human fact is submerged in and subordinated to a world of circumstance, the world of things; it is known only in glimpses, emerging from the danger or the sordidness in which it is implicated. Those writers who by their practice subscribe to the theory of the epiphany are drawn to a particular aesthetic. In the stories of Maupassant, as in those of Stephen Crane, and Hemingway, and the Joyce of *Dubliners,* as in those of Babel himself, we perceive the writer's intention to create a form which shall in itself be shapely and autonomous and at the same time unusually responsible to the truth of external reality, the truth of things and events. To this end he concerns himself with the given moment, and, seeming almost hostile to the continuity of time, he presents the past only as it can be figured in the present. In his commitment to event he affects to be indifferent to "meanings" and "values"; he seems to be saying that although he can tell us with unusual accuracy what is going on, he does not presume to interpret it, scarcely to understand it, certainly not to judge it. He arranges that the story shall tell itself, as it were; or he tells it by means of a narrator who somehow makes it clear that he has no personal concern with the outcome of events—what I have called Babel's lyric joy in the midst of violence is in effect one of his devices for achieving the tone of detachment. We are not, of course, for very long deceived by the elaborate apparatus contrived to suggest the almost affectless detachment of the writer. We soon enough see what he is up to. His intense concern with the hard aesthetic surface of the story, his preoccupation with things and events, are, we begin to perceive, cognate with the universe, representative of its nature, of the unyielding circumstance in which the human fact exists; they make the condition for the epiphany, the showing forth; and the apparent denial of immediate pathos is a condition of the ultimate pathos the writer conceives.

All this, as I say, is soon enough apparent in Babel's stories. And yet, even when we have become aware of his pathos, we are, I think, surprised by the kind of moral issue that lies beneath the brilliant surface of the stories, beneath the lyric and ironic elegance—we are surprised by its elemental simplicity. We are surprised, too, by its passionate subjectivity, the intensity of the author's personal involvement, his defenseless commitment of himself to the issue.

The stories of *Red Cavalry* have as their principle of coherence what I have called the anomaly, or the joke of a Jew who is a member of a Cossack regiment—Babel was a supply officer under General Budenny in the campaign of 1920. Traditionally the Cossack was the feared and hated enemy of the Jew. But he was more than that. The principle of his existence stood in total antithesis to the principle of the Jew's existence. The Jew conceived his own ideal character to consist in his being intellectual, pacific, humane. The Cossack was physical, violent, without mind or manners. When a Jew of Eastern Europe wanted to say what we mean by "a bull in a china shop," he said "a Cossack in a *succah*"—in, that is, one of the fragile decorated booths or tabernacles in which the meals of the harvest festival of *Succoth* are eaten: he intended an image of animal violence, of aimless destructiveness. And if the Jew was political, if he thought beyond his own ethnic and religious group, he knew that the Cossack was the enemy not only of the

Jew—although that in special—but the enemy also of all men who thought of liberty; he was the natural and appropriate instrument of ruthless oppression.

There was, of course, another possible view of the Cossack, one that had its appeal for many Russian intellectuals, although it was not likely to win the assent of the Jew. Tolstoy had represented the Cossack as having a primitive energy, passion, and virtue. He was the man as yet untrammeled by civilization, direct, immediate, fierce. He was the man of enviable simplicity, the man of the body—and of the horse, the man who moved with speed and grace. We have devised an image of our lost freedom which we mock in the very phrase by which we name it: the noble savage. No doubt the mockery is justified, yet our fantasy of the noble savage represents a reality of our existence, it stands for our sense of something unhappily surrendered, the truth of the body, the truth of full sexuality, the truth of open aggressiveness. Something, we know, must inevitably be surrendered for the sake of civilization; but the "discontent" of civilization which Freud describes is our self-recrimination at having surrendered too much. Babel's view of the Cossack was more consonant with that of Tolstoy than with the traditional view of his own people. For him the Cossack was indeed the noble savage, all too savage, not often noble, yet having in his savagery some quality that might raise strange questions in a Jewish mind.

I have seen three pictures of Babel, and it is a puzzle to know how he was supposed to look. The most convincing of the pictures is a photograph, to which the two official portrait sketches bear but little resemblance. The sketch which serves as the frontispiece to Babel's volume of stories of 1932 makes the author look like a Chinese merchant—his face is round, impassive, and priggish; his nose is low and flat; he stares through rimless glasses with immovable gaze. The sketch in the Literary Encyclopedia lengthens his face and gives him horn-rimmed spectacles and an air of amused and knowing assurance: a well-educated and successful Hollywood writer who has made the intelligent decision not to apologize for his profession except by his smile. But in the photograph the face is very long and thin, charged with emotion and internality; bitter, intense, very sensitive, touched with humor, full of consciousness and contradiction. It is "typically" an intellectual's face, a scholar's face, and it has great charm. I should not want to speak of it as a Jewish face, but it is a kind of face which many Jews used to aspire to have, or hoped their sons would have. It was, surely, this face, or one much like it, that Babel took with him when he went among the Cossacks.

We can only marvel over the vagary of the military mind by which Isaac Babel came to be assigned as a supply officer to a Cossack regiment.

He was a Jew of the ghetto. As a boy—so he tells us in his autobiographical stories—he had been of stunted growth, physically inept, subject to nervous disorders. He was an intellectual, a writer—a man, as he puts it in striking phrase, with spectacles on his nose and autumn in his heart. The orders that sent him to General Budenny's command were drawn either by a conscious and ironical Destiny with a literary bent—or at his own personal request. For the reasons that made it bizarre that he should have been attached to a Cossack regiment are the reasons why he was there. He was there to be submitted to a test, he was there to be initiated. He was there because of the dreams of his boyhood. Babel's talent, like that of many modern writers, is rooted in the memory of boyhood, and Babel's boyhood was more than usually dominated by the idea of the test and the initiation. We might put it that Babel rode with a Cossack regiment because, when he was nine years old, he had seen his father kneeling before a Cossack captain who wore lemon-colored chamois gloves and looked ahead with the gaze of one who rides through a mountain pass.

Isaac Babel was born in Odessa, in 1894. The years following the accession of Nicholas II were dark years indeed for the Jews of Russia. It was the time of the bitterest official anti-Semitism, of the Pale, of the Beilis trial, of the Black Hundreds and the planned pogroms. And yet in Odessa the Jewish community may be said to have flourished. Odessa was the great port of the Black Sea, an eastern Marseille or Naples, and in such cities the transient, heterogeneous population dilutes the force of law and tradition, for good as well as for bad. The Jews of Odessa were in some degree free to take part in the general life of the city. They were, to be sure, debarred from the schools, with but few exceptions. And they were sufficiently isolate when the passions of a pogrom swept the city. Yet all classes of the Jewish community seem to have been marked by a singular robustness and vitality, by a sense of the world, and of themselves in the world. The upper classes lived in affluence, sometimes in luxury, and it was possible for them to make their way into a Gentile society in which prejudice had been attenuated by cosmopolitanism. The intellectual life was of a particular energy, producing writers, scholars and journalists of very notable gifts; it is in Odessa that modern Hebrew poetry takes its rise with Bialyk and Tchernokovsky. As for the lower classes, Babel himself represents them as living freely and heartily. In their ghetto, the Moldavanka, they were far more conditioned by their economic circumstances than by their religious ties; they were not at all like the poor Jews of the *shtetln*, the little towns of Poland, whom Babel was later to see. He represents them as characters of a Breughel-like bulk and brawn; they have large, coarse, elaborate nicknames; they are draymen and dairy farmers; they are gangsters—the Jewish gangs of the Moldavanka were famous; they made upon the young Babel an ineradicable impression and to them he devoted a remarkable group of comic stories.

It was not Odessa, then, it was not even Odessa's ghetto, that forced upon Babel the image of the Jew as a man not in the actual world, a man of no body, a man of intellect, or wits, passive before his secular fate. Not even his image of the Jewish intellectual was substantiated by the Odessa actuality—Bialyk and Tchnernokovsky were anything but men with spectacles on their noses and autumn in their hearts, and no one who ever encountered in America the striking figure of Dr. Chaim Tchernowitz, the great scholar of the Talmud and formerly the Chief Rabbi of Odessa, a man of Jovian port and large, free mind, would be inclined to conclude that there was but a single season of the heart available to a Jew of Odessa.

But Babel had seen his father on his knees before a Cossack captain on a horse, who said, "At your service," and touched his fur cap with his yellow-gloved hand and politely paid no heed to the mob looting the Babel store. Such an experience, or even a far milder analogue of it, is determinative in the life of a boy. Freud speaks of the effect upon him when, at twelve, his father told of having accepted in a pacific way the insult of having his new fur cap knocked into the mud by a Gentile who shouted at him, "Jew, get off the pavement." It is clear that Babel's relation with his father defined his relation to his Jewishness. Benya Krik, the greatest of the gangsters, he who was called King, was a Jew of Odessa, but he did not wear glasses and he did not have autumn in his heart—it is in writing about Benya that Babel uses the phrase that sets so far apart the intellectual and the man of action. The exploration of Benya's preeminence among gangsters does indeed take account of his personal endowment—Benya was a "lion," a "tiger," a "cat"; he "could spend the night with a Russian woman and satisfy her." But what really made his fate was his having had Mendel Krik, the drayman, for his father. "What does such a father think about? He thinks about drinking a good glass of vodka, of smashing somebody in the face, of his horses—and nothing more. You want to live and he makes you die twenty times a day. What would you have done in Benya Krik's place? You would have done nothing. But *he* did something." But Babel's father did not think about vodka, and smashing somebody in the face, and horses; he thought about large and serious things, among them respectability and fame. He was a shopkeeper, not well to do, a serious man, a failure. The sons of such men have much to prove, much to test themselves for, and, if they are Jewish, their Jewishness is ineluctably involved in the test.

Babel, in the brief autobiographical sketch to which I have referred, speaks with bitterness of the terrible discipline of his Jewish education. He thought of the Talmud Torah as a prison shutting him off from all desirable life, from reality itself. One of the stories he tells—conceivably the incident was invented to stand for his feelings about his Jewish schooling—is about his father's having fallen prey to the Messianic delusion which beset the Jewish families of Odessa, the belief that any one of them might produce a prodigy of the violin, a little genius who could be sent to be processed by Professor Auer in Petersburg, who would play before crowned heads in a velvet suit, and support his family in honor and comfort. Such miracles had occurred in Odessa, whence had come Elman, Zimbalist, Gabrilowitsch, and Heifetz. Babel's father hoped for wealth, but he would have foregone wealth if he could have been sure, at a minimum, of fame. Being small, the young Babel at fourteen might pass for eight and a prodigy. In point of fact, Babel had not even talent, and certainly no vocation. He was repelled by the idea of becoming a musical "dwarf," one of the "big-headed freckled children with necks as thin as flower stalks and an epileptic flush on their cheeks." This was a Jewish fate and he fled from it, escaping to the port and the beaches of Odessa. Here he tried to learn to swim and could not: "the hydrophobia of my ancestors—Spanish rabbis and Frankfurt money-changers—dragged me to the bottom." But a kindly proofreader, an elderly man who loved nature and children, took pity on him. "How d'you mean, the water won't hold you? Why shouldn't it hold you?"—his specific gravity was no different from anybody else's and the good Yefim Nikitich Smolich taught him to swim. "I came to love that man," Babel says in one of the very few of his sentences over which no slightest irony plays, "with the love that only a boy suffering from hysteria and headaches can feel for a real man."

The story is called "Awakening" and it commemorates the boy's first effort of creation. It is to Nikitich that he shows the tragedy he has composed and it is the old man who observes that the boy has talent but no knowledge of nature and undertakes to teach him how to tell one tree or one plant from another. This ignorance of the natural world—Babel refers to it again in his autobiographical sketch—was a Jewish handicap to be overcome. It was not an extravagance of Jewish self-consciousness that led him to make the generalization—Maurice Samuel remarks in *The World of Sholom Aleichem* that in the Yiddish vocabulary of the Jews of eastern Europe there are but two flower names (rose, violet) and no names for wild birds.

When it was possible to do so, Babel left his family and Odessa to live the precarious life, especially precarious for a Jew, of a Russian artist and intellectual. He went to Kiev and then, in 1915, he ventured to St. Petersburg without a residence certificate. He was twenty-one. He lived in a cellar on Pushkin Street, and wrote stories which were everywhere refused until Gorky took him up and in 1916 published in his magazine two of Babel's stories. To Gorky, Babel said, he was indebted for everything. But Gorky became of the opinion that Babel's first stories were successful only by accident; he advised the young man to abandon the career of literature and to go "among the people." Babel served in the Tsar's army on the Rumanian front; after the Revolution he was for a time a member of the Cheka; he went on grain-collecting expeditions in 1918; he fought with the northern army against Yudenich. In 1920 he was with Budenny in Poland, twenty-six years old, having seen much, having endured much, yet demanding initiation, submitting himself to the test.

The test, it is important to note, is not that of courage. Babel's affinity with Stephen Crane and Hemingway is close in many respects, of which not the least important is his feeling for his boyhood and for the drama of the boy's initiation into manhood. But the question that Babel puts to himself is not that which means so much to the two American writers; he does not ask whether he will be able to meet danger with honor. This he seems to know he can do. Rather, the test is of his power of direct and immediate, and violent, action—not whether he can endure being killed but whether he can endure killing. In the story "After the Battle" a Cossack comrade is enraged against him not because, in the recent engagement, he had hung back, but because he had ridden with an unloaded revolver. The story ends with the narrator imploring fate to "grant me the simplest of proficiencies—the ability to kill my fellowmen."

The necessity for submitting to the test is very deeply rooted in Babel's psychic life. This becomes readily apparent when we read the whole of Babel's canon and perceive the manifest connection between certain of the incidents of *Red Cavalry* and those of the stories of the Odessa boyhood. In the story "My First Goose" the newcomer to the brigade is snubbed by the brilliant Cossack commander because he is a man with spectacles on his nose, an intellectual. "Not a life for the brainy type here," says the quartermaster who carries his trunk to his billet. "But you go and mess up a lady, and a good lady too, and you'll have the boys patting you on the back." The five new comrades in the billet make it quite clear that he is an outsider and unwanted, they begin at once to bully and haze him. Yet by one action he overcomes their hostility to him and his spectacles. He asks the old landlady for food and she puts him off; whereupon he kills the woman's goose in a particularly brutal manner, and, picking it up on the point of a sword, thrusts it at the woman and orders her to cook it. Now the crisis is passed;

the price of community has been paid. The group of five reforms itself to become a group of six. All is decent and composed in the conduct of the men. There is a general political discussion, then sleep. "We slept, all six of us, beneath a wooden roof that let in the stars, warming one another, our legs intermingled. I dreamed: and in my dreams I saw women. But my heart, stained with bloodshed, grated and brimmed over." We inevitably read this story in the light of Babel's two connected stories of the 1905 pogrom, "The Story of My Dovecot" and "First Love," recalling the scene in which the crippled cigarette vendor, whom all the children loved, crushes the boy's newly bought and long-desired pigeon and flings it in his face. Later the pigeon's blood and entrails are washed from the boy's cheek by the young Russian woman who is sheltering the Babel family and whom the boy adores. It is after her caress that the boy sees his father on his knees before the Cossack captain; the story ends with his capitulation to nervous illness. And now again a bird has been brutally killed, now again the killing is linked with sexuality, but now it is not his bird but another's, now he is not passive but active.

Yet no amount of understanding of the psychological genesis of the act of killing the goose makes it easy for us to judge it as anything more than a very ugly brutality. It is not easy for us—and it is not easy for Babel. Not easy, but we must make the effort to comprehend that for Babel it is not violence in itself that is at issue in his relation to the Cossacks, but something else, some quality with which violence does indeed go along, but which is not in itself merely violent. This quality, whatever it is to be called, is of the greatest importance in Babel's conception of himself as an intellectual and an artist, in his conception of himself as a Jew.

It is, after all, not violence and brutality that make the Cossacks what they are. This is not the first violence and brutality that Babel has known—when it comes to violence and brutality a Western reader can scarcely have, unless he sets himself to acquire it, an adequate idea of their place in the life of Eastern Europe. The impulse to violence, as we have learned, seems indigenous in all mankind. Among certain groups the impulse is far more freely licensed than among others. Americans are aware and ashamed of the actuality or potentiality of violence in their own culture, but it is nothing to that of the East of Europe; the people for whom the mass impalings and the knout are part of their memory of the exercise of authority over them have their own appropriate ways of expressing their rage. As compared with what the knife, or the homemade pike, or the boot, can do, the revolver is an instrument of delicate amenity and tender mercy—this, indeed, is the point of one of Babel's stories. Godfrey Blunden's description of the method of execution used by the

Ukrainian peasant bands is scarcely to be read. Nor is it only in combat that the tradition of ferocious violence appears, as is suggested by the long Russian concern with wife-beating as a national problem.

The point I would make is that the Cossacks were not exceptional for their violence. It was not their violence in itself that evoked Tolstoy's admiration. Nor is it what fascinated Babel. Rather he is drawn by what the violence goes along with, the boldness, the passionateness, the simplicity and directness—and the grace. Thus the story "My First Goose" opens with a description of the masculine charm of the brigade commander Savitsky. His male grace is celebrated in a shower of epithet—we hear of the "beauty of his giant's body," of the decorated chest "cleaving the hut as a standard cleaves the sky," of "the iron and flower of that youthfulness," of his long legs, which were "like girls sheathed to the neck in shining riding boots." Only the openness of the admiration and envy—which constitutes, also, a qualifying irony—keeps the description from seeming sexually perverse. It is remarkably *not* perverse; it is as "healthy" as a boy's love of his hero of the moment. And Savitsky's grace is a real thing. Babel is not ready to destroy it by any of the means that are so ready to the hand of the intellectual confronted by this kind of power and charm; he does not diminish the glory he perceives by confronting it with the pathos of human creatures less physically glorious, having more, or a higher, moral appeal because they are weaker and because they suffer. The possibility of this grace is part of what Babel saw in the Cossacks.

It is much the same thing that D. H. Lawrence was drawn by in his imagination or archaic cultures and personalities and of the ruthlessness, even the cruelty, that attended their grace. It is what Yeats had in mind in his love of "the old disturbed exalted life, the old splendor." It is what even the gentle Forster represents in the brilliant scene in *Where Angels Fear to Tread* in which Gino, the embodiment of male grace, tortures Stephen by twisting his broken arm. This fantasy of personal, animal grace, this glory of conscienceless self-assertion, of sensual freedom, haunts our culture. It speaks to something in us that we fear, and rightly fear, yet it speaks to us.

Babel never for a moment forgets what the actualities of this savage glory are. In the story "The Brigade Commander" he speaks of the triumph of a young man in his first command. Kolesnikov in his moment of victory had the "masterful indifference of a Tartar Khan," and Babel, observing him with genuine pleasure, goes on to say that he was conscious of the training of other famous leaders of horse, and mentions "the captivating Savitsky" and "the headstrong Pavlichenko." The captivating Savitsky we have met. The headstrong Pavlichenko appears in a story of his own; this story is his own account of his peasant origin, of the insults received from his aristocratic landlord, of how when the Revolution came, he had wiped out the insult. "Then I stamped on my master Nikitinsky; trampled on him for an hour or maybe more. And in that time I got to know life through and through. With shooting... you only get rid of a chap. Shooting's letting him off, and too damn easy for yourself. With shooting you'll never get at the soul, to where it is in a fellow and how it shows itself. But I don't spare myself, and I've more than once trampled an enemy for over an hour. You see, I want to get to know what life really is." This is all too *raffiné*—we are inclined, I think, to forget Pavlichenko and to be a little revolted by Babel. Let us suppose, however, that he is setting down the truth as he heard it; let us suppose too that he has it in mind not spare himself—this is part, and a terrible part, of the actuality of the Cossack directness and immediacy, this is what goes along with the grace and charm.

In our effort to understand Babel's complex involvement with the Cossack ethos we must be aware of the powerful and obsessive significance that violence has for the intellectual. Violence is, of course, the contradiction of the intellectual's characteristic enterprise of rationality. Yet at the same time it is the very image of that enterprise. This may seem a strange thing to say. Since Plato we have set violence and reason over against each other in reciprocal negation. Yet it is Plato who can tell us why there is affinity between violence and the intellectual life. In the most famous of the Platonic myths, the men of the Cave are seated facing the interior wall of the Cave, and they are chained by their necks so that it is impossible for them to turn their heads. They can face in but one direction, they can see nothing but the shadows that are cast on the wall by the fire behind them. A man comes to them who has somehow freed himself and gone into the world outside the Cave. He brings them news of the light of the sun; he tells them that there are things to be seen which are real, that what they see on the wall is but shadows. Plato says that the men chained in the Cave will not believe this news. They will insist that it is not possible, that the shadows are the only reality. But suppose they do believe the news! Then how violent they will become against their chains as they struggle to free themselves so that they may perceive what they believe is there to be perceived. They will think of violence as part of their bitter effort to know what is real. To grasp, to seize—to *apprehend*, as we say—reality from out of the deep dark cave of the mind—this is indeed a very violent action.

The artist in our time is perhaps more overtly concerned with the apprehension of reality than the philosopher is, and the image of violence seems often an appropriate way of representing the nature of his creation.

"The language of poetry naturally falls in with the language of power," says Hazlitt in his lecture on *Coriolanus* and goes on to speak in several brilliant passages of "the logic of the imagination and the passions" which makes them partisan with representations of proud strength. Hazlitt carries his generalization beyond the warrant of literary fact, yet all that he says is pertinent to Babel, who almost always speaks of art in the language of force. The unexpectedness which he takes to be the essence of art is that of a surprise attack. He speaks of the maneuvers of prose, of "the army of words, . . . the army in which all kinds of weapons may be brought into play." In one of his most remarkable stories, "Di Grasso," he describes the performance of a banal play given by an Italian troupe in Odessa; all is dreariness until in the third act the hero sees his betrothed in converse with the villainous seducer, and, leaping miraculously, with the power of levitation of a Nijinsky or a panther, he soars across the stage, falls upon the villain and tears out his enemy's throat with his teeth. This leap makes the fortune of the Italian company with the exigent Odessa audience; this leap, we are given to understand, is art. And as the story continues, Babel is explicit—if also ironic—in what he demonstrates of the moral effect that may be produced by this virtuosity and power, of what it implies of human pride and freedom.

The spectacles on his nose were for Babel of the first importance in his conception of himself. He was a man to whom the perception of the world outside the Cave came late and had to be apprehended, by strength and speed, against the parental or cultural interdiction, the Jewish interdiction; it was as if every beautiful violent phrase that was to spring upon reality was a protest against his childhood. The violence of the Revolution, its sudden leap, was cognate with this feral passion for perception—to an artist the Revolution might well have seemed the rending not only of the social but of the perceptual chains, those that held men's gaze upon the shadows on the wall; it may have seemed the rush of men from the darkness of the cave into the light of reality. Something of this is suggested in a finely wrought story "Line and Color"—like other stories of the time of Babel's sojourn in France in the early thirties, it was written in French—in which Kerensky is represented as defending his myopia, refusing to wear glasses, because, as he argues very charmingly, there is so much that myopia protects him from seeing, and imagination and benign illusion are thus given a larger license. But at a great meeting in the first days of the Revolution he cannot perceive the disposition of the crowd and the story ends with Trotsky coming to the rostrum and saying in his implacable voice, "Comrades!"

But when we have followed Babel into the depths of his experience of violence, when we have imagined something of what it meant in his psychic life and in the developing conception of his art, we must be no less aware of his experience of the principle that stands opposed to the Cossack's principle.

We can scarcely fail to see that when in the stories of *Red Cavalry* Babel submits the ethos of the intellectual to the criticism of the Cossack ethos, he intends a criticism of his own ethos not merely as an intellectual but as a Jew. It is always as an intellectual, never as a Jew, that he is denounced by his Cossack comrades, but we know that he has either suppressed, for political reasons, the denunciations of him as a Jew that were actually made, or, if none were actually made, that he has in his heart supposed that they were made. These criticisms of the Jewish ethos, as he embodies it, Babel believes to have no small weight. When he implores fate to grant him the simplest of proficiencies, the ability to kill his fellowman, we are likely to take this as nothing but an irony, and as an ironic assertion of the superiority of his moral instincts. But it is only in part an irony. There comes a moment when he should kill a fellowman. In "The Death of Dolgushov," a comrade lies propped against a tree; he cannot be moved, inevitably he must die, for his entrails are hanging out; he must be left behind and he asks for a bullet in his head so that the Poles will not "play their dirty tricks" on him. It is the narrator whom he asks for the *coup de grâce*, but the narrator flees and sends a friend, who, when he has done what had to be done, turns on the "sensitive" man in a fury of rage and disgust: "You bastards in spectacles have about as much pity for us as a cat has for a mouse." Or again, the narrator has incurred the enmity of a comrade through no actual fault—no moral fault—of his own, merely through having been assigned a mount that the other man passionately loved, and riding it badly so that it developed saddle galls. Now the horse has been returned, but the man does not forgive him, and the narrator asks a superior officer to compound the quarrel. He is rebuffed. "You're trying to live without enemies," he is told. "That's all you think about, not having enemies." It comes at us with momentous force. This time we are not misled into supposing that Babel intends irony and a covert praise of his pacific soul; we know that in this epiphany of his refusal to accept enmity he means to speak adversely of himself in his Jewish character.

But his Jewish character is not the same as the Jewish character of the Jews of Poland. To these Jews he comes with all the presuppositions of an acculturated Jew of Russia, which were not much different from the suppositions of an acculturated Jew of Germany. He is repelled by the conditions of their life; he sees them as physically uncouth and warped; many of them seem to him to move "monkey-fashion." Sometimes he affects a wondering alienation from them, as when he speaks of "the occult crockery that the Jews use only once a year at Eastertime." His complexity and irony being what they are, the Jews of Poland are made to justify the rejection of the Jews among whom he was reared and the wealthy assimilated Jews of Petersburg. "The image of the stout and jovial Jews of the South, bubbling like cheap wine, takes shape in my memory, in sharp contrast to the bitter scorn inherent in these long bony backs, these tragic yellow beards." Yet the Jews of Poland are more than a stick with which Babel beats his own Jewish past. They come to exist for him as a spiritual fact of consummate value.

Almost in the degree that Babel is concerned with violence in the stories of *Red Cavalry,* he is concerned with spirituality. It is not only Jewish spirituality that draws him. A considerable number of the stories have to do with churches, and although they do indeed often express the anticlerical feeling expectable in the revolutionary circumstances, the play of Babel's irony permits him to respond in a positive way to the aura of religion. "The breath of an invisible order of things," he says in one story, "glimmers beneath the crumbling ruin of the priest's house, and its soothing seduction unmanned me." He is captivated by the ecclesiastical painter Pan Apolek, he who created ecclesiastical scandals by using the publicans and sinners of the little towns as the models for his saints and virgins. Yet it is chiefly the Jews who speak to him of the life beyond violence, and even Pan Apolek's "heretical and intoxicating brush" had achieved its masterpiece in his Christ of the Berestechko church, "the most extraordinary image of God I had ever seen in my life," a curly-headed Jew, a bearded figure in a Polish greatcoat of orange, barefooted with torn and bleeding mouth, running from an angry mob with a hand raised to ward off a blow.

Hazlitt, in the passage to which I have referred, speaking of "the logic of the imagination and the passions," says that we are naturally drawn to the representation of what is strong and proud and feral. Actually that is not so: we are, rather, drawn to the representation of what is real. It was reality that Babel found in the Jews of the Polish provinces. "In these passionate, anguish-chiseled features there is no fat, no warm pulsing of blood. The Jews of Volhynia and Galicia move jerkily, in an uncontrolled and uncouth way; but their capacity for suffering is full of a somber greatness, and their unvoiced contempt for the Polish gentry unbounded."

Here was the counterimage to the captivating Savitsky, the image of the denial of the pride of the glory of the flesh to which, early or late, every artist comes, to which he cannot come in full sincerity unless he can also make full affirmation of the glory. Here too is the image of art that is counter to Di Grasso's leap, to the language in arms—the image of the artist's suffering, patience, uncouthness and scorn.

If Babel's experience with the Cossacks may be understood as having reference to the boy's relation to his father, his experience of the Jews of Poland has, we cannot but feel, a maternal reference. To the one Babel responds as a boy, to the other as a child. In the story "Gedali" he speaks with open sentimentality of his melancholy on the eve of Sabbaths—"On those evenings my child's heart was rocked like a little ship upon enchanted waves. O the rotted Talmuds of my childhood! O the dense melancholy of memories." And when he has found a Jew, it is one who speaks to him in this fashion: "All is mortal. Only the mother is destined to immortality. And when the mother is no longer living, she leaves a memory which none yet has dared to sully. The memory of the mother nourishes in us a compassion that is like the ocean, and the measureless ocean feeds the rivers that dissect the universe."

He has sought Gedali in his gutted curiosity-shop ("Where was your kindly shade that evening, Dickens?") to ask for "a Jewish glass of tea, and a little of that pensioned-off God in a glass of tea." He does not, that evening, get what he asks for; what he does get is a discourse on revolution, on the impossibility of a revolution made in blood, on the International that is never to be realized, the International of the good.

It was no doubt the easier for Babel to respond to the spiritual life of the Jews of Poland because it was a life coming to its end and having about it the terrible strong pathos of its death. He makes no pretense that it could ever claim him for its own. But it established itself in his heart as an image, beside the image of the other life that also could not claim him, the Cossack life. The opposition of these two images made his art—but it was not a dialectic that his Russia could permit.

IRVING HOWE

The Right to Write Badly

The publication of Isaac Babel's collected stories, coming at a time when the dominant political and cultural trends are deeply hostile to his kind of imagination, is cause for happiness. Most of the stories have appeared in one or another English version, but now to have them in their proper order and thereby to receive their accumulative impact is to know that Babel is not merely, as Maksim Gorky claimed, the most gifted prose writer of post-revolutionary Russia, but one of the literary masters of our century.

This, in a way, is hardly news. Babel's work, when it first came out in the twenties, was quickly praised by the Russian and European critics: anyone with half an ear could recognize that he was, to put it bluntly, a genius. But we live in a culture so committed to opportunism that Babel's work, incompatible with the religiosity and obscurantism that have recently dominated the literary world, needs to be read as if it *were* new, a suddenly discovered gift from an earlier generation.

A few words about Babel's life may help illuminate the quality of his writing. Born in 1894, he was raised in a lower-middle-class Jewish family in Odessa, and during the pre-revolutionary period, when he lived and starved in Moscow as a literary bohemian, he became a protégé of Gorky. After five years of fighting in the revolution and civil war, Babel returned to his writing and won immediate fame as the author of *Red Cavalry*, a book of breathtaking stories that draw from his experiences with a Cossack unit in Budenny's army. But as the Stalin dictatorship hardened its grip, Babel

From *The New Republic* 133, no. 27, 4 July 1955. © 1955 by New Republic, Inc.

wrote less and less (he was not, in any case, very productive) and after a time he lapsed into silence.

In 1934 Babel made one of his rare public appearances, at the first Russian Writers' Congress, partly to join in the ritual of pledging loyalty to the regime, partly to explain his failure to publish. His performance—it is vividly described in Mr. Trilling's introduction—was a remarkable political act. He practiced, said Babel, a new literary genre: he was "the master of the genre of silence." And in the midst of his praise for the regime and the party, he remarked, as if in passing, that they presumed to deprive writers of only one right, the right to write badly. "Comrades," he went on, "let us not fool ourselves: this is a very important right and to take it away from us is no small thing. . . . Let us give up this right, and may God help us. And if there is no God, let us help ourselves."

The right to write badly!—which is to say, to write from one's own feelings, even from one's own mistakes. It would be hard to imagine a more courageous, and a more saddening, gesture on the part of a writer whose every impulse was for the spontaneity, the freedom, the playfulness which his society denied. Babel, who was protected by Gorky and for whom, it was rumored, even Number One had a soft spot, suffered no immediate punishment, other than the continued silence he had imposed on himself. But in 1937 he was arrested and two or three years later he died in a concentration camp. Except for a memorial note on Gorky which appeared in 1938, Babel remained silent to the end, the master of his genre.

The stories in *Red Cavalry,* which form over half the present volume, impress one in endless ways, but their primary impact is shock. "Hard, terse, violent, gorgeously colored, they come upon one like disciplined explosions. Primitive Cossack ways jar against Babel's sophisticated consciousness; the random brutality that is the inheritance of centuries of blackness suddenly lifts itself to a selfless red heroism, and in the very moment of doing so helplessly corrupts the heroism; extremes of behavior, weaving into one another as if to spite all moralists, bewilder Babel as narrator and the reader as onlooker.

The stories turn upon Babel's struggle with a problem that cannot be understood unless it is seen both in the immediate historical context (the Russian Revolution) and in the context of Babel's personal being and tradition as both intellectual and Jew. Though he was not, so far as we know, concerned with politics as ideological definition or power strategy, Babel understood with absolute sureness the problem that has obsessed all modern novelists who deal with politics: the problem of action in both its heroic necessity and its ugly self-contamination, the "tragic flaw" that is at the heart of an historical action which by virtue of being historical must to some extent be conceived in violence and therefore as a distortion and coarsening of its "self." But it must be stressed that Babel sees this problem not as a mere exercise in metaphysics: for him it is part of the very texture of action. And it is in this sense, despite the virtual absence of explicit politics, that the stories in *Red Cavalry* are profoundly revolutionary: under the red heat of Babel's passion, creation and contemplation melt into one.

The problem of historical action also absorbs Malraux and Silone in their best novels, and in Bert Brecht's great poem "To Posterity" it receives its most exalted and its most shameful expression, for here every word is bitterly true yet the poem itself is put to service as a rationale for Stalinism. For Babel, characteristically, the problem turns into one of personal assertion, his capacity to embrace and engage in, yet at some level of awareness to stand apart from, the most terrifying extremes of human conduct.

In his introduction, Mr. Trilling has raised, or perhaps I should say, abstracted, this problem into a kind of timeless moral dialectic. "In Babel's heart," he writes, "there was a kind of fighting—he was captivated by the vision of two ways of being, the way of violence and the way of peace, and he was torn between them." True as this is, I think it misses the center of Babel's concern, which was not so much the choice between "two ways of being" open to men in almost any circumstances and at almost any time, but rather the unbearable—unbearable because felt as entirely necessary—difficulties of being an artist committed to the fate of a desperate revolution. One very important side of Babel was a Bolshevik, or tried hard to be ("O regulations of the Russian Communist Party," begins one story, "You have laid headlong rails through the sour pastry of our Russian tales"), and precisely from this side of Babel came some of the energies and anxieties that give life to his work. Like it or not, we cannot blink this simple fact, nor the equally important fact that Babel, as a writer whose politics and esthetics meet in an appetite for extremes, does not lend himself very easily to those more reasonable modes of feeling which Mr. Trilling has designated as the Liberal Imagination. To deprive a writer of the immediacy, even the distracting immediacy, of his preoccupations is at times to lessen his capacity for disturbing and uprooting us.

Some of the most terrible stories in *Red Cavalry* are directed against Babel himself, against his inability to kill other men and his tragi-comic efforts to adapt himself to the ways of the Cossacks. The Jewish literary man, with spectacles on his nose and autumn in his heart, needs to prove to himself that, *given the historical necessity,* he can commit acts which for the Cossack are virtually second nature. But since he is also a human being and a writer of imaginative largesse, Babel in the course of "lending" himself to the Cossacks falls in love with their gracefulness of gesture and movement. (Mr. Trilling, linking Babel with Tolstoy, has some acute remarks on this.) Above all, Babel admires the Cossacks' sureness of manner, their unreflective absorption in inherited modes of life.

Yet he does not sentimentalize the Cossacks nor use them, as a modern literary man might, to sanction his own repressed aggressiveness. He remains in awed puzzlement before the ancient mysteries of their ways, and even when he achieves occasional rapport with them he does not pretend to understand them. But he grants them every possible human claim, and he trembles beneath the lash of their simple unqualified criticism.

In a magnificent five-page story called "The Death of Dolgushov," a wounded Cossack, his entrails hanging over his knees, begs Babel to shoot him, but Babel, soft and scrupulous, funks it. A comrade of the wounded man does the job and then turns furiously upon Babel: "You guys in specs have about as much pity for chaps like us as a cat has for a mouse." In another five-page masterpiece, "After the Battle," a Cossack curses Babel for having ridden into battle with an unloaded revolver ("You didn't put no cartridge in. . . . You worship God, you traitor!") and Babel goes off "imploring fate to grant me the simplest of proficiencies—the ability to kill my fellow-men." And at the end of *Red Cavalry* another Cossack pronounces his primitive sentence upon Babel: "You're trying to live without enemies. That's all you think about, not having enemies."

As counterforce to the Cossacks Babel turns to the Polish Jews, squatting in their villages while opposing armies trample back and forth, passive and impervious to the clamor for blood. Even as he fights in the Red Army, Babel listens, with the attentiveness of a child, to Gedali, the Hasid who believes that "the Revolution means joy" and who wants "an International of good people." "I would like every soul to be listed," says Gedali, "and given first-category rations. There, soul, please eat and enjoy life's pleasures. Pan comrade, you don't know what the International is eaten with. . . ." "It is eaten with gunpowder," answers Babel, "and spiced with best-quality blood."

The Jews of Poland, with the "long bony backs, their tragic yellow beards," pierce through the taut objectivity of Babel's narrative and stir in him a riot of memories ("O the rotted Talmuds of my childhood!"). He goes back and forth from the Cossacks, strange, cruel and beautiful, to the ghetto Jews, who "moved jerkily, in an uncontrolled and uncouth way, but [whose] capacity for suffering was full of a sombre greatness." If *Red Cavalry* is a paean, ambiguous but ardent, to the force of revolution, it is also an elegy for the dying ghetto, for "the Sabbath peace [which] rested upon the crazy roofs of Zhitomer."

Even to mention Babel's style is to involve one's self in a tangle of contradictions and frustrations. Gestures of bare violence turn abruptly, without notice or preparation, into states of reflective quietness and repose. Objectivity seems the dominant mode, yet few modern prose writers would dare indulge in such lyrical apostrophes and such laments as fill Babel's pages. We have been taught to value terseness and understatement; but in Babel terseness has nothing whatever to do with understatement, since it is actually the consequence of the boldest political and metaphysical generalizations. Indeed, hardly another writer of our time has succeeded so well in making the generalization, even the political slogan, so organically a part of his imagery. One moves in these stories with a dizzying speed from conceptual abstraction to primitive notation: Babel never permits the reader to rest in any mold or style or upon any level of perception, he always drives one from surprise to surprise. In some of the stories there is a surrender to sadness as complete as the urge to motion and violence that accompanies it. In other stories the event itself has been removed from sight, and the surface of the prose is devoted to a few wry ripples of talk and a few startling images of place and weather.

The best observation on Babel's style has been made by John Berryman, who has noted certain similarities to the style of Stephen Crane. In both writers there is an obsessive concern with compression and explosion, a kinesthetic ferocity of control, a readiness to wrench language in order to gain nervous immediacy. Both use language as if to inflict a wound. But the differences are also important. Babel, as Berryman goes on to mention, is warm, while Crane is cold. And more important, I think, Babel has a wider range of effects; by comparison, Crane seems a little stiff-jointed.

The two main literary sources upon which Babel seems to have drawn, Russian and Yiddish, flourished most in the fifty or seventy-five years directly before he began to write; he was one of those writers who spring up at the end of such a creative period and absorb its energies as if they were still at their fullest. The Chekhov strain in Russian literature is strongly evident in Babel's miscellaneous stories (though not so much in *Red Cavalry* or his other group called *Tales of Odessa*); one quickly recognizes the pathos, the warm skepticism of the older writer. The Yiddish literary influence is less likely to be noticed by American critics (Mr. Trilling pays no attention to it). But surely no one who has read Sholom Aleichem can fail to see that in Babel's Odessa stories there is a remarkable parallel of effect: the comic grasp of social relationships, the sardonic arguing with God, the attraction to the undersides of history. Compare Babel's bitter wit with Sholom Aleichem's impudent reverence in writing about Jewish fate.

> [BABEL]: "But wasn't it a mistake on God's part to settle the Jews in Russia, where they've had to suffer the tortures of Hell? Would it be bad if the Jews lived in Switzerland, where they'd be surrounded by first-class lakes, mountain air and nothing but Frenchmen? Everybody makes mistakes, even God."
>
> [SHOLOM ALEICHEM]: "Apparently if He wants it that way, that's the way it ought to be. Can't you see? If it should have been different it would have been. And yet, what would have been wrong to have it different?"

Sometimes the richness of emotion, and often the very phrasing of his idiom, is understandable only in terms of Babel's relationship to Yiddish literature. In a story called "In the Basement" the vulgar-loving rebuke of a grandfather to a boy who tries to commit suicide ("My grandson . . . I'm taking a dose of castor oil, so as to have something to place on your grave") is given its true value and inflection only if one knows that in the Jewish mores suicide is taken to be not merely impious, but in a strictly human sense, shameful.

I shall have to stop in a moment, but before I do a word needs to be said about the underlying quality of Babel's work which gives it a special excitement for our time. Lost as he often is in melancholia and sadness, perplexed and perhaps even a little betrayed as he sometimes is by violence, Babel—through his simple readiness to accept his own desires—makes upon life the most radical of demands: the demand for happiness. In his work one finds a straining toward a union of passion and tenderness, those two elements of feeling which Freud says have become dissociated in the life of modern man and which, because they are dissociated, tend to decline into aggressiveness and impotence. I do not say that Babel often achieves this union, only that he will not let anything, not even "the regulations of the Communist Party," distract him from straining toward it. In his work everything becomes eroticized, everything becomes animated: love and energy come closer.

There is a lovely little story by Babel in which he describes how a baby named Karl-Yankel (half Marxist-half Jew) is being fought over by the two sets of believers. Babel, watching the comic struggle, ends the story by telling himself, "It's not possible . . . it's not possible that you won't be happy, Karl-Yankel. It's not possible that you won't be happier than I."

RENATO POGGIOLI

Isaak Babel in Retrospect

Now, when the American reader has at his disposal the whole body of Babel's narrative writings, may be the time to reassess what is probably the best work of fiction that has ever appeared in Soviet Russia, one written partly within the framework of Soviet literature and partly outside of it. The best way to proceed is perhaps to relive first its author's *curriculum vitae*, which, in the light of the historical experience in which he was actor as well as victim, is both tragic and exemplary.

Isaak Emmanuilovich Babel was born in 1894, in Odessa, of a family of small Jewish merchants. He spent his childhood in Nikolaev, where, as his stories relate, he fully experienced what the life of a Jew under tsardom was really like. From his youth he must have asked himself the question which in "The King" he puts in the mouth of his hero, the gangster Benya Krik: "But wasn't it a mistake on the part of God to settle the Jews in Russia, for them to be tormented worse than in Hell?" In "The Story of My Dovecot" he re-evokes his own early struggle and toil to be admitted into a Russian school, inaccessible to all too few Jewish boys because of the *numerus clausus*; in the same tale and in "First Love" he recalls the murder of his grand-uncle Shoyl during the pogrom of 1905, as well as the humiliation of his father, whose kneeling down before a Cossack officer did not spare his shop from a looting mob, nor himself from ruin.

The work of Babel is often autobiographical, but never pathetic, and only indirectly does it reveal the most intimate secrets of the author's psy-

---

From *The Phoenix and the Spider*. © 1957 by the President and Fellows of Harvard College; © 1985 by Renato Poggioli. Harvard University Press, 1957.

chology and personality. Yet, from the reading of his tales, we easily discover that the writer was deeply affected by a sense of alienation from the world. That sense was rooted in the three curses of his life, which were race, poverty, and his calling as an artist. Perhaps the spectacles on his nose and the books under his arm estranged him from the world at large even more than his being a pauper and a Jew. Babel shared all his life that feeling of loneliness so characteristic of the prerevolutionary intelligentsia, with its unrequited and all too mystical love for the Russian masses. At the same time, as a denizen of the ghetto, or of the worst urban slums, he deeply felt as an added curse, for both the man and the artist within himself, his inability to commune with nature, to experience within his heart and mind all the lively and lovely things that organic life creates for the joy of man.

Babel's isolation is to be seen also in his attitude toward Jewish culture itself. When his family returned to Odessa, he failed to follow the trend dominating the Jewish cultural life of that prosperous and turbulent city. While Vilna was the capital of Yiddish writing, expressing the life of the "pale" in the vernacular language, with a prosaic realism, full of self-pity and irony, Odessa was the moral center of Zionism, and had generated a school of poets returning to the messianic and prophetic traditions of old, singing of the newly promised land in the sacred and symbolic accents of the ancient tongue. Thus his city really deserved the sad praise sung for it by one of the many rabbis we meet in Babel's masterpiece: "Odessa, a god-fearing town—the star of our exile, the involuntary well of our distress." But Babel refused both Yiddish and Hebrew, and chose instead Russian, the idiom of the goyim. He did so not merely to escape from the ghetto, but to turn, through Russia, to Europe and to the West.

In those years he had discovered his masters, who were not only Tolstoy, Chekhov, and Gorky, but also Rabelais, Flaubert, and Maupassant. It was the same urge, the urge to know a broader and nobler world, that led him to settle in Petersburg toward the end of the First World War. The city was then closed to Jews not settled there, and Babel lived in the capital illegally, without means of his own, and with great hardships, in order to start a literary career. His first stories appeared in print in 1917, under the aegis of Gorky, in the review the latter was then editing, *Letopis* (The Chronicle). They had a *succès de scandale,* and got the young writer an indictment for obscenity, but the trial never took place, because of the fall of the tsarist regime. In the meantime Babel had been drafted, and the February revolution caught him while he was fighting the Germans on the Rumanian front.

Babel saw in that great upheaval the first communal experience in which he could share, the first social and historical reality of which he could finally become an active and integral part. After October, although not a party member, he served enthusiastically the new communist order in varied missions and tasks, and was finally attached, first as a civilian, and later in uniform, to the "mounted army" led by Marshal (then General) Budenny in the Polish campaign and in the Civil War. He edited for that army *Krasny Kavalerist* ("The Red Trooper"), a propaganda sheet, and fought with it on the western and southern fronts. Then, after a few years of silence, he started writing again. "It was only in 1923," he stated later, "that I learned to express my ideas clearly and at not too great length." So he wrote down his impressions of those two campaigns in the forms of sketches, which, as they were published, provoked the indignant protest of Budenny, who saw in them a libel against the troops under his command. In 1924 Babel collected about thirty of those sketches in the book known as *Red Cavalry* (or rather, "The Mounted Army," as the Russian title *Konarmiya* really means), which revealed to the Russian public that a new and gifted writer had been born.

Shortly afterwards he published the slim collection *Tales of Odessa*, which, however, passed almost unnoticed. In the meantime Russian social and political reality had been rapidly changing, and Babel did not feel any longer in tune with what was going on, on other fronts as well as the literary one. He was already considered a "fellow traveler," according to the sense which that term had been given by Trotsky in his book *Literature and Revolution*. It was for writers like him that, after the introduction of the new literary orthodoxy represented by the dogma of "socialist realism," Gorky coined the formula of "revolutionary romanticism," so as to justify those mild heretics who still looked back with nostalgia to the tragic and epic years of the civil war, instead of looking forward and celebrating what the regime was now building on the ruins of the past. The changed atmosphere made it difficult for Babel to write anything important or new, although he tried his hand at a novel, and wrote a rather interesting play, *Sunset*, dealing with the same hero and the same milieu he had already treated in the *Tales of Odessa*.

Soon after this, Babel practically ceased to write, as he confessed, rather ambiguously, in a speech he gave at the 1934 Writers' Congress. At that time he was still free to travel abroad, and he went for a while to Paris, where, as he had already tried to do in his youth, he did some writing in French. Upon his return home, his creative vein dried out, and he published nothing but an augmented and revised one-volume collection of all his short stories, which appeared in 1934. Significantly enough, several political and historical allusions, dealing with the revolutionary role of Trotsky, were expunged either by the author or the censor from this text. Babel's signature appeared in print for the last time in 1937; one year later he was arrested at the peak of the purges of Trotsky's followers, supposedly for no other crime than an imprudent joke about Stalin, and he was sent to a concentration camp, where he died in 1939 or 1940. According to one version, he succumbed to disease or hardships; according to another, he was shot. In either case, what spelled his doom was that revolution in which he had so desperately willed to believe, and thus he died in the same alienation in which he had lived. Whatever happened to Babel the man, we know that the writer was officially condemned to death. After his disappearance, his works were proscribed, and his name was condemned to public oblivion.

Red Cavalry, which remains Babel's masterpiece, is a book hard to describe to those who are unacquainted with it. When we read its pages, we see all the western and southern marches of Russia: Volhynia, Podolia, and the Ukraine pass fleetingly by. We ride, in a cloud of powder and dust, amidst bursts of fire, and rattling of sabers, from the flat fields of Poland to the green slopes of the Caucasus. In the distance, among the felled trees and the burned huts, we watch, as they pass before us, the men and women, old and young, who are both the victims and the spectators of our endless raid. Jews in the cities and peasants in the villages look with unseeing eyes at the horsemen and their mounts, both of Cossack blood, that are trampling on their land and their lives. Sometimes, all of a sudden, a horse gallops by without his master, whom a Polish or "White" bullet has nailed forever to the wet mother earth. Some of the riders may turn their heads to salute the lost comrade, but the mounted army will never stop or slow down its relentless race toward war and death. And while riding along, we glimpse on the open skyline the giant shadow of the Russian masses on the move, and we wonder whether their march is an ordeal or a quest.

The reader will never forget the figures who appear fleetingly in the pages of this book. We shall mention a few of them. The mounted army's chief officer, the former tsarist "noncom," Semen Budenny, who smokes and smiles while threatening to shoot anyone who yields or turns back. The youthful giant Savitski, with his legs as handsome as a girl's in his shining boots. The red general Pavlichenko, still smelling of milk as he did when he was a herdsman, who could tame buffaloes and elephants as well as goats and sheep. Konkin, the former ventriloquist, shooting prisoners as if they were clay pigeons. The young officer Kolesnikov, who knows how to do honor to his luck when the fortunes of war raise him to an exalted command. Dyakov, who was once a circus performer, and under whose will and skill a dying nag may still perform like a thoroughbred. And Afonka Bida, with his shrill feminine voice, who weeps over his dead horse and who raids the countryside for days and nights, in order to get himself a new mount as good as the old one.

On the other side there are all the meek and the weak, the poor and the humble, whom for their mischance we shall meet on our path: Apolek, the Polish wandering artist, a heretic and a mystic, portraying peasants, publicans, and country wenches in the saintly figures he paints on the walls of a Catholic church; his German friend Gottfried, the blind musician with white mice as pets; and numberless Jews, among whom there stands out the old Gedali, the Dickensian owner of a curio shop, who is unable to distinguish between counterrevolution and revolution, because he does not know where in the latter the good ends and the evil begins, and who dreams of another, impossible International, one made only of men of good will.

Unlike Gedali, Babel seems to know where the good ends and the evil begins. For him, the revolution is good, and the counterrevolution is bad. He may hope or believe that sooner or later we shall have another International, this time made only of decent people; but he thinks that in the meanwhile we must be satisfied with the Third, and pay for both the present and the future with sweat, tears, and blood. As his hero Benya Krik will later say in the *Tales of Odessa,* in the story entitled "The King": "There are people already condemned to death, and there are people who have not yet begun to live." And many must die so that others may begin to live. By bowing to what one might call either historical necessity or revolutionary expediency, Babel ends by accepting as valid and just the ordeal of war: war taking victims from both enemies and friends, from the strong as well as from the weak. Thus one of the main antinomies of this book is the everlasting conflict between the army and the militia, between the volunteer and the professional soldier, between the man for whom war is an occupation or a calling and the man for whom war is an act of either freedom or necessity. A man with a faith like Babel's will fight out of a sense of ideological duty, and thus will treat any kind of military struggle as a civil war. But for the Cossacks of the unit to which he is attached, the enemy is always an alien or a stranger, and war itself is a job. Strangely enough, the realization of this contrast stirs within the soul of Babel what one might call an inferiority complex, and he feels his own unworthiness before all those martial murderers for whom killing is a natural habit, or a simple routine. Thus he defends the slaughter and the slaughterers from those who fear and condemn them: "She cannot do without shooting," he tells Gedali, "because she is the Revolution." Without being born a killer, he not only joins the killers, but wishes and tries to become one of them, "imploring fate to grant *him* the simplest of all proficiencies—the ability to kill *his* fellow men."

It is with a sense of great humility that he accepts as fully deserved the reproach of weakness leveled at him by those who are soiling their hands while "busy shelling and getting at the kernel for *him*." And he trembles in every vein when a Cossack sees through his chicken heart, all too full of worries, especially with the concern "to live without enemies," all too empty of bravery, even of the simple courage to cut short the torments of a comrade mortally wounded, with a violent and yet merciful death. Thus, in order to gain the friendship of the Cossacks, he beheads a poor goose, and propitiates them with his offering of the slaughtered animal for their evening meal: yet, at night, after the sacrifice, his heart feels stained by the blood he has shed. Despite this, the attitude of Babel toward the Cossacks remains that of an unrequited lover, while at the same time he turns his pity toward the victims of the slaughter, whoever they are, although in the main they are Jews like him. Often he even admires the moral strength of the meek and the weak, as when he says, speaking of the Jews of Galicia and Volhynia: "Their capacity for suffering was full of a somber greatness." The very man who accepts war as the apocalypse, and revolution as the palingenesis, of history, rejects the daily crimes and commonplace misdeeds they imply: "The chronicle of our workaday offenses oppresses me without respite like an ailing heart." Babel is thus of the devil's party, and knows it. His unavowed comradeship may go not to his war companions, but to their victims, and he certainly feels misplaced among the slaughterers whom he wishes to imitate, and cannot help but admire and love. Yet, although unable to fully identify himself with the murderers, he still remains with them, even if only as an outcast.

Mr. Trilling, who has written a penetrating essay about Babel, tries to explain his inner conflict in terms of the contrast between Jew and Cossack, claiming, however, that the writer has tried to reconcile that contrast within his mind and soul: "Babel's view of the Cossack was more consonant with that of Tolstoy than with the traditional view of his own people. For him the Cossack was indeed the noble savage, all too savage, not often noble, yet having in his savagery some quality that might raise strange questions in the Jewish mind." There is some truth in this, but not the whole truth. If the conflict could be reduced only to such terms as those, then its reconciliation would be a purely literary one. Mr. Trilling is undoubtedly right in mentioning Tolstoy in connection with this book. Yet the Tolstoy who has directly influenced *Red Cavalry* is not the youthful author of *The Cossacks*, but the old and classical master of *Hadji Murad*, as we could easily prove by examining Babel's style, and by listing all the reminiscences, especially in the form of images, that the reading of that late Tolstoyan tale has left embedded in the pages of this book. The difference between *The Cossacks* and *Hadji Murad* is not merely that in the latter the Cossacks are replaced by Caucasian Tartars, but that its characters are evoked in heroic rather than in sentimental terms. While in his earlier work Tolstoy looks at Luka and at his fellow Cossacks in the idealized light of a Rousseauistic vision, in his later one he represents Hadji Murad and his followers with objective simplicity, in an epic, not nostalgic, key. It seems to us both evident and significant that Babel's imagination had been influenced by *Hadji Murad* more than by *The Cossacks*: yet from another viewpoint, the inspiration of *Red Cavalry* is rather mixed, and this makes it nearer to *The Cossacks* than to *Hadji Murad*.

What we mean is that both *Red Cavalry* and *The Cossacks* have been written out of a dual mood, out of their authors' double allegiance to opposite attitudes and values. In the case of Babel's book, one could say that the writer has made his own the antagonism between Jew and Cossack, or, as we prefer, between the killers and the killed. In brief, there are two main strains in this work, and neither of them dominates fully its atmosphere or its structure. The first strain is epic in quality, but, despite its power, acts within the book in a fragmentary and spasmodic way, or, in literary terms, as a rhapsody. Babel's epic breath is genuine, but, as in all moderns, rather short. Thus Babel fills the intervals between warlike episodes with a pathetic strain, which is antiheroic in character. Many critics have maintained that the book is based on a contrast between epic and lyrical values. We would say, rather, that the lyrical element appears in and results from only the juxtaposition of the heroic and the pathetic ones. Mr. Trilling must have guessed this when he states that even when recording "violence of the extreme kind," Babel responds to the brutality so recorded "with a kind of lyric joy." In such moments, Babel reconciles within himself the man and the artist, in a reconciliation that is truly poetic, rather than merely literary.

The supreme manifestations of such a reconciliation are to be found in those crucial images through which Babel sums up an entire episode, or closes it. Think of the vision of the newly elected brigade commander, bowing his head under the burden of his responsibility, and yet standing out against the whole horizon while marching toward either glory or death: "And suddenly on the earth stretching away far into the distance, on the furrowed, yellow nakedness of the fields, we could see nothing but Kolesnikov's narrow back, his dangling arms, and sunken, gray-capped head." Think of the scene where the Cossacks ride calmly across the plain, with no other accompaniment but the tune and the words of an ancient ballad: "The song floated away like smoke." Think finally of the vengeance of Prishchepa, who first cruelly punishes all his fellow villagers who pillaged the property of his parents, executed by the Whites, and then ends by burning down his family hut: "The fire shone as bright as Sunday."

Babel submits to this kind of poetic transfiguration only what he has once seen with his own eyes, and feels still alive in his own soul. His imagination, which is strikingly original, prefers to operate at the level where mere invention can be dispensed with. Despite this, in *Red Cavalry* or elsewhere, he never writes autobiographical pieces in the narrow sense of the term. The character using the first person singular in his tales is more of a spectator than an actor; at any rate, he is never a central figure. That character is often identical with the writer himself, and yet he is not so much a person as a point of view. The vision conveyed through his perspective is often static; what the writer tries to recapture is the tension of being, when time seems to stand still, rather than the ever changing and daily drama of man's life. Many critics misjudged this quality, and this led them to accuse Babel of a lack of psychological depth or complexity. Perhaps they failed to realize that in his chosen medium, a short story as brief as a sketch and as tight as a prose poem, there is room for sudden epiphanies, but not for searching and slowly unfolding insights. We forget all too often that while the novel can be musical, the short story is plastic and visual in essence. And Babel works like a painter, representing on a flat surface and in a small space all the massive and colorful variety of reality. Like an old painter he yields to other figures the center of the scene, while tracing his own self-portrait in one of the corners of the canvas. The immediacy of his vision seems to suggest that he always writes under the shock or impact of the event; yet at second sight we realize that he represents the event itself as if it were detached in both mood and time. In his work rage is controlled by order, and the emotion is recollected in tranquillity. This is why these tales look at first as if they were only vignettes, but this impression is immediately corrected by the sense of their perfection, of their finicky polish and finish, which justifies up to a point the Soviet critic who defined them as miniatures. Yet, although many-colored and vivid, their moral contrast is as simple and elemental as the chromatic one between white and black, and this is why they remind us, more than of anything else, of Goya's engravings about the horrors, and even the splendors, of war.

Red Cavalry is not the whole of Babel's literary heritage. The *Tales of Odessa*, although inferior to *Red Cavalry,* as well as posterior to it, could perhaps serve as a better introduction to his work. While *Red Cavalry* is epic and lyric in character, the *Tales of Odessa* are picaresque and picturesque. They do not deal with the world at large, which is the world of history, but with a narrow and peculiar milieu, the Jewish quarter of Odessa, the so-called Moldavanka, of which the author gives us the glorified annals. The main characters of this book are rogues, mainly smugglers and racketeers, and its single hero is Benya Krik, "gangster and king of gangsters," but above all a passionate man, since "passion rules the universe." One could say that this little collection is a kind of *Beggar's Opera* in fictional form, with the difference that Benya Krik is a more human, and less cruel, MacHeath. This representation of Jewish popular life, with its allusions to Jewish folklore, with weddings, funerals, and feasts, goes against the grain of Yiddish writing, since, unlike the latter, Babel treats the denizens of the ghetto as romantic heroes and as plebian caricatures at the same time. Here pathos merges into a kind of sympathetic grotesque, producing an art which reminds us of the engravings of Hogarth, or of the prints of Callot.

If "The Story of My Dovecot" lies halfway between the world of *Red Cavalry* and the *Tales of Odessa,* the piece entitled "Guy de Maupassant" occupies a place of its own within the canon of Babel's work. Inspired perhaps by Chekhov's "Mire," this simple narrative in the first person, certainly autobiographical in character, begins be re-evoking the author's illegal stay, and his bohemian way of life, in Petersburg. To make a little money, the protagonist accepts a position helping a rich Jewish lady with no literary abilities to translate into Russian the whole of Maupassant. The high point of the tale is the dramatic contrast between the plush vulgarity of her person, house, and milieu, and the noble and comic naïveté of her literary ambitions. This awkward situation is handled with great irony and pity, which redeem even the sexual climax of the story, where the two co-translators consummate an embrace in the propitiatory presence of Maupassant's ghost.

No story better testifies to the maturity of Babel's talent than this one. It is therefore only fitting that it contains the whole of his *ars poetica,* so to speak, in a nutshell. The author expresses his views about style, and his ideals of writing, in two statements, which are not merely personal asides, but observations naturally and directly related to the subject matter of the story, which is the translator's (or the writer's) task. Here is the first: "A phrase is born into the world good and bad at the same time. The secret lies in a slight, almost invisible twist. The lever should rest in your hand, getting warm, and you can turn it once, not twice." And here is the second, which is a development of the first: "I began to speak of style, of the army of words, of the army in which all kinds of weapons may come into play. No iron can stab the breast with such force as a period put at the right place." Babel's sympathy for Flaubert and his school justifies Lionel Trilling's claim that at least the first of these two passages has been dictated by an obsessive concern for *le mot juste.* Yet, if we look deeper, we shall find in both passages echoes of ideas that Tolstoy developed in *What is Art?* There is in that treatise an all too neglected page, where Tolstoy says that all art is merely a matter of a "wee bit" less or of a "wee bit" more: of avoiding or omitting here and there a little something insignificant in itself, but the absence or presence of which spells success or failure. What Babel has added to this theory is a series of dynamic and material images, mechanical and military in content. Yet they suffice to change into a skillful craft, or into a cunning strategy, what Tolstoy had conceived of as an intuitive process or a tentative quest. In the same manner, Babel seems also to accept the Tolstoyan theory of artistic communication as a contagion of feeling, although even here he replaces the notion of contagion with a surgical, or even murderous, metaphor. And it matters very little that Babel seems to reduce the sorcery of words to the operation of a well-placed graphic symbol, of a mere sign of punctuation, which is, however, able to pierce our mind, as well as our soul. Perhaps the miracle of his art lies in this power to touch and wound, rather than to calm and soothe, through the magic of words. If this is true, then the best epigraph for the whole of his work was given by the author himself, in the very phrase by which he tried to define Maupassant's writings in this story named after him. We certainly can repeat for Babel's tales what he said of the stories of his French master: that they are "the magnificent grave of a human heart."

FRANK O'CONNOR

The Romanticism of Violence

The two most remarkable storytellers of the First World War were Ernest Hemingway and Isaac Babel. It may be a slight inaccuracy to link Babel with the European war when his connections were mainly with the Russian Civil War, but the two wars and the two men clearly belong together.

The two men have in common what I can only describe as a romanticism of violence. Hemingway's is clear enough. He never makes the mistake of celebrating "Mercy, Pity, Peace, and Love." The only virtue he exalts is physical courage. In reading Irish or Icelandic sagas we have to be prepared to exalt it too, for, like patience and industry, it is a necessary condition of existence, but our society has so conditioned us that we tend to relegate it to policemen and sailors, and even in wartime among the troops there is no particular enthusiasm for the fighting man who is superlatively brave. He is only too likely to get his comrades into trouble.

This is what I call romanticism and Babel shares it with Hemingway. One can only assume that the romanticism goes deeper than the mere accident of finding themselves either brave or timid in the conditions of modern warfare, and that it must be rooted in childish or adolescent experiences of suffering. One who in childhood has got himself the reputation of being a coward and in later life proves his own courage will naturally be inclined to attach more significance to it than the rest of us do.

What Hemingway's experience was we don't know, but it is easy enough to imagine that Babel's must be connected with the suffering and humiliation

---

From *The Lonely Voice: A Study of the Short Story.* © 1962, 1963 by Frank O'Connor. World Publishing, 1963.

of a Jewish boy of genius in a half-barbarous society whose langauge gives us the word we use to describe anti-Jewish atrocities. Isaac Babel would have been a very queer Jewish boy—and indeed, a very queer boy—if he had not often imagined himself as the avenger with the gun.

And yet this fantasy contradicts something that goes very deep in the Jewish character—an instinctive apprehension that though money is excellent and power is good, books are in some way better; a conviction of the supremacy of mind over matter, of the word over the deed. That is why when a Jew turns vicious he turns very vicious indeed, because he acquires the dual character of a criminal and a renegade. Babel's romanticism of violence draws its intensity from the conflict in himself between the Jewish intellectual and the Soviet commissar. Only by romanticizing violence could he live with it.

Babel's most famous work is *Red Cavalry* (1926), a book of stories that influenced me very deeply when it appeared in English. It is not his most characteristic work, nor should I now say his best. There is more of the essential Babel in *Tales of Odessa* which appeared in 1924, and still more in the occasional stories he wrote before he was murdered by the Stalinists on the outbreak of the Second World War.

The early stories already have something of the highly formalized manner of the later ones and which bears such a strong resemblance to Hemingway's manner. Since neither could have been influenced by the other we must trace the style of both to a common source, which is certainly Flaubert. Indeed, considering Flaubert's influence on the modern short story, it would not be too much to say that he should be considered among the storytellers. The extraordinary relationship he established between the object and the style is almost unmanageable in anything so long as a novel, but again and again in the short story we see how it serves to delimit the form, establishes the beginning and the end, and heightens the intensity that is so necessary in a story but so embarrassing in a novel, where everything has to have a sort of everyday quality.

In Babel's earlier stories we see much more clearly the personal need that gave rise to them, and with it, the slight element of falsity we have to correct, unless we are prepared to make the mistake that Lionel Trilling makes in his fine introduction to the stories. Having quoted Hazlitt's remark that "we are naturally drawn to the representation of what is strong and proud and feral," Mr. Trilling replies that "we are, rather, drawn to the representation of what is real." Outside the sagas I am not very much attracted by what is strong and proud and feral, but if I were dependent for my idea of reality on the Odessa gangsters of Babel I should be in a bad plight indeed.

Babel's gangsters are much less real than Hemingway's Chicago gangsters, for these at least have been observed at third hand through the medium of films or *True Detective* magazines ("Cardazzo, the pale-faced, soft-voiced Brooklyn kid, who killed slowly, lovingly, with carefully-spaced thrusts of the knife"), but Babel's gangsters never existed at all outside the wild imagination of a delicate, scholarly Jewish boy, who had been hunted through the streets like an old dog, and whose mind was full of pirates in gorgeous colors.

Take, for instance, the marriage of the gangster's sister, described in the Flaubertian Technicolor of *Salammbô*.

> All that is noblest in our smuggled goods, everything for which the land is famed from end to end, did, on that starry, that deep-blue night, its entrancing and disruptive work. Wines from these parts warmed stomachs, made legs faint sweetly, bemused brains, evoked belches that rang out sonorous as trumpets summoning to battle. The Negro cook from the *Plutarch*, that had put in three days before from Port Said, bore unseen through the customs fat-bellied jars of Jamaica rum, oily Madeira, cigars from the plantations of Pierpont Morgan, and oranges from the environs of Jerusalem.... And now the friends of the King showed what blue blood meant, and the chivalry, not yet extinct, of the Moldavanka district. On the silver trays with ineffably nonchalant movements of the hand, they cast golden coins, rings and threaded coral.

Seriously, is this what Mr. Trilling calls "real"? "With ineffably nonchalant movements of the hand"? But these gangsters are straight out of *The Beggar's Opera*! Look how Benny Krik, the gangster, writes to the unfortunate man from whom he is demanding protection money: "Highly respected Ruvim, son of Joseph! Be kind enough to place, on Saturday, under the rain barrel, etc. If you refuse, as last time you refused, know that a great disappointment awaits you in your private life. Respects from the Bentzion Krik you know of." Does anyone believe that a serious magazine like *True Detective* would even print such stuff as "real"? But there is much better than that. When one of Benny's gangsters shoots an innocent Jewish clerk during a holdup, Benny not only buries the victim in Hollywood gangster style but with equal pomp buries the murderer beside him. Then he delivers a funeral address over the two graves.

"There are people who know how to drink vodka, and there are people who don't know how to drink vodka but drink it all the same. And the first lot, you see, get satisfaction from joy and from sorrow, and the second lot suffer for all those who drink vodka without knowing how. And so, ladies and gentlemen and dames, after we have said a prayer for our poor Joseph I will ask you to accompany to his last resting place one unknown to you but already deceased, one Savely Butsis."

Now, anyone reading that passage might be excused for believing that the original author was Damon Runyon. But perhaps Damon Runyon was also a realist? I should describe it as Jewish humor at its dotty best and Ikie Babel as a liar of colossal genius, but please, ladies and gentlemen and dames, do not let us get our terms mixed up! Whatever it is, it is not realism.

This, of course, is not all there is to the *Tales of Odessa*. There are the stories of the pogrom of 1905, and though I feel sure that Babel, being the romantic he is, has dolled them up, they are too close to what all of us know of the reality of racialism not to move me.

What does concern me about these stories is something that is more important than the question of whether we call them romantic or realistic. It is the question of what the author's personality is really like. There are two personalities in them, that of the Jewish intellectual and that of the Soviet officer, and while one seems to say one thing the other often says the opposite. I am never quite certain which of them I am dealing with—Ike Babel or Comrade Babel. "The End of Saint Hypatius" is a typical post-revolutionary Russian story as is "You Were Too Trusting, Captain"; so, almost to the point of caricature is "Line and Color," a contrast between the vague idealist, Kerensky, and that master of the precise phrase and the revolver, Leon Trotsky. I am not quarreling with the idea—if it is an idea—nor with its expression; I am merely wondering what degree of importance I am supposed to attach to it. Is this the expression of an attitude to human life or merely a mood such as comes over us all at times? I am confused.

I am not confused but confounded by "With Old Man Makhno." In this a Jewish girl is raped by six Russian soldiers in succession. She would have been raped by a seventh except that the rape went by order of seniority, and Kikin, the seventh, realized that in the process she was being raped by another Communist hero reputed to be a syphilitic and, so as not to contract the disease, preferred to nurse a grievance which he expounds to the poor child who has been violated and infected by his comrades. At this point I really want to be vulgar, whip out my notebook and pencil, and ask, "Your point,

Comrade Babel, your point? Are you implying that this is a small, inevitable tragic accident such as is bound to occur with Heroes of the Revolution, or do I detect a hint that hanging—as in certain capitalist armies—might best meet the case? Am I in fact speaking to Comrade Babel or Ike Babel?" But Babel, like Hemingway, is being so infernally tough that he leaves me in doubt about a perfectly simple question as to whether I should regard him as a real writer or as a dangerous lunatic.

Of course, there is the possibility that this is a mere failure in technique, but it occurs again and again. The person I regard as the Jew and genius writes "Karl-Yankel" and "In the Basement," but in "The S.S. *Cow-Wheat*" I am apparently expected to admire the conduct of Comrade Makeyev who reluctantly executes the drunken skipper of a boat that has been commissioned to bring urgently needed wheat to the Moscow region. This gives me the same sort of thrill I experienced when Comrade Shaw described enthusiastically how Comrade Lenin enforced punctuality on stationmasters by shooting them on the spot. Unlike Comrades Shaw and Lenin, I have suffered from stationmasters, and I think I know what can happen in wartime as a result of inferior transport, but I still feel that there are better ways of keeping trains on schedule than by shooting the stationmasters. In fact, unless Russian rail systems are far superior to European ones, shooting stationmasters would be just as ineffective as flogging witches, which is what one of Turgenev's characters did when his enormous carriage refused to start. It is not only wicked; it is silly.

What does emerge from these brilliant stories is an impression of an extraordinary attractive mixed-up Jewish kid. I am happiest with the later stories which are much more overtly Jewish, like the one that describes how the inhabitants of the Old People's Home by the cemetery make a comfortable living by hiring out a coffin which is seized by the Communists. But once more it is not of Chekhov or Maupassant but of Damon Runyon that I think when I read the address of Broidin, the overseer of the Jewish Cemetery, to the old people who have lost their only means of livelihood.

> "There are people who live worse than you, and there are thousands upon thousands of people who live worse than the people who live worse than you. You are sowing unpleasantness, Arye-Leib, and you will reap wind in the belly. You will be dead men, all of you, if I turn away from you. You will die if I go my way and you yours. You, Arye-Leib, will die; ... and you, Meyer Endless. But before you die, tell me—I am interested in the answer—have we by any chance got Soviet power or haven't

we? If we haven't, and I am mistaken, then take me along to Mr. Berzon on the corner of De Ribas and Yekaterininskaya, where I worked all the years of my life as a waistcoat-maker."

This is not "strong and proud and feral" or anything else of the kind; it is plain Jewish fun, and Babel is enjoying his own ability as a liar of genius. One must keep this in mind when approaching a book of stories like *Red Cavalry*. Mr. Trilling merely shrugs his shoulders at the protests of General Budenny who, rightly or wrongly, regarded it as a libel on his troops. I am not saying that atrocities don't occur (I have seen one or two), nor am I arguing that things were not infinitely worse in countries I have not seen, like Poland and Palestine. What I am saying is that when a Jew with an uproarious imagination describes scenes of violence one should ask oneself whether he is describing what he saw or what he thought he should have seen. Some of the things Babel describes I am quite certain he never saw. My own experience of Jesuits and Jews has been moderately pleasant, but as a reader of sensational fiction I realize that my experience is nothing to depend upon, for in sensational fiction all Jesuits are intriguers who have love affairs with sinister society women and all Jews people who drink the blood of Christian children. Babel is a new experience to me, for in him I get a description of Jesuits written by a Jew.

> Bone buttons sprang beneath our fingers, icons split down the middle and opened out, revealing subterranean passages and mildewed caverns. The temple was an ancient one and full of secrets. In its glossy walls lay hidden passages, niches, doors that moved noiselessly aside.
>
> O foolish priest, to hang the bodices of your parishioners upon the nails in the Saviour's cross! In the Holy of Holies we found a trunk with gold coins, a morocco-leather bag with banknotes, Parisian jewellers' cases filled with emerald rings.

I wish some Jesuit would write like this about the synagogue. I know of one priest who puts up quite a good show in his regular monthly tirade, but he is not a Jesuit, and he hasn't the air of imbecilic rapture which Babel adopts. But is it even necessary to be satirical about this sort of thing? Can there be a reader so guileless as not to wonder whether Babel's Jesuit churches came out of Babel's experience or his imagination?

But if the reader and I agree on where the churches came from, what are we to say about the Russian family background as it seemed to an Odessa Jew? Dad, who has turned "traitor" and joined General Deniken's army, captures a Communist detachment which includes his two sons.

> And they took us all prisoners because of that treason and my brother Theodore came to Dad's notice. And Dad began cutting him about, saying "Brute, Red cur, son of a bitch!" and all sorts of other things, and went on cutting him about until it grew dark and Theodore passed away.

Now, we all know that in civil war father is often set against son and brother against brother, and no doubt from time to time they have killed one another. (In fact, when I was a prisoner I knew a father with a son among the guards, and when the father went for a walk the son walked beside him outside the wire and muttered, "Dad, Mother says how are you?" and the father replied sourly, "Go away, you son of a whore!") I have counted up in the pages of Maksim Gorky the number of wives kicked to death by their husbands, but I should still have said that this representation of paternal love was unique, even if it had not been improved by the picture of filial devotion that ensues, for Simon, Theodore's brother, in due course captures Father.

> But Simon got Dad all right and he began to whip Dad and lined up all the fighting men in the yard according to army custom. Then Simon dashed water over Dad's beard, and asked him:
> "You all right, Dad, in my hands?"
> "No," says Dad, "not all right."
> Then Simon said: "And Theo, was he all right in your hands when you killed him?"
> "No," says Dad. "Things went badly for Theo."
> Then Simon asked: "And did you think, Dad, that things would go badly for you?"
> "No," says Dad. "I didn't think things would go badly for me."
> Then Simon turned to us all and said: "And what I think is that if I got caught by his boys, there wouldn't be no quarter for me.—And now, Dad, we're going to finish you off."

I do not think we should blame General Budenny too much, if, lacking an artistic training, he did not regard this as a tribute to his troops. I know a lot of officers, Irish, English, and American, who would have felt just the same.

This is not quoted to exaggerate the element of falsity in Babel's stories. He probably saw things more searing to the imagination than most of us have seen, and, anyway, he was working out an emotional problem that cannot be judged by the literal standards of General Budenny and Mr.

Trilling. We can appreciate that problem in the story of how the narrator irritated his comrades by riding into battle with an empty revolver to make sure that no man's blood would be on his head. We can appreciate it even better in a story like "The Death of Dolgushov," in which the narrator during a retreat finds a mortally wounded man who begs to be dispatched before the enemy can torture him, shrinks away from the terrible responsibility, and as a result is himself almost murdered by his best friend, who having killed the wounded man, says to the narrator, "You four-eyed bastards have as much pity for your comrades as a cat for a mouse."

There, certainly, speaks the Jewish idealist. Nor are all the stories in which Babel celebrates physical violence false and strained. There is nothing faked in "The Death of Dolgushov" nor in another fine story called "Prishchepa's Vengeance," in which a young Cossack whose parents have been killed by the Whites goes from house to house, collecting the few family possessions that have been stolen by unfeeling neighbors and killing the possessors; and then, at the end of three days sets fire to his home and rides off. That might easily be an incident in an Irish or Icelandic saga and impresses us as the terrible incidents in these do, without taking from our feeling of the common humanity we share with their authors.

But I have no such feeling about the other story I have quoted. However attracted a young Jewish intellectual may be by violence, a Jewish father who had flogged his own son to death would not, shall I say, receive an enthusiastic welcome from the community, and a son who had flogged his father to death might even be treated with a certain reserve—at least in the communities I know. I feel the story is literary and faked in the same way as I feel that the description of the Odessa gangsters and the Jesuit church is literary and faked. In this enthusiasm for Cossack violence Babel has denied his ancestry.

For me Babel is always most moving when he remembers it and writes out of the conflict in himself, when he juxtaposes the two cultures—the barbaric culture of the Communists and the humane one of the Jews—and shows them to us in antithesis.

> His things were strewn about pell-mell, mandates of the propagandist and notebooks of the Jewish poet, the portraits of Lenin and Maimonides lay side by side, the knotted iron of Lenin's skull beside the dull silk of the portraits of Maimonides. A lock of woman's hair lay in a book, the Resolutions of the Party's Sixth Congress, and the margins of Communist leaflets were crowded with crooked lines of ancient Hebrew verse. They fell

upon me in a mean and depressing rain—pages of the Song of Songs and revolver cartridges.

One can study the conflict best in a fine story like "Squadron Commander Trunov," where the formal construction is particularly revealing. Chronologically the story tells how Trunov was killing his prisoners and was rebuked by the Jewish narrator for not obeying orders. A squadron of American planes comes overhead, and Trunov and his buddy decide to try and fight them off while the squadron escapes. Trunov is killed and is given a hero's funeral with the fierce Cossack rites, while the narrator, as though seeking comfort for his own disturbed mind, drifts into the Jewish quarter only to find the Jews there quarreling about age-old points of doctrine.

> A section of them—the Orthodox Jews—were extolling the teachings of Adassia Rabbi of Belz. For this they were being attacked by the Hasidim of moderate doctrine, the disciples of Juda Rabbi of Gussyatin. The Jews were arguing about the Cabala, making mention in their discussions of the name of Elijah, Gaon of Vilna and scourge of the Hasidim.

Then in the place where a gypsy is shoeing horses one of a group of Cossacks attacks the Jew for having beaten up the hero Trunov that morning—a story we already know to be false, but the quarrel between the dead hero and the living Jew is becoming legendary.

It is a beautiful story that expresses allusively and movingly the tragedy of the idealistic Jewish lad who had abandoned his own people with their crazy religious squabbles in hope of a better future for humanity but will never be accepted by the wild Cossack throat-slitters whom he admires. It could have been told in direct narrative and chronological order as I have summarized it; it could have been told by a flashback from the wild funeral scene to the death of Trunov and then ended with the antithesis of the Jewish squabbling. Instead, because Babel decided to follow the line of his own troubled thought, it begins with the funeral, goes on to the argument among the Jewish sectarians, and ends with the quarrel over the murder of the prisoners and the heroic death of Trunov. Only in this audacious way could Babel have expressed without propagandist harangues his own final faith in Trunov and the heroic gesture.

There was, I suspect, a lot of Benny Krik in Babel, and he, too, for much of the time seems to have believed that "passion rules the universe." Accordingly, the stories in *Red Cavalry* contain more poetry than storytelling, which may be what I think is wrong with them. Passion can never rule the universe of the storyteller; it leaves too many things unexplained.

Nowadays, I prefer the later stories, like the enchanting Odessa story I have already quoted from, "The End of the Old Folks' Home." This, too, presents us with the antithesis between Communists and Jews, but a certain sly humor in it makes me wonder whether Babel himself had not begun to have doubts about the superiority of the Communists. They also left many things unexplained.

It is almost as though Babel had begun to realize that the uneasy alliance between the Jewish intellectual who went into battle with an unloaded revolver and Comrade Babel who had steeled himself to describe massacre and rape was coming to an end, and that Comrade Stalin whose purposeful prose he had so dutifully admired would soon deal with him and his kind with revolvers that were not unloaded.

ILYA EHRENBURG

The Wise Rabbi (Memoirs)

It was hot in Moscow that summer; many of my friends were living at their *dachas* or elsewhere in the country. I wandered aimlessly about the scorching city. One of those sultry days that precede a thunderstorm brought me an unexpected joy: I met the man who became my most intimate and true friend, the author to whom I looked up as an apprentice to a master—Isaak Babel.

He came to me unheralded, and I still remember his first words: "So that's what you're like." I on my side stared at him with even greater curiosity: so here was the man who had written *Red Cavalry, Tales of Odessa,* "The Story of My Dovecot." Several times in my life I have been introduced to authors whose books I revered: Maksim Gorky, Thomas Mann, Bunin, Andrey Bely, Heinrich Mann, Machado, Joyce; they were much older than I; they were universally recognized, and I looked at them as at distant mountain peaks. But twice I was as excited as a lover who meets the object of his secret love for the first time; it was like that in the case of Babel and, ten years later, in that of Hemingway.

Babel immediately carried me off to a beerhouse. When we entered the dark, crowded room, I was astounded. Here shabby speculators, habitual thieves, cabbies, suburban market-gardeners, down-at-heel representatives of the old intelligentsia forgathered. Someone was shouting that "the elixir of life has been invented, it's disgusting because it's fabulously expensive, so the scoundrels will outlive everybody else." At first no one paid any atten-

---

From *Memoirs: 1921–41*, translated by Tatania Shebunina, in collaboration with Yvonne Kapp. © 1963 by Macgibbon & Kee Ltd. World Publishing, 1964.

tion to the shouter, then his neighbour knocked him over the head with a bottle. In another corner a scuffle broke out over a girl. Blood streamed down the face of a curly-haired young fellow. The girl yelled: "You needn't try so hard. Harry Piel—he's the one I like!" Two men who had drunk themselves unconscious were dragged out by their feet. A little old man, very polite, seated himself at our table. He started telling Babel how his son-in-law had tried to cut his wife's throat "and Verochka, you know, didn't turn a hair, she just said: 'Clear out, if you don't mind'—this girl of mine, you know, she's very refined." I could not stand it any longer: "Shall we go?" Babel was taken aback: "But it's so interesting here."

He looked less like a writer than anyone I have ever seen. In his sketch "The Beginning" he relates how when he first came to Petersburg (he was then twenty) he rented a room in an engineer's flat. After taking a good look at his new lodger the engineer gave orders that the door leading out of Babel's room into the dining-room should be locked and that all the overcoats and galoshes should be taken out of the hall. Twenty years later Babel lodged with an old French lady in the Paris suburb of Neuilly; his landlady locked him in at night for fear he should cut her throat. And yet there was nothing terrifying about Babel's appearance; it was just that he puzzled people: heaven knew what kind of man he was and what his occupation might be.

Mike Gold, who met Babel in Paris in 1935, wrote: "He is not at all like a man of letters or a former cavalryman but reminds one rather of a village schoolmaster." This impression was largely due to his spectacles whose role in *Red Cavalry* had assumed alarming proportions ("They send up chaps like you without asking us, and here anyone wearing glasses can get his throat cut," "You bespectacled fellows have about as much pity for us as a cat has for a mouse," "You've ruined that mount, four-eyes.") He was short, stocky. In one of the stories in *Red Cavalry* he speaks of Galician Jews, contrasting them with "the stout and jovial Jews of the South, bubbling like cheap wine": the stevedores, carters, cabbies, bandits like the notorious Mishka Yaponchik, the prototype of Benya Krik. (The epithet "jovial" is a Gallicism; in Russian we say "jolly," "cheerful.") In spite of his glasses Babel was far more like a jovial Odessan—though one who had known his share of grief—than a village schoolmaster. His spectacles could hide the unusually expressive eyes, now mischievous, now sad. His nose, tirelessly inquisitive, also played an important part. Babel wanted to know everything: what his brother-soldier, a Kuban Cossack, felt when, after a two days' drinking bout, in a fit of melancholy, he had set fire to his own house; why had Mashenka of *Land and Factory*, after cuckolding her husband, taken up biokinetics; what sort of poetry did the White Guard Gorgulov, the French President's assassin, write; how did the old accountant seen once in the window of the *Pravda* office die; what was the Paris lady at the next table in the café carrying in her handbag; did Mussolini keep up his bluster when he found himself alone with Ciano—in short, life's most trivial details. Everything interested him, and it was unimaginable to him that a writer could be without an appetite for life. "A great writer," he said to me about Proust's novels. "But it's boring. Perhaps he himself felt bored when he was describing it all?" Remarking on the promise shown by the young *émigré* writer Nabokov-Sirin, Babel said: "He can write, but he's got nothing to say."

He loved poetry and was on friendly terms with poets quite unlike himself: Bagritsky, Yesenin, Mayakovsky. But he could not stand literary circles. "When I have to go to a writers' meeting I feel as if I'm going to have to put down a mixture of honey and castor oil." He had friends of the most varied occupations: engineers, jockeys, cavalrymen, architects, bee-keepers, cymbalists. He was capable of listening for hours on end to someone else's happy or unhappy love affairs. He had a way of attracting other people's confidences; perhaps they felt that he not only listened to them but shared their feelings. While some of his stories about other people's lives are told in the first person (for instance, "My First Honorarium") there are some which, purporting to be about fictitious heroes, are in fact pages of the author's biography ("Oil").

In his short autobiography Babel related how in 1916 Maksim Gorky "sent him out into the world." He continues: "And for seven years, from 1917 till 1924, I went out into the world. During that time I was a soldier on the Rumanian front, then served in the Cheka, in the *Narkompros* (People's Commissariat of Education), in the Food Detachments of 1918, in the Northern army against Yudenich, in the First Cavalry Army, in the Odessa *Gubkom* (Provincial Commissariat), I was a printer in the Seventh Soviet Press in Odessa, a reporter in Petersburg, Tiflis, etc." And in truth those seven years gave Babel much; but he was "out in the world" even before 1916 and remained "out in the world," too, after he had become a famous author: he could not exist without people. "The Story of My Dovecot" was the experience of a boy told much later by a mature master. During the days of his adolescence and early youth Babel met the heroes of his Odessa tales: bandits and profiteers, near-sighted dreamers and romantic rascals.

Wherever he found himself he immediately felt at home and entered into other people's lives. He did not stay long in Marseilles but when he spoke about the life there, his were not the impressions of a tourist: he spoke of gangsters, municipal elections, the strike in the port, a woman getting on in life—a laundress, I think—who, having suddenly come into a lot of money, gassed herself.

However, even in France, which he loved, he was homesick. He wrote in 1927 from Marseilles: "Spiritual life in Russia is nobler." In another letter to his old friend I. L. Lifshitz he wrote from Paris: "Life in the sense of individual freedom is fine here, but we Russians pine for the wind of great thoughts and great passions."

In the twenties there were many references in our papers to "scissors"; this did not mean the tailor's instrument but the growing discrepancy between the price of bread and the price of cotton fabrics or boots. It makes me think now of another kind of "scissors": the discrepancy between life and the meaning of art; I spent the whole of my life with these "scissors." I often discussed this with Babel. Passionately in love with life, involved in it at every minute, he had been devoted to art from his childhood.

It sometimes happens like this: a man has an important experience, he wants to relate it, it turns out that he does it with talent, and a new writer is born. I have heard Fadeyev say that in the years of the Civil War he never thought he would be drawn into literature; *The Nineteen* was a most unlooked-for outcome of his experiences. But Babel, even while he was fighting, knew that he would have to translate the reality into a work of art.

The manuscripts of Babel's unpublished works have disappeared. S. G. Hecht's memoirs reminded me of Babel's remarkable story "At the Troitsa." He read it to me in the spring of 1938; it is the story of the destruction of many illusions, a wise and bitter story. The manuscripts of the stories have been lost as well as the chapters of an unfinished novel. Babel's widow, Antonina Nikolayevna, sought them in vain. The diary which Babel kept in 1920 when he was in the ranks of the First Cavalry Army has survived by some miracle; a woman in Kiev had preserved the thick exercise book with its illegible entries. The diary is very interesting: it not only shows how Babel worked, but also enables one to understand the psychology of creative art.

From the diary it appears that Babel shared the life of his comrades in arms: the victories and defeats, the attitudes of the soldiers to the local inhabitants and that of the inhabitants to the soldiers; he was deeply impressed by what he saw of generosity and violence, rescue in battle, pogroms, death. Nevertheless, all through there are insistent reminders: "Describe Matyazh, Misha"; "describe the people, the air"; "for that day—it is most important to describe the Red Army men and the air"; "remember—the figure, the face, and the joy of Apanasenko, his feeling for horses, how he leads them, chooses for Bakhturov"; "must not fail to describe the lame

Gubanov, the terror of the regiment, a dashing cavalry officer"; "must not forget the priest in Luszkow, ill-shaven, kind, educated, possibly self-interested—but what self-interest!—a chicken, a duck"; "describe the air-attack, the distant, almost slow, chatter of machine-guns"; "describe the forests—Krivikha, the ruined Czechs, the buxom woman."

Babel was a poet; neither the naturalism of the life he describes, nor the round glasses on his round face can conceal his poetical attitude of mind. He was set alight by a line of poetry, a painting, the colour of the sky, the sight of human beauty. His diary is not of the sort intended for publication: Babel was talking frankly to himself. That is why, when I refer to his poetical nature, I begin with notes taken from his diary:

"Cleared outskirts of forests, remnants of the war, wire, trenches. Majestic green oaks, hornbeams, many pines, a willow—majestic and gentle tree, rain in the forest, roads washed out, an ash."

"Boratin—a solid, sunny village. Hops, a laughing daughter, a silent, rich peasant, eggs fried in butter, milk, white bread, gluttony, sunshine, cleanliness."

"Magnificent Italian paintings, pink Catholic priests nursing the infant Christ, magnificent dark Christ, Rembrandt; Murillo-style (or perhaps Murillo) Madonna, saintly well-nourished Jesuits, a bearded Jew, a small shop, a broken reliquary, the figure of St. Valentius."

"I remember broken frames, thousands of bees buzzing and struggling beside a smashed beehive."

"Aristocratic old Polish mansion, probably more than a hundred years old, mounted antlers, ceilings with ancient painting done in light colours, small butler's pantry, stoves, passages, excrement on the floor, small Jewish boys, a Steinway piano, sofas ripped open to the springs; remember white light and oaken doors, letters written in French dated 1820."

Babel related his attitude to art in his short novel, "Di Grasso." An actor comes to Odessa from Sicily. His acting is conventional, perhaps even exaggerated, but the power of art is such that the unkind have a change of heart; the wife of a profiteer says to her shamed husband as they come out of the theatre: "Now you see what love means."

I remember when *Red Cavalry* was first published. Everyone marvelled at its imaginative power; there was even talk of sheer fantasy. Yet Babel had described what he had seen with his own eyes. The proof of this is the evidence of the exercise book which was with him on the expedition and survived its author.

Here is the story *The Remount Officer*: "Up to the very steps galloped Dyakov on his fiery Anglo-Arabian—Dyakov who had formerly been an athlete in a circus and was now a red-faced, grey-moustached remount officer with a black cloak and silver stripes down his wide red breeches." Further on Dyakov tells a peasant that he will get 15,000 for the horse, and would have got 20,000 if the beast had been a little friskier. "If a horse falls and gets up again, it's a horse; if, to put it the other way round, it doesn't, well then it isn't."

And now here is the entry for 13 July 1920: "The remount officer—fairy-tale picture, r(ed) breeches with silver stripes, a belt with silver trimming, from Stavropol, a figure like Apollo, sh(ort) grey moustache, forty-five years old... was an athlete... about horses." 16th July: "Dyakov arrives. Conversation short: for this sort of horse you can get 15,000, for another sort 20,000. If it gets up it's a horse."

The story "Gedali": here the author meets an old Jewish junkshop owner who sorrowfully expounds his philosophy: "but the Poles shot because they were the Counter-Revolution. You shoot because you are the Revolution. But surely the Revolution means joy. And joy doesn't like orphans in the house. Good men do good deeds... And I want an International of good people, I want every soul to be taken into account and given rations of the first category." This is the description of Gedali's shop: "Dickens, where was your kindly shade that evening? In that little old curiosity shop you would have seen gilt slippers, ships' cables, an ancient compass, a stuffed eagle, a Winchester engraved with the date 1810 and a broken saucepan."

Entry for 3rd July 1920: "A small Jew—a philosopher. Incredible shop—Dickens; brooms and gilt slippers. His philosophy: all of them say they are fighting for justice and all of them loot."

In the diary you will find Prishchepa, and the little town of Berestechko, and the letter written in French that was found there, and the killing of prisoners, and the "pawn" in the battle for Lesznow, and the commander's speech about the Second Comintern Congress, and the "furious sycophant Levka," and the house of the Catholic priest Tuzinkiewicz, and many other episodes and pictures which were later incorporated in *Red Cavalry*. But the stories are not like the diary. In his exercise book Babel described everything as it was. It is a list of events: advance, retreat, the ruined, terrified inhabitants of towns and villages that changed hands; executions, trampled fields, the cruelty of war. In his diary Babel asked himself: "Why am I in the grip of unrelieved misery?" And he replied: "Life is being destroyed, I am present at an endless funeral."

But the book is different: in it, in spite of the horrors of war, in spite of the savage climate of those years, there is faith in the Revolution and faith in man. It is true that there were those who said that Babel had slandered the

Red Army cavalrymen. Gorky intervened to vindicate *Red Cavalry* and wrote that Babel had "embellished" the Cossacks of the First Cavalry Army "better and with more truth than Gogol had embellished the Zaporozhye Cossacks." The word "embellish" that I snatch out of context and the comparison with *Taras Bulba* may cause bewilderment. Besides, the style of *Red Cavalry* is exuberant, hyperbolic. (As early as 1915, when he made his début as a writer, Babel said that what he looked for in literature was sunshine, rich colours; he expressed his admiration for Gogol's Ukrainian stories and regretted that "Petersburg had conquered the land of Poltava. Akaky Akakievich had unassumingly but with horrifying power put Gritsko in the shade.")

Yet Babel did not "embellish" the heroes of *Red Cavalry*: he revealed their inner world. He ignored not only the workaday life of the army, but also many actions which at the time drove him to despair. It was as if he floodlit an hour, a moment when a man reveals himself. That is precisely why I have always looked on Babel as a poet.

Very different kinds of writers like *Red Cavalry*: Gorky and Thomas Mann, Barbusse and Roger Martin du Gard, Mayakovsky and Yesenin, Andrey Bely and Furmanov, Romain Rolland and Brecht.

In 1930 *Novy Mir* printed a number of letters from foreign writers, mainly German, in answer to a questionnaire on Soviet literature. In the majority of letters Babel's name topped the list.

But Babel criticized himself with the severity of a great artist. He often said to me that his style was too flamboyant, that he was trying to achieve simplicity and wished to rid himself of excessive imagery. One day, in the early thirties, he admitted that the Gogol of "The Overcoat" was closer to him than the Gogol of the early stories. He developed a liking for Chekhov. Those were the years when he was writing "Guy de Maupassant," "The Trial," "Di Grasso," "Oil."

He worked slowly, painfully, and was never satisfied with himself. When we first met he said to me: "Man lives for the pleasure of sleeping with a woman, of eating ices on a hot day." One day I went to see him; he was sitting naked, the day was very hot. He was not eating ices, he was writing. When he came to Paris, there, too, he worked from morning till night: "I toil here like an inspired ox, see nothing of the world (and in this world Paris is no Kremenchug"). Later he went to live in the country, a little way outside Moscow, renting a cottage room in the village, where he sat and wrote. Everywhere he burrowed himself away in seclusion to work. This exceptionally "jovial" man laboured like an anchorite.

When at the end of 1932 and the beginning of 1933 I was writing *The*

Second Day, Babel came to see me practically every day, I read out the chapters I had written, and he either approved or criticized: my book interested him, and he was a true friend.

He was very secretive, never said where he was going; his days were like the tunnellings of a mole. In 1936 I wrote of him: "His own destiny is not unlike some of his writings: he cannot unravel it. On one occasion he was coming to see me. His small daughter asked: 'Where are you going?' He had to give an answer and at once changed his mind and did not go. When in danger an octopus ejects ink; all the same they catch it and eat it—a favourite dish with the Spaniards is 'an octopus in its ink.'" (I wrote these words in Paris at the very beginning of 1936, and it horrifies me to copy them now: I could never have imagined how they would sound a few years later.)

Following Gorky's advice, Babel did not publish anything for seven years—from 1916 till 1923. Then one after another there appeared *Red Cavalry, Tales of Odessa,* "The Story of My Dovecot," the play *Sunset*. Then again Babel fell into almost complete silence, publishing at rare intervals short (but remarkable) stories. "Babel's silence" became one of the critics' favourite themes. At the First All-Union Congress of Soviet Writers I spoke against this kind of attack and said that a cow-elephant has a longer period of gestation than a doe-rabbit; I compared myself to the rabbit and Babel to the elephant. The writers laughed. And in his speech Babel made a joke, saying that he was the master of a new literary genre—silence.

But for him it was no joke. Every day he became more exacting with himself. "For the third time I have started to re-write the stories I have written, and realize with horror that another, a fourth, version will be necessary." "My worst trouble in life," he confessed in a letter, "is an abominable capacity for work."

I was not putting it on when I spoke about the rabbit and the elephant: I had the greatest admiration for Babel's talent and knew what high standards he set himself. I was proud of his friendship. Although he was three years younger than I, I often sought his advice and jokingly called him "the wise rabbi."

I had only two conversations with Gorky about literature, and on both occasions he spoke with tenderness, with confidence, of Babel's work; this pleased me as much as if he had been praising me. I was happy when Romain Rolland in his letter about *The Second Day* expressed his admiration for *Red Cavalry*. I loved Babel, and I loved and still love Babel's books.

There is something more I want to say about the man. It was not only in his appearance that Babel was unlike a writer, he also lived differently. He did not have mahogany furniture, or bookcases, or a secretaire. He even did without a desk and wrote on a kitchen table; and in Molodenovo, where he rented a room with the village cobbler Ivan Karpovich, he used a joiner's bench.

Babel's first wife, Yevgenia Borisovna, had grown up in a bourgeois family and found it hard to accustom herself to her husband's vagaries. For instance, he would bring his former army friends to the room where they were living and announce: "Yevgenia, they're going to spend the night with us."

His sensibility as an artist and his culture enabled him to be perfectly at ease with the most varied kinds of people. I heard him talk to Parisian snobs—putting them in their place—to Russian peasants, to Heinrich Mann, to Barbusse.

In 1935 a Congress for the Defence of Culture was held in Paris. The Soviet delegation arrived, without Babel. The French writers, who had organized the Congress, requested our embassy to include the author of *Red Cavalry* in the delegation. Babel arrived late, on the second or third day, I think. He was due to speak immediately. He reassured me with a smile: "I'll find something to say." This is how I described Babel's speech in *Izvestia*: "Babel did not read his speech, he spoke gaily and in masterly French for fifteen minutes, entertaining the audience with several unwritten stories. People laughed, but at the same time they realized that under cover of those amusing stories the essence of our people and of our culture was being conveyed to them: 'This collective farmer has bread, he has a house, he even has a decoration. But it's not enough for him. Now he wants poetry to be written about him.'"

Many times he said to me that the main thing was the people's happiness. He loved animals, especially horses; he said, when writing about his fellow soldier Khlebnikov: "We were in the grip of the same passions. We both looked out on the world as on a May meadow where women and horses roam about."

Life turned out to be no May meadow for him. But to the end he was faithful to the ideals of justice, internationalism, humanism. He understood the Revolution and recognized it as a pledge of future happiness. One of his best stories of the thirties, "Karl-Yankel," ends with the words: "I grew up in those streets, now it is the turn of Karl-Yankel, but they did not fight for me as they are fighting for him, few people had any thought for me. 'It's not possible,' I whispered to myself, 'that you won't be happy, Karl-Yankel. It's not possible that you won't be happier than I.'"

And Babel was one of those who paid with his struggle, his dreams, his books and, finally, with his life, for the happiness of future generations.

Late in 1937 I came to Moscow from Spain, straight from near Teruel.

When I reach the narrative of those days, the reader will understand how important I felt it was to see Babel immediately. I found the "wise rabbi" sorrowful, but his courage, his sense of humour, his story-teller's gift never left him. He told me once about his visit to a factory where books taken out of circulation were pulped to make paper; it was a very amusing and a very terrible story. On another occasion he told me about children's homes to which orphans of living parents were sent. Our parting in May 1938 was inexpressibly sad.

Babel always spoke affectionately of his native Odessa. After the death of Bagritsky in 1936 he wrote: "I recall our last conversation. It is time to leave other people's towns, we both agreed, time to return home, to Odessa, take a small house in the Blizhniye Melnitsy, write stories there, grow old. We saw ourselves as old men, sly old men, warming ourselves in the Odessa sunshine, by the sea on the promenade, and following women steadily with our eyes. Our desires were never realized. Bagritsky died when he was thirty-eight, without having fulfilled even a small part of what he could have done. VIM, the Institute of Experimental Medicine, has been founded in our State. May it find a way to prevent such insensate crimes of nature from ever being repeated."

In our anger we sometimes call nature blind. Men, too, are sometimes blind.

Babel was arrested in the spring of 1939. I learnt about it some time later—I was in Paris. Mobilized soldiers were marching, smart women walked about with gas-masks, windows were being plastered with strips of paper. And I was thinking that I had lost the man who had helped me to stride not across a May meadow, but along the very difficult road of life.

Our kinship lay in our understanding of a writer's duty and our perception of the age: we wanted the new world to find room as well for some very old things: beauty, love, art.

At the end of 1954, perhaps at the same hour when the man with the funny name Karl-Yankel and his contemporaries—Ivans, Pyotrs, Nikolases, Ovaneses, Abdullahs—were leaving the University lecture rooms in a happy crowd, the prosecutor informed me of the posthumous rehabilitation of Isaak Emmanuilovich Babel. Recalling Babel's stories I thought vaguely: it isn't possible that they won't be happier than we.

EDWARD J. BROWN

Isaac Babel: Horror in a Minor Key

Prose fiction [in the Soviet Union] of the early twenties, whether written by proletarians or fellow travelers, had one overpowering and ever-present theme: the Civil War. Every one of the writers who created the literary revival of the twenties dealt with that experience from one viewpoint or another. The fellow travelers tend to be more concerned with the literary style than with the political or social content of their work, but they could not be indifferent to the latter. Thus it has happened that the Russian Civil War is thoroughly documented by literary works, some of them stylistically mannered and obscure, most of them featuring verbal and metaphoric ornamentation, all of them agreed on the need to study either in aesthetic or political terms the moral nakedness of the times. The generation of writers that witnessed the events of the Civil War felt the need of catharsis and found it, partly, in portraying with aesthetic detachment scenes of horror and blood. Sensitive children of a high culture, they had witnessed the ultimate degradation of human passions, and they had observed the actions of men more cruel than beasts. These writers seem to suffer a compulsion to present scenes of extraordinary violence in literary form.

The Civil War stories of the fellow travelers are interesting also for their geographic and ethnographic content. Their authors had been dispersed in the course of the war to all corners of Russia and even outside of Russia, and this dispersion is reflected in their stories, which deal with Volga settlements, Kirghiz tribesmen, Cossacks on the Polish border, Tambov

---

From *Russian Literature Since the Revolution.* © 1963, 1969, 1982 by Edward J. Brown. Harvard University Press, 1982.

Province, the steppes of Siberia, and Don country, as well as with the cold caverns of Moscow and Petrograd. The Marxist critic Kogan, defending the fellow travelers, pointed specifically to this feature of their work:

> In a very short time Russia was described more realistically and in more vivid detail than ever before. The majority of the writers had fought on numerous fronts, held responsibilities both in big cities and in the deep provinces, seen with their own eyes pictures of hunger and inhuman cruelty and also superhuman feats of bravery. They had seen sectarians, superstitions, the age-old customs of tribes and peoples scattered over the enormous expanse.

The principal work of Isaac Babel, a series of short stories concerned with incidents in the campaign of Budyonny's First Cavalry Army in Poland, is typical of Civil War literature in the variety of its characters—Cossacks, Polish lords and peasants, Jews, and Russians—and in the cruel reality which it depicts.

Babel was born in Odessa, the son of a Jewish merchant who educated his son in the Hebrew language, the Bible, and the Talmud. He records that life at home was difficult because of his father's insistence on serious study, but that he found relief from that in school. There he learned French, well enough to write short stories in that language, and he came to love French literature. In Odessa he witnessed the pogrom of 1905, an experience which figures in one of his most moving stories. Literary ambition and the need to escape at any cost from the narrow orthodox world took him to Petrograd in 1915, where he lived miserably in a cold cellar, constantly on watch for the police, since he did not have the residence permit required of all Jews. Only Gorky would accept any of his stories. The prominent Bolshevik editor printed two of these in his journal *Chronicle* in 1916. Because of these stories Babel was brought into court on the charge of subversion and pornography, but, as he reported ironically, the Revolution of 1917 saved him from prosecution. Of these early efforts, which combined eroticism and a certain wit, Babel wrote: "The complete absence of decency in them was rivaled only by their meager content. Fortunately for well-intentioned people, some of them never saw the light of day." Babel records that Gorky's encouragement was one of the most important events in his life, and he claimed to revere the memory of the famous writer.

After this literary misadventure Babel abandoned the effort to write fiction for a number of years, and though he attributes the ensuing period of varied activity to Gorky's advice it was more likely the result of the troubled times. He fought in the Czarist army on the Rumanian front, then joined the Bolsheviks. According to his "Autobiography," written in 1924, he worked with the Soviet security police (*Cheka*), was a functionary in the People's Commissariat of Education, and in 1918 took part in grain-collecting expeditions. He fought against the Whites on the northern front, did editorial work in Odessa, and was employed in the local Soviet administration there. He was assigned in 1920 to the First Cavalry Army, where he was primarily responsible for political indoctrination of the rough Cossack mass that made up Budyonny's army. Out of this curious assignment came his most powerful writing, the collection of stories known in Russian as *Konarmia* (Horse Army), a Soviet neologism for cavalry, usually translated as *Red Cavalry*.

The book on which his fame rests can best be understood if it is approached in the spirit in which it was written. *Konarmia* was intended as a series of anecdotes, each with an ironic twist. In the stories thoroughly absurd human beings in ridiculous situations are occupied with the slaughter of other human beings. We misread Babel if, searching for open or hidden commentary on the Revolution, or horrified by pictures of barbarism, we fail to see that each story is built around a grim incongruity. Consider these priceless anecdotes: A peasant soldier writes a letter to his mother regaling her with all the adventures of the campaign, including among them an account of how his brothers murdered their father; a Cossack remount officer reassures peasants to whom he has given worn-out nags in return for their healthy horses: "If the animal can stand up it's a horse"; a village artist offers to paint a picture of you as St. Francis and of your enemy as Judas Iscariot for a small fee; the same artist tells how Jesus lay with Deborah, a Jerusalem maid of obscure birth, and begot a son who was hidden away by the priests; a Cheka officer, sick of the Revolution and the war, asked to be reassigned to Italy where it's warm and sunny or at least to the Cheka headquarters in Odessa; the Jew Gedali wants to found an International of Good People, where every soul would get "first-category rations"; a mild intellectual assigned to a Cossack platoon earns the respect of his soldier comrades by taking and killing a goose that doesn't belong to him; the same intellectual, after spending the Sabbath with a community of Hasidic Jews, returns to his *agit-train* to finish an article for "The Red Cavalryman." After a town is taken a commissar encourages the stunned and plundered populace: "You are in power. Everything here is yours. No more Polish Pans. I now proceed to the election of the revolutionary committee." The hero is upbraided by a Cossack soldier for going into battle with no cartridges in his revolver: "You're a milk-drinking pacifist. You worship God, you traitor." A rabbi's son, who has rejected orthodoxy for the Revolution, still lives in his father's house, "because he doesn't want to leave his mother."

Ilya Ehrenburg, who wrote the Introduction to the one-volume edition of Babel's work published in the Soviet Union in 1957, claims that Babel's diary, which has not yet been published in full, contains entries proving that these sketches were based in the main on actual occurrences of the Polish campaign, and are therefore "highly realistic." It is possible to agree with Ehrenburg's statement that the sketches contain much firsthand experience, but the term realistic as applied to them is meaningless. On the other hand, Budyonny, leader of the First Cavalry Army (who appears as a character in two of the sketches), fulminated against Babel for his failure to show the heroism of the Cossack horsemen in their struggle for the Revolution. It would seem that Budyonny in rather naïve terms is criticizing the sketches for their failure as realism. But perhaps Ehrenburg and Budyonny both miss the point. The sketches do not purport to give a balanced picture of the Cavalry Army or the Polish campaign. They are a series of sketches or, as Babel called them, "miniatures" based on experiences of the author during that campaign, and held together by the deliberate injection into each one of the author's own personality. The picture of the Cossack fighters is impressionistic and subjective. We have to do with a kind of lyric apprehension of absurd violence, seen through the eyes, indeed through the spectacles, of a sensitive intellectual whose work for the Revolution has brought him into the company of innocent savages. And the Cossacks are innocent men: they shed human blood without reason but almost without malice. When the book is examined as a whole it appears that, far from offering a comprehensive treatment of Budyonny's cavalry or the Polish campaign, only a little more than half of the sketches have to do with that organization or its exploits in war. The rest tell of other things: Hasidic Jews in eastern Poland, the deserted Polish church at Novograd, an assortment of original local characters, old buildings and cemeteries, pogroms, and other matters. What is peripheral to the campaign in Poland becomes central in Babel's cycle of sketches. In a letter to a friend he revealed the anguished experience of human tragedy which dictated the eccentric shape of the cycle:

> I have gone through two weeks of total despair as a result of the fierce and constant cruelty I've seen, and also because I've realized how unqualified I am for the business of destruction. Well then, some will make the Revolution, but I ... I will sing of whatever happens to be on the periphery, or of what is deeper

down. I have the feeling that I will be able to do it . . . that I'll have time enough and room enough.

Conventional Soviet criticism is no doubt right according to its own lights in finding that Babel's work is weighted with the details of brutality, and that he has missed "the rational principle in the Civil War, and the organizing role of the Communist Party." No doubt Babel himself could have constructed a final ironic anecdote featuring the Soviet literary critics who say such things. The great virtue of his stories is precisely their lack of political color, their apparently casual and fragmented structure. Not the least of Babel's ironies is the fact that the ideals of the socialist revolution, wrapped in facile phrases, have come into the possession of Russian peasant warriors incapable of understanding or realizing them. The stories are studded with such phrases as "no more masters," "heroic revolutionary army," "all are now equal," "the teachings of Lenin," "the revolutionary consciousness of the mass," and so forth. Such ideas might have been used by another writer, Furmanov, for instance, to justify and give rational meaning to the bloodshed of the Polish campaign. But in Babel's stories they are always given in mangled, misunderstood form by a moral illiterate who has just performed some needless piece of violence, such as killing an old Jew or shooting a woman in the back. Babel's stories are reminiscent of Blok's poem "The Twelve," where the world is at the mercy of twelve Red guards who kill and plunder to the tune of revolutionary songs and slogans. The hopes and fears of the reformers, idealists, and revolutionaries of the nineteenth century, in *Konarmia* as well as in "The Twelve," find distorted utterance in brutish mouths.

The narrator of the sketches in *Konarmia*, whose job is political propaganda, is present in almost all of the stories, and it is his personal view of things that the reader usually becomes aware of. The fact that he is a Jew is made explicit in some of the stories, and is suggested in others by the organic hostility toward him expressed by the Cossack soldiers. He is a man of peace—the only one, if we except Sandy the Christ, a mild syphilitic moron, who travels with the Horse Army—and he finds it almost impossible to adjust to the folkways of violence. He loses his best friend because he is unable to kill a comrade dying in misery.

> Silhouetted against the setting sun, Afonka Bida came galloping toward us.
> "We're pounding them a little," he cried out gaily. "What's the fuss here?" I pointed to Dolgushov and rode off.

> They spoke briefly, but I didn't hear the words. Dolgushov handed his papers to the commander. Afonka stuffed them into his boot, then shot Dolgushov in the mouth.
>
> "Afonka," I smiled pathetically as I rode up to the Cossack, "I just couldn't do it."
>
> "Get out of here," he said, and his face was white, "or I'll kill you. You fellows in specs have as much pity for guys like us as a cat has for a mouse." And he cocked his revolver.
>
> I went off at a walking gait, without turning around, and I felt the cold chill of death at my back.
>
> "Hey, you," Grishchuk cried out behind us, "are you crazy?" And he grabbed Afonka's arm.
>
> "The filthy snake," Afonka shouted. "He won't get away with it."
>
> Grishchuk caught up with me at a bend in the road. Afonka had gone off in another direction.
>
> "You see, Grishchuk, today I've lost my best friend, Afonka."

He wins their friendship only by brutality, he loses it when he displays a civilized reluctance to kill, maim, or defile another human being. Saddened by his alienation from the Cossacks he "implores fate to grant him the simplest of skills, skill in killing human beings."

Konstantin Paustovsky's reminiscences of Babel and the latter's own stories about the anguish of the Jewish community during the pogroms in Odessa, "The Story of My Dovecot," for instance, reveal with unusual clarity the sharpness of Babel's consciousness that he was a Jew. The scornful remarks of the Cossack about "fellows in specs" are anti-Semitic attacks, and therefore Babel was never allowed to forget the fact of his biography. Paustovsky wrote:

> A tear gleamed behind the convex lenses of his glasses. He took them off and wiped his eyes with the sleeve of his drab patched jacket.
>
> "I did not choose my race," he said suddenly in a broken voice. "I'm a Jew, a kike. Sometimes I think there's nothing I can't understand, but one thing I'll never understand: the reason for this black vileness which bears such a humdrum name as anti-Semitism." He fell silent. I too was silent and waited for him to calm down and for his hands to stop trembling.
>
> "I went through a pogrom when I was a child and survived. But they twisted the head off my dove. Why? . . . I hope my wife

doesn't come in," he whispered. "Lock the door. She doesn't like this sort of talk. And she might easily cry all night. She thinks I'm a very lonely man and perhaps she's right."

Not only do the stories describe peaceful orthodox Jewish communities, Hasidic rabbis and dreamers like Gedali who talk of an International of Good People, but also young Jews who like Babel himself had rebelled against the ghetto and "joined the Revolution." There were many of them in the Odessa Cheka and in the Red Army during the Civil War, and they often reached positions of leadership. This historical fact is beautifully etched by Babel in a single symbolic image:

> Our foot soldiers were entrenched three versts from the town. Before the front line a stoop-shouldered youth in spectacles was walking back and forth. A saber dragged along at his side. He moved with a hopping gait and an air of irritation as though his boots hurt him. This "hetman of the peasants," whom they had chosen and loved, was a Jew, a near-sighted Jewish youth, with the thin, concentrated face of a Talmudic scholar.

Jewish characters and themes are an important ingredient of *Red Cavalry*. Maurice Friedberg has pointed out that the dusty towns through which the Cossack army passed may be peripheral to Russian history, but they occupy an important place in the history of East European Jews. The town of Zhitomir, for instance, was a center of the Hasidic movement, and three of the sketches deal with the Hasidic Rebbe, a follower of his, Gedali, and the Rebbe's son.

Babel had many faces: Chekist, soldier, reporter. The most real and the most important of his many roles was that of writer, and it is the one which he himself took most seriously. The reminiscences of his friend Paustovsky reveal the tortured perfectionism of his attitude toward the craft:

> What I do [Babel said] is to get hold of some trifle, some little anecdote, a piece of market gossip, and turn it into something I cannot tear myself away from. It's alive, it plays. It's round like a pebble on the seashore. It's held together by the fusion of separate parts, and this fusion is so strong that even lightning can't split it. And people will read the story. They'll remember it, they'll laugh, not because it's funny but because one always feels like laughing in the presence of human good fortune. I take the risk of speaking about good fortune because we're alone. As long as I live you mustn't tell anyone about this conversation.

> Give me your word. It is, of course, none of my doing that, I don't know how, a demon or an angel, whatever you want to call it, has taken possession of me, the son of a petty merchant. And I obey him like a slave, like a beast of burden. I have sold my soul to him, and I must write in the best possible way. I guess it's an affliction. But if you take it away from me—either my good fortune or my affliction—the blood will gush out of my veins and my heart along with it; I will be worth no more than a chewed cigarette butt. It's this work that makes me into a man, and not an Odessa streetcorner philosopher.

The trick of Babel's art is to find the stuff of life by indirection, almost by accident. The Cavalry Army itself is a kind of side issue in a world which includes a vivid array of individual peasant soldiers, plundered villages, trampled fields, and indifferent nature itself. The task of political education, of explaining what it means, is abandoned as a grim travesty. The superflux of suffering and violence seems really to serve no rational end, and, therefore, Babel takes the sensations of the moment and transforms them through art into aesthetic experience. One of the means for this transformation is an ornate and elevated style, the texture of which is variegated with elaborate and arresting metaphors: "Blue roads flowed past me like streams of milk spurting from many breasts"; "His long legs were like girls sheathed to the neck in shiny riding boots"; "And we were moving toward the sunset, whose foaming rivers flowed along the embroidered napkins of the peasant fields"; "Crouching at the feet of huge estates were dead little Jewish towns"; "The orange sun rolled down the sky like a severed head"; "The deathly chill of eye-sockets filled with frozen tears"; "The stars put out by ink-swollen clouds"; "Between two and three o'clock of a spacious July day the rainbow web of heat shimmered in the air." By such lavish use of poetic language Babel screens himself and the reader from direct experience of violence. The device makes it possible to treat as matters for contemplation even Afonka Bida's empty eye socket: "In place of the left eye on his charred face there yawned horribly a monstrous pink bulge."

Ilya Ehrenburg in his reminiscences, *People, Years, Life,* devotes several pages to his memories of Babel and quotes from the diary Babel kept in 1920 during the Polish campaign the following passage, containing raw material which went into the story "Berestechko." The entry in his diary demonstrates Babel's method, the gathering of impressions which can be given artistic form but hardly reduced to a rational meaning:

The ancient house of a Polish count, probably built about 100 years ago, horns, old-style paintings on the ceiling, little rooms for the servants, stone blocks, passageways, excrement on the floors, Jewish urchins, a Steinway piano, sofas torn open down to the springs . . . oaken doors, letters in French dating back to 1820.

Like Olesha and many other fellow travelers, Babel produced very little. At the Congress of Writers in 1934 he announced that he was working in a new genre, "silence." In addition to the stories in *Konarmia* he published *Tales of Odessa* (1923–24) which describes in his characteristic exotic manner the Jewish half-world of gangsters and racketeers, a number of short stories, many of them autobiographical, and two plays. When he was arrested in 1939—"on a false charge," according to the Soviet edition of his works—he left behind the manuscript of a number of unpublished stories, some of which appeared during the 1960s and 1970s in various places. He died in 1941 at the age of forty-seven and was cleared of criminal charges in 1954.

ANDREY SINYAVSKY

Isaac Babel

The literary heritage left by Babel is not very voluminous. This leading Russian writer willingly accepted the title "craftsman of silence"; he took a long time maturing and finishing his works and was never in a hurry to turn them over to the public. His care for the perfection of each phrase, for purity of language, seem more the work of a poet than of a prose writer. No one more than he has justifed the famous formula of Jules Renard: "Prose ought to be a poem which is not divided into lines."

The most important work of Babel is *Red Cavalry,* in which his method and his style found their most complete expression. The tales that compose it, published in various periodicals from 1921 to 1924, then collected as a book in 1926, raised him at once to the first rank of Soviet writers.

What strikes one first of all in Babel is the variety of characters, of situations, and of styles. A sublime pathos appears alongside images of the most brutal reality, painted with the precision of a naturalist. Light and shadow, the beautiful and the hideous, are juxtaposed in combinations that are unexpected and often bizarre. The law of contrasts directs the development of subjects, the selection of details, the juxtaposition of words. The choice of heroes in Babel's narratives, of the characters that people *Red Cavalry,* is very significant in this regard. In their psychology good and evil rub elbows and interpenetrate, and in one and the same character, traits cohabit that at first sight seem irreconcilable: cruelty and magnanimity, brutality and tenderness, infamy and innocence. Even the appearance of

From *Major Soviet Writers: Essays in Criticism,* edited by Edward J. Brown. © 1973 by Oxford University Press. This essay was translated by Catherine Brown.

Babel's heroes is often paradoxical: "'Warsaw is ours' howled the Cossack in bast shoes and a derby hat." Such also is the language of the illiterate mass who rise above their ignorance, the common but salty language of disheveled revolutionaries. Political slogans mingle with a frequently obscene argot, journalistic clichés with coarse oaths: "Let's die for pickled cucumbers and the world revolution!"—here is an example of language that is as expressive and as contradictory as the character of the men who use it.

Babel has taken for the material of his tales impressions gathered in 1920 during the Polish campaign of the First Cavalry Army. But this has nothing to do with a chronicle of military history. He is careful to avoid copying events "in their raw grandeur." Deliberately, he condenses colors, alters proportions, creates confrontations between extremes in the life and the consciousness of his heroes. His whole effort is centered on the rough-hewn man of the masses, loaded with defects and vices, but compelling admiration by his courage, even his heroism. Far from idealizing his characters, Babel carries the play of black-and-white to grotesque lengths, accentuating and exaggerating at will, and makes us see in his Red Cavalry the moral and esthetic greatness of these men, even though they are stained with blood and mire.

Several tales, developing an argument which is essential for anyone who wants to grasp the main idea of *Red Cavalry*, present two different points of view: the dream of a good-natured and harmless revolution, without bloodshed, to which is opposed the author's conviction: "It's impossible not to shoot, because it's revolution."

The ideal of virile humanism is embodied in the soldiers and the officers of *Red Cavalry*, who chide the narrator for his softness, his poor adjustment to the rigors of military life. One of the basic points of Babel's style is that the narrator is not necessarily the spokesman of the author and cannot be identified with the real "I" of the writer, which is hidden, camouflaged under the twists and turns of the action. Constantly ironic in regard to his autobiographical hero, Babel takes pleasure in uncrowning, even humiliating him. Their contrast with this pleasantly scatterbrained intellectual makes even more striking the heroic traits of the combatants of the Red Cavalry.

The depiction of characters and the artistic weaving of plot in *Red Cavalry* reveal to us the two sides of the work of Babel. The lucidity of the realist does not chill the impetuous temperament of the romantic. His heroes of flesh and blood bathe "in torrents of luxury and power," in a climate of the marvelous and the extraordinary. Handsome, gaudily clothed, camped in a rich setting, they often seem to us like figures in an epic, whose very appearance compels wonder.

"Savitsky, the commander of the 6th division, rose at my approach and I was struck by the beauty of his giant's body. He rose, and the purple of his breeches, his raspberry-red cap pushed a little to one side, the decorations pinned to his chest, cut the hut in two as a banner cuts the sky."

Babel is prodigal of bright colors, of resplendent, glistening garments. We find "the pearly mist of birches," "clouds sailing like swans," blood flowing "like a brook with coral foam," in short, all the battle gear of romantic literature. The tone rises readily to the emphatic and the sublime. The author can't resist uttering sentiments which suffuse his book with waves of emotion that sometimes seems affected. But this sentimentality is only the canvas for scenes and personages conceived in a quite different register, rigorous and stripped-down to the point of asceticism.

Babel—like his heroes—does what one least expects at any given moment. At points of extreme dramatic tension, these characters manifest a remarkable calm. On the other hand, they sob, tear their garments, pass from despair to jubilation, for reasons which may seem to us very trifling. One of these heroes, Afonka Bida, weeps hot tears on learning of the discharge of his commanding officer, but remains unmoved when it is a question of carrying out the last wish of a mortally wounded comrade. "You must waste a cartridge on me. . . . Those Polish bastards will be coming, they'll make sport of me." In Babel, emotional reaction is in inverse proportion to the event that excited it.

Babel's restraint is extreme. As soon as a heroic exploit or a tragic event comes up, he affects impassivity, letting the action speak for him. His characters die and kill with simplicity, without self-serving poses, without impressive eloquence. All the more moving are those scenes whose very bareness creates their horror and their majesty. This is how squadron chief Trunov goes to certain death by engaging in unequal combat with an enemy airplane:

> He sealed the envelope, sat down on the ground, and, grunting with the effort, pulled off his boots.
> "Here," he said, handing the boots and the envelope to the machine gunners. "They can still be used, they're brand new."
> "Good luck, chief," mumbled the machine gunners in reply, shuffling around, unable to make up their minds to leave.
> "Good luck to you too," said Trunov. "Well, anyway, boys—"

> And he headed toward the machine gun installed on a mound, behind the sentry box. Andrey Vosmiletov, the tradesman, was waiting for him there.
>
> "Well, OK," Trunov said to him, setting up the machine gun. "You're staying with me, right?"
>
> "Jesus Christ!" answered Andrey, terrified. He gave a short sob, blanched, and burst out laughing: "Christ and damn!"
>
> And he aimed the second machine gun at the plane.

In episodes of this kind, the essence of the action is concealed. Babel does not explain to us what is happening. He pretends not to know about motives, and contents himself with relating the action, the bare external facts of the case. It is up to the reader to draw conclusions from them, to confront the facts and see, under the calm recital of events, their deeper significance. Certain phrases spoken incidentally inform us that Trunov is sacrificing his life in order to divert the enemy plane from the wood where the squadron has taken refuge. These phrases are proffered in a tone which gives the impression that it is a question of an unimportant incident.

> The major and his three gunners performed beautifully in this battle. They went down to an altitude of three hundred meters and aimed their machine gun at Andrey first, then at Trunov. All the bullets fired by our men had not done the slightest harm to the Americans; the planes left without noticing the squadron hidden in the wood. So after waiting a half hour we could go and pick up the bodies.

The author sees fit to dilute the heroism of this scene and to send us off on a false scent. Hence the know-how of the American gunners and the ineffectiveness of our machine gunners which might lead one to believe that the death of Trunov and Andrey was useless. And finally that little tag-end of a phrase with such a detached sound: "After waiting half an hour," whose unbearable inner tension is concealed under a bland exterior.

The lack of agreement between the form and the content of a remark, between the meaning of a sentence and its intonation or its vocabulary, is customary in Babel. The terrifying is told gently, the sublime, coarsely. Tragic events are related to us with the vulgar awkwardness of an illiterate, bordering on burlesque. The purpose of this is to deflate solemn bombast, to bring the story down to earth.

The same is true in the brutally physiological descriptions he uses to tell about the habits and the characters of the heroes of *Red Cavalry*. Taboo topics, ultrarealistic images, fill Babel's tales, contrasting violently with the most exalted romanticism. They serve as dissonances in this verbal symphony with its many expressive elements and insert themselves in the romantic context like deep shadow next to brilliant light.

The presence and the interaction in Babel of such different elements (the fantastic and the documentary, the sparkling metaphor and the trivial statement, the lyric flight and the unemotional recital) give to his images and his language an unequaled power of expression. Neutral and colorless phrases are almost totally absent from his texts. The language is laden with sensibility and creates images that are almost physically perceptible, almost dazzling: "The barn was crammed with new-mown hay, as exciting as perfume"; "an odor of lilies pure and strong as alcohol." Supersaturating his style, Babel pushes to the extreme the materiality of the world and the clarity of the image of it that he offers.

The laconic style in which our author excels goes along with this intensity of verbal expression. It is not just a question of the art of brevity in writing. Revealing to us in one of his tales his most cherished thoughts about style, Babel credits his brevity with enormous expressive power: "I am speaking of style, of the army of words, of an army in which all the arms are in movement. No metal can pierce the human heart with such paralyzing violence as a period placed at just the right spot."

It is the quest for the greatest possible expressiveness that motivates Babel's laconic style. The more confined the verbal space, the weightier the significance of each word that penetrates our consciousness like the point of a lance, provoking an explosive reaction. The prose of *Red Cavalry* would be unsuitable for a novel of large dimension: it is made to deliver quick blows, and the violent effects the author is fond of would be weakened if used over too long a space. The style of our epoch, said Babel, consists "in courage, in restraint, and it is full of fire, of passion, of power, and of gaiety."

The maturity and extraordinary originality of Babel's talent are fully manifested in *Red Cavalry*. This said, one may observe how the most unexpected artistic traditions meet and intermingle in his work.

Maksim Gorky played an exceptionally important role in Babel's literary career. Like many other Soviet writers, Babel passed through the school of Gorky. To him he owed his literary debut. It was Gorky who in 1916 published in his review *Chronicle* the first stories of Babel. In them the author of *Red Cavalry* can be only dimly discerned. The tone of the narration is dull, lacking in expression and poetry. This was chiefly the result of the paltry inner experience of the young writer, freshly arrived in Petrograd after a period in a commercial school. In the time that followed, Babel temporarily abandoned literature. He took off on long travels, took part in grain requisitioning campaigns, fought with the Army of the North and in the First Cavalry Army. After these experiences he undertook again the craft of writing. Having plunged, on the advice of Gorky, into the whirlwinds of revolutionary reality, he had not only stored up experiences and impressions, but he had also found his place in the struggles of his times and had taken a position on both the artistic and the ideological level. Such was the road that led him to *Red Cavalry,* which introduced a new stage in his life and work. Very significantly, the gestation of this book was likewise linked with the name of Gorky. Babel sent him his new stories and Gorky replied that "he might begin now." Understandably Babel considered Gorky "his first and principal teacher."

But along with this his style indicated predilections that were quite foreign to Gorky. One must cite to this effect Babel's piece "Odessa" (1916), his first attempt at an esthetic program. Russian literature, Babel affirms, developed till now under the sign of Petersburg, grey, morose, and crepuscular, to which must be opposed another symbol of faith—Odessa, city of the sea and of the sun, blossoming in a perpetual climate of festival and of light.

This sunlit esthetic, proclaimed from the writer's earliest youth, is masterfully embodied in the *Tales of Odessa,* published at the same time as *Red Cavalry,* in 1923 and 1924. The Odessa cycle is distinguished not only by a heady "local color," but also by esthetic principles that are clearly new. The talent of Babel appears in a novel light.

It is a gush of gaiety, of joy, of light. The humor of Babel, purposely suppressed in the accounts of the war, where it served mainly to accentuate the atrocious and the tragic, gives itself free rein here and becomes the preponderant element. The mischievous smile of the author of the *Tales of Odessa* is a sign of exuberance, of energy, of joie de vivre. This laughter is born of youth and health, of the fullness of physical and moral vigor, of a happy springtime acceptance of life. "The boys dragged the girls behind hedges, and the sound of kisses rose over the tombstones."

Descriptions of customs (weddings, burials, marriage proposals, and so forth) occupy the first level of *Tales of Odessa.* But these are fantastic pictures which seduce precisely by their unusual character, the brilliance of their exotic colors. Babel's Odessa is a fairyland where local images and national traits are surrounded by a halo of legend. At Odessa the power of His Imperial Majesty ends, and there begins the realm of Benya Krik, the gentleman-burglar, king of the bandits of Odessa. Here ragged Jews perform prodigies of valor, defy the police, and terrorize the rich. The women have Titanic strength, unheard-of height, and stentorian voices. The beggars drink Jamaica rum and smoke cigars which have come straight from the plantations of John Pierpont Morgan.

Here everything is excessive. "Odessa had never seen and the whole world never will see such a funeral." And so on—up to the drunken workman who sprawls "right in the middle of the universe" and not just in the gutter. Odessa is promoted to the rank of center of the world, it comes to be administered by marvelous laws and traditions. The image of the real city is enriched by the dream of the famished barefoot beggar. And precisely because most of these pictures exist only in the imagination of Odessans, the exaggeration, the bragging became an unending source of comedy. Just the opposite of *Red Cavalry,* the romanticism of *Tales of Odessa* is subordinated to the humor, and performs the function of a conventional device, purposely exaggerated by the author. What in *Red Cavalry* borders on the sublime here provokes hilarity. In *Tales of Odessa* the most prosaic things take on the air of an epic. At a wedding celebration the wine brings forth "belches as loud as a battle trumpet." The account teems with amusing incongruities, absurd comparisons, exaggeration, and droll fakery.

Babel worked very strenuously on the cycles which compose *Red Cavalry* and *Tales of Odessa.* In each of these collections the tales are linked by subject, by material, by theme, and by style.

From 1925 on Babel's pace slows; he spreads himself over a multiplicity of genres and types of writing, tries his hand in the theater and in the cinema (*Sunset,* produced in 1928, the scenario *Benya Krik,* and so forth). His short stories and tales of the second half of the twenties and of the thirties are marked by extremely unorthodox content. His style undergoes noticeable changes. He evolves toward a less expressive prose, toward broader, more circumstantial forms.

In May 1939, Babel was arrested and soon after perished. But his projects and his writings of the last period permit us to say that this was for him a time not only of preparation but also of work in progress on books of great interest.

Publishing only the works about which he felt completely confident, Babel wrote much more than he published and didn't like to divulge his literary projects, his conceptions of art. We can, however, judge of his esthetic ideas, of his searches and his meditations, as indicated in several stories dealing with the theme of art, and chiefly in his autobiographical writings of the years 1925 to 1930. These evocations of the years of childhood came, in order of importance, immediately after *Red Cavalry* and *Tales of Odessa.* A direct line of descent links them to the autobiographical accounts of Gorky. Moreover, the first of these pieces, "The Story of My Dovecot" (*Istoriya moei golubyatnei*), was dedicated to Gorky. Babel here in his way replies to the famous question of Gorky: Why did you begin to write, and what childhood impressions inclined you to your vocation? The emphasis is placed on problems that are of capital importance for Babel: the romantic and the realistic vision of the world, dream and reality, the truth of fact and the truth of fiction. Thus, while recounting his childhood, he analyzes his evolution as a writer and defines his conception of literary creation.

In this connection one must examine the story "My First Honorarium" (*Pervy gonorar*). In order to understand it correctly, one must consider the particular characteristics of Babel's style: the nonconformity of content and form, the tendency to "debasement" through contrast, and to mystification which creates the illusion of the documentary exactness of an autobiographical account when it's really a matter of pure fiction. Whether they were founded on fiction or on authentic fact, the works of Babel should always be viewed in the perspective of art and analyzed according to the logic of art and not of life.

In the story in question, "My First Honorarium," the artist's noble role is degraded to the contrivance of a hoax calculated to shock the conventional taste. His first honorarium, the author says, was the money which, when he was young, a prostitute refused, touched by a story—which was itself shocking enough—that he had reeled off to her. In this pseudoautobiographical form, in this crude representation of the most sordid venal love, Babel offers moral and esthetic ideas rich in exalted poetry and philosophic profundity. The young hero of "My First Honorarium," devoured by the passion to write, and by love for the one who sees in him only a client among many others, tells her a fanciful story of his unhappy childhood. This story, a real work of art, moves the girl to the point where she repays him with a sincere and honest love, really his "first honorarium," and the only thing capable of repaying the torment and the illumination of artistic creation.

The narrative of the hero, presented as a worthy model of the literary craft, is at the same time so unconventional and so simple that the most audacious fiction takes on the force of complete authenticity.

In a general way, the problem of truth and fiction has always obsessed Babel, especially in that new, transitory period of his career as a writer, when his style was changing and when the realistic vision of the world was taking the upper hand. But for Babel, fiction was not the opposite of reality. The truth of fiction helped to penetrate the truth of life and to recreate it much more compellingly than a vulgar copy could. "To invent" is not "to deceive," but neither is it to copy facts just as they were or "are ordinarily." Art is the quest for the unexpected, the unaccustomed, the unique, themselves the source of veracity, for real experience always contains new elements and assumes discovery, creation, and not the repetition of what is already known.

In his speech at the First Congress of Soviet Writers, in 1934, Babel said: "Without elevated thought, without philosophy, there is no literature." His work corroborates this profession of faith. It bears the imprint of noble thought and perfect form. During his lifetime, criticism did not always pay homage to this philosophical aspect of the narratives of Babel. Fascinated by his skilled craftsmanship, it hardly looked beyond the beauties of his style. All the more because the author purposely disguised his thought, refused to impose it, or to present it circumstantially in grandiloquent and ostentatious declarations. In Babel, thought always fosters concrete images which speak by themselves, which form the inner content of a work intended for an attentive and thoughtful reader.

VICTOR TERRAS

Line and Color: The Structure of I. Babel's Short Stories in Red Cavalry

The stories of Babel's *Red Cavalry* have been discussed often, almost invariably as a whole rather than as individual masterpieces. With good reason, for they *are* a whole in more ways than one. The homogeneity of setting and thematics is enhanced by the presence of a constant "I," presumably Babel himself, and by cyclic elements such as recurrent characters, events, and places. Certain conflicts recur so persistently critics have thought that the whole of *Red Cavalry* can be seen as a study in contrast and paradox. For instance: the *contrast* between Babel's "lyric joy" and the horrors of war which he describes; the *paradox* of a bespectacled Jewish intellectual and pacifist appearing not only as a chronicler of the exploits of Budenny's Red Cossacks, but also as their friend and companion-at-arms. Certain recurring stylistic traits, such as the frequent use of *skaz* technique or the lyric pathos which is rekindled in almost every story, add to this impression of homogeneity.

I will not dwell on these unifying traits. They have been recognized and described exceedingly well by Poggioli, Struve and, best of all, by Lionel Trilling. I will, on the contrary, try to put in relief those traits which belong to a given story as such, which establish it as an artistic creation in its own right, which make for its peculiar beauty, harmony, and completeness. Such inquiry is, I think, justified on two counts: first, the *Red Cavalry* stories originally appeared one by one, in several journals, each attracting on its own merits the attention of the public and critics alike; and second, the heterogeneous, even discordant, features of these stories are just as impor-

From *Studies in Short Fiction* 3, no. 2 (Winter 1966). © 1966 by Newberry College.

tant as are the common and the unifying. At least I believe so and will now try to demonstrate why.

If we use Emil Staiger's existential conception of the epic, dramatic, and lyric modes of poetic creation, the main themes of the stories in *Red Cavalry* must, I think, be distributed among all three genres.

There is, first of all, the epic theme of the ride to a strange place where adventure, passion, or even death are waiting: the ride to a rendezvous with destiny. Naturally, the theme appears in "travesty" so to say, Parsifal disguised in the ungainly uniform of a soldier of the revolution, Amfortas wearing the rags of a poor Polish Jew. In the very first tale, "Crossing into Poland," the "I" rides through the intoxicating beauty of a Ukrainian summer night, arriving at the ancient Volhynian town of Novograd past midnight. The poor Jewish home where he is billeted is turned into a haunted place by the grotesque nightmares that plague him when he finally falls asleep. In the end it reveals its solemn mystery. The old man at whose side the intruder has slept is not asleep but dead, murdered by the Poles the day before. His daughter's story then shows the old man to have died the glorious death of a martyr. The ride has taken our young adventurer to a sacred place, as well as to one of horrors.

The ride to a fateful encounter is a feature of several other stories. Pavlichenko, the avenger, returns to the estate of Nikitinsky, his former landlord, to get even with the old man for the wrong he has done him years ago, when the now Red general was herding Nikitinsky's cattle. The bizarre antics of the crazed lady of the manor turn the house into a "castle of horrors." The descent to the vaults of the mansion, where Nikitinsky, trembling for his life, shows Pavlichenko all his treasures, enhances this impression. The murder of the old man, a passionate yet purposeful act, is a fitting finale.

"Prishchepa's Vengeance" is thematically close to Matthew Pavlichenko's story. A young Cossack rides home to recover the property stolen by his neighbors after the Whites killed his parents. It culminates in a nightmarish orgy of revenge, destruction, and despair.

In "The Story of a Horse," a tale in a somewhat lighter vein, Commander Khlebnikov rides a hundred versts in a stretch to the legendary Savicky's haunt, to claim the white stallion he loves. This time it is the intruder who is defeated. Khlebnikov returns without his white horse, a broken man.

In "The Road to Brody," Babel gives the theme of the ride a lyric treatment. The nostalgic ride through the tall cornfields of the Ukraine, under "blazing, winged skies," stops short of the dented stones of the synagogues of the sacred city. It merges with the condemned Cossack's ride to Heaven in Afonka Bida's song. And the song itself joins the ride, "trailing along like smoke."

Some other stories are focused not in the ride, but entirely in the adventure at the end of the ride. In "The Church at Novograd" and in "St. Valentine's Church" the adventurer enters the "aromatically fierce," forbidden and fascinating world of a Catholic church; in "The Rabbi" it is the equally exotic world of a Hasidic synagogue; in "Gedali" it is the strange microcosm of an old curiosity shop.

Several stories are thematically close to the mode of the legend, featuring a saint or a hero. "Sandy the Christ" is a *vita sancti*—in travesty, of course—both explicitly and symbolically. Sandy, the simpleminded syphilitic and singer of songs *is* a saint. He feels it himself; the Cossacks who call him "the Christ" know it no less than their women, who seek solace and comfort from him. And isn't Sandy's stepfather a carpenter, and Sandy his helper? That he surrenders his mother to his stepfather to get permission to hire out as a shepherd, that he sleeps with women, that he is a soldier like the other Cossacks is the "travesty" part of it.

Another *vita sancti* is the story of Pan Apolek, God's fool, drunkard, blasphemer, and artist of genius, who is in a way Babel's double. The solemn proem sets a tone which keeps ringing over the irony of the narrative and triumphs in the clausule:

> The wise and beautiful life of Pan Apolek went to my head like an old wine. In Novograd-Volynsk, a town crumpled in a hurry by the war, amidst twisted ruins, fate threw at my feet a gospel that had lain concealed from the world. Surrounded by the simple-hearted radiance of nimbi, I then made a vow to follow Pan Apolek's example. And the sweetness of meditative spite, the bitter scorn for the curs and swine of mankind, the fire of taciturn and intoxicating revenge—all this I sacrificed to my new vow.

In the stories "The Rabbi" and "The Rabbi's Son," Elijah Bratslavsky, last scion of a proud dynasty, is saint, hero, and prince all in one. The last words we hear from him are, "I got to Kovel . . . The kulaks opened the front to the enemy. I took command of a scratch regiment, but too late . . . I hadn't enough artillery."

The gentle poet, with the body of a boy and the wan face of a nun, was also a born leader of men. But the travesty is present even here: we meet the prince not only in defeat and despair, but also in shame and degradation. Babel shows some other heroes in more conventional epic situations of the human condition: victory or heroic death in battle. "The Brigade Commander" is a bright picture of ambition, strength, and triumph. The bow-legged peasant boy Kolesnikov is awkward and nervous before Budenny, but not so when he faces his brigade, much less the enemy. Budenny, the Cossacks, and the narrator himself, all watch the young man's first, victorious command performance with obvious pleasure. This is a Homeric episode—in travesty, for Kolesnikov, a fine soldier who fights "for glory," as befits the true hero, who after his victory displays "the masterful indifference of a Tartar Khan," is externally a drab and even a ridiculous figure!

Another Homeric episode in travesty can be found in "Konkin's Prisoner." The cocky Red hero, thrice Knight of the Order of the Red Banner, tells without boasting, "in his customary farcical manner," how eight well-armed Polish horsemen are easy game for two battleweary Cossacks, one of whom has been badly wounded earlier in the day. An elderly Polish general is cornered after putting up a brave fight. The old man's love of life gets the better of his honor and he is inclined to hand over his sword. Much as in similar Homeric scenes, the balance, after a good deal of suspense, tilts toward Hades: the general is done in by his captors after all.

"Chesniki" could have been called "Before the Battle," had not the following story been "After the Battle." We see at first Red cavalry getting ready for one of its headlong charges. The demigods Voroshilov and Budenny are personally directing operations. Then, much as it would in the *Iliad*, the scene shifts to an idyllic microcosm. Sasha, the Red amazon, is secretly getting her mare covered by the Commander's prize stallion. The beginning of the following story then brings one of the most stirring battle scenes in all Russian literature: the unforgettable cavalry charge of Chesniki.

In "Squadron Commander Trunov" the glory of a heroic death is only slightly dimmed by the usual travesty. The slaughter of the prisoners by the doomed Trunov acquires a mythic meaning if we perceive them as the sacrificial victims that accompany the epic hero in death. The very futility of Trunov's death has a certain grandeur about it. The American planes of Major Fauntleroy's air squadron, which kill swiftly, efficiently, and inexorably, are like intruders from another, superior world. Trunov challenges them, and dies like an epic hero who has challenged the gods. But the petty, squalid details of the setting disguise the main theme, enough for us to take the heroic epic poem for a naturalistic war sketch.

The elements of travesty are stronger in "The Widow," the story of the death of Commander Sheveliov. He dies, to his last breath a hero and a leader, against a background of revolting animal life. Who would recognize the rivalry for the arms of the slain Achilles in the squabble for the dead hero's earthly belongings? But if we take an unprejudiced look at the theme of this story, and at those of the other "epic" stories in *Red Cavalry*, we see that they are in fact the common themes of the heroic epos of all times. It is most important to note that this is not merely a self-evident concomitant of the fact that Babel is writing about war and that his heroes are soldiers. The point is that the *sujets* of these stories reflect a vision of the human condition which is characteristic of a heroic worldview, of a heroic society.

A good many of the stories in *Red Cavalry* feature a dramatic rather than an epic theme, for example, a conflict based on social tensions. It is to this type of story that many of the interesting things said about Babel do particularly apply. It is mostly in these dramatic stories that Babel's ironies and ambiguities are in evidence: dramatic pathos thrives on such tensions, not epic ethos.

The easiest recognized of these tensions is that between the intellectual, usually represented by Babel's "I," and the Cossack. It may develop along many different vectors: the natural pacifist clashing with the man for whom killing, nay murder, is a business; the abjectness of the thinking man faced with a situation which calls for outright, courageous action—such as putting a bullet through a dying soldier's head to save him from being abused by the approaching enemy; the battle between the subtle irony of "specs," the commissar, and the unsuspecting good humor and exuberant physical vigor of the Cossacks and their handsome giant of a commander, a battle which both parties win and lose: the bespectacled law school graduate cannot help becoming enamored of Savicky's imposing physique and reckless élan, also, for all his outward bravado, he knows all too well that he will always remain but a sorry killer—even of geese; the Cossacks couldn't ever, like their commissar, spy out the secret curve of Lenin's line, they naively see only what the learned man wants them to see as he reads the Leader's latest speech to them. And, the semiliterate Savicky, for all his manly charm, cuts a fairly ridiculous figure as a writer of military prose.

The most dramatic of all the stories in *Red Cavalry* is perhaps "Argamak." The world of *Red Cavalry* is a horseman's world in which the "I" must needs play the role of an intruder. In "Argamak" the intruder becomes doubly odious when given the Cossack Tikhomolov's mount Argamak. Also, while this is never made explicit, the man who is ruining Tikhomolov's glorious stallion is obviously a man of some authority, *viz.*, a political commissar. The tensions developing from this situation are many: Tikhomolov, the disgraced Cossack, fights to recover the horse that must be as dear to him as his life. He finally succeeds, by a feat of extraordinary bravery. The "I" struggles to gain the friendship of the Cossacks—in vain. He also struggles to conquer Argamak, who hates his involuntary tormentor no less than does Tikhomolov. There is also a conflict, hidden and subtle, between "line" and "color." Baulin, the squadron leader, is a genuine Bolshevik: "The path of his life had been laid down, and he had no doubts as to the correctness of this path." Only the *line* matters to Baulin; passion, suffering, beauty are irrelevant. The pathetic story of Argamak is to him a routine disciplinary matter. The emotional, ethical, and aesthetical (yes, for isn't it a crime against beauty to give a great horse to a miserable horseman?) angles do not exist for him; they nearly kill the sensitive Babel.

The conflict between "line" and "color," which erupts openly and with great acerbity in such later stories as the one which actually bears the title "Line and Color," or "Froim Grach," can be recognized in some *Red Cavalry* stories as well. The story "Evening" shows it quite clearly. Galin, the walleyed communist fanatic, is absolutely confident of the victory of his party, whose line is likened to a pair of railroad tracks. It is Galin who utters the following prophetic words:

> You're a driveler, and we are fated to have to put up with you drivelers. We're busy shelling and getting at the kernel for you. Not long will pass and then you'll see the cleaned kernel, and take your fingers out of your nose and sing of the new life in no ordinary prose. In the meantime sit still, you driveler, and stop whimpering around us.

Line will win over color. There is little consolation in the circumstance that Galin pays a price for his victory: he loses the contest for the graces of Irina, the laundress. Having sleepily listened to his tirades, she goes off to bed with Vasily, the cook.

Babel's dramatism depends on tensions between men, classes, nationalities, not on a man's inner conflicts. Dostoyevskian complexities or the isolation of the Chekhovian dramatic hero will not easily be found in *Red Cavalry*. Babel's drama is that of head-on clash. Hostility or loneliness, much rather than alienation or solipsism, trouble the Babelian hero.

Struve has pointed out, very shrewdly I think, that there is something romantically conventional about most of Babel's characters. They do what we expect them to do. Almost invariably we meet them in moments of high crisis and so only see the highlights of their roles, so to speak. In other words, the Babelian character is devised to dramatize one of the tensions inherent in the world of *Red Cavalry*. We are shown the tension, not the whole man.

It is in its dramatic capacity that the Babelian short story takes on some traits of social satire. Such is the case in "Salt," one of Babel's most famous stories, which dramatizes the unholy union between tough revolutionary phraseology and the self-righteous brutality of the semiliterate. Another such story is "A Letter," with the eternal theme of father and sons fighting on different sides. The element of travesty is particularly strong in the latter story, so strong it almost turns it into a satirical allegory. The tragic pathos of fratricidal civil war is dragged through the mud of the narrator's low mentality and dulled by the brutish callousness of the principals of the drama. The heroic combat of Hildebrand and Hadubrand is replaced by two sadistic executions.

Several of the stories not mentioned so far display a strong affinity to a modern genre which for want of a better term I shall call "the nightmare": a piece the mode of perception and structure of which resemble an oppressive dream. "Italian Sunshine" is a good example. Its hero, Sidorov, obviously is an executioner of the Cheka who is on the verge of "cracking up" (or has he already crossed the threshold?). He dreams of being sent to Italy to organize the assassination of King Victor Emmanuel, but would, if worse came to worst, accept an assignment with the Odessa Cheka. The ravings of Sidorov, the "melancholy murderer," are set against a background of the "I's" own, almost somnambulant stream-of-consciousness.

"Zamoste" is another dreamlike piece, shreds from the stream-of-consciousness of a desperately tired man, alternating with dream scenes. The violent clashes in "After the Battle" are experienced as if in a trance: important details remain untold, the sequence of events is sharply discontinuous.

There are a few stories that are rather easily recognized as "poems in prose," thus belonging to the lyric genre. Such are "The Cemetery at Kozin," "The Road to Brody," and "The Song." The lyric mode also prevails in "Gedali" and in "Berestechko." The remaining pieces can be classified as *feuilletons*. There are not too many of them: "Discourse on the *Tachanka*," "The Remount Officer," "The Story of a Horse, Continued," and "Treason."

We see, then, that, while the setting and characters of *Red Cavalry* are quite uniform indeed, the structural-aesthetic thematics of these stories are extremely varied. The same Cossacks and Jews, soldiers and civilians, insensitive brutes and subtle dreamers appear in situations the aesthetic and emotive mode of which may be either epic or dramatic, heroic or satirical, sublime or comical, serious or frivolous. Such heterogeneity does not *per se* suggest that the stories of *Red Cavalry* do not follow the traditional canon of the classical *novella*. We know that it is in the structure rather than in the *sujet* that we find the distinctive traits of this well-defined genre. So let us ask: Do we find in Babel's stories the straight line of action, the limited but compact space, the dramatically coiled spring of time, all of which are characteristic of the *novella* from Boccaccio to Guy de Maupassant?

I believe that the stories written entirely, or almost entirely in *skaz* must be set aside as a separate structural type. Style is here the principal integrating factor. The author's determination to create a credible semblance of uneducated narrative is binding not only stylistically but also structurally. And so Kurdiukov's letter to his mother, Balmashev's letter to the editor of the *Red Trooper*, or the complaint of the three hospitalized Cossacks in "Treason" ramble along, mixing the relevant with the irrelevant, the serious with the comical, the touchingly sincere and poignantly true with the stupidly affected, brazenly phony rhetoric of the semiliterate.

The uneducated or semiliterate narrator finds it difficult to get to the point of his tale as he wades through a morass of irrelevant trivialities; and when he does get there finally, it is awkwardly off balance, and as if by accident. The murders in "Salt" and in "A Letter" seem just to happen, anticlimactically almost; and in "Treason" we discover, late in the story and among other things, that one of the three principals died four days after the incident described by his buddy. The entire narrative in these stories is characterized by what one might call "wrong accents"—stylistically, structurally, and emotionally.

While the stylized stories are among the best remembered, they do not, I believe, represent Babel's art at its loftiest. I think that Babel's claim to immortality rests entirely with those stories which reveal the stream-of-consciousness of a cultured, sophisticated, aesthetically and emotionally sensitive young man—young even though there may be "autumn in his heart."

Clearly, plot in the conventional sense (the Russian *fabula*) is not what gives unity to most of Babel's stories. In fact, the tales in which plot seems to play its customary role are mostly those written in *skaz* and, in my opinion, the least ambitious artistically. In many of the other stories we observe a curious phenomenon: what would have to be the plot of the story is condensed into a brief scene, or even into a single phrase, and made a distinct, concrete part of the narrative. Figuratively speaking, the plot is then a single figure on the face of a rug, not a pattern woven into the whole rug.

The martyr's death of the old Jew in "Crossing into Poland" is told in a few lines at the very end of the story. In "The Rabbi's Son" the story of Elijah's heroic stand and tragic failure appears as if in parenthesis. In "The

Rabbi" the fascinating image of the last prince of the dynasty remains in the background and the story of his rebellion, glory and tragic end is only hinted at, even though Elijah is the hero of that tale also.

In "The Church at Novograd" the story of Pan Romuald's treason and death flashes by in a subordinate clause. In "Italian Sunshine" the mad, sordid career of Sidorov, the ex-anarchist and now Chekist, emerges from the chaos of the second page of his letter; his roommate, who tells the story, dared not look for the beginning.

Some stories are veritable mosaics of intriguing, dynamic themes, each of which would be good for a fine short story. In the difficult-to-analyze story, "Berestechko," for instance, there are introduced, in order: an old Ukrainian with a bandore, singing of the ancient glory of the Cossacks; the murder of an old Jew, accused of spying; mad ninety-year-old Countess Raciborska, who would beat her son with a coachman's whip because he had given the dying line no heir; the echo of a story of love and separation in the fragment of a French letter, dated "Berestechko, 1820."

While Babel seems to be scornful of plot in the conventional sense, the clausule (Russian *kontsovka*) of the classical *novella* is very much in evidence throughout. However, much as with the plot, what looks like the "clausule" is sometimes a separate entity, independent of the rest of the story.

It may come in the form of an elegant conclusion of the plot, as for instance in "Argamak," "Konkin's Prisoner," or "Afonka Bida." It may come as a lyric recapitulation of the subjective, emotional mood of the story, as in "Gedali," "My First Goose," or "After the Battle." As a rhetorical peroration, as in "The Rabbi's Son," "Berestechko," or "The Cemetery at Kozin." As a brief, poignant gnome, as in "The Church of Novograde," "Story of a Horse," or "The Life and Adventures of Matthew Pavlichenko."

In many instances we see a definite rondo pattern (Russian *kol'tso*): the clausule returns to the proem, as for instance in "Squadron Commander Trunov," "Evening," "Pan Apolek," or "Gedali."

Clearly, there couldn't be any greater variety. The same can be said of the exposition. A terse, matter-of-fact statement in the style of a military communiqué is the usual introduction ("Our division took Berestechko last night."). But this is deceptive. What follows is more often than not a colorful image—a landscape, a portrait, or a *nature morte*. Besides, Babel has many other ways to start a story: with a rhetorical proem ("The Rabbi's Son," "Pan Apolek," "Evening"), with a dialogue ("The Rabbi"), by taking the reader *in medias res* with a narrative passage ("The Death of Dolgushov"), or by raising the curtain with a description ("My First Goose").

Really nowhere—with the exception of the *skaz*-type stories—do we have anything resembling conventional epic narrative. There are but few dialogues of any length. What we have is a kaleidoscopic sequence of descriptions of town and country; goyaesque scenes of violence and suffering; brief, racy dialogues (always "stylized"!); stream-of-consciousness-type passages; dreams and nightmares; rhetorical passages ringing with emotion; gnomes and *bons mots*; anecdotes, biographies, legends compressed into a single paragraph; scraps of "confessions"; a torrent of similes and metaphors which often enough are motives in their own right. Here, for example, is a breakdown into motives for "Crossing into Poland":

An introductory line in the tone of a military communiqué. Then, as early as in the second sentence, "color" joins "line" in the form of first an adjective (the rearguard of the advancing army is called "clamorous"), then an adjective phrase which is a story all in itself ("over the highroad from Brest to Warsaw built by Nicholas I upon the bones of peasants"). Half a page of elaborate landscape painting follows. Towards the end of this description the movements and noises of the army marching through the peaceful countryside take over. The connecting phrase "Far on in the night we reached Novograd" opens up a very different picture, the *intérieur* of a poor Jewish home, with its silent, puppet-like occupants.

At this point, the first dialogue line: "Clean this up," I said to the woman. "What a filthy way to live!" The Jews silently clean up and make the unwanted visitor's bed: a brief, but oppressive, nightmarish description.

After the connecting phrase "Silence overcame all," another lyric nature image (of the moon). Then another connecting phrase and a vivid, dramatic, grotesque nightmare dreamt by the "I." It is disrupted, finally, by the phrase "and here I woke up, for the pregnant woman was groping over my face with her fingers."

Here then comes the first significant dialogue line which, flash-like, brings the woman to life: "Good sir," she said, "you're calling out in your sleep and you're tossing to and fro. I'll make you a bed in another corner, for you're pushing my father about." And now the ghastly revelation, in curt, dispassionate words, that the intruder had been pushing about a man whose throat "had been torn out and his face cleft in two."

Finally, the Jewess tells the story of her father's death. The narrator inserts an observation on the intonation of her voice. The woman's last words, which conclude the story, form a rhetorical question, uttered "with sudden and terrible violence": "I want to know where on earth you could find another father like my father?"

The story is quite typical of *Red Cavalry*. In longer stories we have, of course, even more different motives. The question arises: how are these many different motives, which are often quite heterogeneous in more than one respect, put together to form the marvellously integrated organism of the Babelian short story? This question is all the more legitimate as Babel himself is reported, by a reliable source, to have seen his creations as assemblages of motives, integrated by painstaking craftsmanship:

> When I write down the first version of a story, the manuscript looks disgusting, simply horrible! It's an aggregate of more or less successful bits, joined together by the dreariest connecting links, so called "bridges," a kind of dirty ropes.... This is where my work begins. I check sentence after sentence, and not once, but many times. First of all I throw out the superfluous words from each sentence.... And so I go on, retyping the text each time, until I get to a point where, despite the most savage captiousness, I couldn't find a speck of dirt in the manuscript.
>
> (Paustovsky)

This gives us a valuable hint: we may view Babel's stories as compositions rather than as narrative prose in the conventional sense. As far as their genesis is concerned, they are closer to the lyric poem than to the epic narrative. A Babelian short story owes its completeness and unity to composition, more than to an inherent thematic or structural principle (such as plot, adherence to the established rules of a specific genre, or a dominating character).

Some recurring structural devices of Babel's stories resemble lyric more than epic or dramatic technique. The importance as well as the various specific types of the clausule are a trait which the *novella* shares with the lyric poem, and so is the rondo form found so often in Babel's stories. However, more often than not the proem, or the clausule, or both, are distinctly lyrical, particularly when they consist of an image or of a rhetorical ejaculation, which is often. It is also my impression that the frequent recurrence of a motive (usually an image) in the same story resembles a lyrical refrain as much as it does the "falcon" of the classical *novella*. I am thinking here of such items as the blood trickling through the bandage wrapped around Trunov's head, the shepherd-saint motive in "Sandy the Christ," or the blinking of Galin's walleye.

Babel's is a static space, filled with vivid, sensuous images. Savicky's gigantic frame cleaves the hut "as a standard cleaves the sky." Afonka Bida comes galloping "framed in the nimbus of the sunset." Kolesnikov walks to glory "Bathed in the crimson haze of a sunset that seemed as unreal as oncoming death." A comparison of Babel's space to that in the paintings of the young Chagall has been rightly suggested. The space of both artists is color without a boundary, none even between heaven and earth. In this continuum of color there float images—some beautiful, some sordid; some delicately ethereal, some coarsely naturalistic; images of the peasants and Jews of Red Russia, their little towns, their huts, their horses and their cattle; and the moon in the most incredible, yet so real shades of color.

For the poet, "color" is of course a somewhat broader concept than for the painter, although in Babel's case the literal (rather than metaphoric) meaning of that word applies often enough. "Color" is the enchanting moonlit night into which are cast "dreams leaping about like kittens," "a satin-clad Romeo singing of love," Sidorov's mad letter under a flickering candle, a squabbling Jewish couple, a melancholy murderer's dream of Italian sunshine. "Color" is the fiery sunset over peaceful Ukrainian cornfields in "Crossing into Poland," "The Death of Dolgushov," "The Brigade Commander," and "The Road to Brody." "Color" is the "burning brilliance of the skies" over "blue dust and Galician mournfulness" in "Squadron Commander Trunov." "Color" is the melancholy Sabbath eve atmosphere in "Gedali" and "The Rabbi."

The arrangement of images, shreds of dialogue, scraps of confession and stream-of-consciousness, rhetorical passages and aphorisms in this space of color likewise resembles the composition of Chagall's paintings. Time in *Red Cavalry* is not time as we know it from the classical *novella*, or even from the Chekhovian short story. It may be the leisurely change of evening to night, or of night to morning. It may be the unnoticed flow of the "I's" stream-of-consciousness, often quite timeless like a dream. Never is it the sharply felt time of anticipation or of regret. When there is action, time seems to be standing still. The cavalry charge of Chesniki is for us the static image of a "deathlike wall of black uniforms and pale faces" and Captain Yakovlev awaiting the charge with unsheathed saber, a gold tooth gleaming in his mouth and his black beard lying on his chest "like an icon on a dead man."

Not that the Babelian short story has not got line. What it hasn't got is a line typical of it, as the curve is of the Chekhovian short story. In *Red Cavalry* a good deal seems to depend on the theme of each story. In the more "epic" stories the initial bold sweep of the line that one sees in the opening paragraph of so many stories does not altogether dissolve into color, but continues, sometimes firm and clear, sometimes a mere hazy outline, straight to the climax of the story. Such are the stories featuring the epic ride to a rendezvous with destiny.

The stories of the life and death of a hero, or of a saint, tend to follow the rondo form. The substance of the "legend" is revealed in the solemn proem, the story itself then brings various vivid details, not necessarily in chronological order, and the conclusion is another encomium, echoing the mood, or even the image of the proem. Such is the pattern of "Pan Apolek," "Squadron Commander Trunov," or "Sandy the Christ."

As to the dramatic tales, they all share the permanent unresolvedness of their conflicts. The tension between Cossack and bespectacled Commissar that is felt at the very beginning of "My First Goose" or "After the Battle" is only heightened by the several clashes that make up the plot of the story. The conclusion underscores, in each case, that the rift is irremediable. In this may lie the completeness of the story.

The ironies and ambiguities of Babel's art do not, I believe, create a "curve." The irony, if present, is constant and almost immediately obvious, so in the *skaz*-type stories, where the stylistic contrast between Babel's introductory words and the following *skaz* creates tension immediately. (Here I may be in slight disagreement with Matthewson who says: "[skaz] is a device Babel frequently uses to effect those human exposures that are his main concern. It is the technique of the slow disclosure of a situation through the naive view of a participant who comprehends dimly—if at all—the consequences or meanings of what he is describing—*The Positive Hero in Russian Literature*. In my opinion the real point of the *skaz*-type stories lies in the exposure of the gaping chasm between the sensibility of the uneducated narrator and that of Babel himself. The rift is immediately patent in every case, although one may become more aware of its abysmal depth as the story proceeds.) Neither does the mask of Babelian travesty deceive us: we soon recognize heroes and saints, leaders and martyrs, good men and murderers, in spite of their disguise.

A few times an ambiguity does seem to make for a structural break. In "Gedali" one has the feeling that the narrator is presenting to us a historical relic, a glimpse of the vanishing past, for which reason has but little regret, in spite of heart's nostalgia. Then suddenly this line: "She cannot do without shooting, Gedali, because she is the Revolution." This changes the mood of the story and introduces the ambiguity. With the brash young revolutionary having nothing better to offer to refute Gedali's simple philosophy, the old man's naiveté becomes wisdom.

In "The Rabbi" the atmosphere suddenly changes when, among the possessed, the liars, and the idlers, we perceive suddenly "a youth with the face of Spinoza, with Spinoza's powerful brow and the wan face of a nun." A little later the Rabbi chants: "Blessed is the Lord God of Israel Who hath chosen us from amongst all the nations of the earth." This would have been pure irony with Cossack horses neighing under the windows of the synagogue—but for the presence of the chosen youth, the prince. In "The Rabbi's Son" the break comes when we hear, to our intense gratification, that Elijah had proven himself a prince not only in spirit but in action as well. Yet this kind of structural break effected through the introduction of an ambiguity is not really typical of the stories in *Red Cavalry*.

So much, then, for "line." We know from Babel's diary that virtually every detail of *Red Cavalry* is based on actual observations. Babel said himself that he lacked "fantasy." The secret of his art, he said, lay in the way he reassembled the sundry scraps of a reality which was not in itself poetic. There are those who say it is essentially "style" that keeps Babel's stories together. This may be too simple an answer. I think that it is really composition, the details of which are different for every single story and practically for every single juncture.

I have already discussed "line." There are a few stories in which suspense is a factor. Will Ivan Akinfiev kill the Deacon, or won't he? Ironically, the story breaks off before the suspense is lifted. Will Konkin kill his prisoner? He does—as an afterthought, so to speak. But much more often suspense is momentary, a distinct, particulate entity—like images, gnomes, and rhetorical tirades. It comes and it goes, for instance, in "The Death of Dolgushov" or "After the Battle," where for a moment Liutov's life hangs in the balance.

By and large Babel's stories are examples of ideological disinterestedness. But a few times it seems there is an epiphany which casts light upon the whole story. In "Sandy the Christ," I think that the following passage is pivotal:

> "For the love of God, let me go, Tarakanych," Sandy begged once more.
> "All the saints used to be shepherds."
> "Sandy the Saint!" guffawed the stepfather. "Caught syphilis from the Mother of God."

It is this brief dialogue that establishes Sandy as a saint in travesty. It is not difficult to detect allegory in this, and in a few other stories. But, I daresay that, once again, the allegory is a distinct motive rather than an element underlying the structure of the whole story.

There are a few lyric pieces in which lyric parallelism is the significant structural pattern ("The Road to Brody," "The Cemetery at Kozin"), and one or two where contrast seems to act as the structural pivot. In "The Song" the squalor of poverty is set opposite the beauty of a song. In "Berestechko" the reeking Jewish ghetto stands opposite a genteel French letter, and a communist party meeting takes place at the foot of the castle of Count Raciborski.

Yet by and large, and surely in most of the stories in *Red Cavalry*, the composition must be accounted for motive by motive, transition by transition. Such great stories as "Pan Apolek" or "The Rabbi's Son" are original compositions which cannot be reduced to any particular pattern, or even to any particular genre.

The Babelian short story at its best seems to realize that poetic balance between thought and image, line and color, movement and structure in a way which is characteristic of great lyric poetry. The emphasis is on image, color, and structure, rather than on thought, line, and movement. Ehrenburg is quite right when he calls Babel a poet. Such non-lyrical ingredients as philosophical abstraction, plot, irony, and rhetoric are transformed by him into concrete verbal units, small and light enough to float about in Babel's space of color. Babel also displays a healthy dose of that Goethean "narrowness, enamored of reality," which is proper to the true lyric poet. In many respects Babel's art in *Red Cavalry* resembles that of the acmeist-imaginist school of lyric poetry, in particular that of the great acmeist poet Osip Mandelstamm.

KONSTANTIN PAUSTOVSKY

I Promise You Maupassant

The Seaman printed a short story called "The King." It was signed I. Babel.

It was the story of an Odessa bandit chief, Benzion ("Benny") the Scream, who married off his ageing sister Dvoira to an ailing, whining thief. The thief married her out of terror of Benny.

This was one of the first of Babel's "Moldavanka" stories.

Moldavanka was a district near the goods station, with a population of two thousand bandits and thieves.

He had moved into the district to study its ways. He stayed with an old Jew, Tsires, who was being scolded into his grave by his shrewish wife, "Aunt Khava."

Soon after renting a room from this meek old man, who looked like a Lilliputian, events were to develop at breakneck speed and Babel had to flee for his life from the flat with its overpowering smell of fried onions and moth-balls.

But more of this later.

"The King" was written in a precise, terse language. Its freshness hit you in the face like a splash from a syphon.

Ever since my schooldays the work of certain writers had seemed to me a form of magic. When I read "The King" I realised that a new magician had joined their ranks, and that nothing he wrote could ever be limp or colourless.

"The King" dealt with a world completely outside our experience. The characters, their motives, their circumstances and their vivid, forceful talk—

From *The Story of a Life: Years of Hope*. © 1968 by Harvill Press and Pantheon Books. This essay was translated by Manya Harari and Andrew Thomson.

all were strange to us. The story had the vitality of a grotesque. The smallest detail showed the sharpness of the author's vision. And suddenly, like a burst of sunshine through the window, you came upon some exquisite fragment, or the unexpected rhythm of a sentence balanced like a translation from the French, measured and rich.

This was new, exciting prose. It had the tone of voice of a man still covered with the dust of the Cavalry Corps campaigns, but who could draw on all the riches of the culture of the past—from Boccaccio to Leconte de Lisle and from Vermeer of Delft to Alexander Blok.

Izya Livshitz brought Babel to *The Seaman*'s office. Never had I seen anyone look less like an author. Stooping, almost neckless because of his hereditary asthma, with a duck's bill of a nose, a creased forehead and an oily glint in his little eyes, he was anything but fascinating. At first sight you would have taken him for a commercial traveller or a stockbroker. But this, of course, was only until he opened his mouth.

At his very first words everything changed. His voice had an undertone of insistent irony.

Many people couldn't bear to meet his eyes; they drilled through you. Babel was a born unveiler of truth. He enjoyed cornering people, and was known in Odessa as an awkward, dangerous man.

He arrived at the office with a book of Kipling stories under his arm.

Talking to the editor, Ivanov, he put it down on the desk but kept looking at it with greedy impatience. He fidgeted in his chair, got up and sat down, obviously on edge. He wanted to read, not to make polite conversation.

He soon changed the subject to Kipling, saying that everyone ought to write his kind of steely prose, and to visualise in the clearest detail what he was about to write. A story should be as accurate as a military report or a bank cheque. Even the handwriting should be firm and clear, as on a cheque or an army order—which Kipling's, incidentally, was.

He finished on an unexpected note. He took off his spectacles, and this at once gave him a benign and helpless air.

"We Odessans," he said with a hint of mockery, "will never have our Kipling. We are peaceful hedonists. But we will certainly have our Maupassants—because we have plenty of sea and sun, and pretty women, and plenty to think about. That much I can promise you."

He went on to tell us of his visit to Maupassant's last flat in Paris—the sun-warmed frilly pink lampshades, like the underclothes of expensive courtesans, the smell of brilliantine and coffee, and the vast rooms which frightened the sick author, who for years had schooled himself in the tight framework of his plots and the shortest way of telling a story.

Babel recalled with delight the Paris he had known. He had an excellent French accent.

From some of his comments and questions, I realised that Babel was a man of incredible persistence, tenacious as a leech, wanting to know everything and never squeamish about the truth, a man outwardly sceptical to the point of cynicism but who, in fact, believed in the simple goodness of the human soul. He was fond of quoting the Bible: "Strength makes thirsty; sorrow slakes the heart."

I watched him from my window as he walked away along the shady side of Marine Boulevard. He walked slowly, for no sooner had he left the building than he opened his book and began to read. At times, he stopped to let someone pass, but not once did he look up.

People went by and glanced back puzzled, but no one spoke to him.

Soon he disappeared in the shadow of the plane trees, their velvet leaves fluttering in the stream of Black Sea air.

After that, I often met Babel in town. He was never alone. Swarming round him like midges were the "Odessa literary boys." They caught his jokes in mid-air, flew round town with them, and ran his countless errands without complaining.

He told them off for carelessness, and drove them away ruthlessly when he had had enough of them. But the rougher he treated them, the better they seemed to like it.

Nor were they alone in their hero-worship of Babel. Old, established authors (there were several in Odessa at the time) treated him with as much respect as did the young local writers and poets.

The reason was not only that he had exceptional gifts—it was also that Gorky liked and appreciated him as a writer, that he was just back from Budenny's campaigns and shared in their legend, and above all, that he was our first authentic Soviet writer.

It has to be remembered that Soviet literature at the time was scarcely born, and that not a single new book had reached us in Odessa except Blok's *The Twelve* and a Russian translation of Barbusse's *The Fire*.

They produced a shattering impression on us—they already flashed with the distant lightning of new poetry and prose, and we learned Blok's poems and the austere prose of Barbusse by heart.

It was not till late summer 1921 that I got to know Babel really well. He was living at Ninth Station in Fountain. I was on holiday, and Izya and I rented a dilapidated villa not far from his.

One of our walls overhung a sheer cliff. Chunks of bright pink plaster often broke away and went skipping gaily down to the sea. So it was safer to sleep on the verandah facing the steppe.

Our garden stood waist high in grey weeds. Tiny poppies, the size of finger nails, struggled through them and looked like drops of fresh red paint.

We saw Babel often. Sometimes we spent nearly all day on the beach, fishing for bullheads and listening to Babel's leisurely stories.

He was a wonderful storyteller. Those he told were even more powerful and accomplished than those he wrote.

How can I describe that gay yet sad summer we spent at Fountain in 1921? It was made gay by our youth but sad by the vague anxiety continually in our hearts. And also, perhaps, because of the pitch-black southern nights. They dropped their curtain right in front of us, on the top step of the stone verandah.

You could stand on the verandah and stretch your hand into the night and snatch it back, having felt the chill of cosmic space at your fingertips.

The gaiety was in the bright patchwork of our conversations, jokes and hoaxes (the Odessa word for them, "roulette," soon spread to the rest of the country).

The sadness was unaccountably embodied for me in a clear light which shone on the horizon every night.

It was a star low over the sea. It watched us with friendly insistence night after night, yet none of us knew its name.

The sadness was also, for some reason, in the smell of the stone highway as it cooled in the evening, and in the light centres of the wild verbena growing outside our door, and in our strong sense of the quick passing of time.

The world was still beset by troubles. But for us youngsters they were already next-door to happiness, because the times were full of hope of a rational outcome, of an end to persistent misfortune, of the flowering bound to follow the seemingly endless winter.

That summer, I think I understood for the first time what is meant by the "power of genius."

Everything was made absorbingly interesting for us by Babel's presence. We lived in his reflected light.

The people I had met until then had rarely made a lasting impression on me. I forgot their faces, voices, their words, their way of walking. But now they etched themselves on my memory.

Babel often returned from Odessa by the evening horse-tram (it had replaced the electric tram, now forgotten). The tram went no further than Eighth Station, and you could hear it from a long way off, clanking all its loose bolts.

From there, Babel walked, and arrived dusty, tired, but pleased.

"You should have heard two old women talking in the tram! About eggs! Let me tell you. You'll laugh till you cry."

He described the conversation, and we not only laughed until we sobbed, we rolled on the floor, helpless.

Then Babel would pull us each by the sleeve and ask in the querulous voice of the market woman we knew at Tenth Station:

"Have you gone completely barmy, young fellow? Or what?"

You had only to close your eyes when you listened to him, and there you were, sitting in the Odessa tram, looking at the passengers with as much insight as if you had been their bosom friend all your life. Perhaps they didn't really exist and Babel had made them up from scratch. But what did we care so long as we could see them in front of us, complete, living, earthy, grunting, coughing, winking at each other and nodding at Babel, who already was said in Odessa to be as clever as Gorky.

Long before the stories were published, Babel told us about old Guedalla who dreamed of an "International of men of good will," and the incident with the salt at Fastov Station, and the furious cavalry charges, and Budenny's dazzling smile, and we heard from him some wonderful Cossack songs. There was one he liked particularly; we often sang it afterwards in Odessa and its poetry never ceased to astonish us. By now I have forgotten all but a couple of lines:

> The star of the fields above my father's house,
> And my mother's grieving hands.

It was that "star of the fields" that got me every time. I even dreamed of it at night, a quiet, solitary star high up above the dark, familiar, barren fields.

Babel was a ready talker, and told us much about Gorky and the revolution, and how he, Babel, once took up unofficial residence in the Anichkov Palace in Petersburg, and slept on the divan in Alexander the Third's study, and took a peep in the desk, and found a box of cigarettes presented by the Sultan of Turkey, Abdul Hamid. They were fat, pink cigarettes with an Arabic inscription in gold. With an air of great mystery, Babel handed us one each, and we smoked them that evening on our verandah. A delicate aroma drifted over Ninth Station, but we both got splitting headaches, and, for a good hour, reeled like drunkards, clutching at the walls.

It was then I also heard from Babel the strange story of Tsires. Babel stayed with Tsires and his sluggish, morose wife, Aunt Khava, at the very centre of Moldavanka. He had decided to write several stories about this suburb of Odessa and its turbulent way of life. He felt drawn by the strangeness and originality of such undoubtedly gifted natures as the already legendary bandit Mike the Jap (Benny the Scream). He wanted to study them closer, and Tsires's dingy flat was the obvious look-out post.

It stood firm as a rock amidst the rampaging violence of the thieves' dens and the deceptive respectability of quiet homes, with crochet mats and silver candlesticks on the sideboard, where bandits sheltered under their parents' roof.

Surrounded by daring and well-armed young men, the flat was as safe as a fortress with an armed guard.

When Babel confided the purpose of his research work to Tsires, the old man was anything but pleased. In fact he was frankly worried.

"Oi, Monsieur Babel!" he said, shaking his head. "And you, the son of such a well-known papa! And your mother a famous beauty in her time! Courted by Brodsky's own nephew, they say. Take my word for it, Moldavanka is no place for you, writer or no writer. Forget it. I'm telling you here and now, you won't have a pennyworth of success here, and you might collect a pocketful of trouble."

"What kind of trouble?" Babel asked.

"Do I know?" Tsires replied evasively. "How can I tell what crazy notion even a peaceful man like Five Roubles might get into his head—not to speak of Lyuska Chicken and the rest. Better not risk it, Monsieur Babel. Go home quietly to Catherine Street, to your papa. I tell you honestly, I'm sorry I ever let you that room. But how could I refuse such a pleasant spoken young man!"

Sometimes Babel spent the night in his room at Tsires's and heard Aunt Khava scolding the old man in whispers for letting a stranger into the house.

"What will you get out of it, you old miser? A wretched hundred thousand a month! And for that you'll lose your best clients? Lazar Broide will have a good laugh on you. They'll all go over to him, I swear by our late Idochka."

"The cops are only waiting to jump on your Broide," Tsires said uncertainly.

"Mind they don't jump on you first. He'll ruin you, that lodger. Nobody will give you one per cent. What will become of us in our old age?"

Tsires worried, tossing and turning in his bed.

So did Babel, trying to guess what Aunt Khava meant. He didn't like these mysterious conversations at night. He felt they hinted at some dangerous secret.

The nights were long in Moldavanka. A bleary light from a distant street-lamp fell on the peeling wallpaper. The walls smelt of acetic acid. At rare intervals the sound of brisk, businesslike footsteps came from the street, or a high-pitched whistle, or even a shot close-by, and a woman's hysterical laugh. It came from behind brick walls. The sobbing laughter seemed to be immured in them.

Rainy nights were particularly bad. Water tinkled in the drain-pipe. The bed creaked at the slightest movement, and all night long something nibbled at the rotting timbers behind the wallpaper.

Babel felt like going home to Catherine Street. There, behind thick walls, his room was peaceful, dark, safe, and the manuscript of his latest story, revised and rewritten a dozen times, lay on the desk.

Babel would go up to it and stroke it gingerly like a half-tamed beast. He often got up at night and reread three or four pages by the light of a wick-lamp, hemmed in by thick dictionaries standing on their side. Every time he found a few more unnecessary words and triumphantly crossed them out. "Language is clear and powerful," he used to say, "not when there is nothing more to add to a sentence, but when there is nothing more you can cut out."

All who saw Babel at work, especially at night (though few ever did, as he went into hiding when he wrote) were struck by the sadness of his face and its unusual expression of kindness and distress.

During those barren Moldavanka nights he would have given much to go back to his manuscript. But, as a writer, he felt he was a soldier on reconnaissance, who must put up with any hardship in the way of duty: the loneliness, the stench of the extinguished oil-lamp which brought on his attacks of asthma, and the screams of tormented women from behind the walls of the houses.

One such night it suddenly dawned on him: obviously Tsires was a common "crib-spotter," a scout for thieves, who tipped them off about the places they should raid. He got his "cut"—his percentage of the proceeds. That was how he made his living. Babel was indeed an inconvenient lodger!

He could frighten away Tsires's reckless yet cautious clients. Who would want to take an extra risk because stingy old Tsires, tempted by an extra hundred thousand, had let a stranger into Moldavanka's very heart?

And the stranger had turned out to be a writer and therefore twice as dangerous as any ordinary card-sharper or pimp!

At last Babel understood Tsires's hints about "a pocketful of trouble" and decided to move out in a few days. He needed these few more days to get Tsires to tell him all the interesting things he knew. For Babel was conscious of his powerful gift for squeezing people dry, gutting them with ruthless persistence or, as they said in Odessa, "drawing their very souls out of them."

But this time he failed. A bandit, Simon Lop-Ear, beat him to it, and there was nothing metaphorical about the way he parted Tsires from his soul.

One day when Babel had gone to town, Tsires, at home in his flat, was stabbed to death with a Finnish dagger.

Babel returned to find the police in the house and the head of the criminal investigation department in his room. He sat at Babel's desk, writing his report. A polite young man in dark-blue riding breeches and top boots, he dreamed of becoming a writer and therefore treated Babel with respect.

"I must ask you to take your things and leave this house at once," he said. "Or I can't be responsible for your safety even for the next twenty-four hours. You know Moldavanka!"

So Babel fled, shuddering, pursued by Aunt Khava's wails and the curses she called down upon Simon Lop-Ear and all others whom she believed to be connected with the murder.

They were terrible curses. The polite policeman advised Babel:

"Don't listen to her ravings. She was in her right mind this morning and was able to give evidence. But now she's gone quite mad. The ambulance from the asylum is coming for her in a moment."

Beyond the partition, Aunt Khava steadily tore her hair, flung away the tufts, and screamed, sobbing and swaying to and fro:

"May you, Simon, get drunk on vodka with rat poison and die in your vomit! And may you kick your own mother Miriam, the old witch, for giving birth to such a fiend of hell! May all the Moldavanka boys sharpen their pen-knives and cut you into pieces during twenty days and twenty nights! May you, Simon, burn and burst in your own sizzling fat!"

Soon Babel learned everything there was to know about Tsires's death.

"Everything" was the fact that he had brought his fate upon himself. So not a living soul in Moldavanka pitied him, except Aunt Khava. He had proved to be dishonourable, and after that nothing in the world could save him from death.

This is what actually happened. The day before his death, Tsires called on Simon Lop-Ear.

Simon was shaving in the hall, in front of a magnificent cheval-glass in an ornate black frame.

He squinted at Tsires and said:

"Mixed yourself up with a nark, have you, Monsieur Tsires? Well, you know the new Soviet law—if you call on a man when he's shaving, state your business and buzz off. You're allowed twelve words, like at the central telegraph office. Any more, and your cut goes down by two hundred thousand a word."

"Were you born with that unfortunate sense of humour?" Tsires asked with a sugary smile, "or has it grown on you?"

Tsires was a coward in life and even in business, but, in his position of senior crib-spotter, he could afford to be cheeky in conversation.

"All right, you old clown," said Lop-Ear, drawing his razor up and down through the air like a violin bow. "Get on with it, before I run out of patience."

"Four billion wage money," said Tsires very softly, "delivered tomorrow at one at the Concordia."

"Right. You'll get your cut. No deductions this time."

Tsires went home, but he wasn't altogether happy. He hadn't liked Lop-Ear's manner; it was too frivolous. Simon had never joked over a business deal before.

He confided in Aunt Khava, who turned on him at once:

"How long must you go on being such a fool? And don't look at Idochka's photograph, it's you I'm talking to, not her. Of course it's not a job for Simon. He'll never put himself out for a measly four billion. You'll have worked for nothing, that's all."

"What am I to do then?" groaned Tsires. "They'll drive me crazy, those bandits."

"Go to Five Roubles. He might be tempted by your phoney billions. At least there's a chance, and you won't look such a fool."

So Tsires put on his lustrine cap and trudged off. Five Roubles lay asleep in the shadow of a white acacia in the cool of his garden. He heard Tsires out, and said drowsily:

"You'll get your cut."

Tsires went off, delighted. He felt like a man who has just insured his life for pure gold. "The old woman was right. You can't count on Lop-Ear. He's like a butterfly. Moody like a pregnant woman. What does it cost him to make a deal, and then play about with his razor and change his mind if it looks like too much trouble?"

But for the first and last time in his life, Tsires had blundered.

Next day, at one o'clock, Simon and Five Roubles met in front of the cash desk at the Concordia. They looked each other in the eye, and Simon asked:

"Would you mind telling me who tipped you off?"
"Old Tsires. And you?"
"Old Tsires."
"So?"
"So old Tsires won't be with us much longer."
"Amen," said Five Roubles.

The two thieves parted amicably, keeping to the unwritten law that if two of them met on the same job, it was called off.

Forty minutes later, old Tsires was killed in his flat, while Aunt Khava was hanging the washing in the yard. She hadn't seen the murderer but knew it must be Simon or one of his men. Simon never forgave those who double-crossed him.

PATRICIA CARDEN

Red Cavalry: *Art Renders Justice*

> *"Your Holiness," lame Vitold, the fence for stolen goods and watchman at the cemetery, then replied to the vicar, "In what does the all-merciful God see truth, and who will tell the ignorant folk about it? Isn't there more truth in the pictures of Pan Apolek which satisfy our pride, than in your words, full of blame and aristocratic wrath?"*
>
> ("Pan Apolek")

Thus in the fifth story of *Red Cavalry*, Babel makes his first statement of the theme of the work: art should "satisfy our pride." It is characteristic of Babel's elusiveness that he has withheld an explicit statement of theme until the fifth story in the cycle, allowing the earlier stories to strike with full, unmediated force upon the reader's sensibilities. But the fifth story, "Pan Apolek," opens with a direct statement to the reader:

> The excellent and wise life of Pan Apolek went to my head like old wine. In Novograd-Volynsk, in that hastily shattered town among twisted ruins, fate threw at my feet a gospel hidden from the world. Surrounded by the naive radiance of haloes, I then gave my vow to follow the example of Pan Apolek. And the sweetness of the dreamer's wrath, the bitter disdain for the curs and swine of mankind, the flame of silent and intoxicating revenge, I sacrificed to my new vow.

The hagiographic style is arresting, but even more so is the sense of relief we experience in at last coming upon a straightforward statement of belief. From the beginning of *Red Cavalry* our senses and our minds have been

---

From *The Art of Isaac Babel*. © 1972 by Cornell University. Cornell University Press, 1972.

assaulted by shocking episodes told in an elliptical style free of explanation. The stories present a glittering, portentous, but resisting surface to the reader. He feels that he has been dealt a blow with a powerful instrument, but he cannot yet determine to what purpose. "Pan Apolek" is a story about art, it is a story setting forth a particular view of humanity, and it opens with a resounding affirmation from the author-narrator that this is his view of art, his view of humanity. The door opens wider. Here is a good place to enter Babel's world.

In each of the stories of *Red Cavalry* the narrator appears in the guise appropriate to the situation: as Red armyman, as *intelligent,* as Jew, as the observing eye. In "Pan Apolek" he appears for the first time as "writer," as "author of the work." His statement of belief in his role as writer occurs three times in the story: in his "vow" that opens the story, in the description of Apolek's paintings, and in the parable of Christ and Deborah. The writer in his vow renounces "the sweetness of the dreamer's wrath, the bitter disdain for the curs and swine of mankind, the flame of silent and intoxicating revenge." The belief is restated from the affirmative side in the description of Apolek's paintings, which "have elevated [the common people] to sainthood in their lifetimes." Apolek's parable about Deborah and Christ sums up the views of man that inform his art. According to Apolek, Deborah could not lie with her husband on her wedding night because, being filled with fear, she was seized with hiccups and vomiting. She was shamed before her family and the guests, but Christ, "seeing the unusual anguish of the woman, who longed for her husband, yet feared him, put on the bridegroom's raiment and, full of compassion, was joined with Deborah, lying in her vomit." Apolek's parable indicates that true humanity demands not only the acceptance of man in those attributes that elevate him, but also in those attributes that we despise. The parable underlines the writer's vow to reject his "bitter disdain for the curs and swines of mankind," but seems to require something beyond mere indifference to curs and swine.

The story binds together in the central symbolic figure, Apolek, two views of man. The first of these is the Christian view, which finds its place in Apolek's gospel when purged of the "aristocratic wrath" that is opposed to the Christly principle that the meek shall inherit the earth. Apolek is the preacher and exemplar of this Christianity of the meek. He takes his name Apollinarius from the heretic who "established so close a connection of the Logos with human flesh, that all the divine attributes were transferred to the human nature and all the human attributes to the divine and the two merged in *one* nature in Christ" (William Smith and Henry Wace, eds., *A Dictionary of Christian Biography*). The narrator tells us that "chance almost made of the gentle wanderer the founder of a new heresy." It is of the essence of Apolek's art that he elevates the common people to sainthood, not by painting idealized portraits of them, but by painting them exactly as they are. When he paints "the Jewish girl Elka, daughter of unknown parents and mother of many bastard children," as Mary Magdalene, he unveils the truth about the Magdalene's humanity, for she was, as the narrator puts it, "the fornicatress from Magdala." Apolek does this not from a cynical desire to lower the saint in our eyes, but to point out that the human is inseparable from the godly. In the parable of Christ and Deborah, the price that Christ pays for his act of charity is mortality. "Jesus stood apart. A deathly sweat broke out on his body and the bee of sorrow stung his heart. Unnoticed by anyone, he went out of the hall of the feast and went off into the desert, to the east from Judea where John the Baptist awaited him." Jesus could not have remained God had he evaded the act of compassion, but having put on the bridegroom's raiment he cannot evade his humanity. A godliness lacking in specifically human attributes would have been of no use to Deborah or to mankind.

The other tradition upon which Babel draws in the story is the classical humanist tradition. Apolek's view of man requires from Christianity the emphasis on the lowly, the meek, the grotesque, that quality that Erich Auerbach designates by the Latin word *humilis* and that he interprets thus: "In the Christian context everday things ... lose their baseness and become compatible with the lofty style; and conversely, the highest mysteries of the faith may be set forth in the simple words of the lowly style which everyone can understand" (*Literary Language and Its Public in Late Latin Antiquity and in the Middle Ages*). Apolek's art is far from the idealized statuary of Greece. But from the classical tradition he (and Babel) requires the emphasis on physicality. Apolek's name also suggests Apollo, patron of art, and when he and his blind companion Gottfried play and sing in the courtyard of Shmerel's inn, "it looked as though the organ had been brought from St. Indeghilda's Church to Shmerel's and as though all the muses had sat down in a row at the organ wearing varicolored quilted scarfs and hobnailed German boots." In this single image Babel weds the Christian and classical traditions with the mundane world of the present. As important as the spiritual message of Apolek's art is his acceptance of the body. When the innkeeper sets out to catch Apolek, who has paid his bill by presenting Shmerel's wife with her sketched portrait, he is converted from the way of wrath by the memory of "the rosy body of Apolek, streaming with water and the sun in his yard and the quiet hum of the accordion."

In Apolek's painting the truth of the body ever asserts itself:

> The new church was full of the bleating of herds, of the dusty gold of sunsets and of straw-colored cows' udders. Oxen with threadbare hides plodded under the yoke, dogs with rosy muzzles ran before the flocks and fat infants rocked in cradles swung from the straight trunks of palms. The cradle was surrounded by the brown tatters of Franciscan monks. The crowd of Wise Men was gashed by shining bald heads with wrinkles blood-red as wounds.

Here Babel uses a favorite device, the startling transformation over the space of the period from plural noun ("fat infants rocked in cradles") to singular noun ("The cradle was surrounded"). The switch from plural to singular points to the combination of specificity and generality in Apolek's painting and in his view of man. Each man is individual and unique, especially in the possession of his body with its distinguishing characteristics, just as the things of the world have distinguishing characteristics and thus become particular like the intricately carved Chinese rosary that one of the wise men fingers in the painting. But man also participates in a larger spiritual identity that is shared by all men, which is our humanity. So the infant Christ is plural and singular, plural in his symbolic identification with the innocence of infants, singular in his mortal existence. Hence also the "substitution" of one individual for another—Elka for Mary Magdalene, lame Yanek for the Apostle Paul, the Novograd priest for one of the Wise Men. The substitutions are made in such a way that the individual quality of the person, both physical and spiritual, is preserved. Yanek, the convert, "a timid-looking lame man with a ragged black beard, a village apostate," painted by Apolek in his individuality, reveals the human individuality of the Apostle Paul, also a convert and an epileptic. Sometimes the association between the actual and the mythical subjects of the paintings is elusive. One is puzzled at first by the painting of John the Baptist:

> The long figure of John the Baptist descended straight upon me out of the blue depths of the niche. A black cloak hung solemnly on that implacable, disgustingly emaciated body. Drops of blood shone in the round clasps of the cloak. John's head had been cut off at a slant from the jagged neck. The head lay on a clay dish held tightly in the large yellow hands of a soldier. The dead man's face seemed familiar to me. A premonition of the secret touched me. The dead head which lay on the clay dish had been painted from that of Pan Romuald, the fugitive priest's assistant. From the grinning mouth looped the tiny body of a snake with glittering

scales. Its tenderly rosy head, full of animation, powerfully set off the dark background of the cloak.

Pan Romuald, the priest's assistant, is described in another story, "The Church at Novograd," as "a eunuch with a giant's body and a nasal twang" and as a "faithless monk, with . . . plump hands and [a] soul gentle and pitiless as the soul of a cat." He turns out to be a spy and is shot by the Reds. The conceit of the snake reveals Apolek's divination of Romuald's treacherous character, but whence the identity with John the Baptist? The key seems to lie in the "implacable" nature of John, so opposed to the compassionate humanity of the Christ of Apolek's parable. Romuald is the representative of the Church, indifferent to humanity, pitiless in his judgments. It is also significant that Romuald and John are "eunuchs" and thus deprived of their humanity at the deepest level, as the Christ of Apolek's parable is not. Romuald's external differences from John are stripped away to reveal his identity with the implacable life-denying core of the Baptist, which betrays the Christian doctrine of forgiveness. Christ and Apolek possess the gift of compassion. It is this gift that the author-narrator proclaims essential to a humanistic art.

But beyond the attitude to be proclaimed in art lies the fact of art itself. It is here that Apolek unites at the most literal level the physical world of the body with the world of the spirit. In Pan Apolek the power of sight consumes and remakes the world. The remarkable intensity of the power of seeing is set off all the more by the presence in the story of Apolek's "eternal friend," blind Gottfried, in whom the faculty of hearing is as intensely concentrated as the faculty of seeing in Apolek: "Old Gottfried is beating out the tune with his shaky fingers. The blind man sits motionless in the yellow, oily glow of the lamp. Bowing his bald head, he listens to the endless music of his blindness and the mumbling of Apolek, his eternal friend."

What might be the power of an art that combines the vitality of physical presence with a redefined humanism? Babel answers in another story, "In St. Valentine's Church," whose narrator sees the church in two aspects: first, as an aesthetic object, then as a spiritual symbol. The movement from one view to the other constitutes the essential action of the story. The narrator's change of view subtly enlarges the connections between Babel's new humanism as expounded in "Pan Apolek" and the task of the artist.

The story opens with an anecdote about the priest of St. Valentine's, one Tuzinkiewicz, who, "disguising himself as a peasant woman, . . . fled from Berestechko before the entrance of [the Red] troops." The narrator discovers two facts about him, that he was a good priest, "beloved of the

Jews," and that he was responsible for the restoration of the three-hundred-year-old cathedral. On the day the newly restored cathedral was dedicated, Tuzinkiewicz was honored by prelates of the Church "in silk cassocks" and by peasants, "who knelt before him and kissed his hands." The anecdote suggests the effect of the cathedral's physical presence on the spiritual life of the community.

Seeking respite from his duties at staff headquarters, the narrator goes to the window and looks out at the church, "powerful and white. It glowed in the cool sun like a porcelain tower. Midday lightning flashed in its glossy sides, whose convex lines lightly ran down from the cupola's ancient green. Rosy veins smoldered in the white stone of the foundation and at the tops were columns thin as tapers." Later the narrator says, "The church stood before us, dazzling as a stage set." He enjoys the visual feast it provides but refuses to take the church seriously as a house of the spirit. Thus the action of the old woman who comes in, crawls before him, and kisses his feet seems grotesque, disconnected as it is in his mind from any motive. He has heard the organ pealing forth from the church and at that very moment sees the old woman appear in the staff headquarters, but the two events are not tied together in any way for him. Throughout the story he suffers from the inability to make the connection between events and motive, until he has the flash of revelation that makes his experience whole.

The old woman has come to appeal to him to save the church from the vandalism of the Cossacks. This fact gradually dawns on him as the organ "grew quiet and then guffawed in bass notes." The scene is masterly, with swift cutting between the sound of the organ, the old woman's pleas, and the narrator's fear of ridicule. Nowhere in the paragraph is there so much as a word of explicit statement. We are told what the narrator hears (the organ), what he sees (the purblind old woman embracing his feet), and what he does (he glances at the other men in the staff and tries to drag the old woman from his feet). No words are exchanged, nor is the narrator's dawning understanding stated. Only his action in running to the church makes clear his comprehension of the situation.

As the narrator runs, he sees another of those scenes in which dissociated elements strike the senses with equal force: "The side doors [of the church] were open and the skulls of horses dangled on the graves of Polish officers." As he enters the altar room, he comes upon yet another strange scene. The nurse Sasha is rummaging through vestments. Cossacks enter and, pushing her down on the piles of materials, pretend to rape her. "And only then, passing through the altar, we entered the church," the narrator tells us. Why "and only then"? The narrator does not tell us, for he does not yet know that this is but one of several acts of desecration he is to witness.

As he enters the sanctuary, he is struck again by the beauty of the church, "full of dancing sunbeams, airy columns, a kind of cool gaiety," and by the paintings of Apolek that adorn the interior. Two paragraphs are devoted to the paintings. The first describes what is seen; the second, Apolek's "point of view toward the mortal sufferings of man." The paintings, like the paintings of Novograd-Volynsk, insist upon man in his physical aspect. The infant Jesus appears with "his toes protruding [from the cradle], his body lacquered with the hot sweat of morning." The twelve apostles appear, "their faces so close-shaven as to be blue, their flaming cloaks thrust out by round bellies." "In that church saints went to their deaths picturesquely as Italian singers and the executioners' black beards gleamed like the beard of Holophernes." Throughout the church and the paintings the mood is gay, and this gaiety seems to render frivolous the sufferings depicted. After examining the paintings, the narrator makes a cool judgment: "At first I did not notice any traces of destruction in the church, or at least they seemed slight to me." His casual modification of his judgment comes from this observation: "Only St. Valentine's shrine had been broken. Bits of decayed wadding lay strewn under it with the ridiculous bones of the saint, more like the bones of a hen than anything else." While the first traces of "destruction" strike him as laughable and negligible, he is even more inclined to dismiss the next "desecration."

> And Afonka Bida was still playing the organ. Afonka was drunk, wild and all hacked up. He had returned to us just the day before with the horse he had seized from the peasants. Afonka was stubbornly trying to pick out a march on the organ and someone was trying to persuade him to stop in a sleepy voice: "Drop it, Afonka, let's go eat." But the Cossack wouldn't drop it. They were many, the songs of Afonka. Every sound was a song, and each sound was torn from another. The song, its dense melody, lasted a second and gave way to another. I listened as I looked about me. The traces of destruction seemed slight to me.

The narrator's view of Afonka is framed by his two assertions that no damage has taken place. From his point of view the church is intact, since the church is for him an aesthetic object. The harmonious structure is unharmed, even enhanced from the aesthetic point of view, by the destruction of the shrine. Even less is Afonka's song, so sympathetically apprehended by the narrator as an outpouring of spirit, a desecration of the sanctuary. As the narrator quickly notes before the paragraph ends, "But Pan Ludomirski, the bellringer of St. Valentine's Church and the old woman's husband, did not agree." We are thus moved from the narrator's point of view, in which the church is seen as an object, to Pan Ludomirski's point of view, in which the church is seen as a sanctuary.

The gestures of Pan Ludomirski appear grotesque to the narrator, as once again he fails to make the connection between gesture and motive. The old man falls to the floor in a gesture that recalls the grotesque supplications of his wife before the narrator: "The bellringer fell to the blue-tiled floor and raised his head, his blue nose rising above him like a flag over a dead man." The compelling picture of Pan Ludomirski is broken by the unveiling of Apolek's painting of Christ:

> His blue nose trembled above him and in that moment the velvet curtain over the altar swayed, and trembling slid aside. In the depths of the uncovered niche, on a background of sky furrowed by clouds, ran a bearded figure in an orange Polish coat, barefooted with torn and bleeding mouth. A hoarse howl rent our hearing. The man in the orange coat was being pursued by hatred and overtaken by the chase. He thrust out a hand to ward off the impending blow. From the hand blood flowed in a purple stream. A Cossack boy standing next to me cried out and, lowering his head, turned to run, though there was nothing to run from. The figure in the niche was no one but Jesus Christ—the most unusual depiction of God I have seen in my life.

Babel blurs the boundary between painting and external reality. The howl of hatred of the painted crowd is "heard" by the people observing the painting, and the Cossack boy runs as if being pursued. The mysterious falling away of the curtain suggests the Biblical event of the rending of the veil in the temple. The revelation of the painting to the narrator is full of the suggestion of mystery, but the painting contains no more mystery than Apolek's daring in identifying Christ's suffering as a recognizably human suffering.

> Pan Ludomirski's savior was a curly-haired Jew with a ragged beard and a low furrowed brow. His sunken cheeks were painted carmine; delicate red brows arched over eyes closed with pain. His mouth was torn like a horse's lip. His Polish coat was clasped with a precious belt and beneath the coat writhed porcelain feet, painted, bare, pierced by silver nails.

The Christ of Pan Apolek's painting is both aesthetic object and spiritual symbol. The painting arouses the narrator's aesthetic enthusiasm (as we understand from his description of it) and Pan Ludomirski's religious fervor. Infused by the religious power of the painting, Pan Ludomirski is moved to action.

> Pan Ludomirski stood in a green frock coat under the statue. He raised a withered hand over us and cursed us. The Cossacks gaped and hung their yellow forelocks. The thundering voice of St. Valentine's bellringer anathematized us in the purest Latin. Then he turned away, fell on his knees and clasped the savior's feet.

For the first time the grotesque action becomes ennobling: falling upon the knees is a sign not of weakness but of power. The mediation of the painting makes the sources of Pan Ludomirski's secret power accessible to the narrator. Aesthetic sensibility opens the door to spiritual awareness. His view is changed:

> Upon returning to staff headquarters, I wrote a report to the division commander about the outrage to the religious feelings of the population. The church was ordered closed and the offenders, being liable for disciplinary action, were brought before a court martial.

The story returns at the close to the official military tone with which it opened. (Compare "Our division occupied Berestechko yesterday evening. The staff headquarters were set up in the house of the priest Tuzinkiewicz.") The coldness of the communiqué ironically conveys the narrator's new sensitivity, for the offense he points to is not the physical destruction of the shrine but the outrage to the religious feelings of the population. Thus, feeling takes its place among the realities that justice has to take into account.

The question arises, what did the narrator see in the painting that led to this reversal? The style of the story is cryptic. Scenes of pure description alternate with short statements of opinion. No explanation of motive bridges the gap between fact and decision. The reader must ask himself, what in the nature of the facts justifies the narrator's decision? In the episode with Afonka Bida the narrator makes clear that he sees Afonka's "song" as no desecration but as an outpouring of spirit related to his earlier suffering, perhaps more appropriate to the sanctuary than empty ritual. He thus shows himself to be a man keenly aware of spiritual potential. Earlier he had understood that Pan Ludomirski's wife was outraged in her religious sensibilities, since he ran to the church to see what was happening there; yet his description expresses ridicule for those feelings. How does he come to take them seriously?

I would suggest that the answer lies in the nature of sacrilege as revealed by Apolek's painting: sacrilege is an outrage to humanity rather than to God. Apolek's picture of Christ suffering in the flesh conveys to the narrator the suffering of Pan Ludomirski in the spirit. The barrier between man and God is erased in Apolek's painting as God becomes flesh and man participates in the godly spirit. The spirit of outrage for suffering is one that the narrator can share with Pan Ludomirski. Religion is no longer a silly superstition for him but an embodiment of this sense of outrage.

Aesthetic sensibility is linked through the mediation of the painting to moral sensibility. Artistic creation as an outpouring of the spirit is a moral act. The narrator's moral intuition about the roots of suffering that feed Afonka's wild behavior leads to aesthetic awareness, the hearing of the "song." In turn, his aesthetic response to the painting extends his moral sensibility. In the final turn of the wheel, the simple man Pan Ludomirski responds through his consciousness of suffering to Apolek's painting.

If Afonka Bida's action is condemned by the same principles used to justify it, what is the distinguishing feature that leads the narrator to his decision? The cold tone of the closing lines and the failure to mention Afonka Bida specifically (that he was the culprit responsible for the breaking of the shrine is made clear in the story "Afonka Bida") suggest a withdrawal before the dilemma imposed by judgment, an attempt to repress the sympathy that the narrator cannot help feeling for Afonka's act. It is in the nature of justice that a choice must be made, and the narrator as judge does not hesitate to choose—on the first occasion in the story for Afonka, on the second, against him. The explanation, which we must once again try to determine from the "facts" as presented, would seem to be that Afonka in the expression of his own suffering fails to respect the general suffering. One might go further and say that the decision is based on the inferiority of Afonka's art, which is private and chaotic, expressing his suffering only and failing to symbolize the greater suffering. If art is an expression of the quality of spiritual life, then to make a moral judgment on this basis is not absurd.

The story takes its movement from three bravura grotesque scenes, the old woman grasping the unwilling feet of the narrator, Afonka Bida at the organ (Peter Quince at the clavier!), Pan Ludomirski on his knees before his God. The story is crowned by the sublime grotesquerie of Apolek's painting. These scenes cut through the fabric of the narrator's meditations on the beauties of the church. Because they cannot be made to fit into his conception, the conception is shattered. The narrator is forced toward a broader understanding. It is easiest for the narrator to enter sympathetically into

Afonka's feelings and to grasp the "song" behind his wild outpourings of sound because he knows the story of Afonka's suffering over the loss of his horse and his joy at the possession of a new horse. The sounds that are unintelligible to uninformed ears are for the narrator the melody of Afonka's self-expression, his own primitive art. The grotesque gestures of Pan Ludomirski and his wife remain opaque to the narrator until Apolek's art mediates between him and these incomprehensible people.

The revelation of the painting illuminates not only the central event of the story but even the most casual and peripheral aspects of the narrator's experience. The Polish officers' skulls on the graves glimpsed as he ran to the church take their place among the desecrations he has witnessed. Once grotesque as the hen bones of the saint, the skulls now become emblems of suffering. Now, too, it becomes clear why Tuzinkiewicz, who loved the church and was loved by his parishioners, abandoned both, seemingly so frivolously. The grotesque picture of the priest fleeing in the clothes of a peasant woman takes its dignity from its identity with the fleeing Christ of Apolek's painting. Each event of the story, easy for the narrator to dismiss individually because trivial or grotesque, becomes dignified in the symbolic act of desecration rendered by the painting.

The story suggests that what is grotesque becomes human and even sublime when traced to its source in the spirit. (I hesitate to use another word. No other word seems to have the breadth and dignity appropriate to the all-inclusive quality of human responsiveness examined by Babel.) The elevation of the grotesque makes accountable much that would otherwise be puzzling in the tone of Babel's work. It is clear in these parables about art that one should not take the presence of the grotesque in Babel's work as a sign of irony directed against the characters. On the contrary, the grotesque is accepted here and elsewhere as the revealing sign of the individually human quality, the divinely human.

RICHARD W. HALLET

Babel the Dramatist

Babel's early connections with the theatre can only be surmised. A childhood romance with the medium is suggested in the story "Di Grasso," published in 1937. The fourteen-year-old narrator, who trades in tickets, is held spellbound by the performance of the head of a Sicilian touring company, but his youthful reactions constitute a flimsy basis for any assertions about the author himself. Exactly why Babel turned his attention briefly to drama is also a matter of conjecture. His liaison with an actress, his work on film dialogue, a simple desire to test his talents in a new setting—all these are speculative factors.

Critics generally have concentrated almost exclusively upon Babel the story-teller (especially upon the author of *Red Cavalry*) and given Babel the dramatist little more than a polite nod. It is true that he is known to have written only two plays. It is true also that his mastery in the short story is not matched in his writings for the stage. Further, as I have mentioned already, there is an almost complete absence of data concerning his theatrical credentials. Yet none of these considerations excuses the reluctance both to examine at due length Babel's stature in the Soviet theatre and to consider his plays in relation to the remainder of his work.

Sunset, Babel's first play, appeared in 1928. Almost immediately it received an enthusiastic welcome from a contributor (G. A. Gukovsky) to the first book of criticism entirely concerned with Babel's art: "At this very moment, when our new and still young drama is wandering in the dark and quite often straying from the right path, a drama by a writer such as Babel

---

From *Isaac Babel*. © 1972 by R. W. Hallet. Bradda Books, 1972.

cannot fail to be an event." Later in the same year Stanislavsky's Moscow Art Theatre gave *Sunset* its Russian première, although it had originally been performed first in Baku and then Odessa in October 1927. The state of the Soviet theatre in 1928 was, as Gukovsky suggests, not particularly healthy. Because of the more immediate impact drama can produce upon its audience, Soviet writers were permitted less latitude when creating plays than when creating novels, poems or short stories. Towards the end of the 1920s, moreover, the Soviet writer found his freedom of expression becoming alarmingly circumscribed. After 1917 up until approximately the midtwenties he had enjoyed comparatively wide scope, but, as Stalin's position at the apex of power grew more secure, so his grip upon the organs of opinion tightened, and the situation of the writer began rapidly to deteriorate.

1928 marked the beginning of the First Soviet Five-Year Plan. Writers were enjoined to record the nation's future hopes and present achievements. Particular pressure came to be exerted upon so-called fellow-travelling writers (Babel among them) who gave at best only tepid support to the Communist Party and its ambitious programme. The play, *Sunset*, did not, however, treat of current events. Instead it harks back to the prerevolutionary Odessa of 1913 and to the narrow world of the Moldavanka. It is instructive to observe how the short-story writer adapts his talents and compositional habits to meet the exigencies of a different medium. Of course observation is enhanced by the recent discovery of the story from which the play developed. An essential feature of Babel's style is his brevity, whether applied to sentence structure or to plot, and though *Sunset* almost equals "The Story of My Dovecot" in length, it had to be expanded before a full-length play on the same subject could result. An unusual insight offered, therefore, by a comparison between story and play is of Babel working against his natural inclinations and adding to, rather than subtracting from a particular work.

Brevity is attained in other ways, however. The play consists of eight scenes, some extremely short and none especially long. The dialogue, moreover, reflects Babel's ingrained laconism, though with one important difference. In the story he uses dialogue more sparingly, providing most of the necessary background information through third-person narrative. A play, on the other hand, must rely almost entirely on dialogue to convey details of plot. For this reason Babel's stage characters speak at greater length, and the pithy and purposely formal-sounding witticisms of the story have to be interspersed with what, from the purely literary point of view, is rather more mundane material. As if to compensate for this dilution, Babel includes detailed remarks about scenery, stage directions and cast in the style of his short stories. It is as though he were anxious to sacrifice as little as possible of his proven technique on the altar of the theatre and had determined to cater for his past readership as well as for the future playgoer.

Whilst the plot of the drama remains fundamentally the same as in the short story, it is enriched by much that is new. Nowhere can this better be illustrated than by reference to Mendel Krik, whose characterisation is deepened and whose attempts to defy his advanced years acquire additional pathos. More than before Babel isolates him within his own family. In the earlier version he could always count for support on his wife, but in the play she fulfils a smaller and more sympathetic role, resenting her husband's tyranny just as much as do her children.

Before Mendel appears on stage, the violence of the opposition to his patriarchal authority has already been demonstrated. Dvoyra, his "overripe" daughter, becomes hysterical over the disappearance of a favourite dress. She is expecting a prospective suitor, Boyarsky, but not for the first time Mendel has tried to wreck her chances of marriage, as he is too mean to supply a dowry. Both her brothers sympathise. Lyovka, the younger, voices open contempt for Mendel, while the gaudily clad Benya says little but hovers menacingly in the background.

The patriarch is introduced in person with powerful dramatic effect. He enters carrying a whip, casts it aside and sits down in silence for his wife to remove his boots. Totally ignoring Boyarsky, he questions an employee about Lyovka's impudence in giving orders without his father's permission. As a sign of displeasure he then sweeps everything off the kitchen table and declares his sole authority over the household and the business before storming out. The inevitability of a clash between Mendel and his children is further emphasised in the following scene (which did not appear in the original story), when Benya commits the unheard of act of entering his parents' bedroom at night to complain of the noise.

Another completely new scene set in a tavern successfully puts Mendel's position in perspective and gives his characterisation an extra dimension. As at home he acts the petty despot, behaving violently when his commands are not obeyed and disporting himself destructively without any thought for others. In a drunken state, however, he also reveals self-deception and inability to face facts, for despite his sixty-two years he still believes himself invincible. His dream is to start a new life in Bessarabia with a twenty-year-old mistress, Marusya. Here we see a change from the plot of the short story in which Benya made pregnant a girl of the same name, but Mendel was not shown as anything but a faithful spouse. Another fresh factor is Mendel's decision to sell his carter's business without consulting his sons, and this finally precipitates against him the smouldering family revolt.

Again new light is shed on Mendel's character in the fourth scene, which cleverly conveys his infatuation with Marusya. Whereas previously he has been depicted as brutal and dictatorial, here he shows himself gentle, submissive and even pitiable. As the girl and old man prepare for bed, she chatters away nonstop, while the solitary word he utters during the entire proceedings is the affectionate diminutive of her name.

Only in the fifth scene, set in a synagogue, does Mendel not make an appearance. It is at this juncture that Benya learns of his father's intention to sell up and move away. In the scene which follows, the long threatened confrontation between Mendel and his sons takes place at last. As in the story he proves physically more than a match for them but Dvoyra's intervention is not called upon this time, Benya resolving the struggle with a blow from his revolver. Stage directions throughout indicate with no great subtlety what is to ensue as well as underlining the significance of what has happened already. The scene begins at sunset. When the fighting breaks out, "the sky is bathed in blood." Immediately after Mendel's defeat, the sun sinks still lower. The final direction rounds off the scene as follows: "Silence. Evening. A blue darkness, but above the darkness the sky is still purple, set in a glow, and pitted with cavities of fire."

In the last two scenes Benya becomes the focus of attention in his new capacity as head of the family. Mendel, on the other hand, has been transformed into a dispirited wreck of a man whose "face is blue and swollen like the face of a corpse." As in the short story this transition is too total and too sudden to surprise in an entirely convincing way. As in the story, too, Lyovka protests at Benya's ill-treatment of Mendel, who laments his lost power and begs for freedom in one of the play's most emotionally charged speeches: "Why won't you unlock the gate . . . ? Why won't you let me out of the yard in which I have passed my life? (The old man's voice strengthens and a light blazes at the base of his eyes). It has seen me, this yard, a father to my children, a husband to my wife, and a master over my horses. It has seen my strength, my twenty stallions, my twelve ironbound drays. It has seen my legs, as large as pillars, and my arms, my devilishly strong arms. . . . And now open up for me, dear sons, let today be as I want it. Let me out of this yard which has seen too much." His appeal, however, remains unheeded, and the scene ends with another elderly Jew (Ar'ye-Leyb of *How It Was Done in Odessa*) likening Mendel's insatiable appetites to those of the ageing King David.

In the final scene Benya celebrates his triumph by throwing a party. Only towards the end of it does Mendel enter and even then is allowed but a single remark. Significantly Benya interrupts him to announce his father's gift of a large sum to charity—a gesture quite out of keeping with Mendel's nature but one calculated to win Benya admiration and popularity. From now on it is the eldest son who rules the family, having reduced its former despotic head to the status of an impotent subject. In conclusion the most distinguished guest, Ben Zkhar'ya, the local rabbi (who does not figure in the original story) pronounces the last word in the play and draws a somewhat commonplace moral with regard to Mendel's fate: "All his life he wanted to bake in the heat of the sun, all his life he wanted to stand in the place where mid-day had found him. But God has policemen in every street and Mendel Krik had sons in his home. Policemen come and impose order. Day is day, and evening is evening. Everything is as it should be, Jews. Let us drink a glass of vodka!"

Most of the differences between the play and the story arise from the fuller characterisation of Mendel. This involves in turn a wider variety of scenes and a larger cast of characters with the result that the Jewish ambience is conjured up in greater density. Basically, however, the play has much in common with the Moldavanka stories and Babel's other earlier work as regards both tone and technique. Though making unavoidable concessions to the theatre medium, he succeeds in other ways already mentioned in maintaining the characteristic economy of expression. Moreover, the aura of violence pervading his Moldavanka and *Red Cavalry* stories is established from the very beginning of the play and the ultimate explosion in the sixth scene is if anything excessively prepared for and delayed. As before Babel depicts an exotic jungle of a community in which only the strong and ruthless flourish. Idiosyncratic juxtapositions are used as ever to jolt the reader. In the synagogue scene talk of money-making and a proposed robbery mingle with the prayers of the congregation; and Ar'ye-Leyb's instruction of a child in the scriptures precedes the decisive battle between the Kriks. Of the typically grotesque details in the play the most curious occurs when the priest in the synagogue, finding his complaints about rats going unheeded, pulls out a revolver and shoots one during the service! Another memorably bizarre phenomenon is the choir of blind Jews which sings for Mendel in the tavern.

Apart from the bedroom scene between Marusya and Mendel there is little erotic content of the kind to be found in several earlier (and later) works. A more striking difference is the moral expounded by the rabbi at the end, which sounds strange coming as it does from an author mostly at pains to refrain from judgements of any sort. A final distinction between the play and the Moldavanka tales specifically is that the larger-than-life characters of the latter (especially Benya) assume more human proportions when appearing in the flesh and speaking for themselves. *Sunset* the play tends therefore to be a little less extravagant and a little more down-to-earth than "Sunset" the short story.

Compared with most other new plays staged in the late 1920s *Sunset* seemed something of an anachronism. Not only was it essentially remote from the Revolution in subject and spirit, but also it did not lend itself easily to a socio-political interpretation advantageous to the Soviet régime. P. Markov, a critic respected by Babel, could view the play as an attack upon the Moldavanka way of life only by disregarding that there is no more evidence of condemnation here than in the earlier stories and that the triumphant Benya is hardly a positive hero dedicated to building socialism.

Sunset remains far superior to most other dramas of the time in the quality of its writing, though perhaps more impressive as literature to be read than a play to be performed. Babel expressed disappointment that the first production had failed to convey those subtleties he believed present beneath its surface and Markov, a member of the Moscow Art Theatre, perceived a conflict of attitude between author and producer, declaring himself on Babel's side. Ominously, however, he found the play's philosophy alien to the epoch and after sixteen performances it disappeared from the repertory.

Babel's second play, *Maria*, forsakes pre-revolutionary Odessa for post-revolutionary Petrograd. The action is said to take place "during the early years of the revolution," but a reference to the likelihood of war with Poland indicates 1920. The place and period chosen offered not only rich dramatic possibilities but also ample scope for a writer with Babel's stylistic tendencies.

1920 was a year of political uncertainty, social transition and economic hardship. Although the Bolsheviks controlled much of the country, particularly the large cities, the Civil War was by no means won and a new way of life was still emerging from the chrysalis. Babel re-creates the atmosphere of the period by concentrating mainly on representatives of the old order, over whose future in a socialist society hung a disturbing question mark. Those who had decided to remain in Russia are shown adapting to radically changed circumstances in a variety of ways. A former prince, Golitsyn, literally scrapes a living by playing the cello in taverns and finds dockers most appreciative of his sad melodies. An unnamed professor is mentioned as having entered the sausage trade since the revolution. Dymshits, a Jew, smuggles in black-market goods with the aid of maimed war veterans. His girlfriend, Lyudmila Mukovnin, thinks only of having a good time and exploits her beauty to obtain it. In contrast, her elder sister, Maria, works selflessly in the political section of the Red Army and is attached to a division commanded by a former blacksmith. The fates of these and other characters are played out against a background of privation and fear, with the necessities of life in short supply and people afraid to walk in the streets at night lest they be stripped of the clothes they stand in.

The juxtaposition of old and new had been a feature of *Red Cavalry*. In *Maria* it consists in examining how former privileged persons survive at a time when their privileges have ceased and they themselves are in danger of being trampled underfoot by the class upon whose oppression their high standard of living had once depended. From their point of view the situation had the quality of a nightmare. Babel increases the general luridness by a selection of physiological details which connote decay and disintegration: the grotesquely mutilated bodies of Dymshits's accomplices; the rape of Lyudmila by Viskovsky, a former army officer; and Lyudmila's consequent venereal disease. Unfortunately, in attempting to shock, Babel veers into melodrama which is not only more acceptable in the exotic world of the Moldavanka but was also more skilfully handled for the theatre in his earlier play, *Sunset*. For example, the shooting of Viskovsky is poorly motivated, and the writhing of General Mukovnin during a heart attack contributes little or nothing by taking place on stage. Both instances were intended as powerful dramatic situations prior to the fall of the curtain but risk arousing nervous laughter rather than horror.

Maria recalls *Sunset* in its length and its eight scenes. On the whole, however, it is the inferior play, as regards not only tone, but also construction. The heroine, Maria, never in fact appears, and, though her expected arrival in the seventh scene does engender considerable tension, it leads also to a theatrically stagnant fifth scene devoted almost entirely to the reading aloud of a letter she has sent from the Ukrainian front. Babel here firmly establishes her idealism, contrasting it with the selfishness and emptiness of Lyudmila and other characters who had been nurtured by the tsarist régime, but he does so in a somewhat crude literary manner and utilises none of the potentialities offered by the stage medium.

Some characters who do appear in person possess little more substance than the absent heroine. Golitsyn, the former nobleman who takes refuge in religion, remains an interesting embryonic character insufficiently developed; the depraved Viskovsky never really comes to life; and Dymshits contributes nothing new to Babel's gallery of Jewish rogues. Babel's love of brevity serves him less well than in *Sunset*, where the Moldavanka milieu had already become familiar through earlier stories, and the extravagant conduct of the characters was more or less acceptable in context. In setting his play in Petrograd at such a complex period of history, however, Babel needed to concentrate on fewer characters or alternatively to expand the play's length if he were to do justice to his theme.

The final scene of *Maria*, in which preparations are in train for a working family to move into the Mukovnins' former apartment, does not entirely succeed. Obviously such an ending aims to emphasize the rapid and radical nature of social change at the time in question, but to introduce so many new characters at such a late stage requires more theatrical expertise than Babel possessed, and the play concludes somewhat lamely in consequence. In sum, though full of interest for Babel's view of 1920, *Maria* does represent a technical regression by comparison with *Sunset*.

In a letter to his mother and sister in May 1933 Babel described *Maria* as a Herculean task which would probably bring him trouble because it did not accord with the party line. His fears proved all too justified. Though allowed to appear in print in March 1935, it incurred official displeasure and was eventually excluded from the repertory. Like *Sunset* in 1928 it may be regarded as alien to the philosophy of the epoch. In this instance Babel failed to meet the requirements of Soviet Socialist Realism which commended works revealing the positive side of Russian life, and deplored those featuring prominently scenes of sex and violence. The total absence of his positive heroine from the action suggests that any attempt to compromise with the new literary doctrine was at most half-hearted. On the other hand, the critic I. Lezhnyov wrote, in an unenthusiastic review accompanying the original published text of the play, that it represented the first part of a trilogy and that Maria would eventually appear in person. As far as is known, however, the other two parts never materialised and Babel's career as a dramatist ended briefly and unfortunately. In the history of the Soviet theatre he stands out as an unusual and isolated figure. Unsurprisingly, in view of his relative lack of experience, he was not entirely at ease with the medium. Nevertheless, in only two plays he revealed unmistakable stage talent, and it is a matter for regret that he did not continue to enliven the Stalinist theatre and relieve the general mediocrity of the drama it produced.

JAMES FALEN

The Odessa Tales: *An Introduction*

Odessa is a miserable town. Everyone knows what they do to the Russian language there.... but all the same, quand même et malgré tout, *[the place] is extraordinarily, quite extraordinarily, interesting.*
—"Odessa"

Upon his demobilization in 1920 Babel had to find a means of supporting himself and his wife; accordingly, rather than embark immediately upon the uncertain path of a writing career, for a short time he took a job with a government printing house in Odessa. The settled routine and the duties that kept him from his own work were not to his liking, however, and he soon abandoned Odessa to work toward a happier destiny as a reporter in Tiflis.

During the years 1921 to 1923, Babel, in order to supplement his income, published an occasional short story in addition to his newspaper pieces, but for the most part he resisted the temptation to rush prematurely into print. With the greatest care and the highest sense of purpose, he was carefully planning, executing, and reworking the two ambitious cycles of stories that were to be his real occupation for the next several years. Following Gorky's advice, Babel had served his apprenticeship to life as well as art and now felt himself ready to undertake their imaginative fusion. The years of revolution and war just behind him had left him with a wealth of confused but startling impressions, and he was determined to explore to the utmost the ambiguities and paradoxes in which they were clothed.

Babel's service with Budyonny's Cossack Cavalry had been one of

---

From *Isaac Babel: Russian Master of the Short Story.* © 1974 by the University of Tennessee Press, Knoxville.

those profound experiences to which he responded, in a sense, for the rest of his life. The war was the catalyst that set Babel on the path to self-discovery, and it helped to shape the patterns of the art through which he would express and combat his personal alienation. The depiction of violence and conflict, far more than a mere device or technique, becomes a controlling feature of his fiction, and it clearly lies at the heart of both of his famous collections, *Tales of Odessa* and *Red Cavalry*. The artistic relationship between these two cycles of stories and the role that the war played in the genesis of each are somewhat clarified by an understanding of the time and sequence of their composition.

Both in the Soviet Union and abroad, the prevailing view has been that the *Odessa Tales* were written later than *Red Cavalry* and that they represent a decline in the author's powers. Actually Babel had written at least three of the four stories collected in *Tales of Odessa* by the spring of 1923; two of them had even been published, one as early as 1921. The first appearance in print of any of the *Red Cavalry* stories, however, was in February 1923, when Babel published five stories in the Odessa *Izvestija*. Furthermore, Babel published these latter stories to alleviate financial worries and only reluctantly did he release what he called "excerpts." The remainder of the *Red Cavalry* stories, on which Babel was apparently still working in 1923, appeared separately over the next two years, while the first collected edition was not issued until 1926. The date of 1920 which accompanies many of the cavalry stories and which has misled the critics must consequently be understood to refer not to the time of composition, as has been assumed, but to the time of the action described. It seems clear now that many of the *Red Cavalry* stories were only finished in 1924 and 1925, at a time, that is, when the *Odessa Tales* were already complete. The proper sequence of composition thus established, the actual path that Babel's creative development took and the peculiar relationship these two cycles of stories bear to one another become clearer.

Written almost simultaneously, the two sets of stories share certain themes and attitudes and have as a common setting a background of passion and chaos. Though the Odessa stories possess a surface of broad comic intent, they, like those of *Red Cavalry*, have conflict and violence at the heart of their world. While *Red Cavalry* portrays soldiers engaged in actual combat, in legally sanctioned war, the Odessa characters are criminals, men at war with the society and their fate. The life of the Jewish underworld depicted in *Tales of Odessa* shows traditional moral and cultural values as fully under assault, and in much the same way, as they are in *Red Cavalry*. Furthermore, in both cycles the moral questioning of violence is linked to certain common attitudes toward Jewish identity. Thus, in spite of differences in style, tone, and point of view, these two sets of stories are like two contrasting but complementary expressions of a single creative impulse, two interrelated versions of a dichotomous, perhaps flawed, but nevertheless single artistic vision which informs all of Babel's art. Let us examine first the *Odessa Tales* since these are the earlier and more properly introductory pieces to Babel's mature work.

As far back as 1918, Babel had treated of Jewish lore and anecdote in his story "Šabos-naxmu." In *Tales of Odessa,* as in that story, there is much to remind us of older Yiddish literature; though he wrote in Russian, Babel owes much to such Yiddish writers as Sholom Aleichem. Obviously there is the theme of Jewish culture, both as a complex, self-contained phenomenon and as a tradition surrounded and beleaguered, but not submerged, by a very different and largely hostile culture. But it is not only through his interest in the closed world of the Jewish community that Babel is related to the Yiddish literary tradition: the very texture of his language and the quality of his humor, with its peculiar mixture of the sardonic and the highly emotional, are best understood in the light of that tradition.

At the same time, the *Odessa Tales* are strikingly different in tone from the work of other Jewish writers. Babel does not share the basic attitudes toward ghetto life which are common to Yiddish literature and which are still implicit in his 1918 prewar story "Šabos-naxmu." The war seems to have confirmed in Babel a less indulgent attitude toward Jewish experience, and when he turned once again to Jewish themes and characters he did so in the light of his anomalous position as a Jew who had lived and fought side by side with the Cossacks. Hershele, the folk hero of "Šabos-naxmu," is a recognizable stereotype: the comic, pathetic, but resourceful misfit frequently encountered in prerevolutionary caricatures by both Russian and Yiddish writers. Hershele's world, though a ghetto, is essentially the self-congratulatory milieu of Jewish folklore, and in this sense "Šabos-naxmu" may be said to belong to the older tradition.

Yiddish literature, associated with a people who everywhere in Europe constituted a minority, understandably reflected the efforts of Jews to preserve both their traditional values and a sense of community. Their attempt to maintain a distinct religious identity was met with especially hostile opposition not only from the differing religious traditions of the larger culture, but also from the largely secularized atmosphere of contemporary Western society. Both internal and external pressures, therefore, resulted in the closing off to Jewish experience of many of the main currents of Western life, of the opportunity to share fully in the broader social and political milieu in which Jews were a cohesive but isolated minority. As a result of this insulation the literature that concerned itself with Jewish fate in the Diaspora was liable at its worst to accept all of its traditions uncritically and to succumb to nostalgic self-indulgence or to eulogies to the obscure or picturesque. At its best, as in Sholom Aleichem, such literature was capable of both skepticism and sympathy, of irony as well as affection, and it was able without sentimentality or idealization to affirm the values of Jewish life and to revere its culture, learning, and humanism.

For Babel, however, insulation from the mainstream was a deprivation. As a man of preeminently modern sensibilities he found the cultural walls of Jewish life yet another aspect of the ghetto. Returning from war and revolution, after participating in a great historical event, he views the backwater of Jewish life with new distaste, with a conviction that the ghetto had paid too great a price for its production of saints, scholars, and artists. In these years of upheaval Babel welcomes the destructive winds of change which he hopes will topple not only the physical ghettos created by the old decayed society, but the spiritual and emotional ghettos of Jewish life as well, those shackles which have deprived human beings of the experience of joy.

The hope of chaos is a desperate hope and indicates a profound sense of social alienation in the man who holds it. In Isaac Babel the estrangement from traditional cultural values in general, and from the milieu of his birth in particular, is dramatically underlined by his admiration for the Cossack soldiers of the Revolutionary army in which he had served. There is a striking anomaly and no small paradox in this reaction on the part of a Jew to men whose way of life seems so antithetical to his own deepest traditions; but for Babel those who wield the cleansing sword of destruction are figures of heroic significance. He minimizes neither their violent instincts nor their primitive morality, but at the same time he delights in the animal grace and beauty of their bearing and in the spontaneity and directness of their physical passions. In the conflict between these virtues and the values of Jewish tradition, Babel often seems ready to forego the latter. His experience outside the ghetto had touched the deepest places of his being, and for the moments of wild and exultant freedom that he craved he was prepared at times to abandon traditional Jewish ideals such as intellectual eminence or moral dignity as irrelevant and incongruous, as marks of the imprisoned and deprived Jews of the ghetto. He sought instead to extract from within the Jewish experience something to compare with his vision of the Cossack ethos, something that would permit him, as a Jew, to participate in that same primitive celebration of life.

As a new ideal Babel creates a Jewish version of the Cossack: a man schooled in violence, immune to the vacillations of the intellectual or the moralist, and reveling in all the physical pleasures and challenges of life. In his *Odessa Tales*, Babel sought to portray a Jewish hero who was *in* but not *of* the ghetto. The gangster Benja Krik and his cohorts represent an antitraditional image of the Jew; they are aggressive and powerful fighters who challenge authority and answer violence with violence: if they are outcasts at all it is only in the sense that they have elected to cast themselves out into the world and accept no external limitations on their right to experience. Although the deprived and suffering Jew of the ghetto is still present in Babel's stories, he is placed in the shadow of this physically towering, resplendent, outrageous new folk hero.

Tales of Odessa is a collection of four stories interrelated as to characters, themes, milieu, and narrative tone. In the first, "The King," we make the acquaintance of Benja Krik (Benny the Yell), leader of the exotic underworld of the Moldavanka. We learn how he came to be married to the rich Eichbaum's daughter, and we see how he and his men forestall a police raid (planned to catch the gang while celebrating the wedding of Benja's forty-year-old sister) by setting fire to the police station. In "How It Was Done in Odessa" we are told the story of Benja's rise to fame and power, how he robbed the rich and clever Jewish merchant Tartakovsky, how he meted out punishment to the overzealous member of his band who killed Tartakovsky's clerk, and, finally, how the murdered clerk was accorded the most sumptuous funeral Odessa had ever seen. In "The Father" we learn of Benja's marriage to Basja, the gigantic daughter of the red-headed, one-eyed gangster Froim Grach, and of how these two great bandit families are united by ties of blood and marriage. And in the last story, "Ljubka the Cossack," we meet a kind of female counterpart to Benja, the formidable Ljubka Schneeweiss, whose family name is incongruously embellished with the awesome nickname "the Cossack" and whose inn is the rowdy home of Odessa's smugglers and gangsters when they relax.

But a bare plot synopsis of these tales is less than useless because they are primarily phenomena of style and tone, experiments in narrative composition, and masterpieces in the use of colorful language. Babel once declared that his main interest as a writer was the "how" and "why" of things rather than the "what." His *Odessa Tales*, above all, require a proper understanding of this aspect of his imagination.

The stories are an intricate blend of many rich ingredients, and although these ingredients are words they are so visually and palpably effective that they make an almost physical impression upon the senses. Part of the problem in trying to describe the secret of these tales lies in the inimitable quality of Babel's version of the Odessa speech, a jargon that defies translation or paraphrase and that cannot be adequately described by an analysis of its grammar. Odessa had been famous long before the Revolution as the home of a characteristic brand of regional anecdotal humor. Its unique and colorful local idiom, strongly influenced by Yiddish and Ukrainian folklore, had developed a characteristic accent and rhythm as well as its own special way with a word or turn of phrase. In one of several essays on Odessa written early in his career Babel spoke of the great literary potential in the rich Odessa speech. He predicted that the city would experience a cultural renascence, that it would bloom again with its own "bright and self-made word." Because of his own fascination with this Odessa "word" and his intimacy with it from childhood, Babel himself was in no small measure responsible for the eventual truth of his prediction.

Odessa did indeed give to Soviet literature in its earliest period a number of prominent writers, including Eduard Bagritsky, Vera Inber, Valentin Kataev, and the team of Ilf and Petrov. The work of these writers, while by no means of a piece, shared a sufficient number of traits to give rise to the notion of a "southern school." Their lack of respect for classical rules, as well as their richly metaphorical language, was not exclusive to any particular school, of course, but in their penchant for the picaresque and for the use of exotic speech and local color, as well as in their peculiar union of romanticism with humor and ironic modes of narration, all of these writers shared something of a common aesthetic.

Babel reveals something of the Odessa flavor in a short piece he wrote as an introduction to a projected collection of stories by seven young Odessans (including Ilf, Bagritsky, and the immigrant Odessan Konstantin Paustovsky): "In Odessa every youth—until he marries—wants to be a cabin-boy on an ocean-going ship. The steamships putting into our port enflame our Odessan hearts with a thirst for beautiful new lands." Then after a brief word about each of the seven young authors and the "melancholic," the "mellifluous," and the "miraculous" things they have to tell, Babel closes with a typically ironic and self-mocking variation on his opening: "The whole point of this book is that in Odessa every youth—until he marries—wants to be a cabin-boy on an ocean-going ship. There's only one trouble with us—in Odessa we are extraordinarily insistent on marrying."

In the four stories that collectively bear the name of his native city, Babel has reproduced the intonations of the Odessa speech. He is extremely careful to make his literary version of this salty jargon both representative and comprehensible to the general reader. He avoids an excessive dosage of dialect and relies instead on the judicious use of characteristically distorted

The Odessa Tales: *An Introduction*   149

syntax and morphology, or on other slight deviations from the norms of standard speech. Part of his success in capturing the flavor of speech is accounted for by his creation of a diction and speech rhythm for his heroes. They speak in proverbs and formulas, they mix levels of discourse, and they misuse clichés, thereby making them newly vivid. Dialogue at times has a kind of comic brevity, a clipped staccato quality which is heightened by the use of truncated repetitions. Often it proceeds in the sort of circuitous question-and-answer style that is typical of much Jewish humor. Through his mastery of speech patterns Babel achieves both comedy and characterization, and he conveys with precision the milieu to which his speakers belong.

The language of Benja Krik, the King himself, is a spicy verbal counterpart to his wildly improbable career. Never at a loss for a phrase, Benja will laconically toss off an aphorism or invent a graphic image as vivid as a line of comic verse: "My brains stood on end along with my hair when I heard this news." Again, this time pleading with the wealthy dairyman Eichbaum for the hand of his daughter, Benja is carried away by the enthusiasm of his suit to heights of impassioned rhetoric [the following is from *Isaac Babel: The Collected Stories*, trans. and ed. Walter Morison. I have occasionally made slight changes in this and subsequent citations.]:

> "Listen, Eichbaum," said the King. "When you die I will bury you in the First Jewish Cemetery, right by the entrance. I will raise you, Eichbaum, a monument of pink marble. I will make you an Elder of the Brody Synagogue. I will give up my own business [Benja's business is robbery and extortion!] and enter yours as a partner. Two hundred cows we will have, Eichbaum. I will kill all the other cow-keepers except you. No thief will walk the street you live in. I will build you a villa where the streetcar line ends. Remember, Eichbaum, *you* were no Rabbi in your young days, either. Who was it that forged that will, but we won't talk too loud about that. And your son-in-law will be the King—no snotnose, but the King, Eichbaum."

The speech is effective both as comedy and as characterization. Benja's supralogical, rapid-fire sequence of thoughts has Eichbaum dead and magnificently buried before making him owner of two hundred mythical cows, and the offer to kill off the competition (with an obliging "except you" for a prospective father-in-law) is hardly calculated to instill confidence in a man whose own funeral has just been painted in such glowing colors. Without pausing for either breath or logic, Benja next promises to protect Eichbaum from thieves in the district (a bitter pill under the circumstances); then to build him a dacha on the outskirts of town; and, finally, he ends the entire peroration with a thinly veiled threat neatly and irresistibly sandwiched between a humble admission of human frailty and a proud boast of superhuman power. It is no doubt shrewd not to be a saint if one intends to indulge in blackmail, and being a "King" instead of a "snotnose" lends credence to the threat while at the same time appealing to Eichbaum's vanity.

Benja's ever-present aplomb is conveyed through his language. When Manja, the sixty-year-old "progenitress" of the bandits, lets out with a piercing whistle to celebrate the burning of the police station, Benja is quick with a typical reproof, one that contains a neat "Krikism" in its translation of the French term *sang-froid*: "'You're not on the job, Manja,' observed Benja, 'a little more cool-bloodedly, Manja!'"

Another example of Odessa bandit palaver can be seen in this excerpt from a conversation (from "How It Was Done in Odessa") between Benja and Froim Grach (Ephraim Rook). Benja is applying for membership in Grach's band:

> "Take me on. I want to moor to your bollard. The bollard I moor to will be the winning one."
> Rook asked him:
> "Who are you, where do you come from, and what do you use for breath?"
> "Give me a try, Ephraim," replied Benja, "and let us stop smearing gruel over a clean table."
> "Let us stop smearing gruel," assented Rook.
> "I'll give you a try."

After accepting the difficult assignment of raiding the wealthy Tartakovsky, Benja once again displays his mastery of style in the extortion note he writes; it is similar, the author tells us, to all letters of this type:

> "Highly respected Ruvim son of Joseph! Be kind enough to place, on Saturday, under the rain barrel, etc. If you refuse, as last time you refused, know that a great disappointment awaits you in your private life. Respects from the Bentzion Krik you know of."

During the raid Benja as usual is a model of self-composure:

> "A little calmer, Solomon," observed Benja to one who was shouting louder than the rest. "Don't make a habit of being nervous on the job."

One member of the gang, however, loses his head and murders Tartakovsky's clerk, Muginstein. Tartakovsky's ensuing accusation against Benja is an example of the fusion, common to the Odessa jargon, of humor with an underlying philosophical seriousness:

> "You hooligan's snout," he cried, perceiving the visitor, "you bandit, may the earth cast you forth! A fine trick you've thought up, killing live people."

Benja too displays a philosophical side when, referring to the murder (in what must surely be termed an exaggerated understatement) as a "tremendous mistake," he pleads with Muginstein's mother for understanding:

> "—if you need my life you may have it, but all make mistakes, God included. A tremendous mistake has been made, Aunt Pesja. But wasn't it a mistake on the part of God to settle Jews in Russia, for them to be tormented worse than in Hell? How would it hurt if the Jews lived in Switzerland, where they would be surrounded by first-class lakes, mountainous air, and sheer Frenchmen? All make mistakes, God not excepted. Listen to me with all your ears, Aunt Pesja."

A sardonic tone like that of Benja's lament is a characteristic feature of Jewish humor that has been well exploited in Yiddish literature. For instance, Sholom Aleichem's work, which Babel knew well, has running through it just such rueful disputes with God, and the blending of humor and seriousness peculiar to such street-corner philosophizing does much to create the special flavor of the Odessa jargon that Babel imitates so well. It will be noted also in this passage how Benja's use—or misuse—of words ("first-class lakes, mountainous air, and sheer Frenchmen") helps to delineate his personality and background.

Examples of Babel's Odessa jargon might be selected at random from any of the stories: the intonations, the syntactical and semantic patterns, and the mental styles they exhibit are common to almost all of the characters. What is of interest from a structural point of view, however, is that the narrative frame itself often echoes these speech peculiarities. The narrator will introduce dialogue by using the same inflections, the same staccato rhythms and comic repetitions, that later appear in the dialogue itself. By thus anticipating his characters' language the narrator not only contributes to comic unity; he lends a pronounced oral flavor to the entire story. As a result of this oral structure, the narrative style and tone take on significance and the narrative voice becomes a major character in its own right.

Cases where one can identify the narrating voice as that of a "disinterested author" are relatively rare. Such tonally neutral lines as do occur are kept to the minimum required for moving the plot, and they are distinguished from other narrative passages by their isolation and brevity as well as by their placement, usually at the beginning of paragraphs.

Frequently in Babel the narrative technique involves a blending of voices, an interlacing of varied speech masks into a richly textured pattern. Actual mimicry of his characters is only one of the oral devices in the narrator's bag of tricks. He may, for example, assume a philosophical or biblical pose and express himself in maxims or proverbs. The effect is often one of comic or ironic incongruity, as in this explanation (from "The King") of how the seating was arranged for Dvoira Krik's wedding: "Not according to their years did the wedding guests take their seats. Foolish old age is no less pitiable than timorous youth. Nor according to their wealth. Heavy purses are lined with tears."

Sometimes the narrator's voice highlights an exaggeratedly farcical scene through the device of inappropriate matter-of-factness. By keeping the tone, if not the words, calm and brusque, he pretends to be unaware of his story's outlandish comic proportions. Here, for instance, is the narrator's description of how Benja comes to ask the man he has just robbed for his daughter's hand:

> Two days later, without warning, Benja returned to Eichbaum all the money he had taken from him, and then one evening he paid the old man a social call. He wore an orange suit, beneath his cuff gleamed a bracelet set with diamonds. He walked into the room, bowed politely, and asked Eichbaum for his daughter's hand. The old man had a slight stroke, but recovered. He was good for another twenty years.

Only in the final short sentence, a rapidly delivered aside, is the comedy of the scene permitted to break through to the narrative surface.

In "The King" the narrative voice includes still another tonal range: the poetic. Belonging neither to the Odessa dialect nor to a disinterested author, this poetic tone lies mainly beneath the narrative surface. Usually it is subdued and channeled into one of the other narrative strains, but sometimes it shows itself through other speech patterns, and occasionally it bursts into full-throated song. The timbre of this other, unidentified voice is sometimes lyric, sometimes epic, by turns ironic and solemn. It is a voice betraying a heart full of romantic longings and a mind bemused by the word-fragrance of books. Though we cannot identify it as Babel's voice, the personality it invokes is close indeed to the figure offstage. This impression is strengthened because the lyric quality we detect appears inconsistent with the more dominant tones of the narrative; as a result, the narrative voice at these times seems to belong to an outsider, to a man who admires the world he describes, but who nonetheless stands apart from it.

This implied onlooker stance of the narrator's represents both a calculated rhetorical device and an integral part of the story's thematic structure. As rhetorical device it gives to the recital of the story an authority independent of the characters. Thematically, it introduces enriching elements of contrast and irony, since the partially repressed romantic lyricism in the onlooker's voice paradoxically serves to both beautify and expose the reality it describes. The hyperbolic tone, so obviously at variance with the general features of the stories' milieu, results in an ambiguous and delicately balanced tension between encomium and parody.

Consider the poetic color, the luxuriant wordiness and the crescendo-like structure of the following two passages describing the wedding feast in "The King":

> At the wedding feast they served turkey, roast chicken, goose, stuffed fish, and fish-soup in which lakes of lemon gleamed like mother-of-pearl. Over the heads of defunct geese, flowers swayed like luxuriant plumages.

The prose in the next passage (the quotation represents less than half of a long and elaborate single paragraph) vibrates at an exaggeratedly heightened pitch. It is a description of the exotic fare smuggled from distant places for the enjoyment of Odessa's bandit élite and, as the narrator tells us in the declamatory last two lines, of their attendant beggars:

> All that is noblest in our smuggled goods, everything for which the land is famed from end to end, did, on that starry, that deep-blue night, its entrancing and disruptive work. Wines not from these parts warmed stomachs, made legs faint sweetly, bemused brains, evoked belches that rang out sonorous as trumpets summoning to battle. The Negro cook from the *Plutarch*, that had put in three days before from Port Said, bore unseen through the customs fat-bellied jars of Jamaica rum, oily Madeira, cigars from the plantations of Pierpont Morgan, and oranges from the environs of Jerusalem. That is what the foaming surge of the Odessa sea bears to the shore, that is what sometimes comes the way of Odessa beggars at Jewish weddings.

This passage produces a number of conflicting impressions. It gives a sense of Hebrew tradition, of feasting rich in religious symbolism. Beggars and noble bandits share wine together at this repast, and we recall the words of the Haggadah of the Passover: "Blessed art thou, Lord, our God, King of the Universe, who dost create the fruit of the vine," and "He lifts up the poor from the dust, from dungheaps he raises the lowly, to seat them with nobles, with the nobles of his people." But the occasion is essentially nonreligious, or at least nonspiritual, and such associations seem ambiguous and mocking. In the light of religious suggestion, the passage inflates and distorts what it tells, describing ceremoniously what is after all (as the ensuing description shows us) an occasion of wild drunkenness. Ultimately, however, the effect is not to ridicule the proceedings, but rather to separate the occasion from those religious associations which are an incongruous and unnecessary appendage. The feasting is after all only feasting, but its magnificence is undiminished.

If the celebratory atmosphere is not the result of religious symbolism, neither is it the result of any alternative set of values inherent in the meaning of the words. The effects are achieved through the sheer phonetics of the sounds themselves, from the heavy weight of sonorous Russian words and the rhythm of rolling cadences. The goods enumerated in this passage are fit for a king because they sound exotic; the ship *Plutarch* is not a real ship, but a legendary vessel bringing nectar for the feast of godlike men and illustrious heroes. Port Said, Jerusalem, and the plantations of Pierpont Morgan, all contribute not only their lush southern delicacies, but the splendor and melody of their names as well. The language, with its repetitions and alliteration, its profusion of adjectives and its imagery, is itself intoxicating; the prolonged, clause-laden sentences go to the reader's head like the wines and rich foods they describe.

One of the most striking qualities of the passage is the way Babel's delight in the exoticism of the setting colors his portrayal of actual things. His adjectives and modifiers tend to dominate and submerge the inert nouns they describe; the ordinary reality of things retreats before the power of his rhythmic phrasing. The lavish tone of the description subordinates actions and things to a decorative vision. As in poetry, this is accomplished through the prominence given to particular words. As ornaments on the textured surface of the style, these words become entities in their own right; their phonetic properties take on new weight and importance. Freed of their responsibilities to be merely signs for things, they become the rhythmic ingredients for a musical prose composition.

Babel intends, of course, that his word-musical view of things will invest them with a new reality, with a hard brilliance and an almost sensuous beauty. What he despises and rejects is the tyranny of things as possessions. When viewed in this way, as they typically are by the middle-class, things are gray and lifeless; paradoxically, it is they who possess their owners. The Moldavanka bandits, on the contrary, display an attitude toward things that is more "aristocratic." Here, for example, is the description of how they bestow their gifts on the newly wedded pair in "The King":

> And now the friends of the King showed what blue blood meant, and the chivalry, not yet extinct, of the Moldavanka district. On the silver trays, with ineffably nonchalant movements of the hand, they cast golden coins, rings, and threaded coral.

In Babel's hand language itself becomes a means of escape from life's drabness. Through his ornamental style he forces his reader to view the commonplace through a topsy-turvy kaleidoscope or, to use one of his own images, through a pair of magic spectacles. In order to convey a new and magnified reality he employs all manner of linguistic, stylistic, and thematic devices of creative distortion and exaggeration. In delineating characters he even approaches the grotesque. Here, for example, are some of the phrases describing the girl Basja in "The Father":

> Rook ... saw ... a woman of gigantic height. She had enormous hips, and cheeks of a brick-red hue.

> She had put on men's boots and an orange frock, and she wore a hat bedizened with dead birds.

> She weighed five poods and a few pounds over.

> Mounds of linen would glide across her great straddled knees.

Description is not only bizarre and exaggerated; it is frequently expressed, even in minor details, in boldly physical terms:

> The child strained toward her, bit at her monstrous nipple, but achieved no milk.
>
> ("Ljubka the Cossack")

> Policemen, their buttocks waggling, were rushing up smoky staircases.
>
> ("The King")

> The old crones would lave fat infants in troughs, slap their grandchildren on their shining buttocks and wrap them up in worn-out skirts.
>
> ("The Father")

Babel is attracted by the primitive and vital aspects in the life force. He constantly draws attention to living, functioning flesh and to bodily processes; the reader of his stories is likely to find himself assaulted by a barrage of sensuous imagery. In addition to the abundant detail which Babel devotes to actual physical attributes—to arms and legs, bosoms, buttocks, and pregnant bellies—there are the lavish descriptions given to food and drink, as well as frequent reference to blood, sweat, and spittle. Even the sense of smell is enlisted to invigorate the reader's perception of people or things, often in a context of strange or jarring juxtapositions:

> From their wide hips wafted the odors of the sea and of milk.
>
> ("How It Was Done in Odessa")

> Each ware had its own price, each figure they drank down with Bessarabian wine that smelt of sun and bugs.
>
> ("Ljubka the Cossack")

> The old man drank down some vodka from an enameled teapot and ate the hash, fragrant as a carefree childhood.
>
> ("The Father")

Still another device that emphasizes the primitive physicality of Babel's fictional world is the frequent attribution of animal features to its human inhabitants. Sometimes the implication is of weakness: Dvoira's husband in "The King" is likened to a mouse; the murdered clerk Muginstein, bachelor son of Aunt Pesja the poultry dealer, is described in "How It Was Done in Odessa" has having spent his life "like a bird on a bough"; and Basja's beloved in "The Father" is named Capon. More often, however, the attribution of animal features tends to magnify the human, to endow it with animal energy. Dvoira is as carnivorous as a cat; Benja is likened to a cat, a lion, and a tiger; other of the Moldavanka bandits are characterized in a similar fashion by the use of animal names: Froim Grach (rook) is a scavenger and thief like the bird whose name he bears; another of the gangsters goes by the blunt and enticing sobriquet of Levka Byk (Lefty the Bull); while Benja and Dvoira, though they lack specifically animal names, share the aggressive implications of their family surname, Krik (the Yell), which reminds us that in the beginning was not the word, but the yell—barbaric and uncivilized. In his figurative language, too, Babel frequently uses animal imagery, as in these examples:

> Velvet-spread, they [tables] wound their way down the yard like so many serpents with variegated patches on their bellies.
>
> ("The King")

> Sweat with the pinkness of fresh blood, sweat as pink as the slaver of a mad dog.
>
> ("The King")

> They wore black frock coats with silk lapels and new shoes that squeaked like sacked suckling-pigs.
>
> ("How It Was Done in Odessa")

> After him like sheep went all the lawyers, all the ladies with brooches.
>
> ("How It Was Done in Odessa")

> The pregnant women, nibbling at this and that, would fill up with juice as a cow's udder fills on the pastures with the pink milk of spring.
>
> ("The Father")

> It [the sun] climbed to the middle of the sky and hung there quivering like a fly overcome by the heat.
>
> ("Ljubka the Cossack")

> The sun lolled from the sky like the pink tongue of a thirsty dog.
>
> ("Ljubka the Cossack")

> A moon that skipped through black clouds like a stray calf.
>
> ("Ljubka the Cossack")

Babel's use of the intensely physical, even the erotic, is intended partly to shock the reader into new perceptions. But Babel also celebrates the erotic in its own right, as an essential ingredient of the full life. It represents a challenge to the squeamish gentility of the bourgeoisie and an antidote to the blanched dullness of their lives. Babel rejects the urban middle-class denial of the biological truth of human nature, and in his art he turns to a freer, more aggressive world, one where primitive physicality is allowed ample expression. To provide a proper setting for his celebration of this physical principal of existence, Babel creates a lush and exotic background. His fictional Moldavanka is the direct antithesis of all that is lifeless or gray; its bizarre people live in a carnival world, in an atmosphere of lurid color. Dark and light, set closely together, heighten each other like the color effects of an impressionistic painting:

> The purple eye of the sunset, groping over the earth, that evening lit on Rook as he snored beneath his cart. The impetuous ray fastened with flaming reproach on the sleeper and led him out to Dalnitskaya Street, dusty and gleaming like green rye in the breeze.
> ("The Father")

> Evening had long since turned to night, the sky had grown black, and its milky ways were filled with gold, glitter, and coolness.
> ("The Father")

In the following passage, touches of pale color help to characterize the foreign asceticism of the Tartar pilgrims who pass through Odessa on their return from Mecca; the effect of the scene is to transfer for a moment the sun-struck religious impulse of the distant, bleached, and holy desert to the urban landscape of modern Odessa: "Inflexible striped robes stood stiffly on the Tartars, flooding the pavement with the bronze sweat of the desert. White towels were wound around their fezzes, and these distinguished such as had bowed to the dust of the prophet" ("The Father"). The transfer is accomplished, however, only for a moment, and with the inevitable accompaniment of mockery. One of the pilgrims, an old Turk covered with "pearly sweat," is dying in the courtyard of Ljubka's inn, where his religious conviction in the face of death is subjected to brutal and insensitive ridicule. The descriptive language, with its stately repetitions, amplifications, and its selection of a bright color, manages to give subtle sustenance to the dying Turk by linking his death with the vibrance of growing things: "An old Turk in a green turban, an old Turk green and light as a leaf, lay on the grass" ("The Father").

The color green is used frequently by Babel in conjunction with motifs of death or decay. It serves to emphasize the ultimate triumph of living processes as well as to point to the harsher truth that life must feed upon death in order to rise above it. There is a passage in "The Father" that describes old Mendel Krik, defeated and disfigured by his own sons. Despite the element of travesty on the theme of resurrection, there is a somber grandeur in the old man's struggle to deny decay. The peculiar presence in the passage of the word "green" seems especially remarkable:

> Mendel Krik sat at one of the tables drinking wine from a green tumbler and relating how he had been crippled by his own sons—the elder Benja and the young Ljovka. He yelled his tale in a hoarse and terrible voice, exhibiting his ground-down teeth and getting people to feel the wounds on his belly.

The linking of death with greenness and the resultant intimation of life's persistent vitality are made early in "How It Was Done in Odessa":

> Reb Arye-Leib was silent, sitting on the cemetery wall. Before us stretched the green stillness of the graves.

The story will end where it began—in the cemetery—and though there may be an ironic truth to the fact that all stories must have their final act played before the eyes of Arye-Leib, sitting atop his cemetery wall, it is a truth that Babel seeks to circumvent by subjecting even death to the distorting lens of his fantasy. The solemn stillness of the graveyard is shattered at the story's climax by a burst of noise and color as life—through Benja and his men—asserts its unconquered power. Midway through the story, when the clerk Muginstein is about to die at the hands of one of the gunmen, Babel, with a few quick strokes, changes the pallid specter of death into a living reality of color. The clerk, within the space of several short lines, is described as "white as death," "yellow as clay," and "green as green grass." The colors summarize and predict for us not only Muginstein's immediate future, but his ultimate destiny as well: he is seen, almost at once, as corpse, as body interred in the earth, and then transmogrified into the grass that will grow above his grave. At the later funeral ceremonies death is again decked out in nature's greenery.

In "The Father" the closing scene is once more set against the backdrop of a Russian cemetery. It is not a place of solemn stillness, but one where "Lads were then dragging lasses behind the fences, and kisses re-echoed above the tombstones." Life has chosen an unexpected and incongruous spot to reassert its power, and death is perhaps partly subdued by being associated with vast, revivifying natural processes.

Babel's fantasy greatly depends on the striking use of color: silver, gold, blue, white, black, yellow, green, and purple all add their specific hues to the kaleidoscopic world created by the writer's imagination. But Babel's favorite color, the one most common to these stories, is red. In a great variety of shades, reds and related colors such as orange serve as a kind of prism through which people and objects are refracted and changed; it is as if the spectacles through which the narrator views the world are rose-colored, and as if the author himself were wearing similar glasses and asking the reader to do the same. So pervasive and dominant are the reds that the resultant impression is something of a cross between a garish nightmare and a child's drawing in which a single color is boldly and illogically used for everything.

Babel's reds have a thematic as well as a decorative function. They stand for energy and exuberance, for passion and life:

> Kate, the whole-hogging Kate, was still heating up for Benja Krik her many-colored, Russian and rubicund paradise.
> ("The Father")

> Little Dave looked at him in amazement and waggled his little raspberry legs bathed in infant sweat.
> ("Ljubka the Cossack")

> There awaited her Mr. Trottyburn, a man like a pillar of russet meat.
> ("Ljubka the Cossack")

> An orange star which had slid to the very brim of the horizon gazed wide-eyed at them.
> ("Ljubka the Cossack")

> The pink milk of spring.
> ("The Father")

> The sky was red like a red-letter day.
> ("The Father")

> On the other side, draped in orange shawls, were the honorary dairy-maids from Bugajevka.
> ("How It Was Done in Odessa")

> Sweat with the pinkness of fresh blood.
> ("The King")

The most vivid characters are also imbued with hues of red: Froim Grach has red hair; his daughter Basya has brick-colored cheeks; Benja

Krik drives a red car and he promises Eichbaum a monument of pink marble; Benja and his men wear outlandish and colorful costumes in which red and orange play a prominent role:

> He wore an orange suit, beneath his cuff gleamed a bracelet set with diamonds.
>
> ("The King")

> Aristocrats of the Moldavanka, they were tightly encased in raspberry waistcoats. Russet jackets clasped their shoulders, and on their fleshy feet the azure leather cracked.
>
> ("The King")

> Here Benja paused. He was wearing a chocolate jacket, cream pants, and raspberry boots.
>
> ("How It Was Done in Odessa")

Everything about the gangsters is exaggerated and fantastic. They are the Moldavanka's élite, of a different stamp from ordinary tradesmen, and their passage through the town is a truly incredible procession:

> All the shops on Dalnitskaja had now shut, and the gangsters were driving past to Glukhaja Street, where Jo Samuelson kept his whorehouse. In lacquered carriages they drove, dressed up like birds of paradise, their jackets all colors of the rainbow. Their eyes were agoggle, each had a leg jutting out on the footboard, and each held in an outstretched arm of steel a bouquet wrapped in tissue paper. Their lacquered jaunting cars moved at a walking pace. In each carriage sat one gangster with a bouquet, and the drivers, protuberant on their high seats, were decked with bows like best men at weddings.... [T]he sons of the shopkeepers and shipwrights envied the kings of the Moldavanka.
>
> Little Solomon Capon the grocer's son and Monja Gunner son of the smuggler were among those who tried to turn their eyes from the blaze of an alien glory.
>
> ("The Father")

All of this decorative color enhances and enlarges the characters depicted, makes them bigger than life, epic in stature. The bandits have "steel shoulders" and "burning eyes," they are bolder and stronger than ordinary men, they do everything on a grander scale. Their attire is like the plumage of exotically colored birds, or like the armor of famous knights; their lacquered carriages resemble fabled steeds; and in "The King" they carry long poles like spears or lances. "Aristocrats of the Moldavanka," they are a special class within the Jewish community, a warrior caste amid the clerks, tradesmen, herders, and women. Because of their physical attributes and their legendary deeds of plunder and adventure, a special glory attaches to them alone within the tribe.

The element of fable that Babel exploits in these tales lends them a curious quality of timelessness, so that in spite of the fact that the stories take place in a modern city the sense of historical reality is suspended and nebulous. Rather than the reactionary and troubled post-1905 era that constitutes the actual historical setting for these stories, the evoked atmosphere suggests a tribal or feudal past. There is no direct reflection in the tales of the two revolutions or of the contemporary reordering of social institutions. On the contrary, there is a distinct sense of ancient modes of behavior and of old, tribally limited loyalties—rather as if Babel, by appropriating elements of epic tradition, were seeking to re-create, half seriously and half satirically, a heroic tradition for the Odessa Jews.

In Arye-Leib the "Moldavanka knighthood" has its court chronicler or bard; he is a Jewish Homer whose words impart the sagas of the giants to the young, and we shall see later how his use of biblical diction contributes to the aura of myth. Benja himself is a mythic figure, a knight and avenger, a king among figures as splendid and colorful as himself. When he ventures forth he is surrounded by a retinue of attendant warriors; to reflect further glory on his person his exploits are compared in epic fashion to the deeds of other illustrious heroes. He and his men are both bold and crafty; they triumph over great adversaries: the law and the power of oppressive wealth. The bandits indulge in Homeric feasts, and there is an epic quality to the frequent poetic enumeration of foods and other goods. It is significant that for the most part the lists of things are not of possessions to be accumulated, but of things to be used and enjoyed: the fare at the wedding feast in "The King"; the delicacies of Capon's grocery in "The Father"; the wares found in the inn of "Ljubka the Cossack."

At the funeral in "How It Was Done in Odessa" the mourners are tradesmen and clerks, dairymaids and poultry dealers, but Arye-Leib's narration makes them a stately procession passing in salute to the illustrious dead. The narrative style idealizes the bandits—particularly Benja, whose heroic stature is disclosed in the Homeric simile that Arye-Leib uses to describe him: "and the sun rose above his head like an armed sentry." Situation and psychology as well as narrative language cast Benja in an

Achillean mold. Like the Greek hero who felt a sense of personal guilt in the death of his friend Patroclus and who avenged him by killing his slayer, Benja avenges Muginstein by slaying the murderer Savka Butsis. Also like Achilles, he arranges a splendid funeral for his departed brother, a ceremony that serves not only to ease the deceased's passage to heaven and to console those left behind, but to assuage Benja's personal sense of responsibility as well.

There is a further suggestion of the Homeric epic in Arye-Leib's recital of how the Jews outwit a hostile gang during a pogrom by staging a mock funeral with a machine gun in the coffin instead of a body. At the appropriate moment, after the procession has penetrated into enemy territory, the weapon is brought into action and the enemy routed. The situation is a travesty of the legendary Trojan horse episode and carries the suggestion of a bitter new adage: Beware of Jews bearing coffins.

Of course there is a comic incongruity to much of the epic tone in these tales. The heightened pathos at times sounds distinctly ironic and often gives rise to an impression of satire or parody. The ironic note, however, is neither simple nor consistent, and the author is often apparently at odds with himself. There is a level at which the stories constitute a kind of parody of the epic conventions they imitate. The various rites and ceremonies, the initiation trials (for example, Benja's being sent in pursuit of Tartakovsky's wealth), the emphasis on sensual rather than spiritual experience, and the roguish hero himself—all suggest a satirical picaresque variant of the medieval romance, a burlesque of the religious or symbolic functions of the epic hero.

At the same time there is a strong element of mockery in the treatment of the heroic characters themselves. With their inimitable jargon and outlandish clothes, Babel's Moldavanka bandits are a decidedly urban phenomenon, more Damon Runyan in intonation than ancient warrior or medieval knight; nor are they convincing as modern Robin Hoods. The Homeric simile as applied to the bandits is at times distorted into a comic parody of itself and of them: "Wines not from these parts . . . evoked belches that rang out sonorous as trumpets summoning to battle." For all their rejection of the ordered life of bourgeois merchants, they remain essentially the product of their milieu. Even Benja the King is not immune from mockery. He outwits the police and extorts money from the rich, but he bows to the power of tradition and custom: he would prefer to sit down with "Monsieur" Tartakovsky and discuss like a business transaction the terms of his extortionary demands; he is annoyed because he doesn't receive a prompt and civil reply to his extortion note; he argues until hoarse over the pension

Tartakovsky will pay Muginstein's mother and in the end settles for a mutually agreeable compromise. There is similar bargaining between Benja and Eichbaum and between Benja and Froim Grach over the terms of marriage contracts, and Benja accepts Tartakovsky's reproach about "killing live people."

The other Moldavanka aristocrats are mock-epic figures too. In "The King," for example, the narrator explains how the gangsters fire their revolvers into the air "because if you don't fire into the air you might kill someone." In their bourgeois respect for caution and tradition, the bandits reveal that ultimately they share, for all their daring, in the same underlying attitudes toward Jewish folkways as do the bankers, tradesmen, rabbis, and clerks. The effect is to satirize such traditional values as moderation and compromise and to ridicule such homely virtues as gentleness and concern with family and community. All four of the *Odessa Tales* deal in a farcical way with Jewish communal ceremonies or institutions—with weddings and arranged marriages, with feasts and funerals, and with family and community life in general. The bandits are thus, in part at least, mock-chivalric figures, and Benja is the warrior and lover of a mock epic. The operatic melodies of Benja's automobile (the horn of his car plays a march from *Pagliacci*) invoke a comic-opera quality that mocks the bandit élite as much as it affronts their supposed antithesis, the staid bourgeoisie.

Yet beneath all the mockery Babel's use of the ironic voice conceals an authentic longing for heroic action, and he continues to find the epic a viable mode for the artistic embodiment of his most profound desires. But as the modern condition mocks the rebellious human spirit, and the unheroic fact confronts the heroic act, Babel, like many modern writers, finds that the antiheroic minor key is the necessary counterpoint to a contemporary epic. Under these conditions the ironic mode is far more than a rhetorical device; it becomes literally indispensable to the preservation of any vestige of the heroic spirit.

A useful term for the kind of treatment Babel gives to epic themes has been provided by Victor Terras in a discussion of *Red Cavalry*. He speaks of Babel's approach to the epic as travesty, that is, "replacing (or distorting) the form of an original without, however, changing the content," which is to be distinguished from parody—"replacing (or distorting) the content of an original, while retaining the form" [reprinted here]. The application of this concept of travesty to Babel is highly suggestive for it illuminates a trait that recurs through most of his work. In *Red Cavalry* especially, but even in *The Odessa Tales,* Babel disguises and conceals his epic themes, but he does not parody them. He reclothes (to use a formulation close to the etymological meaning of the word "travesty") his epic heroes in an unusual and incongruous modern garb; but despite the distortion of the outward form, they retain an epic cast.

The claim of an underlying earnestness in Babel's *Odessa Tales* may seem surprising at first, but some sort of didacticism would seem to be common to all manifestations of the epic impulse. In echoing those traditions Babel is concerned to reveal, to celebrate and proselytize, a distinctive style of life. His *Odessa Tales,* for all their seeming ahistoricity, are rooted in a specific time and place. Their setting, though only implied, is still the reactionary post-1905 era, and Odessa, for all its cosmopolitan charm and color, was then a city in which the Jew-hunting Black Hundred and the Union of the Russian People were able to thrive as well. The pogrom was a common occurrence; even the national government, immoral and opportunistic, encouraged and supported such an anti-Semitic horror as the Beilis trial of 1913. The Jews were a special target in this moment of revolutionary hiatus, as they often are in times of national crisis, self-hatred, and fear.

Babel's Odessa stories are not, however, as might be expected, aimed directly at anti-Semitism. Written after the revolutionary upheavals of 1917 and the Civil War which confirmed them, they exclude a retrospectively buoyant, almost exultant sense of release; they have a brash and—as it seems now—an overly confident tone that takes the destruction of the old order for granted. They celebrate somewhat prematurely a success not yet tasted. But despite his humor and the hope engendered in him by the new vistas opened to Russia at the beginning of the twenties, the author is unsure. Babel wrote *Tales of Odessa* after his own participation in the Civil War as a comrade-in-arms of the Russian Cossack, and he is celebrating in them his own sense of liberation and enlarged experience. But he remains divided and perplexed about the meaning of his Jewish past, about the nature of the present, and also about what he wants the future to become.

Despite the surface gaiety of the tales, their inner view of contemporary man is rather dark. Violence remains the corrosive center of the world, and the dominant figure of its city landscape is the cemetery. Urban degradation is the underside of Babel's vision, and although he seems to want to smother this awareness it constantly threatens to expose the bright exterior itself as illusion. The stories, as a result, are an extremely volatile mixture of uncertain attitudes and irresolvable conflicts. The multifaceted style as well as the proliferating ironies that give the stories their unique flavor reflects the author's own inner ambivalence.

The situation of the Jew, and in particular of the East European Jew, fraught with overtones of exile and estrangement, has often been taken as a paradigm for the phenomenon of contemporary alienation. As with many modern Jewish writers, Babel's rejection of the ghetto involves more than an attack upon Jewish conditions: it reflects an awareness of the urban ghetto as the modern condition of all men. In its yearning for another place Babel's work suggests an almost mythic search for the uncitified past. But at the same time there is a certain specifically Jewish quality in Babel's alienation. His *Odessa Tales* repudiate and mock many traditional features of Jewish life, and they do so with the bitterness of the apostate. The kind of joy and fulfillment that Babel sought from existence lay outside the limits of Jewish experience and seemed to demand not merely transcendence of that experience, but repudiation of it. Babel attempted, partly as a response to the war, to displace the Jewish mores of his heritage with an altogether alien ethos. It is clear that the displacement, radical though it was, meant a kind of release; he identifies his sense of liberation with a liberation of the senses, with a newfound joy in physical life. At the same time, however, this joy is inseparably bound up with a feeling of guilt. This rejection of Jewish values produces in Babel a lingering suspicion of self-betrayal, and in the end he is as unable to rid himself of his past as he is to forego his claim to a larger future. Babel's dilemma goes beyond the confines of the specifically Jewish element of his experience to that conflict, not uncommon in Russian literature, between aesthetic and worldly pleasures and the claims of any rigorous and insistent morality.

In Benja Krik, Babel tried to create a figure who would embody the liberation for which he himself was searching. Benja may not have fully emerged from the ghetto, but like his creator he has elected to do battle with life in a larger arena of experience and, so far as he is able, without the emcumbrance of either Jewish morality or Jewish exclusiveness. Benja is larger than his environment, not completely defined by it; with regard to the mores of the Jewish community he is an iconoclast, and it is this that makes him unique even among his fellow "aristocrats." Only Benja is prepared to accept the onus of the tenth raid on Tartakovsky and the possibility of murdering a fellow Jew. And he alone has fully enjoyed the pleasures of the non-ghetto world, partaking, for example, of the prostitute Katya's "many-colored, Russian and rubicund paradise." These two aspects of Benja's self-expression, his ready violence and his open sexuality, seem crucial. As viewed by Babel—and this is where he runs afoul of humanist criticism—these qualities are not so much the result of struggle against injustice, a reluctant election of violence as the only alternative to annihilation; they are the essentials of Benja's free personal existence. Benja is not merely fighting to survive; he is demanding to live, to matter, and he chooses to define himself by taking from life what he needs. Though this does not make him attractive to the humanist tradition, it does place him securely within a major branch of modern literature. Babel makes of Benja a kind of profane messiah, an exemplar-rogue whose very knavishness demonstrates the possibility of a self-expressive joy. Benja's will to be is essentially and of necessity anarchic; to exist at all he must constantly challenge authority, whatever its source. "Where there's an emperor, there is no room for a king," is the policeman's response to Benja Krik, and the assertion is an inadvertent tribute to the force of Benja's self-proclamation, to the challenge he hurls in the face of the world. But Babel appears to find this external challenge easier to meet. Benja's more serious adversary resides in the communal values that remain alive and strong within himself, in that cultural heritage that retains its authority over him even as he tries to renounce it.

It is for this reason that Benja's advent, if glorious, is also comical. Something in Babel's ambivalent attitudes, a perversely skeptical sense of reality or a finely ironic sense of truth, forces him to mock his hero as much as he does his other targets. Benja remains the product, in many respects, of the very community his actions ridicule; his kingly attributes and his exploits are travesties of its values and dreams. Even his kingly title is conferred upon him by the community, and the biblical overtones in the stories, though they mock religious values, nevertheless link Benja with ancient Hebrew prophetic and messianic traditions.

If the sublime and the ridiculous are never far apart, Babel brings them perilously close. His reasons are not difficult to ascertain. The use of comedy and irony, like the use of crude naturalistic detail, can forestall the charge of sentimentalism; more specifically, it helps to parry any possible accusation that Babel has a too ready and uncritical acceptance of his exemplar-hero. Pure fantasy, like unadulterated didacticism (and Babel's work contains elements of both), may produce a counterreaction in the reader, turning him against what he is meant to admire. Benja Krik's story is really a fairy tale, and the danger for Babel, one that he recognizes, is that fairy tales are untrue. A dose of mockery is therefore a healthy corrective, an injection of reality into the realm of romantic dreams. The question remains, however, does the device work? In Babel's *Odessa Tales* it is, at best, only partly successful.

At first the elements of parody and irony are totally confusing. We are not immediately certain where the author stands in relation to his major figure and ultimately to the Jewish world of the stories. Ambiguity is almost universally regarded as a virtue by the modern sensibility, and we are prepared, almost reflexively, to grant Babel his pervasive ambiguities—especially when self-mockery plays as prominent a role as it does in his work. But Babel's mockery is one-sided; it is directed almost exclusively against values that are characteristic of Hebrew and humanist culture. Insofar as this irony is leveled against the author himself or against author-related figures such as the narrators, it seems a legitimate device; such figures are adequately representative of their cultural milieu, and we are able to infer their virtues as well as to accept the negative accusations made against them. But as applied to Benja the same mockery seems inappropriate, since the ethos that he represents is openly presented in the tales as the antithesis of that tradition which the narrative voices embody. To criticize or ridicule Benja for the bizarre surviving traces of his bourgeois upbringing is not to criticize him at all. To mock Benja in earnest would be to mock him where he is most himself, where he most diverges from his milieu and poses an alternative to its central values. But Benja as a creature of brute violence and animal physicality, Benja as didactic exemplar of a new path to joy, is in fact exempted by Babel from mockery; we are allowed the approving laughter that helps to make ferocity more palatable, but we are permitted to direct the laugh of condemnation only against the gentler, more "civilized" attributes. Since we have grown to expect irony and ambiguity, the lack of it here at the central and most vulnerable point of these tales comes as both a surprise and a disappointment.

Many readers are fooled by Babel's ability to conceal the blunt purpose of his central hero. At least one American critic has reacted to these stories with extreme distaste:

> Babel respected the Jews only when they answered the violence done to them with violence of their own.... These stories of Odessa seem to me unpalatable. Aside from their moral dubiousness, they affect a folksy amiability and relaxation which are not appropriate to their intense violence and chicanery. Unlike the stories of *Red Cavalry* they seem to have been "gotten up" into literature, but Babel's deliberation over them was unproductive of finer and more humane judgments.
>
> (Steven Marcus)

Yet Babel does not espouse violence as an answer to violence. He has gone beyond this toward an understanding of the creative possibilities of the aggressive instincts. He sees how modern urban societies repress spontaneous self-expression, how they throttle the sensual and emotional life, and in the face of this frustration he reasserts the claims of "natural" man. It is true that Babel comes close at times to affirming violence itself as a positive value, but at his best he is capable of establishing the truth of primitive passions without himself becoming a barbarian.

The reader may still find this unpalatable, of course. He may feel that in exalting strength and scorning weakness Babel has obscured what would otherwise be insistent moral dilemmas. He may argue that Babel's characters are stereotypes, grotesque distortions that are unfair to the finer realities of Jewish culture. But such a view, concentrating on individual characters, misses the point that none of the heroes, whether strong or weak, bandit or bourgeois, is psychologically real. Babel's Odessa heroes are essentially static figures, types rather than persons; taken individually they cannot express the kind of conflicts we look for in complex fictional portraiture. The reader who seeks a recognizably human hero in a recognizably human dilemma must look beyond the psychological implausibilities of Babel's characters to the structural center of his stories, to the narration itself. It is in the narrator (and implicit behind him, the author) that the various static and conventionalized types converge to create a portrait of considerable moral complexity. The author, not the actors, sees the irony in Eichbaum's marrying his daughter to the man who has robbed him, in Grach's search for a son-in-law in a whorehouse, and in the sumptuous funeral given by the bandits for their victim. The stories come alive, finally, in the hidden person of the author, for whom the various characters are only different masks.

We are thrust back then to the heavy burden carried by style in Babel's short stories, to the way in which the clash of opposed views permeates the very language. Narrative and authorial identities sometimes flow together, sometimes diverge; lyrical pathos contrasts with the earthy jargon of the characters; narrative and descriptive coloring clashes with its own content and sounds parodic; the cliché follows hard upon the poetic image; and vulgarity alternates with high sensitivity. Comic incongruity, however, is really only the obverse of poetic congruity, and though these apparently contradictory impulses appear irreconcilable in the tales both have their source in the author. It is he who manipulates the strings and weaves the strange patterns, and the irony and ambiguity of his art are rooted in his vision of himself. In truth, almost all the irony is self-irony, and when this is grasped it becomes clear how insistently moral are Babel's central concerns. In the end Babel's irony is probably self-defeating for it keeps him fatally estranged from both the real and the ideal; but it does exonerate him from the charge of having devised a mindless defense of violence.

If Babel's attempt to depict a new Jewish ethos ultimately fails, it nevertheless marks the beginning of his effort at self-identification, at understanding his own Jewishness. His attack upon Jewish tradition was necessary precisely because that tradition was so strong a force in his own consciousness, and beside the harshness of his attack should be placed the powerful affection for Jewish experience that exists in the very core of his work—in his language. In the verbal dimension of his art, despite the grotesqueness of his characterizations, one finds an underlying sympathy. The variety and profusion of Babel's verbal energy link him directly with Jewish sources; his interweaving of history, poetic myth, and metaphysical speculation with the mundane and prosaic is true to the spirit of ordinary Yiddish conversation, and his very irony and humor reveal a belief in words that relates him to the nonviolence of the ghetto at its best.

Babel's violence, too, is a thing of words: he murders in art. For Babel art is an investigation and trial of the possibilities of life; it is a necessary surrogate for the jungle or battlefield, and he transposes the violence of existence to the relatively manageable arena of words. He has a profound personal need for the catharsis and sublimation of aesthetic creation, and as a result, his stories record the painful but always awesome and rare struggle of the human spirit against itself.

SIMON MARKISH

The Example of Isaac Babel

Isaac Babel fits perfectly into the landscape of Soviet literature of the 1920s. Thematically, his collection of short fiction, *Red Cavalry,* takes its place alongside the stories of Vsevolod Ivanov, Dmitri Furmanov's *Chapayev,* Alexander Fadeyev's *The Rout,* and innumerable other works on the civil war. The naturalism of *Red Cavalry*—its brutal depiction of elemental forces unleashed by the revolution—is not more remarkable or more terrifying than what can be found in Vsevolod Ivanov or Artem Vesely; its style is not more colorful than the bewitching verbal tissue of Andrei Platonov, or the inimitable palette of Mikhail Sholokhov's *And Quiet Flows the Don.* As for the exotic underworld of Babel's *Odessa Tales* and of his play, *Sunset,* both of which reflect a general interest in criminal life (as well as in subjects related to the borderlands and "aliens," Jews included), this finds parallels in such works as V. Kaverin's *The End of Khaza,* or Leonid Leonov's *The Thief.* Even Babel's notorious silence, his catastrophically low output after *Sunset* (1928), and the relative weakness of that work compared with his work of the 1920s, are merely an extreme form of the disease and crisis that afflicted all of Soviet literature at the turn of the decade.

It was no slip of the tongue and no exaggeration when Stalin called 1929 the "year of the great breaking point." That year marked the threshold not only of great economic and social upheavals—the destruction of the peasantry, industrialization, the beginning of the new autocracy and of a new terror—it also signaled the fundamental reconstruction of the young

---

From *Commentary* 64, no. 5 (November 1977). © 1977 by the American Jewish Committee.

Soviet culture. For all the blindness and randomness of the Great Purges, which struck out right and left indiscriminately, there is no denying them a certain logic, which can be discerned in their results: everything was liquidated that stood out from the rank and file, that did not blend with the general mass, or was unable to fall into line behind the party leadership, without hesitation or complaint. Naturally, there were exceptions, but it was not by chance that Titian Tabidze or Pavel Vasiliev disappeared, while Nikolai Tikhonov and Alexander Prokofiev were spared and allowed to flourish. Nor was the destruction of Babel a matter of chance. Soviet literature of the 1940s and 1950s had no place for the likes of him.

And yet Babel does stand out obviously and sharply among his contemporaries. The reasons for this preoccupied critics during his lifetime, and have done so since his posthumous rehabilitation. Some have spoken simply about his talent and its uniqueness. Others have offered explanations based on his experiments in genre, his special brand of romanticism, the peculiarities of his character and his personal fate. Without rejecting any of these arguments, I would like to concentrate exclusively on one circumstance of fundamental importance, Babel's tie to Russian-Jewish literature.

I do not mean Babel's Jewish origin or his Jewish mentality. Others have written on that before, and continue to do so. Thus we read in an article by Pavel Novitskii, published in 1928: "Babel has a passionate, dry, precise Jewish mind.... A solemn seriousness and concentrated severity make his work true and sharp.... He is wearied by the dense melancholy of memory. The past (in his phrase, 'the rotted Talmuds of his memories') holds him fast in its grip. He is incapable of drastic action." More recently, the French critic Judith Stora-Sandor has similarly stressed Babel's Jewishness: his religiosity, his knowledge of Yiddish, his youthful study of Hebrew, the Bible, and the Talmud; his loyalty to Jewish traditions, both familial and social; his passion for Hasidism which, in Miss Stora-Sandor's view, led him on to Tolstoyanism. Her conclusion: "It was precisely due to his Jewish interests that Babel, the *Soviet* writer, became also a *Jewish* writer. In making himself the mouthpiece of his fellow Jews, without locking himself up within the close confines of their restricted community, as the Yiddish writers did, Babel tried to demonstrate the practical possibility of uniting two souls, the Jewish and the Russian."

Where Novitskii connects the Jewish "past" with weakness and indecisiveness, and with these alone, Miss Stora-Sandor wraps her definition of what makes a "Jewish" writer in an equally dense fog of half-understanding or even total misunderstanding. Babel, in fact, did not "become" a Jewish writer, he had always been one. He did not choose to write in a particular language, as did Mendele Mokher Seforim, or Hayyim Nahman Bialik; for him the Russian literary tradition was natural, organic, and the only one possible. As for the supposed opposition between Yiddishist exclusivity and Babel's "universality," that is as senseless as the notion of his striving to unite the Jewish and Russian "souls."

By the time of Babel's first literary efforts, a Russian-Jewish literature already existed. It had arisen immediately after the first shoots of Jewish Enlightenment (Haskalah) appeared on Russian soil in the nineteenth century. This movement, which aimed at bringing the Jews out of their isolation in the ghetto, had as one of its main objects the introduction of the Jews to the culture and especially to the language of the indigenous population. In Germany, where the movement originated, the German language was assimilated quickly and successfully, owing partly to its closeness to Yiddish and partly to the greater material well-being of the Jewish population. In the Russian empire, the followers of Moses Mendelssohn, the father of Haskalah, encountered enormous difficulties. Yet despite the appalling poverty and congestion of the Jewish masses; despite the inconsistency of government policy, first fostering the enlightenment of the Jews, then obstructing it, first hoping for their assimilation, then fearing "Jewish domination"; and despite the decisive turn to repression and restriction under Alexander III, Russian-Jewish literature did indeed develop, and it generated its own growing readership.

Already by the turn of the twentieth century, then—or at any rate by the eve of World War I—Russian had become one of the languages of the Jewish Diaspora. Notwithstanding the unquestionable predominance of Yiddish, a certain section of the Jewish intelligentsia, notably in Odessa, Kiev, and St. Petersburg, had become Russian-speaking; there was widespread and accomplished Russian-Jewish journalism, historiography, belles-lettres; periodicals and books were being published in large numbers. The rise of Russian-Jewish literature at the beginning of the twentieth century was enhanced by emergent Zionism, which rejected Yiddish and adopted Russian as a stepping-stone to Hebrew, a language undergoing its own renaissance.

The Russian-Jewish literature of the prerevolutionary period was a literature written in Russian by Jews for Jews, and one way or another charged with Jewish themes. Even if a Russian-Jewish writer succeeded in attracting the attention of the Russian reading public—as was the case with the poet Semyon Frug or, later and with greater significance, David Aizman and Semyon Iushkevich—he still remained outside the bounds of Russian literature proper, and was perceived as an alien or exotic phenomenon. And so indeed he was.

The Revolution changed things fundamentally. Leaving aside the social and political changes which turned the life of Russian Jewry inside out, let us consider one circumstance of a general nature which seems not yet to have received the attention it merits. Since the Revolution the Soviet regime has in truth created a new, unified culture—not "socialist in content, national in form," as the official formula has it, but an imperial *Russian* culture which continuously absorbs the best (by whatever standard) that is created in the provinces. Only translation into Russian, performance on the Moscow stage, exhibition on the Moscow screen or in Moscow galleries confers real life on an artistic production. And that, with very few exceptions, is what every artist works for. This has produced a curious analogy to the imperial culture of ancient Rome, which was created by the united efforts of the Italians, Gauls, Spaniards, Africans, and Greeks—and in which, with the passage of time, the proportional contribution of the provinces became more and more significant. Thus Soviet literature today is inconceivable without Vasil Bykov (a Byelorussian), Okudzhava (a Georgian), Faizul Iskander (an Abkhaz), or Genghis Aitmatov (a Kirghiz), all of whom either write in Russian or translate their own work into Russian. Another parallel with ancient Rome: just as the label "provincial" covers Seneca (whose Spanish origins are undetectable in his work) and Apuleius (clearly a Hellenized North African, in literature as in life), so Okudzhava is Georgian in name only, while Oljas Suleimenov is a passionate Kazakh nationalist. In other words, the national markings of the alien who has entered imperial Russian-language literature fluctuate within very wide limits, so that in extreme situations new branches emerge; thus, in the case of Suleimenov, we are plainly dealing with a Russian-Kazakh, or possibly Russian-Turkic, branch of Soviet literature.

All this must be borne in mind in order to understand the fate of Russian-Jewish literature and its role in the Soviet period. As an independent and isolated cultural phenomenon, it was liquidated along with neo-Jewish (Hebrew) literature. This was a politically motivated, violent action, one of the important moves in the Bolsheviks' struggle against Zionism and national-cultural autonomy, and it represented a systematic carrying out of the Bolshevik program as drawn up before the Revolution.

In the course of the 1920s, all the Russian-Jewish periodicals were gradually closed down, and the leading figures of Russian-Jewish literature either died, emigrated, or fell silent. But from the very beginning a considerable number of Jews had gone into Soviet-Russian literature. Many of them never in any way evinced any connection with Judaism, even in those far-off times when to be a Jew was positively encouraged. Examples are Benjamin Kaverin, the prose writer, and the poet Alexander Bezymenskii (the level of talent is irrelevant here); in a later period one might cite Emmanuel Kazakevich, who began writing in Yiddish but went over to Russian after the war and in the entire corpus of his Russian work betrayed not a hint of anything Jewish. Among Russian writers of Jewish origin, however, a fair number exhibited (and continue to exhibit) national characteristics, though in very varying quantities and forms, depending on general circumstances and personal situation. The 1920s and 1930s are particularly rich in examples of this, revealing a freshness and directness in literary reminiscences of distinctively Jewish life, made possible by the absence of official anti-Semitism. By contrast, the last years of the Stalin regime, which saw the peak of anti-Semitic terror, are almost totally sterile. Then, in the second half of the 1950s and the 1960s, came a resurgence of a new kind, an explosion of a people's frustrated dignity (no matter that its positive self-awareness, its cultural "baggage," might be scant or even nonexistent).

However disparate the forms and quantities involved, works with a Jewish orientation do constitute a certain whole—for which two claims, at least, can fairly be made: they represent the first—and, up to now, the most significant—non-Russian branch of Soviet-Russian literature; and despite their inseparability from the imperial literature described above, they are the direct descendants of pre-revolutionary Russian-Jewish literature, and can be studied and understood only in relation to the latter. (To these two claims a third might well be added: it is that Russian-Jewish literature of the Soviet period might instructively be considered alongside such parallel phenomena as contemporary American-Jewish, Anglo-Jewish, and Franco-Jewish literature from a whole range of standpoints.)

At the very headwaters of the Russian-Jewish literature of the Soviet period stands Isaac Babel. Or perhaps one should say that he himself was the main source—to which its peculiarities, its development, and its role within Soviet literature are in large measure traceable.

The daily life and cultural background from which Babel came played an important role in his creative life. He grew up in Odessa, in a family that was economically comfortable. (It may be pertinent to note here that many details in his quasi-autobiographical Odessa stories are invented out of whole cloth, as for example the assertion, "I come from a poverty-stricken wreck of a family.") A substantial part of the Jewish population, which in the year of Babel's birth, 1894, formed one-third, and on the eve of the revolution one-half, of the total population of Odessa, had left the old traditional and enclosed Jewish life far behind. Theirs was the path of assimilation—in the original and literal meaning of that term, "becoming like"; what they had in view was adaptation, perhaps even the first step toward integration. Despite pogroms, persecution, and discrimination, the situation in Odessa was not unlike that in America: a blending with the surrounding milieu, and at the same time a secure sense of group community, with the synagogue as spiritual and organizational (rather than purely religious) center. This situation was unique in Russia; there was nothing like it in any of the other centers of Jewish culture, neither in St. Petersburg, Kiev, nor Vilna. That the contribution of Jewish Odessa to the nascent Soviet culture proved so large was thus no accident.

According to Babel's sister, at home the parents spoke Yiddish to each other and Russian to the children. This may have been the case—it was typical enough in Odessa at the time. And yet (as we learn from his letters, published in English in 1964 as *Isaac Babel: The Lonely Years*), Babel knew Yiddish well enough to edit the collected works of Sholom Aleichem in Russian translation, expressed the desire to translate "Tevye the Dairyman," and did in fact translate David Bergelson's tale, "Dzhiro-Dzhiro." What is even more important, he read Yiddish not simply for professional reasons but for his own pleasure, sitting before the fire at his *dacha* outside Moscow; in one letter to his mother, he calls Yiddish "our language."

Babel studied at a commercial school, together, according to his "Autobiography," with "the sons of foreign merchants, children of Jewish brokers, imposing Poles, Old Believers, and many overgrown billiard players." In that motley place, and in the dockside cafes and billiard halls, he not only absorbed the language of the Russian classics, he also fell in love with that special Odessa dialect, half-Russian, half-Ukrainian, in which even today the strong Jewish intonation and phrasing are evident. In school he also learned French, so well that after only two years he was writing stories in that language. But during the same period, for about six years, from age ten to sixteen, he was studying biblical and talmudic teaching as well, and was thus able (in 1926) to approve the Hebrew translation of six of his tales.

Miss Stora-Sandor asserts that Babel was religious. This seems not quite accurate; he is on record too often with public denials of God's existence (for instance, the end of his speech at the First [Soviet] Writers' Congress), and no one who knows his life and work would accuse Babel of hypocrisy. Yet religious traditions were an inseparable part of his nature. He punctiliously sent greetings to his parents on the High Holidays in the fall and at Passover, always mentioning that he himself intended to celebrate as far as possible, and lamenting that his possibilities were so meager and poor. In his letters he asks his mother if she has been to the synagogue, and, after attending the synagogue in Odessa himself for the New Year service, he tells her how "everything was so painfully familiar, I am terribly glad I went and, as always, I prayed in my own way to my own, other God, above all for you both" (that is, his mother and his sister).

The "above all" is not an exaggeration. Babel's love and attachment to his family, which may seem surprising and excessive to the present-day generation, is an age-old and important tradition of the Jewish Diaspora, and Babel clearly understood the nature of his family feelings. So when he says that every minute and every hour he is sharing in spirit the sufferings of his family, and would give everything to be able to do so physically, he adds the comment: "Look what a classic Jewish family-man I've become." Again and again in his letters he recalls his late father: he swears to carry out everything he had promised this father who had always expected success, not complaints, from his children; thus, thoughts of his father give him strength and drive away despair. In consciously accepting tradition, Babel was also trying to sustain it, if only symbolically, in the family which had been torn apart by his wife's emigration from Russia. When his daughter was born in Paris, he asked his wife to give her a real Jewish name—in vain: instead of "Judith," Natasha made her appearance in the world in 1929.

It is understandable that Babel should have loved Odessa as no other city in the world. He regarded it as the only place where he could really work, and he dreamed of returning there to live, traveling to Moscow only on business. It is understandable too that each visit, no matter how impoverished and provincialized the city had become, should bring him great pleasure. His spirit and his brain were refreshed. His ears were caressed by the Odessa accent. Newspaper boys, garbage collectors, janitors would greet him on the street and engage him in the most improbable conversations, of a sort that could only be heard in Odessa. After an evening at the theater, where he delivered a few utterly unmemorable remarks, thousands of young people lined the streets and blocked the path of his car. So it is understandable that he should have refused to emigrate with his mother, his wife, and his sister. Apart from his genuine Soviet patriotism—of which more later—the feeling was too strong in him of belonging to Russian Jewry, to that cultural milieu, in the broadest sense, which existed nowhere else in the world and of which the focus, the quintessence, was old Odessa. Even for so "poignant" a writer as Babel, the nostalgic lines he wrote about Odessa, in his brief note on Edward Bagritskii, sound unusually poignant: "I remember our last conversation. We agreed it was time to get out of strange towns, time to go home, to Odessa, to take a little house on Blizhnie Melnitsy, to write chronicles, to grow old.... We saw ourselves as old men, sly, portly old men, warming ourselves in the Odessa sun, on the boulevard by the sea, and following the women with a long gaze."

Still, the Jewish background, Jewish traditions and emotional attachments, are not in themselves enough. The writer or artist may recall his Jewish youth with tenderness and yearning, he may prefer gefilte fish with red-hot horseradish above all other food and drink, he may indulge himself with matzot and even pop into the synagogue a couple of times a year, but none of that entitles him to a place in Jewish culture, or in a Jewish encyclopedia. This can only come when his entire creative life, or a good part of it, has taken form under the influence of Jewish self-awareness. Babel's moment of self-awareness and choice arrived rather early, and antedates his appearance in print. Two crucial pieces of work, written at the end of 1915, provide the evidence—"Childhood II: At Grandmother's," and a fragment, "Three O'Clock in the Afternoon"—both of them entirely Jewish in theme and, more importantly, in the subjectivity that informs them.

The first is a sketch of a day spent at his grandmother's. House and grandmother together evoke this response in the boy: "Everything seemed strange to me. I wanted at the same time to run away from it all and to stay there forever." Here a familiar routine and atmosphere undergo an abrupt transformation, take on a piercing novelty, inspiring simultaneously horror (or perhaps revulsion) and a feeling for what is "one's own," ineluctable and permanent. Here we have essentially the whole Jewish Babel, the basis of his social and emotional values and the foundation of his aesthetics. Jewishness of whatever kind—the steadfastly traditional, the *shtetl*-hasidic, or the urban-emancipated—is perceived dualistically. The heritage is at once accepted and rejected, a fact which precludes simple social realism along with apologetics and denunciation—the three characteristic stances of the old Russian-Jewish literature. What appears in their stead is a fresh perspective from a new vantage point; sheer astonishment is no small part of it. Here is the source of that exoticism of the quotidian, that fantastic sharpness of line and violent emotionality which are the mark of Babel's style. But here, at the same time, is the source of his loneliness; dooming him to the role of outsider, always and with everyone.

The fragment, "Three O'Clock in the Afternoon," was published in an obscure journal only in 1971, and is generally unobtainable. It has been described by a Soviet critic, however, as a combination of "plotless lyrical narration saturated with precise psychological details which constitute a second level" and a vivid story "with heightened emphasis on individual speech." Thus, long before *Red Cavalry* and the *Tales of Odessa,* but at the time when his general position had crystallized (and, obviously, as a result of that crystallization), Babel discovers, at least in principle, the expressive means and the manner which were to become his hallmark. The moment of registering this self-awareness is the moment of Babel's self-invention as a writer.

The novelty of his position involved a new approach to his subject matter. Until then it had not been possible to imagine a work of Russian-Jewish literature on a non-Jewish subject. Now the author's attitude to his material acquires greater importance: his dual vision, from within and without, deepens his imagery and gives it a dimension which it had not and could not have known before.

But if the approach "from outside" had been construed only negatively, as synonymous with "not inside," if the phrase "I wanted to run away from it all," had simply signified flight, then we would not be able to speak of the dimension that comes from binocular vision. The Bolshevik Revolution gave Babel a second vantage point, another feeling of belonging, as indisputable as the first. I have already remarked that even the best and most famous Russian-Jewish writers were alien beings to the non-Jewish reader. But these writers felt themselves to be aliens in Russian literature, guests at best. For Babel, however, Soviet-Russian literature was as much hearth and home as it was to Vsevolod Ivanov, and I am convinced that Babel's loyalty to the Soviet regime, his love for Soviet Russia, his importuning of his family to return from emigration, especially in 1934–35, are in many ways connected with this. After returning from his first trip abroad, he wrote that he felt well in his native land, even if there was poverty and a great deal of misery; here he had his language and his material, the only things he found truly and inexhaustibly interesting. This disposition remained intact even during the 1930s—like the Jewish heritage, Soviet life was for him his rightful property, and more: his creation.

It follows that until this dual support was found, the real Babel did not exist. His first stories, published in 1916, are equally feeble, whether they have Jewish themes ("Ilia Isaakovich and Margarita Prokofievna") or non-Jewish ("Mama, Rimma, and Alla"). His first success, *Red Cavalry*, was destined to prove his largest one as well—because here, as in no other work, he drew on *both* his supports with such assurance and strength.

Kirill Vasilievich Liutov, the narrator and protagonist of *Red Cavalry*, is not Babel, even though the writer gave him the name under which he himself had served in the First Cavalry Army as correspondent for a military newspaper. Liutov is half of him, the Jewish half that is frantically in quest of a complementary, revolutionary, Bolshevik half. "'Gedali,' I said, 'today is Friday and it's evening already. Where can I get hold of some Jewish biscuits, a Jewish glass of tea, and a bit of that pensioned-off God in the glass of tea?'" ("Gedali"). Jewishness gives him his bearings in the savage and bloody, longed-for and unattainable, Revolution. Thus, although the death of the hero and pillager, Trunov, is not connected with the Galician village of Sokal, except geographically, Liutov nevertheless gives a detailed (detailed, that is, for Babel—two paragraphs) account of the ancient synagogues and torn gabardines, of the noisy wrangling of the Orthodox and Hasidim, and he concludes: "Heavy-hearted because of Trunov, I too went pushing among them, shouting along with them to ease my sorrow" ("Squadron Commander Trunov"). The ending of the famous "Discourse on the *Tachanka*," which appears at first glance to have no connection with the rest of the text, is in fact a most important paragraph on the Jews of Galicia and Volhynia. The son of a Zhitomir rebbe, "the last prince of the dynasty," the Red Army man Bratslavskii, a party member who had prayed in his father's synagogue because he felt unable to leave his mother, comes to understand that "in the Revolution a mother is only an episode," and, sent by his organization to take charge of a combat regiment, dies of typhus on the filthy floor of the news-correspondents' railroad car. The contents of his trunk are as mixed as those of his brief biography: "Agitator's orders and booklets of a Jewish poet, portraits of Lenin and Maimonides, pages from the Song of Songs, and bullets for his revolver." "He died, the last prince, amid verses, phylacteries, and leg windings. And I, barely able to contain the gales of my imagination within my ancient body, received the last gasp of my brother" ("The Rebbe's Son").

The Red Army man Bratslavskii is more than Liutov's brother, he is his double. He sacrifices all, asking for nothing and claiming nothing, except revolutionary solidarity. Yet he dies in solitude, under the indifferent gaze of "Cossacks in red baggy trousers" and "two big-breasted typists in sailors' jackets," having been wrested by his "brother" from the mass of typhus-ridden peasants who "rolled before them the customary hump of a soldier's death" and "wheezed and scratched and flew on wordlessly." He had been alone even in that crowd; indeed, his "brother" recognizes him by his solitude: he is the only one to reach out for a pamphlet, while all the others vie with each other to grab the potatoes Liutov is scattering from the wagon. The narrative of the story is addressed to an unknown Vasilii, whose name is mentioned insistently, almost importunately, five times in two pages. This persistence rests on the opposition of brother with stranger; to the latter, no matter how hard you try and how many times you call him by name, nothing can finally be explained.

Yet the rebbe, Motele Bratslavskii, the Red Army man's father, is one of Babel's own, albeit no "brother." The dialogue between him and Liutov, in the story "The Rebbe," is a conversation between people who understand each other intuitively. Joy, laughter, merriment are what Liutov craves as he wanders voluntarily through the convulsions and carnage of the class war, and the rebbe seeks the same with his pupils, as does the rag-and-bone man Gedali—which is why Gedali's praise of Hasidism has the ring of the author's own judgment. By contrast, the argument with Gedali (in "Gedali"), the champion of the "sweet Revolution" and the "International of good people," rings hollow. Liutov answers the ragman's "abstract humanism" with only two arguments, quite summarily presented: the Revolution "cannot help shooting, because it is the Revolution," and the International "is eaten with gunpowder and seasoned with the finest blood." In fact, these are something less than arguments. The principal refutation of Liutov's position, however, lies elsewhere: immediately after his menacing reference to gunpowder and blood comes the plaintive request, quoted above, for some Jewish biscuits and a glass of Jewish tea. "There isn't any," Gedali replies: "There isn't any. There's a tavern next door, where good people used to do business. But people don't eat there anymore, they just weep there."

Liutov has nowhere to go. The old world, from which he fled but which still retains its hold on him, has been destroyed by the new, toward which he is striving with all his heart, but which will not accept him, and repels him with its ugliness and bloodlust. The loneliness and desperation of the intellectual in the Revolution—a frequent enough literary theme in the 1920s—are compounded by the loneliness of the Jew; the Jew, moreover, being of a particular kind, split down the middle in his attitude to Jewishness, as the intellectual is split in his attitude to the Revolution. As a result, in the strength and tension of the tragic principle, the insolubility of its conflict, *Red Cavalry* may well take pride of place among books on the civil war.

The sharpness of the conflict is intensified by a vision so unsparing in its precision as to suggest at times the moral indifference of an aesthete:

> Right in front of my windows, some Cossacks were executing an old silver-bearded Jew for spying. The old man yelped and struggled. Then Kudrya, from the machine-gunners, tucked the old man's head under his arm. The Jew fell silent and spread his feet apart. With his right hand, Kudrya took out his knife and carefully cut the old man's throat, avoiding the spurting blood.
>
> ("Berestechko")

But this precision is itself the result of a sense of apartness and alienation that often borders on active hostility. (Simple compassion for "one's own," whether in ethnic kinship or common cause, would have blurred the vision and robbed the picture of its distinctive severity.) In the same story, "Berestechko," the Jewish way of life is delineated with a hostility that marks even the vocabulary ("the warm putrefaction of the old world," "the stifling decay of Hasidism," "the traditional wretchedness of this architecture," and so on); and this hostility is underlined by the contrast: "The village stinks, waiting for the new era, and instead of people, it is inhabited by fading schemata of frontier misfortunes. By the end of the day I was fed up with them and I left the town, climbed the hill, and found an entry into the ruins of the Raciborski castle." Liutov is not shocked by the abomination of desolation in what was once the seat of a Polish aristocrat; his descriptive detail—the nymphs with their eyes put out, a fragment of a hundred-year-old letter—sounds, rather, elegiac.

But even sharper and more merciless is the vision he turns on his comrades-in-arms. Here the alienation of an intellectual is augmented by ethnic alienation—and Liutov recoils in horror. He wants to admire and approve, and from this willed desire derive both the romantic phantasmagoria of landscapes and the infatuated portraits of his heroes, such as that of Savitskii, the divisional commander, in the opening paragraph of "My First Goose." But the romantic, technicolor film often snaps, and then one sees in the gaps the "raw fingers" and "fleshy, loathsome face" of another hero, another divisional commander, Pavlichenko in "Chesniki." The horror is even clearer in the stories told by narrators other than Liutov; between them and him lies an abyss of non-understanding and fear. With fear and bewilderment the intellectual Liutov registers the dense and savage suspiciousness of the barbarian ("Betrayal"); but for Liutov the Jew, much more terrible is the fanatical savagery of the "*goyim*," trampling the enemy to death ("The Life Story of Pavlichenko"), ready to kill for a bag of salt ("Salt"), capable of parricide and the murder of a son ("The Letter"). It would be wrong to see Liutov's reaction to all this as reflecting only a sense of moral superiority, millennia of living with the biblical commandment, "Thou shalt not kill," for it reflects as well millennia of passive martyrdom, the heritage of discrimination and intimidation.

On the whole, as I have already remarked, the author of *Red Cavalry* stands above his hero. His dual position is stable and productive. Despite his apartness, he is still his own man in both elements, in the old and in the new, in the Jewish and in the Soviet. He is not with the Liutov who is fed up with the Jews of Berestechko, or who confesses, "I am tired of living in this Red Army of ours" ("Evening"). He corrects Liutov through Gedali; and he cuts short Liutov's complaining with Galin's words: "You're a ditherer, and it's our luck that we have to put up with ditherers like you.... We are taking the nut out of the shell for you. Soon you'll see the nut right out of its shell, then you'll stop picking your nose and start singing the praises of the new life in unusual prose. Till then, just sit quiet, you ditherer, and don't whine around our feet" ("Evening").

This astonishing harmony-in-duality is what makes *Red Cavalry* a unique book, in Soviet as well as Russian-Jewish literature. It is Babel's best work, also his most Jewish—despite its non-Jewish subject matter—because at its center stands Jewish restlessness and yearning, gripped momentarily by the prospect of finding self-transcendence in the great common cause. That this hope was unrealizable, that the cause, "seasoned with the finest blood," would turn into an endless bloodbath, Babel did not know, and to indict him on this ground would be wrong.

Babel's works on purely Jewish subjects turn out, in a sense, to be less Jewish, precisely because in them the confidently sustained duality of position is weaker by comparison with *Red Cavalry*—when it is not, as in the early story "Shabbes Nakhamu" (1918), entirely absent. The latter is a rather pallid rendering of several anecdotes, or oral tales, about Hershele Ostropolier, the Jewish variation of the trickster-hero to be found in the folklore of almost every people. Babel, however, evidently gave this experiment (which, despite its subtitle, "From the Cycle, 'Hershele,'" he never continued) special significance, for in *Red Cavalry,* in reply to Reb Motele's question, "What does the Jew do?," Liutov replies, "I am rendering the adventures of Hersh of Ostropol into verse."

The *Odessa Tales* were probably written at the same time as *Red Cavalry*. They are marked, however, not only by different themes: the narrator is different, as is his relation to his material. Babel writes of the gangster life of Jewish Odessa in the first person, but at one point allows the narrative to pass to the synagogue beadle (*shames*), Arye-Leib, who refers to the narrator in rather disparaging terms: "You have spectacles on your nose, and autumn in your soul." Nevertheless, the poetics and intonation, as well as the emotional background of all four tales, are identical. The narrator is as much in love with the fat, juicy, fleshy, full-blooded, expansive Odessa of robbers, rich men, and cemetery-gate beggars, as is Arye-Leib himself. Arye-Leib says of the rich man nicknamed "Jew-and-a-half": "Tartakovskii's got the soul of a murderer, but he's one of us. He started as one of us. He's our flesh and blood, just as if the same mother bore us" ("How It Was Done in Odessa"). *Mutatis mutandis,* Babel might have said the same thing about all of old Jewish Odessa—as old Odessa might about him. He is here at home among his own; of the urge to escape and the self-division, all that remains is the conventional pair of spectacles on his nose, contrasting with the eagle eyes of the horse-and-cart drivers, the thieves, and Tartakovskii.

None of this is intended to diminish the qualities of the *Odessa Tales*. I merely mean to emphasize one thing: despite their stunning stylistic discoveries and innovations, despite their nostalgia for a recent but already irrevocable past, despite the utterly new and unexpected appearance of a bandit-hero in Russian-Jewish literature, the *Odessa Tales* continue and perhaps crown the prerevolutionary tradition of social observation in this literature, whereas *Red Cavalry* opens a new period and establishes a new tradition.

The four stories of the autobiographical cycle were written later than *Red Cavalry* and *Odessa Tales*. Two of them are dated 1925 and two 1930. These sad Jewish tales of sad Jewish childhood, with pogroms, penury, insane relatives—as I mentioned above, at least half the events and details are imaginary—would not stand out among the childhood reminiscences in which Russian-Jewish literature abounds but for the fact that here the author regards his past from a different, completely non-Jewish world. He has not broken with his former world demonstratively or noisily; he has simply left it, slipped away from it, into "nowhere," and he looks back with mixed feelings of nostalgia and fear, like the majority of children who have turned adult. Jewishness here is not the theme but the background against which the tragedies of childhood are reenacted: tragedies of love, deception, humiliation. Naturally, they are all strongly conditioned by the background, especially as, in the first two short stories, "The Story of My Dovecot" and "First Love," the background is a pogrom, but the tragedies themselves are universal, not linked to any one place or time or people. And the heart of each tale lies precisely in these universal tragedies; perhaps that is why the narrator, in focusing on his past sufferings, renders them with Babel-like tension and insight, observing everything else—the pogrom itself, his murdered grandfather Shoil, the Cossacks and their horses, the pogromists themselves—with a gaze that is clear, clam, and at times even admiring. This contrast represents not merely the special strength of Babel's autobiographical stories, but also an innovation of the greatest significance for the modern Jewish literatures of the Diaspora.

Babel's first play, *Sunset*, fulfills a singular role in his fate as a writer. Written in 1926, revised and finished in 1927, it was first produced and published in 1928, on the eve of the "great breaking point." The general atmosphere of the play, as well as the characters and even the plot, had all been anticipated in the *Odessa Tales*. But the change of literary genre—from narrative to dramatic—in and of itself brings drastic alterations in the message. Gone is the narrator in love with his material, and what had the air of a story told with relish about big-city sharpers now takes on the oppressive seriousness of life and becomes tragedy. It may suffice to recall the embryonic plot of *Sunset* as we find it in the tale, "The Father":

> Lamps were already burning in the wine-cellar and music was playing. Old Jews with heavy beards were playing Rumanian and Jewish songs. Mendel Krik was at a table, drinking wine from a green glass and recounting how his own sons, Benya and Levka, had beaten him up. He bawled out his tale in a hoarse and dreadful voice, he showed where his teeth had been knocked out, and he let them feel the wounds on his belly. Porcelain-faced *tsaddikim* from Volhynia stood behind his chair and listened dumbfounded to Mendel Krik's bragging. They were amazed at everything they heard, and Grach despised them for it. "Old braggart," he mumbled about Mendel, and ordered himself some wine.

Jewish themes must not be considered the indisputable monopoly of Jewish literature. So, here, it is not so much Babel's thorough knowledge of and feeling for the milieu that makes this play about the age-old tragedy of generational conflict the peak of Russian-Jewish drama as it is the fundamentally Jewish angle of vision, the presence of a Jewish wisdom two millennia old. Events are summed up by the old man, Ben Zekharia, "the rabbi of the Moldavanka," clown and jester, "crook and wise man":

> Day is day, and evening is evening, Jews. Day drowns us in the sweat of our labor, but evening is waiting to fan us with its heavenly breezes. The prophet Joshua, who stopped the sun, was a wicked madman. And here is Mendel Krik, a member of our synagogue, who turns out to be no smarter than Joshua. All his life he's wanted to broil himself in the blazing sun, all his life he's wanted to stand on the spot where noonday found him. But God has policemen on every street, and Mendel Krik had sons in his house. Policemen come and put things in order. Day is day and evening is evening. Everything is in order, Jews. Let's have a glass of vodka!

What are these beautiful and menacing allegories, "stealing from afar toward a goal not everyone can see," as Babel himself might have said ("The End of the Old Folks' Home")? what is this lofty and heartrending acceptance of the inevitable, if not a variation on the eternal bitterness and wisdom of Ecclesiastes? "To everything there is a season, and a time to every purpose under the heaven. A time to be born, and a time to die; a time to plant, and a time to pluck up that which is planted." Everything is in order because "One generation passeth away, and another generation cometh; but the earth abideth forever," and Arye-Leib's lamentations over Mendel's "lacerated and powdered" face are authentic catharsis in the classical Aristotelian sense. And when he "laughs and cries," wiping away his tears with the handkerchief which Mendel offers him, we are witnessing not hysterics, but catharsis, the recovery of emotional balance and good spirits through the contemplation of another's suffering. Everything is in order, life goes on.

Still, the play is not called *Sunset* for nothing. It is about what is passing away, not what is to come; it is about destruction and death. The commodious symbol of sunset refers to much more than the collapse of past greatness and the outdated expectations of the horse-and-cart driver Mendel Krik, to more even than the decline of old Odessa. It is the entire old order that is collapsing, its very foundations crumbling into dust. However dubious Mendel Krik may seem in the role of patriarch, he is nevertheless the father, and we know what the father means in Jewish tradition, and especially for Babel. "Honor thy father and thy mother, that thy days may be long." "Whosoever curses his father or mother shall be put to death." "You shall rise up before the hoary head and honor the face of an old man." Yet here the face of the old father has been beaten and lacerated by the leaden fists of his sons.

"The sun also ariseth, and the sun goeth down." What this rising sun would be and what sort of world it would illuminate, Babel did not know as he worked on *Sunset*. It would be straining interpretation to assert that he was lamenting with Arye-Leib the decline of the old Jewish tradition, however bound to it he was emotionally and even, as it were, umbilically; it would be still less defensible to see in the gangsters Benya and Levka a caricatured allegory of the new, revolutionary order of things. But there is no blinking the way grief and anxiety in *Sunset* predominate over the "bubbling joviality" (the phrase is from "Discourse on the *Tachanka*") of the *Odessa Tales*.

Sunset proved the beginning of Babel's own sunset. The "great breaking point" broke his backbone, too. There would still be some flights—and high ones; but there would no longer be any confident or consistent ascent. Among the chief reasons was the departure of the Jews from the Russian scene—not Mendel Krik, but the whole of that Jewry which was Babel's own. Assimilation was proceeding at breakneck speed. To the new forms of Jewish life permitted and encouraged by the authorities at the end of the

1920s and beginning of the 1930s, Babel apparently remained indifferent. As far as I am aware, he made no comment whatever on the Jewish "province" of Birobidzhan. In 1931, the Society for the Agricultural Settlement of Jewish Workers wanted to show him the new Jewish agricultural settlements in the Ukraine. He mentions this briefly in his letters, without any interest, and fails even to say whether or not he took up the invitation. He was not really interested or involved in Yiddish culture, despite his love of Sholom Aleichem, his connection with the Yiddish theater and friendship with the actor Solomon Mikhoels, and his good relations with certain Yiddish writers. The Russian-Jewish writer had had the ground cut out from under his feet.

The ascents of the last decade are, in the main, connected with the Jewish theme or with the narrator Liutov's manner of perception in *Red Cavalry*: the last two stories of the autobiographical cycle (1930), and the superb "The Road" (1932) are pure Liutov. Liutov's spirit also permeates Babel's masterpiece, "Guy de Maupassant"—published in 1932, but, according to the author, dating from 1920–22. I am inclined to assign another remarkable story, "Dante Street" (1934), to this category, for its emotional key—the most important component of the story—is desperate loneliness: "There is no loneliness more desperate than loneliness in Paris." As for the *Odessa Tales*, their manner extends to "The End of the Old Folks' Home" (author's date 1920–29, published 1932 with the subtitle "From the Odessa Tales") and "Froim Grach" (submitted for publication 1933, published posthumously). One can hardly call the latter an "ascent," but the two stories are linked (and detached from the *Odessa Tales*) by the motif of departure, death, and regret for what is gone which is particularly sharp in "Froim Grach."

In 1935, Babel announced: "I would like to tell the world everything I know about old Odessa; after that I will be able to go on to the new Odessa." In fact he had undertaken to confront the new Odessa earlier, in 1931, when he published his story, "Karl-Yankel." But the attempt was not a success—as Babel himself realized. In a letter written in February 1932, he expresses astonishment that the critics should pay any attention to such rubbish, and he calls the story simply bad. He cannot handle the new Odessa because he has no tender feeling for it. The scandal about the circumcision of the newborn Karl-Yankel in the story of that name is inflated not merely in itself, but is inflated and artificial for Babel, who is forcing himself and cannot disguise the fact. The same element of artificiality appears in the stereotype, Ovsei Belotserkovskii, who stockpiles farm supplies with the help of the Balta and Tiraspo district party committees. It appears in the feeding of the infant by the Kirghiz woman—a sugary vignette illustrative of the "indestructible friendship of the peoples of the USSR"—and in the pathos of the narrator's concluding exclamations. On the other hand, there is nothing false, despite some crude grotesque, in the "little operator" Naftula Gerchik; the page and a half devoted to him are Babel at his best.

Throughout the 1930s, Babel was searching for a new style. Both his letters and his public speeches are full of complaints about the agonizing difficulties of the search. He was looking not only for new expressive forms but, above all, for another atmosphere, another milieu, new ground under his feet. Beyond the bounds of Russian-Jewish literature, however, success would not favor him—even though he knew the Soviet Union very well, loved it devotedly, was himself loved and surrounded everywhere by friends. As I have said, the reasons for this are various and each has its own measure of validity; still, it would appear that the loss of his dual position, his dual vision, had a crucial effect. It is not in evidence—nor could it be—when he is regarding something entirely alien, as, for example, the high aristocracy (in the play *Mariia*), even if by accident of revolution a Jewish speculator has managed to worm his way into its midst. Gorky, incidentally—who justifiably disliked *Mariia*—wrote to Babel: "I especially don't like Dymshits. . . . You make him too easy a target for the Judeophobes." I imagine such apprehensions had never occurred to Babel. The Jewish writer portrays a Jewish villain as naturally and unselfconsciously as a Russian writer would a Russian villain, and neither would worry about what the Judeophobes or the Russophobes might say. Even so, there is no dual vision when one examines a thing of one's own making: in the two surviving fragments of a lost novel about collectivization ("Kolyvushka" and "Gapa Guzhva"), Babel is truthful, that is, true to himself—but he is unable to detach himself from the material, to stand to one side, and the sharpness, clarity, and depth of his account suffer in consequence.

Babel is the most important figure in Russian-Jewish literature of the Soviet period, the model of the Jewish writer in Soviet-Russian culture. The Russian-Jewish literature that was reborn after Stalin takes its bearings from him, and is measured against him. To imitate Babel is impossibly difficult, to repeat him impossible—just as his fate is unrepeatable, just as old Odessa and turn-of-the-century Russian Jewry are beyond recall. But one can compare, assess, learn. It is unlikely that anyone today will be tempted by Babel's second standpoint, the Russian Revolution. But his feelings and views suggest the possibility of another much more attractive "bifurcation." I have in mind some such oppositions as these: insularity, rigidity, inhibition, hypertrophied rationalism—as against openness, emotional release, fullness of feeling, the joy of existence. That is what the dialogue in the bedroom of the old Kriks in *Sunset* is all about. Nekhama nags her husband: "Look how other people live. For supper, other people have ten pounds of meat, they make soup, they make cutlets, they make compote. The father comes home from work, everybody sits at the table, everybody eats and laughs. But what do *we* do?" And Mendel snarls back: "Pull out my teeth, Nekhama, pour some Yiddish soup into my veins, break my back." Here is the root of Babel's ill-concealed delight in his gangsters, in the violent, dangerous crank Simon-Wolf, in grandfather Levi Yitzhok, the ex-rabbi who lost his post for crooked dealing in currency, "the laughing-stock of the town, and its embellishment" ("In the Basement," "Awakening"). Here also is the sense of the ending of "The Story of a Horse," a remarkable paragraph which has been endlessly quoted: "Khlebnikov was a quiet man, like me in character. We were both rocked by the same passions. We both looked on the world as a meadow in May, a meadow where women and horses moved about."

Not to reject tradition, not to turn away from one's own history, not to wallow either in the fruits of the Diaspora or in its rubbish, but instead, to leap into freedom, into open space, to burst free from one's chains, to know the taste, color, scent, texture of everything denied us by the ghetto wall, the Pale of Settlement, and that invisible pale which we put around ourselves and in which we suffocated for century upon century. And to find harmony in dichotomy.

This is not written in Babel's work, it is only implied. But the idea of this paradoxical harmony, which is not at all the same thing as peace and quiet and heavenly grace, comes to mind constantly when one looks at the old guard of the kibbutzim, the settlers of Palestine in the 1930s. It comes to mind with increasing frequency as one thinks of the Jews of Silence, who have now become the Jews of courage.

MAURICE FRIEDBERG

Yiddish Folklore Motifs in Isaak Babel''s Konarmija

To a Russian or, for that matter, a Ukrainian reader the locale of Isaak Babel''s *Konarmija* is the epitome of provincial backwaters, and the drab little towns in which its action unfolds evoke no significant associations. A student of literary trivia may recall, if only through Chekhov's *Tri sestry* [*Three Sisters*], that Berdičev is the place where Balzac had married. Not so a reader familiar with the Jewish tradition. Peripheral to Slavic history, the dusty and muddy towns of the Ukraine through which Babel' takes his reader occupy a very important place in the annals of East Europe's Jewry. It was there that in the second half of the eighteenth century Hasidism made its appearance—a movement that sprang up in opposition to an overly intellectualized Judaism, emphasizing instead an emotional and joyful community with God. A map of the Ukraine appended to a recent volume of Hasidic teachings barely notes the existence of some of the Ukraine's major cities and completely ignores others (for instance, Xar'kov, for a time the capital of the Soviet Ukraine, does not even appear on it). On the other hand, the map prominently indicates the towns that Babel''s *Konarmija* made familiar to millions of people throughout the world—Berdičev, Ostropol', Belaja Cerkov', Novograd, Brody, Žitomir.

While Jewish subject matter is found in most of Babel''s work, three stories from *Konarmija* deal more specifically with the world of the Hasidim. All three, "Gedali," "Rabbi," and "Syn rabbi," are set in or refer to the town

---

From *American Contributions to the Eighth International Congress of Slavists*, vol. 2, edited by Victor Terras. © 1978 by Slavica Publishers and Maurice Friedberg.

of Žitomir, and their central protagonists are, respectively, a follower of the Hasidic *Rebbe,* the *Rebbe* himself and his rebellious son.

To a greater extent than most writers, Babel' shows little concern for the authenticity of details in his descriptions of *byt.* We do not refer here merely to *improbable* situations introduced by Babel' for the sake of heightened exoticism—which are the hallmarks of his prose—but to virtually impossible ones. Thus, in the story "Rabbi" the *Rebbe*'s son is shown smoking in his father's presence on the Sabbath, with his cigarette then snatched away by the *Rebbe*'s court jester Reb Mordxe [Mordecai]. Later, Reb Mordxe also accepts money offered to him by Babel''s narrator. Observant orthodox Jews, of course, would no more handle fire or money on the Sabbath than they would eat pork. Still, in matters more central to the unfolding of the three stories of *Konarmija*—"Gedali," "Rabbi," and "Syn rabbi"—we may assume that the author exercised greater care in his choice of detail.

Rebbe Motalè of Žitomir is described as a member of "the Černobyl' dynasty." It is true that Hasidism was popular in Žitomir since the latter part of the eighteenth century. Similarly, the existence of a Černobyl' dynasty of Hasidic *rebbes* is a matter of historical record. Babel''s *Rebbe* Motalè, however, is emphatically presented as "the last *rebbe*" of the Černobyl' line, and his son Il'ja as "the last prince of the dynasty." The fact of the matter is that the Černobyl' dynasty is not extinct. It continues to exist, among others, in Europe, Israel, and the Americas. Before hastening to relegate this detail to academic pedantry, let us also recall that members of the Černobyl' dynasty bore the last name of Tverskij (Twersky). Thus, the last name of Babel''s *Rebbe* Motalè and his son—Braclavskij—contains a revealing clue. That name is associated with one of the most unusual Hasidic groups, one whose founder, *Rebbe* Nahman ben Simhah of Braclav (1772–1811) was also its last living leader. Alone among Hasidic groups which center around the person of the *rebbe,* the Braclaver (or Breslover) have no living leader. They are led, so to speak, by the memory of their founder. Often taunted by their rivals as the "dead Hasidim," the Braclaver are fond of replying, "better a dead *rebbe* who *lives* than a living *rebbe* who is *dead.*" During Rebbe Nahman's lifetime the Braclav sect had little success (it consisted but of a few impoverished followers), although, a century later, "Bratslav Hasidim continued to exist in Podolia in the Soviet regime" (*Encyclopedia Judaica*). At present, paradoxically, the Braclaver are among the more successful Hasidic groups, with four religious seminaries (*yeshivot*) in Israel and an impressive number of adherents in the United States. Indeed, the Braclav Hasidim retains strong memories of its geographic origins:

As recently as 1963, a group of eleven young American Breslover Chasidim received special permission from the Russian authorities to visit the burial place of the Rebbe in the city of Uman.... The cemetery in which the Rebbe had been buried no longer exists. Small country houses have been created in that place. But the tzaddik's [righteous man's—MF] grave has miraculously managed to survive the change of time. It remains to this day, in the yard of one of the Russian citizens of the area.
(Gedaliah Fleer, *Rabbit Nachman's Fire: An Introduction to Breslover Chassidus*)

Echoes of *Rebbe* Nahman's life and work are scattered throughout Babel''s work. Gedali, a name much favored among the *rebbe*'s followers, was given to one of Babel's most famous stories and also to its central character, the founder of the messianic International. By contrast, Ar'e-Leib, "the grand old man" of Špolja and Rebbe Nahman's chief detractor, bequeathed his to the old skeptic of Babel''s "Kak èto delalos' v Odesse" ("How It Was Done in Odessa"). Our concern here, however, is a more basic one: what was it that attracted Babel' to the Hasidic *rebbe*?

The answer is, of course, that *Rebbe* Nahman was himself no less unusual as a religious leader than his followers were to become as a sect, and Babel' was neither the first nor the last Western intellectual to be fascinated by him. Early in this century the writings of *Rebbe* Nahman were edited and published by the philosopher and theologian Martin Buber, and more recently by the Franco-American novelist Elie Wiesel. There is also evidence that they were admired by Franz Kafka. Babel', who was fluent in Yiddish and could read Hebrew with ease, most likely read some of the works of *Rebbe* Nahman of Braclav that were frequently republished early in the twentieth century.

Rebbe Nahman of Braclav's unique appeal to Babel' (and later also to such authors as Elie Wiesel) was almost certainly the fact that he, too, was a creative writer. In 1806, *Rebbe* Nahman declared, "I can see that my ideas have no effect on you, therefore I shall tell you stories; and I shall tell them in Yiddish, so as not to give you the excuse of having misunderstood." He also said, "If one believes what people say, stories are written to put them to sleep; I tell mine to wake them up" (Elie Wiesel, *Souls on Fire*).

Babel''s affinity for *Rebbe* Nahman of Braclav extended even further. Consider Eli Wiesel's description of the *rebbe*'s tales:

All are inhabited by princes and sages. By haunted creatures seeking one another, one in another. By survivors of calamities, refugees, fugitives, messengers and innocent children, orphans and beggars endlessly roaming the world.

Not surprisingly, many contemporaries disapproved of *Rebbe* Nahman's literary activities:

> That a Rebbe should waste his time and that of his faithful inventing fables, well, one could accept that. But that his tales should speak not of saints and miracle Rebbes but of princes and shepherds, of anonymous beggars and horsemen, of sages and messengers—and not even Jewish ones at that—could only dismay them. . . . But Rebbe Nahman was stubborn: he cared about his beggars and his princes.
>
> (Wiesel)

"Princes and Shepherds, anonymous beggars and horsemen, sages and messengers—and not even Jewish ones at that"—is this not a reasonably accurate list of characters from Babel''s *Konarmija*? Is not this, and Babel''s other works, concerned above all with "survivors of calamities, refugees, fugitives, messengers and innocent children, orphans and beggars endlessly romaning the world"?

There was yet another feature of *Rebbe* Nahman of Braclav's legacy that probably attracted Babel', and that was the *Rebbe*'s insistence on the virtue of joy and the perils of sadness. Thus, in Rabbi Nathan of Nemirov's transcription of *Rebbe* Nahman's *dicta* we read:

> Joy is a vessel to draw fresh understanding. . . . Even repentance should be attained through joy. We should rejoice so much in God that it will arouse in us regret for having offended Him. . . . God dislikes melancholy and depressed spirits. Joy is a cure for illnesses caused by melancholy. It is a duty of the joyful person to endeavor to bring to those in sadness and melancholy a portion of his mood.
>
> (*The Hasidic Anthology: Tales and Teachings of the Hasidim*)

On another occasion Rebbe Nahman was more explicit:

> Sadness and depression are extremely destructive and give power to the evil inclination. Therefore, one must vigorously strive to maintain a joyous state of mind at all times. . . . *Sometimes one must resort to superficial frolic or jest in order to cause the rekindling of inner happiness and joy, for all of our strength is*

> *dependent upon this happiness,* according to "rejoicing with God, that is our strength" (Nehemiah, 8:10).
>
> (Fleer)

The above may help explain an otherwise puzzling scene in the story "Rabbi." *Rebbe* Motalè inquires about the narrator's occupation, to which he replies that he is "setting in verse the adventures of Hershele Ostropoler." Hershele was to East European Jews what Tyll Eulenspiegel was to the Germans or Mulla Nasreddin to the Turkic peoples, and there was nothing remotely sacred or even edifying about his exploits. Astonishingly, *Rebbe* Motalè's reaction is one of awe:

> "A great labor," the *rebbe* whispered and closed his eyelids. "A jackal groans when he is hungry and every fool possesses enough foolishness for sadness, but only the wise man rips open with laughter the curtain of existence."
>
> ("The Rabbi's Son")

The incident appears less enigmatic when one assumes that *Rebbe* Motalè was an adherent of Nahman of Braclav. It also accounts for the *Rebbe*'s satisfaction with the narrator's seemingly "irresponsible" goal in life, which is expressed in a single word, "Joy" (*vesel'e*).

Explicit references link the story "Syn rabbi" to both "Rabbi" and "Gedali." In fact, it was in "Rabbi" that we first meet the *Rebbe*'s son. The references to the son's strong physical resemblance to Spinoza are, of course, a signal that the son is a thinker, a heretic and, like Spinoza in the seventeenth century, will be "excommunicated and cut off from the Nation of Israel" (*Encyclopedia Judaica*). When we meet him again in "Syn rabbi" the *Rebbe*'s son is a Red Army soldier running a high fever and on the verge of death. We learn that young Braclavskij was already a Communist when we first made his acquaintance, but would not leave his mother. Curiously, *both* his rebellion against his father and his love for his mother are echoed in the writings of *Rebbe* Nahman of Braclav. The assumption that young Braclavskij was brought up in the house of a Braclav *Hasid* also necessitates a revealing of the scene in which the dying soldier's belongings reveal, "side by side," a portrait of Lenin and one of Maimonides. Traditionally, this was interpreted as Braclavskij's attempt to reconcile his religious Jewish heritage with the teachings of Communism—much as Gedali, in the story of the same name, would like to say "yes" to the Revolution, provided this did not also require saying "no" to the Sabbath. If, however, the Braclavskijs were followers of *Rebbe* Nahman, the scene acquires a different meaning. Although Maimonides

(1135–1204) is generally acknowledged as Judaism's greatest spiritual leader in two thousand years, and his *Guide to the Perplexed* was intended to strengthen the faltering faith of skeptics, there were those who disapproved of the tractate. Specifically, *Rebbe* Nahman of Braclav forbade his disciples to read philosophical works, "Maimonides included" (Wiesel). The choice between Lenin and Maimonides was thus not between heresy and tradition, but between *two brands of heresy,* each offering advice to the perplexed— with Lenin, ironically, *not* officially proscribed the Hasidic master. Similarly, the mention of *The Song of Songs* contains some ambiguities. Although interpreted by the Rabbinic sources as an allegory of love of the People of Israel for the Lord, in some Hasidic circles it was associated with mystical eroticism.

The younger Braclavskij's name, Il'ja, a Russian version of the Hebrew Élija or Élijahu, has three major associations. In the Biblical traditions (Kings I and II), Elijah appears as an intransigent prophet, ruthless and fearless in his defense of the faith from unbelievers. In the oral tradition of the Aggadah, Elijah's appearance heralds the advent of the Messiah; it is also in this role that Elijah appears at the Passover ceremony. Finally, in Jewish folklore Elijah is "portrayed as the heavenly emissary sent on earth to combat social injustice. He rewards the poor who are hospitable and punishes the greedy rich" (*Encyclopedia Judaica*). Clearly, all three associations blend well with Babel''s Il'ja Braclavskij, an uncompromising fighter for what he views as a just and happy future.

The death of "the last Prince of the dynasty" is presented by Babel' both as a result of the incompatibility of Il'ja Braclavskij's military inexperience and sentimentalism with the stern realities of the Revolution, as well as an outcome of his overall "exhaustion": readers are shown that *in any case,* Il'ja Braclavskij could not possibly sire any progeny. His death is thus simultaneously violent—an outcome of the war—and natural. And if the death of Il'ja Braclavskij marks the end of an old Hasidic dynasty, it may also be interpreted as the death of the *founder* of a *new* dynasty of *Communist* Braclavskijs. Viewed from the vantage point of the tradition of the Hasidim of Braclav, Il'ja's death is not to be construed as the defeat of his cause. Quite the contrary—his cause, weak during his lifetime, shall gain adherents after its founder's death. It is in this sense that one may understand the narrator's closing words—"I accepted the last breath of my brother" (*Ja prinjal poslednij vzdox moego brata*).

Significantly, neither *Rebbe* Motalè nor his son Il'ja are allowed to theorize on the nature of Hasidism: a leader and a would-be leader, they should be content with the carrying out of functions the movement assigns to them. The honor of commenting on the doctrine of Hasidim falls to Gedali, the frail owner of the old curiosity shop. Before taking the narrator to spend Sabbath eve with *Rebbe* Motalè, Gedali says:

> "Windows are shattered and doors are smashed in the impassioned edifice of Hasidism, but it remains immortal, like a mother's soul. . . . Even with its eye sockets empty, Hasidism remains standing at the crossroads of history's furious winds."
>
> ("The Rabbi")

Earlier, in the story bearing his name, Gedali shares with the narrator a few misgivings about the Revolution and also his dream of an "International of kind people." Let us examine these in the light of Gedali's self-proclaimed adherence to Hasidism, specifically to the teachings of *Rebbe* Nahman of Braclav, and his acquaintance with the Talmud (*Ja učil kogda-to talmud*).

Gedali's indignation at the fact that the Reds, who came to Žitomir as liberators, requisitioned his record player is no mere concern for private property. Rather, it reflects the fear that this may be a portend of worse misfortunes, for *Rebbe* Nahman taught: "He who is ready to steal is prepared to commit every offense" (*The Hasidic Anthology*). And conversely, Gedali's readiness to voluntarily give up all record players to kind people (*Privezite dobryx ljudej, i my otdadim im vse grammofony*) is in full accord with *Rebbe* Nahman's commandment: "Be not ungrateful either to a Jew or a non-Jew" (*The Hasidic Anthology*). It also supports the medieval *Sefer Hasidim* which "holds up a noble act performed by a Christian as one most worthy of emulation by Jews" (*Encyclopedia Judaica*).

Gedali's readiness to believe in the advent of a quasi-Messianic Revolution that would sweep away injustice and want is, again, consonant with the teachings of *Rebbe* Nahman who said, over a century earlier, that "Many of the non-Jewish nations are near to repentance" (*The Hasidic Anthology*). Similarly, Gedali's famous utterance "And I want an International of kind people, I want every person to be registered and given first category rations"—every person, whether Jew or Gentile—is firmly rooted in Talmudic and Hasidic tradition. Thus, in this world the "Talmud enjoins that Gentile poor be supported with charity like Jewish poor (Git. 61a) and does not even tolerate the charging of interest to Gentiles (BM 706)" (*Encyclopedia Judaica*). As for the post-Messianic era, the Talmud insists that the righteous of all nations will equally share in its blessings. And who are Gedali's "kind people"? *Rebbe* Nahman of Braclav admonishes his followers to seek out goodness among *all* human beings, including personal enemies: "A man should also seek the good in another and judge every man in the scale of merit; this applies even to those who abuse and quarrel with him" (*The Hasidic Anthology*). At the end of the story "The Sabbath is ushered in. Gedali, the founder of an International that will never be, went to synagogue to pray." As *Rebbe* Nahman of Braclav taught, "The Sabbath candles increase peace," and "Peace brings good tidings." However impractical, the old man's vision of an International of kind people was a noble one. That was recognized by Isaak Babel', who named his slightly built hero Gedali. In Hebrew, Gedali means "great."

Isaak Babel', the writer, may have felt a sense of kinship with the following dicta of *Rebbe* Nahman of Braclav:

1. He who is able to write a book and does not write it, is as one who has lost a child.
2. Every author should weigh his work to determine whether it has any connection with the "Book of Humanity," namely whether humanity will receive any benefit from it.

(The Hasidic Anthology)

A question may arise: if Babel' was, in fact, so indebted to *Rebbe* Nahman of Braclav, why did he not acknowledge that debt other than giving a hint in the name "Braclavskij"? An answer was provided nearly two centuries ago by *Rebbe* Nahman himself:

It is oftentimes easy for the man of culture to discover whether an author has originated the ideas included in his book, or whether they are merely copied by him.

(The Hasidic Anthology)

GREGORY FREIDIN

Fat Tuesday in Odessa: Isaac Babel's "Di Grasso" as Testament and Manifesto

> *I am ashamed to take a close look at Babel.*
> —VICTOR SHKLOVSKII, "I, Babel': A Critical Romance"

If one were to search among the painters of the past for an illustrator who could do justice to the collected works of Isaac Babel, the name of Peter Bruegel the Elder, the Hellish Bruegel, would surely be the first to come up. For even though they were separated by four centuries, both the artist and the writer looked at life in a similar way—as a ceaseless combat between the upside-down world of Carnival and the grim and right side-up world of the philistine Lent. The editor of this hypothetical illustrated collection of Babel's writings would most likely assign "Di Grasso" (1937) the ultimate place. Written two years before the author's arrest and disappearance, the story deserves to be read as a testament or, better still, as a retrospective manifesto that Babel issued as a parting festive shot at the encroaching army of Lent. The story's very title would justify the editor's choice, for the title "Di Grasso" refers not only to the central character of the tale but also to the festival, central to the carnival tradition, namely, Shrove or Fat Tuesday, Mardi gras or, in Italian, Marte*di Grasso*.

Indeed, carnivalesque vision, to borrow the term from Mikhail Bakhtin, informs most, if not the whole, of Babel's fiction. He promised to

---

From *The Russian Review: An American Quarterly Devoted to Russia Past and Present* 40, 2 (April 1981). © 1980 by the Russian Review, Inc. (Hoover Institution, Stanford, California).

develop this tradition as early as the programmatic sketch "Odessa" (1916), and his stories—from the first major cycle *Tales of Odessa* (1921–23) to the penultimate "Di Grasso"—demonstrate that he never failed in this pledge. His seemingly incongruous but highly effective and well-ordered style that allowed him "to speak in the same voice about the stars above and about gonorrhea" (Viktor Shklovsky, "Isaac Babel: A Critical Romance") comes from the same allegiance to the carnival tradition with its festive world whose image Babel cherished in the works of Gogol, Maupassant and, of course, Rabelais. But the carnival is not the only aspect of "Di Grasso" that lends the story its significance as a testament-manifesto.

As often happens in Babel, "Di Grasso" is structured around an epiphany, in this case, in fact, two epiphanies—one of passion and violence, the other of tranquility and contemplative beauty. The echoes of Nietzsche's *The Birth of Tragedy* reverberate through "Di Grasso" with as much power as in an earlier story "Pan Apolek"—a story about a Polish painter who imitated in his name and life the Dionysian demi-god Pan and the god of plastic beauty Apollo. In "Di Grasso," as in many other of his stories, Babel's concerns with an integral aesthetic, encompassing beauty and ugliness, pleasure and pain, runs parallel to his preoccupation with psychological problems of individuation, the quest for manhood, and, of course, sex, especially sex. His search for truth and justice in the humble, "primitive" form of popular culture, so obvious in *Tales of Odessa*, also finds its way into "Di Grasso." Finally, the story contains a number of motifs that reappear throughout the body of Babel's writings with remarkable regularity. These are various forms of decapitation in an erotic context, transfer of masculine attributes to a female (or the other way around), as well as the motif of paternal threat, whether it comes from the father himself or from father-like authority figures. Keeping all these observations in mind, I propose, then, to examine "Di Grasso" both separately and in relation to a number of other stories in the hope that a discussion of this sort will help to illuminate some of the underlying and, therefore submerged, patterns which shape and support the complex edifice of Babel's fiction.

Written in the form of a childhood recollection, "Di Grasso" nevertheless is rather different from Babel's other fictional reminiscences, such as "The Story of My Dovecot," "In the Basement," "First Love," and "The Awakening." First of all, it is much shorter both in the amount of time that it covers and in its actual length. Secondly, its thematic content, packed into a compact frame, possesses an unusual depth, since the main narrative incorporates within itself another narrative, a play performed by a travelling troupe of di Grasso. Yet, the story's matter-of-fact beginning ("I was fourteen years old") assumes the reader's familiarity with Babel's other "childhood" stories, thereby suggesting that the author planned to include "Di Grasso" into a cycle of autobiographical fiction, analogous to the *Tales of Odessa* and *The Cavalry*. But now, before proceeding with the discussion, I would like to pause in order to present the story in a brief outline.

At the time of the story, the narrator is a fourteen-year-old boy who is making money by scalping tickets at the Odessa Theater. The season has not been profitable and in order to maintain himself in the business, the boy had to steal his father's gold watch and pawn it for cash to the head of the scalpers, Kolia Schwartz, a man of habit, who preferred drinking Bessarabian wine, instead of tea, for breakfast. Considering Shaliapin's fee too steep, the theater impresario decided in desperation to invite an inexpensive Sicilian troupe led by a tragedian actor di Grasso. The sight of the troupe, which looked like a band of gypsies on peasant carts, did not bode well. Nor did di Grasso himself inspire much confidence in the bankrupt scalpers. Upon arrival in the city, he went to the market with a humble shopping bag and, carrying the same shopping bag, appeared at the theater before the performance.

Things were going from bad to worse. The opening play, a "Sicilian folk drama," was singularly unassuming—ordinary "as the change from day to night." The daughter of a well-to-do peasant betrothed to a humble shepherd (di Grasso), abandons him in favor of Giovanni, a city slicker, who came to the village for the country fair. During the intermission between act 1 and act 2, the girl has ripened for the ultimate betrayal. Neither the shepherd's passionate pleas nor his invocation of the Holy Virgin can change her frivolous mind, and in the third act the audience sees di Grasso taking revenge on the haughty Giovanni. As a barber was shaving Giovanni in the middle of the village square, di Grasso—suddenly and in apparent defiance of the laws of man and nature—leaps across the stage in a single bound and, landing on Giovanni's shoulders, bites through his neck and proceeds to suck the blood out of the wound. The curtain falls, thus concealing the murderer and his victim. This quite literally transcendent leap brings down the house and earns di Grasso the title of the "greatest tragedian actor of the century," so, at least, in the next morning's paper.

The success of the first performance turns out to be so great that the scalpers hawk the tickets at five times their nominal prices, and the boy makes enough money to redeem his father's watch. But Kolia Schwartz, a man of habit, has by now gotten used to the gold watch and refuses to return it even though he has already accepted the boy's money. The character of the boy's father was no different from that of the unyielding Kolia

Schwartz, and, terrified by the prospect of his father's wrath, the boy resolves to run away to Constantinople. But he cannot leave Odessa before paying his last homage to di Grasso, the great actor, who has taught him that "in the frenzy of noble passion there was more hope and justice than in the joyless rules of this world."

Luckily for the boy, Kolia Schwartz brings to the final performance his wife, a woman "fit to be a grenadier and as long as the steppe with a crumpled-up little face at the edge of the horizon." Leaving the theater and touched to tears by di Grasso's passionate performance, Madame Schwartz gives a dressing down to her husband, scolding him for all the "animal things" he has done to her without any display of love or affection. The boy, who followed the couple from the theater, is now weeping nearby. Madame Schwartz takes pity on the boy and, speaking from the position of emotional strength commensurate with her size, orders her husband to return the watch. Left alone, with his father's watch regained, the boy experiences an epiphany of tranquility and beauty which serves as a counterpoint to the earlier epiphany of di Grasso's passion and pain. The end.

"Di Grasso" is obviously one of those stories which may be characterized by their central thematic intent: art, no matter how "primitive," and passion, no matter how violent, redeem life. This is not a new theme for Babel. Some of his more famous stories, such as "Pan Apolek," "The Rabbi," "In the Basement," "The Awakening," "Guy de Maupassant," and "My First Honorarium," make the same point. All of them, likewise, possess a strong carnivalesque quality, expressed in the motifs of debasement, often androgyny and sexual license, and always laughter. But in none of them is the carnival as much in the foreground as it is in "Di Grasso." The theatrical nature of the carnival is presented here as it were directly, in the framed "Sicilian *folk* drama," while the line that separates the life of the audience from the life on stage is erased as completely as it can only happen in a true carnival where everybody is an actor and a mask. Here is how Babel describes the transformation of the money- and status-conscious Odessa following the first performance of di Grasso:

> A stream of dusty, pink sultry air was let into the Theater Lane. Shopkeepers in felt slippers took out into the street small barrels with olives and large green bottles of wine. In huge vats before the shops, macaroni was cooking in boiling frothy water, and the rising steam was dissolving in the distant skies. Old women wearing men's boots were hawking sea shells and souvenirs, and yelling in loud voices, were pursuing the hesitant customers.

Rich Jews with their parted well-combed beards were arriving at the Hotel North and were knocking softly on the doors of the mustachioed fat brunettes, the actresses from di Grasso's troupe. Everybody was happy in the Theater Lane, except for one man, and that man was I.

All the constraints that have been giving shape to the "official" (Bakhtin's term), non-festive life have been loosened: food and wine are in abundance and are brought out into the street, age and gender distinctions have become blurred, and even the respectable Jewish patriarchs are now indulging their sexual appetites with unusual abandon.

This carnivalesque blending of theater and life in Babel's narrative makes it legitimate to analyze the characters without paying much attention to the distinctions between the main and the framed story. Two groups of characters emerge once these distinctions are put aside: one festive and the other "Lenten." The first group includes the "Lord of Misrule" di Grasso, who is the shepherd of the play, and the androgynous and emotional Madame Schwartz together with her protegé, who is the narrator of the story. Opposed to them are the Lenten combatants: the comic Kolia Schwartz, who is the unfair lord of the scalpers, the play's Giovanni, and the oppressive shadow of the boy's father, who shares some nasty attributes with Mr. Schwartz. Given this set-up, the plot of the story may be represented as a carnivalesque uncrowning of the official king (Kolia Schwartz and, by implication, the boy's father) and the establishment of the rule of the carnival—the fat day, Mardi gras or Martedì grasso.

Babel was thoroughly familiar with French literature (some of his juvenilia was, in fact, written in French), and there can be little doubt that he knew and appreciated the carnival tradition, especially in the monumental work of Rabelais. It is in the context of this tradition that the dispute over the *father's watch* acquires an unmistakable archetypal significance. Time, over the ages, has become firmly associated in this tradition with the father of Zeus, Kronos. The primarily oral dissemination of the myth is, to a large extent, responsible for the eventual obliteration of the difference between Kronos (κρoνoς) and Chronos (χρoνoς), which in the popular consciousness helped to fuse the story of succession with the mythic concept of time. Perceived at once as an attribute of the warring father and son, time has become an ambivalent entity, a "carnivalesque" image, implying indivisibility of death renewal. In the nonfestive culture, however, with its inflexible hierarchical structure of authority, time belonged to the "elders," who frustrated the process of renewal, as the mythic Kronos attempted to do when he kept swallowing his own children. A father and a god, an authority figure *par excellence,* Kronos was unwilling to yield his place to his own progeny, preventing the new generation from supplanting him—in short, he wanted to stop time. The Roman festival of Saturnalia (sometimes known as Kronia) served a ritual function of loosening the grip that Father Time, in his negative connotation, held on the succession of generations. Mardi gras, a direct descendent of Saturnalia, functioned in very much the same way, uncrowning and putting to death the mock king at the end of the festivities. In his book on Rabelais, Bakhtin cites an incident that Goethe recorded in his *Italian Journey* in order to demonstrate how deeply the theme of rivalry between the father and son, the old and the new time, was embedded in the tradition of the Roman carnival, Martedi grasso. On Shrove Tuesday, as the festival was drawing to a close, Goethe saw a boy blow out his father's candle while calling out: "Sia ammazzato il signor padre!" ("Death to you, sir father!")

In Babel's work, this theme of the father, preventing his son from asserting himself, plays a prominent role. While other themes may obscure it in such stories as "The Story of My Dovecot" and "The Awakening," it comes to the foreground as the main vehicle of the plot in *The Sunset,* the play and the companion story with the same title. There, Mendel, the father of the famous Benia Krik, schemes to abandon his old wife and marry a young Russian girl, Marusia. But his wish comes to naught when he is beaten into a pulp by his children who are as concerned with the fate of their inheritance as they are with maintaining the natural succession of generations:

> "Benia," he said, "let us pluck up our courage, and people will come and kiss our feet. Let us kill our father, who is no longer called Mendel Krik by the Moldavanka. The Moldavanka calls him Mendel Pogrom."
>
> "This is not the time," Benia replied, "but the time *is* coming. Listen to its footsteps and make way for it."

It should not take a great effort to see in this story a version of the archetypal mythos of Kronos, struggling to defeat his father Uranus, or the well-known sequence to it, the story of Kronos defeated in a similar manner by his own son Zeus.

In "Di Grasso," the heavy burden of playing the role of the archetypal Saturn falls on the feeble shoulders of Kolia Schwartz, the mock alter ego of the boy's father. And just as in the myth of Kronos, it is the god's wife, Madame Schwartz, who delivers the child from what seemed like sure perdition. Now the father will get back his watch and spare his son, following Kronos, who swallowed instead of Zeus a stone wrapped in swaddling clothes. All of this is the work of the Lord of Misrule, di Grasso, who has transformed the formidable Kronos-Schwartz into a mock king to be ritually put to death at the end of Martedi grasso.

The "Sicilian folk drama" in which di Grasso played the role of a superhuman shepherd functions as a pivot around which the plot of the story turns, for it establishes the pattern according to which the events in "real life" will actually unfold. The everyday, as it were "Lenten," life of Odessa where money and wealth threaten happiness and renewal will yield in the third part of the story to the "frenzy of noble passion," eros, that will transcend the "rules" and will set the world aright. The humble shepherd whose being is embedded in the succession of cycles in nature has defeated the young city lord (*barchuk*) Giovanni, who tried to impose the joyless rules on the natural order of things. Erotic passion gives di Grasso the power to make his transcendent leap and to murder the haughty Giovanni. But the unusual manner in which di Grasso performs this crime of passion—"he landed on Giovanni's shoulders and, having bitten through his throat, began, growling and with his eyes darting sideways, to suck the blood out of the wound"—that unusual manner requires special elaboration.

As I have mentioned earlier, the motif of decapitation, partial or complete, reappears throughout Babel with uncanny regularity. I use the term "decapitation" as a shorthand for the motif, since it includes not only beheading proper but other forms of damage inflicted on the uppermost part of the body, namely, the neck and the head. It would, of course, be possible to dismiss this group of images as just another instance of a modernist's penchant for grotesque violence, but the fact that these images consistently appear in a highly charged erotic context begs for a more careful treatment. So, let us put our shame aside and take a close look at Babel.

Indeed, in the very first story of *The Cavalry*, "Crossing the Zbruch," a story that is not even two pages long, the motif appears at the emphatically "thin necks" of the Jews hosting Liutov for the night, the eyes of the Brigade Commander that fall to the ground after he is shot in the eyes by Savitskii (Liutov's dream), and finally, the "ripped out throat" of an old Jew, the father of the pregnant woman who wakes up Liutov from his nightmare.

Likewise, Pan Apolek's icon of the decapitated John the Baptist presides as the central image in the two stories taking place—one in the Cathedral of Novograd, the other at St. Valentine's Church in Berestechko ("Pan Apolek" and "At St. Valentine's"). In "Pan Apolek," we find out that Pan

Romuald, the castrated aide of the Novograd priest ("The Church at Novograd") served as a prototype for the cut-off head of John the Baptist, an icon that regularly elicits raptures from the narrator of *The Cavalry*.

> John's head was cut off at a slant from his jagged neck. It rested on a clay platter clasped firmly by the big yellow fingers of a warrior. The face of the dead man looked familiar. I sensed the augury of a mystery. On the clay platter, I saw the dead head copied from Pan Romuald, the aide of the run-away priest.

Pan Apolek, the one who painted the icon, struggled with the Church's denial of robust sensuality and with its fastidious haughtiness and he eventually prevailed, affirming the "lowly," base, and natural forms of art and existence. Such was the mystery whose solution Liutov sensed in the icon of John the Baptist, linking the decapitated prophet with the *castrated* sexton of the Novograd Church.

In "Berestechko," the scene of another decapitation, this time of a Jew accused of spying by the Red Cossacks, Babel points to another aspect of the motif, seeing in it, albeit ironically, a form of a fertility ritual. But even though he encloses his statement in an ironic parenthesis—the murder is a cruel absurdity—the blood that flows out of the cut throat of a helpless victim cannot but suggest a ritual slaying, preparing the ground for the birth of a new era. It was, after all, in a similar manner that the murder of John the Baptist paved the way for the victory of Christianity.

> I walked out into the street. Notices were already posted announcing that the Division Commander Vinogradov will give a speech in the evening about the Second Congress of the Comintern [read: will preach the new Gospel, G. F.]. Right in front of my windows, several Cossacks were trying to shoot an old Jew with a silvery beard who was accused of espionage. The old man was screaming and tried to tear himself away from the Cossacks. Then Kudria from the machine gun regiment took him by his head and tucked it under his arm. The Jew grew calm and straddled his legs. With his right hand, Kudria drew out his dagger and carefully cut the old man's throat without besplattering himself.

"In St. Valentine's Church" offers another instance of Babel's use of the motif, reminiscent of Nietzsche's words about the voluptuous, "seductive" aspect of Christian martyrdom:

This Berestechko church possessed its own seductive point of view on the mortal sufferings of the sons of man. In this church, the saints marched to the execution with the picturesque air of Italian singers, and the black beards of executioners were shimmering like Holophernes's beard [the first chord of the motif, G. F.]. Right above the altar, I saw the sacrilegious picture of John the Baptist, belonging to the heretical and intoxicating brush of Apolek. On this icon, the Baptist was beautiful with that ambiguous and reticent beauty for the sake of which the concubines of kings lose their half-lost honor and blooming life.

Even Liutov himself, this puny bespectacled Jew, who had "suffered greatly on the field of learning," is drawn into the decapitation revelry of the Cossack world. In the famous "My First Goose," which properly ought to be called "My First Gander," Liutov is sent through the rites of passage by the "giant and beautiful Savitskii" who alerts him to the Cossacks' habit of cutting up people for wearing spectacles. This, it should be remembered, is the same Savitskii who in Liutov's nightmare ("Crossing the Zbruch") performed a symbolic castration on the Brigade Commander for ordering his soldiers to retreat. At first utterly despised by the Cossacks, Liutov eventually wins their favor by proving to them that he can speak their ritual language nearly as well as they can:

"God, soul, mother—fuck you all!" I muttered in annoyance, shoving my fist into the old woman's chest. "I am not gonna waste my words on you...."

And turning away from her, I saw somebody's saber lying nearby. A severe-looking gander was loitering around the yard, carelessly preening its feathers. I caught up with him, pressed him to the ground, and the gander's head burst under my boot—burst and emptied itself out.

"The guy will suit us fine," one of the Cossacks said about me.

The erotic symbolism of this incident, taken in isolation, may not be obvious. It is worth recalling, therefore, the advice that the quarter master offered Liutov before introducing him into the regiment: "If you mess up a lady, and the cleanest lady at that, then the soldiers will love you." Liutov proved to be a fast study, and he passed the test admirably by crushing the gander's head (symbolic castration) and by debasing a helpless old woman (symbolic rape).

Seen from this perspective, the choice that confronts Liutov again and again throughout the action of *The Cavalry* may be summarized in the following manner: he with either join those who behead and debase, renewing time with robust sensuality, violence and often cruelty, or he will remain with those humane, sacrificial victims whose heads will inevitably roll. Babel carefully links the moral and politial dilemma that faces Liutov to his narrator's problematic virility, for Liutov, as he remarks once in an off-hand manner, had been married and abandoned by his wife before joining the Red Cavalry. What this implies is that Liutov entered the Cossack army at the point in his life and history when people like him, those with weak eyes, so to speak, were offered an opportunity to transform themselves into the far-sighted *Übermenschen* of the dawning age. But Liutov, an intellectual and a Jew with a law degree from St. Petersburg University, is naturally wracked by ambivalence. Torn between his allegiance, on the one hand, to the "emasculated" Jewish world and the humanistic values of his education and, on the other, his wish to remake himself in a new image, he never takes the full advantage of the historical opportunity. Nevertheless, as he ponders over the choice in story after story, he continues to shape the world of the narrative according to the pattern of his inner conflict which echoes polyvalently the various versions of the Kronos myth.

The theme of revolution, of course, lends itself easily to the personal and collective mythology of death and renewal, but Babel used his version of the myth consistently even in the stories which either thematically or chronologically had nothing to do with the Revolution. A little-known story of his, "Barat-Ogly and the Eyes of His Bull" (1923), which takes place in timeless and exotic Central Asia, is one such example. In this story about a bull's gelding, Babel makes the association of eyes with male genitals quite explicit. Given this link, Aleksandr Kerensky's proverbial myopia ("Line and Color," 1924) acquires, as it were, a lower significance. Babel's view of his profession as a writer likewise fits into this pattern. "My First Honorarium" (1922–28) and a companion version of the same story, "A Reply to an Inquiry," belong to the same category, as does the famous "Guy de Maupassant" (1932). In this last tale about art and seduction, the motif of beheading appears once again, and it is worth pausing for a moment in order to examine how Babel weaves the motif into the pattern of the story.

As in "Di Grasso," the characters of "Guy de Maupassant" are divided into two groups: those who have displaced their erotic energy onto the acquisition of wealth (the males of Raisa's household), and those who can respond to the call of "noble passion," specifically, the inept translator of

Maupassant, Raisa, and the young aspiring writer who is helping her with the translation. Married to a rich Jewish merchant, Raisa lives in an opulent house, so well fortified with the philistine values of her husband that the destitute writer, who narrates the story, would have forever remained in his garret if it were not for the translation project which left the back door open to the youthful champion of art and love. The theme of seduction, the main plot line of the story, is developed in two stages. At first, the narrator wins Raisa over to his view of a writer's art with the often quoted motto which becomes erotically suggestive in the context of the story: "No steel is capable of penetrating the human heart with the icy precision of a timely full stop." As the narrator went on with his lecture, Raisa

> was listening with her head bent and her painted mouth half open. A black ray was gleaming in her polished hair, parted and smoothly pressed. Her legs, glazed in tight stockings, with their powerful and tender calves were spread apart on the carpet.

The actual seduction, that "timely full stop" in the other sense, is reserved for the end of the tale when Babel leaves Raisa and the narrator alone, having carefully dispatched the other members of her family to the opera house. And while the two are enjoying each other's company, intoxicated by wine and Maupassant, Raisa's relatives are made to watch Shaliapin, playing the role of Holophernes in A. Serov's opera *Judith*. Babel kills his two favorite birds with one stone: he beheads, albeit by implication, the moneybags while paying homage to the good old god of noble passion.

The story, however, ends on a more somber note, with a beheading of another sort, when the narrator, following the seduction, descends into the nether world in order to catch a glimpse of the underside of festive art and eros. Unable to go to sleep after he returned home, he reads a biography of Maupassant where he finds out that his idol was afflicted with congenital syphilis to which he finally succumbed after attempting suicide:

> Fertility and joy, contained in him, resisted the disease.... He struggled furiously, dashed around the Mediterranean in a yacht, fled to Tunisia, Morocco, Central Africa—and wrote all the while. Having achieved fame, he cut his own throat, lost a lot of blood but survived. They locked him up in a madhouse. There, he crawled on all fours.... The last notation in his painful record reads:
> "Monsieur de Maupassant va s'animaliser" ("Mr. Maupas-

sant has turned [sic] into an animal"). He died at the age of forty-two. His mother survived him.

I finished the book and got up from my bed. The fog has approached the window and concealed the universe. My heart contracted. I sensed the augury of truth.

The sentence with which Babel concluded the story appeared once before when the narrator of *The Cavalry* approached the secret of Pan Apolek's art, recognizing in the icon of John the Baptist the face of the castrated sexton Romuald: "I sensed the augury of a mystery" ("Predvestie tainy kosnulos' menia"). Then as now, this was the mystery and the truth of the ambivalent eros, Eros-Thanatos, and the formative role played by this mythic pattern in the aesthetic representation of reality. In its specific Babelian interpretation, this pattern defined the fundamental shape of the author's vision, and in the "childhood stories" of the 1920s and 1930s, Babel explored the origins of this by no means new intuition in the fictional record of his early life.

"First Love" (1925), the story of a childhood trauma, offers an insight into one of the more powerful sources of Babel's unique view of art and reality. At the time of the story, October 1905, the ten-year-old narrator is madly in love with a young married woman, Galina Rubtsova, whose full name includes a rather suspicious-sounding patronymic: Apollonovna. The narrator, as we know from the companion tale "The Story of My Dovecot," has just narrowly escaped death at the hands of one of the participants in the famous pogrom that followed the announcement of the Tsar's October Manifesto. At the end of "The Dovecot," the boy has learned that his great-uncle was not so lucky. He sees the grotesquely disfigured corpse of the old man with a still fluttering fish that the murderers stuck in his mouth. The other fish lay stuck in the fly of his trousers. These details are important, but Babel focusses on them not merely to manipulate the reader's emotions but, rather, in order to establish an analogy between the sexual and respiratory organs, the analogy that he will exploit in "First Love."

The boy, though still alive, does not look much better than his great-uncle: the intestines of the pigeons that he bought on the eve of the pogrom are still covering his face. He thus arrives at the house of his old passion Galina, who is now harboring his family from the pogrom. Galina takes the "little rabbi," as she calls the boy, to the kitchen to wash his face, and as the two are walking there, the boy's head is pressed against Galina's hip—the "hip that was moving and breathing." Borrowed from the famous story of

The Cavalry cycle, a goose is roasting on the stove above which, appropriately, Babel hangs the portrait of the pogrom Tsar, Nicholas II:

> Galina washed the remains of the pigeons off my face. "You'll make a good bridegroom, my pretty boy," she said, kissing me on the lips with her slightly swollen mouth, and turned away.

While the narrator was thus taking advantage of the unexpected physical proximity with Galina of the swollen mouth and the breathing hips, his dishevelled father was outside, rolling in the dust, pleading with a passing Cossack regiment to save his shop from the pogrom crowd. All in vain, needless to say. After the father, called in by the boy, walks into the room, the boy's mother begins to shame him for his love of money:

> "Cursed pennies," said mother as we were entering the room, "your life, our children and our unhappy happiness—all you have squandered for their sake. . . . Cursed pennies," she shouted in a coarse voice, twitched and fell silent.

It is at this point, when all the critical ingredients of the Babelian brew have been measured out, that the boy's hysterical hiccups begin. After Galina admonished him for these involuntary spasms—"You ought to be ashamed, my pretty boy"—his mind begins to spin out a heroic fantasy in which, as a member of the Jewish self-defense, he is fighting an enormous pogrom crowd. As he runs out of ammunition and is about to lose his life, Galina is watching him from an "embrasure" at the top of a "giant purple tower," while her half-dressed officer husband is affectionately kissing her exposed neck.

The narrator focusses once again on the boy's hysterical symptom later on in the story and, as before, he does so in the context of the mother invoking shame: "Look, how our child is suffering, why can't you hear his hiccups, why, Manus?" Isaac *Emmanuilovich* Babel, even in this fictional account of the events that probably had never taken place, did not hesitate to use his father's real name.

The boy seems to be the only member of his family who is capable of transcending shame. His passion for Galina and the shock and fear of death are so powerful that they absorb his entire being and for a moment overshadow even shame. Yet, his condition has been getting worse and worse:

> A roaring sound was bursting out of my chest. A tumor pleasing to the touch was swelling on my neck. The tumor was breathing,

swelling, blocking my windpipe and bulging out of my collar. . . .
And when in the evening I ceased to be a big-eared boy that I had
been all my life, when I became a writhing ball, then, my mother,
wrapping herself in a shawl and looking taller and more slender,
went up to Galina who by now had grown deadly pale.

"Dear Galina," my mother said in a melodious and strong
voice, "we are disturbing you and your whole family . . . I am so
ashamed, my dear Galina."

Her cheeks blushing, my mother was trying to ease Galina out
of the room, then she dashed toward me and shoved her shawl in
my mouth in order to stifle my groans.

"Please stop, sonny," she was whispering in my ear, "stop for
your mother's sake."

And even though it would have been possible for me to stop, I
would not, for I no longer felt any shame.

Thus began my illness. I was ten then. In the morning, they took
me to the doctor. The pogrom went on, but we were spared. The
doctor, a fat man, diagnosed a nervous disorder.

Enough examples have been cited by now to demonstrate that in those stories of Babel where the decapitation motif occurs, necks and heads function as phallic images, just as does the "swollen neck" in "First Love." But in no other story does this image seem so polyvalent as in "First Love." Sexual arousal and sexual frustration of a ten-year-old boy are merely one aspect of it. Death is another. The father's willingness to humiliate himself for the sake of money before the Cossacks and the mother's readiness to humiliate her husband in front of Galina contribute equally to the boy's predicament. The mother's excessive sense of shame which prompts her to stifle her child rather than face embarrassment, too, finds its way into the grotesque image. The historical events, the Revolution of 1905 and the October Manifesto which, according to the story, triggered the pogrom, likewise left their imprint. In fact, since Babel wrote "First Love" (1925) shortly after completing most of *The Cavalry,* one may see in the boy's swollen neck one of the fictional sources of Liutov's symbolic rhetoric which draws a sharp distinction between the world of the virile Cossacks and the passive world of the Jews where men have emphatically thin necks and exceptionally poor eyesight.

Nietzsche's intuition concerning the dual origins of art and life, which is so important in Babel, also becomes integrated into the story's central image. It is, after all, Galina *Apollonovna* with her progressively distant beauty who nearly causes the boy, speaking literally and figuratively, to lose his head. And it is the same daughter of Apollo who gives refuge to the boy and his family from the grisly "Dionysian" orgy of the pogrom—indeed, a Bacchanal, for the boy's great-uncle was killed not by men but, expressly, by Russian women (*katsapki*).

Returning to "Di Grasso" after this lengthy detour, it becomes easy to recognize in the grotesque murder of Giovanni—named so, of course, after John the Baptist—the decapitation motif that runs like Ariadne's thread throughout the terrifying and playful labyrinth of Babel's fiction. In fact, if one is to believe one of Babel's fictional asides, the preoccupation with the motif constituted an old family obsession, going as far back as Babel's grandfather, the author of a never-finished volume of memoirs, entitled *A Man Without a Head* ("In the Basement"). At this point, a psychoanalytically minded critic would, of course, be tempted to reduce the significance of the motif to the author's or, to be more sophisticated, to the authorial persona's castration anxiety and, thus, would call it a day. But this would be grossly unfair to Babel, for the curse of this anxiety, in one way or another, is said to afflict the whole of humanity, while only a select few can make as much out of it as did Isaac Babel. No doubt, the profound multilevel significance of this motif in "Di Grasso" *is* related to the "universal castration complex," but so is an acorn related to a mature oak tree. Yet, only by looking at the tree, and not the acorn, can one come closer to an understanding of what is both unique and universal in this individual member of the species and begin to decipher the record left on it by the seasons and the earth.

When Babel was writing "Di Grasso," the acorn had already grown into an oak tree, and to his readers, the central element of the motif—Giovanni's neck—came as a highly complex metaphoric and metonymic image, a product of a lifetime's condensatin and displacement. This metaphor of an uncertain virility, individuation from the tyranny of the family, the tribe, and the state—of what is fearsome in life and needs overcoming—contains also the metonymic record of Babel's growth as a writer and an imprint of his environment, his age. To appreciate the complexity of this image, one needs only to recall the gelded bull of Barat-Ogly in whose doleful eyes Babel's narrator once beheld his own wasted youth, manhood, and innocence.

In "Di Grasso," treading softly, almost imperceptibly, Babel arranges the key images of his fictional life—Odessa, popular and classical art, sex, and carnival abandon—around the totem pole of Giovanni's throat. Once established, the polyvalent image begins to radiate the allusive energy of the entire motif accumulated in the body of Babel's fiction. One of the century's gods who gave Babel perhaps the most powerful insight into the mystery of art and life, Pan-Apollo or, simply, Friedrich Nietzsche, presides invisibly over the feast of epiphany prepared for the boy from Odessa. But though invisible, as befits a true deity, he is generous when it comes to divine manifestations. And woe unto those who cannot read his signs. They will be either bitten in the neck or shamed by their wives in the presence of children. Or they will have to give up their gold watches and be cut off, pun intended, from the regenerative power of time.

But think how lucky are those who are able to recognize the god's Dionysian features in the confusing kaleidoscope of life and pay homage to him by imitating his passion. Their necks will grow strong and invincible. They will become great artists, reap box-office success, and if they are too young, will command premium prices at the theater where the god is celebrated. They will also be allowed to get away with pawning their father's gold watches. Time will be theirs.

For those few among them who can also recognize the god's other face, the face of Apollo, there is an even more precious gift. In order to qualify for it, one has to be able to appreciate the order and magnificence of Doric architecture, the contemplative serenity of sculpture and the dream-like tranquil restraint of classical art—so, at least, according to *The Birth of Tragedy,* the foremost among the god's gospels. At the conclusion of "Di Grasso," this mystery is revealed to the boy from Odessa:

> I stood alone, clutching the watch. Suddenly, with the kind of clarity that I had never experienced before, I saw the columns of the City Duma running upwards, the illuminated foliage of the boulevard, Pushkin's bronze head gleaming opaquely in the moonlight—I saw for the first time what surrounded me as it really was: tranquil and ineffably beautiful.

Judging by Babel's writing this gift must have been the shield of Perseus, for what else could allow one to fight Medusa so successfully without looking into her eyes but only at her reflection?

Unfortunately, as all gods' gifts to mortals, this one, too, came with a proviso. The shield's magic could work, it seems, only as long as it was possible to celebrate Martedi grasso. But after Fat Tuesday came lean Wednesday and with it the long Lent. That happened some time in the late 1930s (experts differ on the exact date), when the Great Lenten Father of all progressive people suddenly realized that he had run out of fatted calves, but, seeing that they were no more, he did not close his slaughterhouse.

EFRAIM SICHER

Midrash and History: A Key to the Babelesque Imagination

Isaak Babel was a notorious hoaxer who enjoyed mystifying both in real life and in his fiction; he was doubly ambiguous and ironical when it was politically unsafe to speak his mind. After the Bolshevik Revolution he created a myth of his literary career which has misled serious scholars and readers alike ever since, but which was necessary in order to claim acceptable credentials as a Soviet writer. In that marvellous story of 1924 which he called his "Avtobiografiya" ("Autobiography"), Babel has us believe that he lived with a drunken waiter in a Petrograd cellar in 1915 and was on the run from the tsarist police. Babel attributes his "sole debt" to Gorky, who published his first stories in the November 1916 issue of *Letopis,* which brought Babel an indictment under the tsarist obscenity laws. Gorky then sent the twenty-two-year-old writer "into the people" for seven years. Babel speaks of beginning to write again only in 1923 and he dates his literary career from the appearance of some of the Red Cavalry and Odessa stories in Mayakovsky's *Lef* in 1924. In a revision of "Avtobiografiya" dated 1932, Babel writes that *Red Cavalry* (*Konarmiya,* the first edition of the collected Red Cavalry stories, 1926) and the Odessa stories were completed "over two years." There then followed another period of "silence" and "wandering"—by 1932 Babel had to account for a further seven years of not producing a major work.

In actual fact, the first story known to us appeared in 1913 in the Kiev journal *Ogni* as a contribution to the regular column on the Jewish Ques-

From *The Slavonic and East European Review* 60, no. 4 (October 1982). © 1982 by the University of London (School of Slavonic and East European Studies).

tion. During his studies at the Kiev Institute of Financial and Business Studies Babel mixed with the emancipated, assimilated Jewish intelligentsia and Babel's real literary début must be seen in the light of Babel's lifelong interest in the fate of Russian Jewry. The story "Staryy Shloyme" ("Old Shloyme") describes how, rather than see his son assimilate under social and economic pressure into Russian society, the senile Jew Shloyme turns to the almost forgotten faith of his forefathers . . . and to suicide.

Among the stories on which Babel was working in the pre-Revolutionary years was one about a Jew Yankel who attempts to free from prison the son of his landlord, the priest Father Ivan. Another, "Detstvo" ("Childhood"), subtitled "U babushki" ("At Grandmother's") and dated 1915, would appear to be the genesis of the later cycle of stories dealing with a Jewish childhood, of which the first, "Istoriya moyey golubyatni" ("The Story of My Dovecot"), was published in 1925. These so-called "autobiographical" stories do not, of course, strictly relate to the facts of the writer's life, and this story shows the deliberate mythicizing that was to be typical of Babel's first person narration. [Babel's father, for example, was not an impoverished shopkeeper, but dealt in agricultural machinery, though he was not a particularly successful businessman, and Babel's mother Fenya, as Nathalie Babel has testified, was quite unlike the Rakhel of the Childhood stories.] It is clear that the centrality of Jewish themes in Babel dates back to his earliest writing, as evidenced, also by his work for a Jewish welfare organization in Odessa and possible involvement in Zionist groups. Unfortunately, insufficient attention has been paid to Babel's roots in Judaism, in Hebrew and Yiddish literature of the turn of the century and in the Odessa of Bialik and Mendele Mokher-Sforim.

The fiction that he was first published by Gorky said nothing, moreover, of the sketches which Babel published in Petrograd magazines in 1916–18, including what amounts to his literary manifesto, "Odessa" (1916), at a time when he was living not uncomfortably with an engineer's family, the Slonims. This account conveniently glossed over Babel's descriptions of the horrors of revolutionary Petrograd in Gorky's newspaper *Novaya zhizn*, which Lenin closed down in July 1918 for its scathing attacks on the Bolshevik regime. On the other hand references in his "Avtobiografiya" to service on the Rumanian front, then in the Cheka and Narkompros divert attention from Babel's absence from the stage of the October Revolution.

Far from remaining "silent" in his years "among the people," Babel wrote a number of stories about war (under the heading *Na pole chesti* (*On the Field of Honour*), published Odessa, 1920) or about sex and prostitution (the uncompleted series *Peterburg 1918* and *Oforty*, published Odessa,

1922–23). Several later works, published in the late twenties or thirties, were begun in these years (among them "Gyui de Mopassan" ("Guy de Maupassant") and "Doroga" ("The Journey"). Contrary to earlier theories, it seems from the evidence of archival notes that Babel was working at the same time on both the Odessa and the Red Cavalry stories, composing them in Odessa in 1921–23 and while working as a newspaper correspondent in Tbilisi in 1922; despite the stylistic and structural differences of the two cycles they belong to an identical hand. The Odessa stories began to appear in Odessa from 1921: "Korol" ("The King"), "Spravedlivost' v skobkakh" ("Justice in Parentheses") and most of the Red Cavalry stories were printed in Odessa during 1923 in much the same form as they were later republished in Moscow. Babel made hardly any attempt to introduce significant conformity with the ideological demands of Budyonny and Marxist critics into *Red Cavalry* between first publication of the separate stories and the first edition of the book; indeed, Babel made a stand against proposed cuts and alterations. [If most of the Red Cavalry stories had been completed by 1923, then Babel cannot have had much intention of mollifying his critics by revising existing stories and adding some ten to twenty more to give a less "negative" picture of the Red Army, as he suggested he would to his editor at Gosizdat, Dmitry Furmanov, between December 1924 and March 1926.]

Conniving at, or actually creating, an apocryphal aura about his person as well as his writing helped put off the track those establishment bloodhounds who criticized the ahistoricity of Babel's work and who denounced the author's "silence" or rather his failure to produce new and ideologically acceptable stories. And redating subsequent republications of stories on themes that might be accused of being "dated" or "repetitive" was only one of Babel's attempts to deceive readers and critics.

The "real" letters dictated to the narrator in *Red Cavalry* as well as the dates and places given at the end of some of the stories may be taken as similarly deceitful attempts to provide some illusion of factual veracity. The narrator likewise "authenticates" the mythology of the Odessa stories by speaking of "our famous rabbi, Ben-Zkharya" or mentioning that "none other than Doctor Zilberberg" operated on the murdered informer Aron Peskin.

The use of myth in Babel's fiction gives an illusion of the epic while mocking it and reads both unorthodox interpretations and essential truths into history. For Babel the myths of history and religion were a subtle and ironical medium for allegorical parallels as well as allusions to a moral message.

In the space of an article one can hope to pick out only a few of the mythological strands in the multivalent, sophisticated play of Babel's laconic prose. Using previously unavailable archive material and textual analysis of the unexpurgated texts of Babel's short stories of the nineteen-twenties I should like to suggest how Babel's use of myth illustrates principles of the stylistic and structural composition of his fiction.

Babel draws on biblical references and, indeed, on the whole gamut of Judaeo-Christian culture not only in symbolic imagery, but also in the plot construction of the prophetic and apocalyptic vision of *Red Cavalry*. This article will concentrate on the use made of the messianic myth, particularly its treatment in the art of the Polish painter in *Red Cavalry*, Pan Apolek.

Apolek is himself an instance of the introduction of myth. Like the French avant-garde poet Apollinaire, Apolek is christened Apollinarius, which identifies him with the muse Apollo, god of poetry and music, representative, in direct opposition to Dionysus, of the intellect and of civilization. Apollo has a confused history in Greek mythology, but out of his many functions it is as Apollo Smintheus that Apolek is recognized: Apolek wanders the earth with two white mice tucked behind his shirt, although here they are a Babelian epithet for the archetypal victim. Apolek lacks his classical forbear's lyre, but he does have the blind musician Gottfried to play to him. The prototype of the blind musician who plays Heidelberg songs can be traced back to Windermeier, the blind musician from Tübingen in "Kontsert v Katerinenshtadte" ("A Concert in Katerinenstadt") (1918), and it is in Western Europe (to whose influence Babel, as an Odessa Jew, was naturally predisposed) that we must seek clues to Babel's hagiography of Pan Apolek.

In the diary which Babel wrote while on the Polish-Soviet front in 1920 and which served as raw material for the later Red Cavalry stories there is no mention of a Polish painter, but in the ruins of Catholic churches and in the home of the priest Tuzinkiewicz with its ancient tomes and Latin manuscripts he stumbles upon the Catholic mystery, which provides him, a Jew from Orthodox Russia, with a startling revelation.

The narrator first comes across the art of Pan Apolek in the story "Pan Apolek." In his introduction to the story the narrator takes vows to the aesthetic ideal of Apolek's art, a "gospel hidden from the world," and writes with hindsight that the saintly life of Pan Apolek "went to his head like old wine": it later transpires that Apolek is a drunken heretic.

The invented aesthetic model of the Polish painter expresses in characteristically visual imagery Babel's concept of art and history. It is an ideal, moreover, which awakens a sense of destiny and a sense of his own failings in the mind of the alienated Jewish intellectual torn between his roots in his doomed ancestral past and the Revolution. It is an ideal which juxtaposes the real and the ideal. The narrator chats to Apolek about the romantic past of the Polish gentry and about Luca della Robbia, the fifteenth-century sculptor who created a spiritual beauty in his church art, but the treatise on Apolek's artistic ideal ends with the narrator returning to the gruesome reality of his plundered Jews and with his loneliness, homelessness and impossible idealism reflected in nature:

По городу слонялась бездомная луна. И я шел с нею вместе, отогревая в себе неисполнимые мечты и нестройные песни.

[A homeless moon loitered around the town. And I walked along together with the moon, warming in my heart impracticable dreams and dissonant songs.]

The first of Apolek's chefs-d'oeuvre to be exhibited is his portrait of St John. This is a portrait of St John the Baptist, for his head lies on a clay dish after his execution, but at the same time it is of St John the Apostle-Evangelist, for out of the mouth issues a snake, a reference to the legend in which a snake saved St John the Apostle's life by extracting the venom from a poisoned chalice. The dead St John's face seems familiar to the narrator and he has a presentiment of the truth: the severed head is drawn from Pan Romuald. Pan Romuald, we recall, was the treacherous viper of "Kostyol v Novograde" ("The Church at Novograd"), the runaway priest's assistant who was later shot as a spy. His venomous character is introduced in that story by the image of his cassock snaking its way through the dusk (*gde-to v zmeinom sumrake izvivales' sutana monakha*) and his soul is merciless, like a cat's. Incidentally, the association of Romuald with the serpent and the cat makes him both the natural and mythological enemy of Apollo the mouse god and slayer of the python. The monkish eunuch Romuald, like the ascetic yet decadent theology of the established church (in which he would have become a bishop had he not been shot as a spy), stands in direct contrast to the aesthetic and doctrinal heresy of Apolek. [Pan Robacki, who pours anathema on the heretical painter in "Pan Apolek," is also likened to a cat and his "grey ears" help to equate him with the "grey old men with bony ears" in "Kostyol v Novograde," all senile attributes of a dead world opposed to the life-giving, joyful art of Apolek.]

The narrator finds himself half-way towards solving the riddle of Apolek's iconography when he spots the Madonna hanging over the bed of Pani Eliza, the priest's housekeeper, for it is she who is portrayed as a rosy-cheeked Mary. Apolek first came to Novograd-Volynsk thirty years before, as the narrator relates in his apocryphal rendering of the coming of this questionably "holy fool" who sparked off a long and bitter war with the established church. Like Michelangelo in the Sistine Chapel, Apolek climbs along the walls of the Novograd church and paints into his frescoes a psychological, though ahistorical, truth. The lame convert Janek is depicted as Paul—who was disabled with blindness in the story of his conversion (Acts 9:1–19). The scene of the stoning of the adulteress (compare John 8:3–11) is referred to as the stoning of Mary Magdelene, who is appropriately depicted as the Jewish prostitute Elka, for all three are "fallen women." Apolek's heresy is to elevate ordinary folk into mythical heroes with the haloes of saints, while bringing the divine, supernatural myths to the level of comprehension of mortals. In the same way that Renaissance painters flattered their patrons, Apolek wins a smile and a glass of cognac from the old priest who recognizes himself among the Magi, and he peoples the homes of the local population with peasant Josephs and Marys. For an extra ten złoty their enemy can be depicted as Judas Iscariot. Apolek even offers to paint the narrator as St Francis of Assisi, with a dove or a goldfinch on his sleeve, an ironical reference to the horse's head insignia on the sleeve of the narrator's Red Cavalry uniform.

Apolek realizes in ordinary folk with all their human vices their potential for spirituality and epic deeds. Above all Apolek brings out the aesthetic beauty of human flesh, which he colours like a "tropical garden." Lush and sensuous, Apolek's paintings beatify mundane existence as if mythical, while the mythical is revitalized to reveal hidden truths. Apolek's scenes of the Nativity resemble Babel's impressions of the religious paintings of Rembrandt, Murillo, and the Italian masters which he saw in a Polish church in Beresteczko. The hint at the pre-Christian and pagan origins of the Church in the "Chinese carved rosary" which the Novograd priest holds as he blesses the infant Jesus in Apolek's painting is also clear in the description in Babel's diary entry for August 7, 1920:

> великолепная итальянская живопись, розовые патеры, качающие младенца Христа, великолепный темный Христос, Рембрандт, Мадонна под Мурильо а л(ожет) б(ыть) Мурильо, и главное—эти святые упитанные иезуиты, фигурка китайская жуткая за покрывалом, в малиновом кунтухе, бородатый еврейчик, лавочка, сломанная рака, фигура св. Валента. Служитель трепещет, как птица, корчится, мешает русскую речь с польской, мне недьзя прикоснуться, рыдает. Зверье, они пришли, чтрбы грабить, это так ясно, разрушаются старые боги.

[Wonderful Italian painting, pink priests rocking the infant Jesus, a wonderful mysterious Christ, Rembrandt, a Madonna after Murillo or perhaps a real Murillo, and the main thing is these saintly, well-fed Jesuits, a weird Chinese figure behind the veil, in a raspberry-coloured cloak, a bearded little Jew, the little store, the broken shrine, the figure of St Valentine. The beadle trembles like a bird, cowers, mixes up his Russian with Polish, I mustn't touch, he sobs. The beasts, they came to ransack, it's so clear, the old gods are being destroyed.]

The scene of the ransacking of a church, from which this extract is taken, is transformed into the desecration by the Cossacks in "U svyatogo Valenta" ("At St Valentine's Church"). This transformation tells us much about Babel's recognition of the power of myth to make supernatural or historical events relevant to the present day, an aesthetic concept which the author places at the centre of the art of that mythical myth-maker, Pan Apolek, and which is without doubt modelled on the masters of the Renaissance. The result is a new and unexpected historical perspective in which the historical is seen as real and the real as legendary. Jesus, a bleeding, suffering, persecuted Polish *shtetl* Jew, in the epiphany revealing Apolek's crucifix and reminiscent of the rending of the veil in "U svyatogo Valenta," frightens a Cossack soldier in the Polish-Soviet war whose comrades and forbears have persecuted so many Jewish communities. This brings us into the realm of *Midrash*, the homiletic rereading and supranarration of Jewish history and lore. [Jewish legends of the desecration of the Temple are appropriate to the persecution of East European Jewish communities in 1919–20. For example, Talmud, Gittin 56b relates how Titus entered the Temple and committed an obsenity on the Scroll of the Law. Then he drew a sword and pierced the curtain in front of the Holy of Holies in the middle of the Temple. By a miracle blood oozed out and he started to shout that he had killed the God of the Jews. (Compare the version in vayikra raba 20, 5.) In Babel's story the Cossacks commit an obscenity with the brigade nurse Sashka.]

Apolek's reweaving of the Gospel stories, like Babel's imagery in general, transposes the sacred and the profane, rendering the supernatural grotesquely earthy and the everyday almost superhuman. As the fence and cemetery watchman Witold declares in Apolek's defence to the church dignitary investigating the local outbreak of blasphemy, Apolek's art conveys to the sinful, ignorant masses the sort of truth Jesus told, which was as unpalatable to the Establishment then as now. And is there not more truth, he asks, in Apolek's paintings, which ennoble the spectator, who is also depicted as participating in them, than in the angry and condescending words of the clergy? Italian prelates and Polish priests, it would seem, are not at all out of place in nativity scenes set in the Renaissance, painted in the 1890s and viewed by the narrator in 1920 when the Roman Church was being sacked by Slav hordes.

The messianic theme is related to the Revolution and the Civil War not only through the device of Apolek's paintings. One sabbath eve at the Zhitomir rebbe's the narrator sees in the rebbe's son an unrecognized herald of the Messiah in a violent apocalypse. This Elijah (Il'ya) profanes the sabbath by smoking, he has the "emaciated face of a nun" and the "forehead of Spinoza"—that other Jewish heretic—and the Hasidim around him are likened to "fishermen and apostles." Like the boy-narrator in Babel's Childhood stories and like the Jewish intellectual narrator of the Red Cavalry stories, Il'ya has tried to escape from the traditional Jewish home and ancestral past—he is described as a recaptured "runaway prisoner." Later, in "Syn rabbi" ("The Rebbe's Son"), he renounces his mother (reminding us of Matthew 12:46–50) in the name of a new messianic ideology, the Revolution. Il'ya dies, sexually impotent, and while the narrator, his ancient Jewish memory stirred, identifies with his spiritual brother, it is clear that the synthesis of Jewish values (Song of Songs, Maimonides and phylacteries) with revolutionary ideals (communist leaflets, Lenin and revolver cartridges) remains an impossible dream.

There is evidence in Babel's 1920 diary and in the drafts of the Red Cavalry stories that he wished to build the messianic theme into the framework of *Red Cavalry* and that he intended historical and religious myths to convey a topical message. [In the draft "Smert' Trunova" ("The Death of Trunov") there is direct mention of the coming days of the Messiah: "И я поверил бы в воскресенье Илии, если бы не аэроплан, который заплывал и т. д." "And I would have believed in the resurrection of Elijah, if it had not been for the aeroplane which was winging its way, etc." But in the story "Eskadronnyy Trunov" ("Squadron Commander Trunov") the Elijah whose name is shouted by the quarreling Jews is Elijah the Vilna Gaon (1720–97), the antagonist of the Hasidim: the Jews argue over old sectarian differences as if there were no war or revolution.] A projected story, "Demidovka," refers several times to Jeremiah and was based on an incident in a *shtetl* on the Fast of the Ninth of Av, when Jews mourn the anniversary of the destruction of the Temple and read Jeremiah's lament over the fall of Jerusalem. As Babel recorded in his diary, the Cossacks forced the local Jews to cook food for them on the eve of the fast, which happened to be a sabbath when all work is prohibited. Everything was as in the days of the destruction of the Temple, Babel wrote, and elsewhere he speaks of the "same old story" when time and again he has to witness the pillaging and torture of the long suffering Jewish population at the hands of Poles and Cossacks. [For example, the diary entry for 18 July 1920 specifies the point for point repetition of history in a description of a Jewish cemetery which has seen Khmelnitsky and now Budyonny, a parallel important for understanding the subtext of "Kladbishche v Kozine" ("Cemetery in Kozin").]

Indeed, the Cossacks marching into Beresteczko in *Red Cavalry* pass the watchtower of the hetman Bogdan Khmelnitsky where he was routed by the Poles in 1651. An old man crawls out of the Cossack burial mounds to sing of past glories. In the tradition of Khmelnitsky the first act of the Cossacks on entering the town is to murder a Jew. The irony is that the Cossacks marching past the memorials of their epic past are greeted by silence and shuttered windows. The Jewish quarter of Beresteczko "reeks in anticipation of a new era." The town's ex-masters are a lunatic countess and her impotent son. A fragment of a letter in French, a fragment of the past dated 1820, one hundred years before the incursion of the Bolsheviks and the arrival of the narrator, recalls the Napoleonic Wars and Napoleon's death. As the narrator reads the letter, apparently from a mother to a husband long departed for war but which epitomizes the Raciborskis and the dying Polish nobility, a revolutionary council is being elected below the old Polish château. The historical parallel between the Napoleonic and Revolutionary wars, between the dying Polish nobility's romantic past and its degenerate heirs, also involves a stylistic contrast and leads to an ironic story ending: power is supposedly being handed over to a bewildered petty bourgeoisie and to plundered Jews.

Allusion to historical and religious myths and specifically to the apocalyptic motif can be seen too in the viewpoint of the alienated Jewish intellectual. The sun has set over the traditional Jewish past from which he is trying to break out, but he is instinctively drawn to his roots and childhood memories, to Gedali's Dickensian Curiosity Shop with its Winchester dated 1810. Gedali's is the name of the governor of Judaea after the destruction of the First Temple (586 B.C.), whose assassination symbolized the destruction of the Jewish nation (see Jeremiah 41). Messianic mysticism is alluded to by the anomaly that the Zhitomir rebbe, Motale, is named Bratslavsky and called "last rebbe of the Czernobyl dynasty." This presages the apostasy and death of his son. Yet the Czernobyl dynasty belonged to the Twersky, not the Bratslav, sect of Hasidism, and the Bratslav rebbe, Nakhman, had left no male heir at his death in 1810 (the date engraved on Gedali's Winchester, as if time had not moved forward for East European Jews). Bratslav may be considered as the most messianic of Hasidic sects, and it is surely significant that the fictional son of a long-dead rebbe should be known as Elijah. Indeed, anti-Semitism has through Jewish history reawakened messianic expectations based on the writings of the Hebrew Prophets, as may be witnessed by the following for the false messiah, Shabatai Tsvi, in the wake of the 1648 Khmelnitsky massacres. The scenes of despair and devastation in *Red Cavalry* are accompanied by a hope for future justice and salvation which stems from this tradition.

"Perekhod cherez Zbruch" ("Crossing the Zbrucz"), the opening *Red Cavalry* story, ends with a plea for humanity from a pregnant Jewess who has witnessed the killing of her father and the sacking of her home in a pogrom. The crossing of the river in that story suggests a road on the way to a red Calvary under apocalyptic portents in the blood-red sky. A drowning soldier defames the Virgin Mary. The fording of the river takes place amid nocturnal chaos and death. The Zbrucz—here confused with the Słucz—may be interpreted as a symbolic boundary which relates the crossing to the Exodus from Egypt, with all the overtones of redemption in the Passover story, evoked by the smashed Passover crockery, fragments of the narrator's Jewish past which he encounters on entering the home of the pregnant Jewess. If the first half of the story is permeated by violation of nature (note the monastic and virginal image of the buckwheat) and death in nature, then the second part introduces the idea of unborn life and future deliverance out of death and destruction, an idea embodied in the Jewish mother-to-be. And her plea for compassion at the end of the story is echoed by the prayer for justice and respite from death for the Jewish victims of persecution in "Kladbishche v Kozine."

Karl-Yankel, in the Odessa story of that name, is another such symbol of salvation, the first-born who heralds an era of justice. But the hope that the unfortunate baby, named after the Marxist and Biblical patriarchs Karl Marx and Jacob (Yiddish *Yankel*), will benefit from the struggle over its fate is ambiguous and fraught with ironies.

Benya Krik the gangster is nicknamed "The King" in "Kak eto delalos' v Odesse" ("How It Was Done in Odessa") after the Lord of the Universe, but also after Jesus of Nazareth. He is proclaimed "King" by Arye-Leyb, an eloquent Aaron speaking on behalf of a lisping Moses. Arye-Leyb speaks out of a burning bush on Mount Sinai (*sic*) and proclaims Benya "King" after Benya has spoken from "on high" at the funeral of Joseph Muginshteyn, a strange kind of sermon on a mount in which he declares Joseph to be a scapegoat (note the biblical symbolism) for the whole working-class. This is, of course, a perverse irony, as is his earlier complaint that God made a mistake in settling the Jews in Russia where they were tormented worse than in hell, for he is mostly concerned with buying off his guilt for Joseph's death during the gangsters' raid on the premises of Reuben Tartakovsky.

Nevertheless, as we are reminded in the play *Zakat* (*Sunset*), Benya is Bentsion, the "son of Zion," and Benya's *coup* in the Krik household puts an end to the injustices of Mendel's reign of terror and reinstates the natural order of cyclical change-over from father to son. The allegory of King David's love for Batsheva in scene seven is instructive, for Mendel wishes to cheat his sons of their inheritance by running off to Bessarabia with Marusya but they seize the throne in their father's old age (compare 2 Samuel 11:1–26 and 1 Kings 1:1–40). The repeated references to sunset and the coming of the sabbath reinforce the idea that historical change is cyclical and no force can halt the setting of the sun. [In the stage directions sunset coincides with the beating up of Mendel and later Benya speaks of making the sabbath a sabbath.] In the play's concluding speech the rabbi Ben-Zkharya warns that Joshua the prophet (compare Joshua 10:12–15 and Midrash Kohelet 111, 114) and Jesus of Nazareth (a reference to Luke 23:44–55, omitted in all but the first edition of the play) were mistaken in thinking that they could alter the natural, divinely ordained course of events by symbolically stopping the sun:

> День есть день, евреи, вечер есть вечер. День затопляет нас потом трудов наших, но вечер держит наготове веера своей божественной прохлаеы. Иисус Навин, остановивший солнце, был всего только сумасброд. Иисус из Назарета, укравший солнце, был злой безумец. И вот Мендель Крик, прихожанин нашей синагоги, оказался не умнее Иисуса Навина. Всю жизнь хотел он жариться на солнцепеке, всю жизнь хотел он стоять на том месте, где его застал полдень. Но бог имеет городовых на каждой уаице, и Мендель Крик имел сынов в своем доме. Городовые приходят и делают порядок. День есть день, и вечер есть вечер. Все в порядке, евреи. Выпьем рюмку водки!

> [A day is a day, Jews, and evening is evening. Day crushes us with the sweat of our labours, but evening holds in readiness the fan of its divine coolness. Joshua the Prophet, who stopped the sun, was a bit crazy. Jesus of Nazareth, who stole the sun, was a malicious madman. And Mendel Krik here, a member of our synagogue,

turns out to be no wiser than Joshua the Prophet. All his life he wanted to bask in the heat of the sun, all his life he wanted to stand where the midday sun stood. But God has policemen on every street and Mendel Krik had sons in his house. Policemen come and make order. A day is a day, and evening is evening. Everything is in order, Jews. Let's drink a glass of vodka!]

There are many possible interpretations of Babel's play *Zakat,* and the allegorical sunset of traditional Jewish society in Russia is only one of them. Moreover Benya does not fulfil any mission as a saviour and, while the sun literally salutes the zenith of his power in "Kak eto delalos' v Odesse," his role as King of the gangsters is something of a comic parody. Only in the later play *Marya* (1933, published 1935 but repressed while in rehearsal), which contains clear marianic motifs as well as quotations from the Gospels, is there a portrayal of the new social order. The final curtain falls in *Marya* on a scene somewhat reminiscent of Petrov-Vodkin's painting *1918 in Petrograd*; the worker Safonov's pregnant wife stands by the window in the sunlight, admiring the apartment of General Mukovnin's family which is now their home.

In *Red Cavalry,* however, the red dawn of the promised Bolshevik utopia fails to brighten the horizon and Ilya Bratslavsky lacks sufficient artillery to bring a Messiah to the apocalyptic confrontation between Bolshevik Russia and Catholic Poland.

By contrast with the semen-oozing seductive crucifixes of the established Church, described in "Kostyol v Novograde," the portrayal of Jesus himself presents a rather un-messianic, earthly figure. Apolek's, or rather Babel's, Jesus is as aesthetically sensual and human as the virginal theology of the "winking madonnas" is ascetic and inhuman.

Apolek's parable of Jesus and Deborah, in the Red Cavalry story "Pan Apolek," may have some basis in popular folklore, but it certainly demonstrates Babel's love of the apocryphal. Apolek not only demythicizes Jesus, but rewrites the Gospels, relating that the wedding night of the Israelite virgin Deborah ended in tears of shame when she took fright at her approaching bridegroom and vomited. Jesus takes pity on her by dressing in the clothes of her bridegroom, just as it is Jesus who sends the angel Alfred to Arina in "Iisusov grekh" ("The Sin of Jesus") (1922, first published as a reworked version of "Skazka pro babu" ["Tale About a Woman"] in 1924). The all-embracing love of Jesus in Apolek's parable is specifically a union of the flesh. Lying in holy adultery with Deborah, Jesus proves his compassion more just than the law. Deborah is Hebrew for a bee, and Babel clearly means this to refer to the "bee of sorrow" which stings Jesus:

Смертельная испарина Выступила на его теле, и пчела скорби укусила его в сердце.

[A deathly sweat broke out on His body and the bee of sorrow stung His heart.]

Stung by post-coital remorse, Jesus leaves unnoticed to join John in the desert.

The bee may represent here the deadliness of human passion and we may compare the bestial desire of Dvoyra (the Yiddish form of Deborah) who drags off her bridegroom at the end of "Korol" looking at him like a cat holding a mouse. The bee also figures prominently in Afonka Bida's parable of the crucifixion in "Put' v Brody" ("The Road to Brody"). The bee, by extension of the Christian virtue of industriousness essentially a proletarian creature, refuses to sting Jesus on the cross out of class solidarity, for Jesus came from a carpenter's family. The context, of course, is ironic, as the narrator is mourning the Cossacks' destruction of the Volhynian beehives and the "daily atrocities." Ironically, too, the Jews in the synagogue scene in *Zakat* are stung by the bee of grace (*pchela blagodati*).

The propensity for suffering and compassion are the attributes of Jesus which are brought out in the syphilitic shepherd Sashka Konyayev, whose meekness earns him the nickname "The Christ." It is by explicitly sexual compassion and an earthy acceptance of "sin" that Sashka, like Jesus in Apolek's parable, becomes himself something of a Jesus figure. His stepfather Tarakanych is a carpenter, like Mary's husband Joseph. Sashka begs his stepfather to be allowed to become a shepherd, because "all the saints" were shepherds, but Tarakanych mocks the idea of a saint with syphilis. That night Sashka has a vision from heaven in which he sees himself in a rosewood cradle hanging from the sky on two silver cords. A syphilitic Russian peasant, he too has aspirations to be supernaturally born. There is, however, an unstated irony in Sashka's exchange of his mother's sexual purity for permission to join the shepherds.

Babel was not interested in the Classical myths themselves, his use of biblical sources is, to say the least, unorthodox, and as a nonbelieving Jew he was not particularly concerned with the literal message of the Gospels. He did not share the Symbolists' attraction to mysticism. Nor was he seriously interested in allegorical interpretations of the role of the Christian saviour, such as in Blok's *The Twelve,* although the background of Marxist and religious messianism in pre-Revolutionary and Revolutionary Russia is relevant here. Babel's retelling of myth aimed to convey the contemporary mores of the Cossack and Russian masses. Matvey Pavlichenko in his saintly *zhizneopisaniye* [biography—that is, his hagiography] in *Red Cavalry* differs from his patron saint (compare Matthew 5:38–39) in not being able to turn the other cheek. His cheek burns with personal as well as revolutionary vengeance and in retribution he tramples his former master to death. The *skaz* story "Iisusov grekh" ("The Sin of Jesus") is a hilarious indictment of the drunken lust of a Russian peasant woman who crushes the angel Alfred in her inebriated sleep and then refuses to forgive Jesus for her life of incessant sex and pregnancy.

The Roman Catholic churches in *Red Cavalry* are as unredeemably doomed as the Jewish *shtetl*, yet despite the aesthetic revelations they offer, the disoriented Jewish intellectual does not feel for them the nostalgia and sympathy evoked by the Jewish areas he visits. It is, however, Pan Apolek who offers a version of Babel's own aesthetics, suggesting, as Babel declared in his speech at the First Congress of Soviet Writers in 1934, that art must emphasize the unexpected, surprising the reader with a renewed perception of life.

Myth and mystification throw serious scholars into confusion because Babel disregards the niceties of geographical and historical accuracy, not to mention ideologically acceptable historicity. Instead, the inventive fantasy of imagination vividly visualizes inner truths and historical parallels in much the same way that the boy-narrator of the childhood story "V podvale" ("In the Basement") transforms the dull, unpoetic details of a book about the life of Spinoza into a dramatic account of old Amsterdam, ending with a fantastic scene of the heretic's relentless, lonely death-struggle while Rubens (anachronistically!) stands by his bed taking a death mask. Just as the lies of the "untruthful little boy" expose hidden truths about his grandfather, so too Babel's sophisticated and complex play on historical and religious myths poeticizes the narrator's view of actuality and thereby affords a fresh interpretation of the contemporary meaning of legendary or supernatural events. In the transformation of myth several key devices of Babel's style are at play, such as the use of parallelism and the juxtaposition of the real and the ideal, the sacred and the profane, or the divine and the earthly. The lurid rich colours which stream from Pan Apolek's palette are Babel's own and in the author's taste for the heretical and the apocryphal may be sensed his belief in the potential of ordinary mortals for the epic and the spiritual.

Often, it must be said, Babel needs myths for no more than a playful means of irony. The scene of the Adoration of the Magi in the Odessa story "Lyubka Kazak" ("Lyubka the Cossack"), for example, should not be taken as a literal allegory, as at least one commentator has done. The babe to whom Lyubka tries to give the breast is indeed named after the royal house of David. Three guests arrive from strange lands and present exotic gifts to the Jewish mother—traditionally one of the wise gentiles is dark-skinned, although in this case he is a Malay, not an Ethiopian—and, as the three sailors dance, an orange star speeds across the sky, looking down on them (compare Matthew 2:9–12). These are not, however, gifts for a holy infant, but contraband Lyubka is purchasing. If the baby apparently lacks an earthly father, then this only emphasizes Lyubka's masculinity. She is, after all, a failed mother. The sleight of hand performed by Tsudechkis is, in a way, a "miracle," as perhaps implied by the Jewish dealer's name (cf. Polish *cud,* miracle). But if there is any allusion to the christological myth it is as an ambiguous hope for the new breed of Jews represented by the first-born Davidka and Karl-Yankel, born into the aftermath of the pogroms and on the eve of a new era. That hope was to be disillusioned after the Revolution. Benya Krik is eliminated by the Reds at the end of the film *Benya Krik* (1926), a fate shared with the old Odessa life in "Konets bogadel'ni" ("The End of the Old Folks' Home") and *Froim Grach,* just as the rebbe's "last son" Il'ya Bratslavsky dies, as has been mentioned, in "Syn rabbi."

The historical parallels in Babel's stories are also not without ironic paradoxes, but these in no way detract from the author's serious intent. A good illustration of the structural function of historical myth is the narrator's apostrophe in "Kostyol v Novograde":

Нищие орды катятся на твни древние города, о, Польша, песнь об единении всех холопов гремит над ними, и горе тебе, Речь Посполитая, горе тебе, князь Радзивилл, и тебе, князь Сапега, вставшие на час!

[Beggarly hordes are descending on your ancient cities, oh Poland, the hymn of unity of all serfs roars over cities, and woe to you, *Rzeczpospolita,* woe to you, Prince Radziwiłł, and woe to you, Prince Sapieha, who have risen momentarily!]

Prince Janusz Radziwiłł (1880–1939/40), head of the Polish Conservatives, and Prince Eustachy Sapieha (1881–1963), Polish Foreign Minister, are continuing, as it were, their ancestors' ancient conflict with Muscovy as part of Piłsudski's plan to resurrect the Poland of the eighteenth century. (Lew Sapieha, 1557–1633, planned to include Muscovy in the Polish-Lithuanian Commonwealth, and Janusz Radziwiłł, 1612–55, sent punitive expeditions against Khmelnitsky, the legendary forebear of Budyonny.) Such perceptive and sophisticated use (or creation) of historical myth calls up the historical background without need for an ideologically risky elaboration, as in "Perekhod cherez Zbruch" ("Crossing the Zbruch"), where the Red soldiers march along the "ever-memorable highway from Brest to Warsaw built on the bones of peasants by Nicholas I." Novograd, taken by Soviet troops in this story, is situated on the Słucz, not the Zbruch, a hundred miles to the south-west, and fell on 27 June 1920, at which time the rearguard could not have been strung out along the Brest-Warsaw road. What Babel wishes to convey, however, in the succinctness of his fiction is the symbolic nature, historically and artistically, of the crossing of the Zbruch, which signalled the reversal of the Polish invasion of the Ukraine, as well as stressing the personal significance of the narrator's entry into Poland and into the world of the First Red Cavalry. The army of Cossacks and peasants, treading the path of destiny of tsarist serfs along the road built by them (there is a pun here in the Russian), form part of the Bolshevik advance through Brest in the direction of Warsaw—the goal on the way to international revolution, which was, of course, never reached.

The play on historical and religious myth was to become muted in Babel's prose of the late twenties and thirties, and is absent from the fragment that has survived of the "povest' Yevreyka" ("The Jewess," begun around 1927), which draws a poignant picture of the final demise of the Jewish *shtetl*. Similarly, Babel came to deploy his colourful metaphors and sensuous imagery more sparsely and thus more devastatingly in his search for a new style and form after the mid-twenties. He nevertheless remained aware of the aesthetic power of myth as demonstrated in his mythicization of the Cossack and peasant masses and in his demythicization of Jesus or the oft-stereotyped Jewish world.

PETER STINE

Isaac Babel and Violence

By temperament Isaac Babel was a spy in the service of eternity. When asked why he was drawn to figures like KGB executioner Yezhov and their merchandise of death, he replied, "I don't want to touch it with my fingers—I just like to have a sniff and see what it smells like." It became his mission as a man and as a writer to breathe this polluted air, feigning impassivity for close access in order to bear witness to the violence of the Revolution. But never to touch it. Babel sprang from a Jewish ghetto into the romantic élan of the October insurrection and embraced the early course of events. They seemed at one stroke to free the Russian Jew from the czarist prison into an arena of limitless social possibility. But as a reign of terror set in, his origins became manifest in a complex pacifism, and a more subversive role became clear. "I can't make anything up," he admitted to Konstantin Paustovsky. "I have to know everything down to the last wrinkle, or I can't even begin to write. Authenticity, that's the motto, and I'm stuck with it." Such truth-telling was not something the Revolution could long afford to tolerate. Getting "to know everything," Babel refined his loot of perceptions into an art of epiphany that exploded all ideology in a restorative act of literary violence. Drawing a bond of brotherhood between himself and the Revolution's victims, this *agent provocateur* forged the ironic secret of his art and so revived the ancient proscription—Thou Shalt Not Kill—that had been banished to the dustbin of history. That such a reverence for life led to his disappearance into the Gulag during the purges seems now a tragic yet inevitable destiny.

From *Modern Fiction Studies* 30, no. 2 (Summer 1984). © 1984 by the Purdue Research Foundation, West Lafayette, Indiana.

Judging from his stories of his childhood, we may conclude that Babel knew death as illumination from an early age. It came with an outbreak of anti-Semitism, that "black vileness" that he admitted to Paustovsky was the one thing he could never comprehend. Indeed his indelible images of violence seem to suggest a state of lucid, mesmerized incredulity. In "The Story of My Dovecot" the short, weakly, ten-year-old prodigy passes his exams into the secondary school of Nikolayev, only to be victimized by a czarist-sponsored pogrom the day he goes to claim his reward. His elders herald his feat as a victory over "the foes who had encircled us and were thirsting for our blood," but this Jewish faith in learning is exploded when the boy is assaulted with his beloved pigeons by a legless cigarette vendor in the murderous streets:

> I lay on the ground, and the guts of the crushed bird trickled down from my temple. They flowed down my cheek, winding this way and that, splashing, blinding me. The tender pigeon-guts slid down over my forehead, and I closed my solitary unstopped eye so as not to see the world that spread out before me. The world was tiny, and it was awful. A stone lay just before my eyes, a little stone so chipped as to resemble the face of an old women with a large jaw. A piece of string lay not far away, and a bunch of feathers that still breathed. My world was tiny, and it was awful. I closed my eyes so as not to see it, and pressed myself tight into the ground that lay beneath me in soothing dumbness. This trampled earth in no way resembled real life, waiting for exams in real life. Somewhere far away Woe rode across it on a great steed, but the noise of the hoofbeats grew weaker and died away, and silence, the bitter silence that sometimes overwhelms children in their sorrow, suddenly deleted the boundary between body and the earth that was moving nowhither. The earth smelled of raw depths, of the tomb, of flowers. I smelled its smell and started crying, unafraid I was walking along an unknown street set on either side with white boxes, walking in a getup of bloodstained feathers, alone between the pavements swept clean as on Sunday, weeping bitterly, fully and happily as I never wept again in my life.

Here violence tears a veil from reality, compelling wonder, as the boy dies from innocence, even selfhood, into a zone of perceptual joy beyond fear or shame. Such is the mental state of one upon returning, as it were, from the dead—and this would be the ground of the *joie de vivre* and sunlit aesthetics of this deeply eschatological writer. Yet if the world for the survivor is renewed in a cosmic embrace, he also has special obligations. Returning home, the boy comes upon his grandfather murdered, fish stuck in his mouth and trousers, one "still alive, and struggling." This symbol of degradation would later take voice in the undercurrents of Babel's art: a subterranean link with the victims of violence affixed forever.

Yet the clairvoyant spy must be attracted to a degree by the deeds he is exposing. "First Love" traces the purely psychological impact of this trauma on Babel's nascent sense of manhood. First love is Galina, a Russian woman whom the boy has spied upon sexually dominating her husband (an army officer) and who harbors the Babels for the duration of the pogrom. From her porch, he witnesses his father pleading on his knees to a member of a Cossack patrol, who, "raising his hand in its lemon-colored chamois glove to the peak of his cap," divinely ignores the looting of their store. Such a dispersion of parental authority sends the boy into hysterical hiccups. To blot out the day's nightmarish revelations he now fantasizes himself as *someone else*, "a member of the Jewish Defense Corps" shooting at the murderers with a "useless" rifle—a fantasy that then fades into a feeling of "immanent death" and a vision of Galina being seduced "high in the world's blueness" by her "half-clad" officer. This fantasy, which passes from vengeance to his own voyeuristic nonexistence in a world of morbid sexuality and military force, is interrupted by the impotent grief of his father, and the boy's verging mental breakdown soon dictates a family retreat to Odessa. In such memories, Babel concludes, "I find . . . the beginning of the ills that torment me, the cause of my early fading."

Babel's emergence as a passionate ironist, then, was in part a reflection of a deeply divided psyche. On one hand, he was baptized into moral and aesthetic consciousness by violence, providing the radiant backdrop ("a bitter silence that sometimes overwhelms children in their sorrow" ["The Story of My Dovecot"]) to his retrospective fiction. Yet as a persona inside his own narratives, he was also seduced by the spectacle and held a captive to its model of manhood. This he suffered, quite consciously, as the "incomprehensible ailment" of a vulnerable Russian Jew who desired to escape his fate as a traditional victim. Babel's awestruck admiration for aspects of the Cossack ethos, most notably in *Red Cavalry*, can best be grasped as a dream of rescue—born of witnessing his father's humiliation before that patrol's life-dispensing power. Fortunately, this "ailment" opened the portals of discovery, enabling Babel as an artist to keep his sense of identity fluid and open, receptive to the historical moment. Indeed his own *repulsion/attraction* to violence ran parallel to the moral self-debate of a revolutionary generation in its often parricidal struggle with its own past. But there the parallel ends. The Revolution was to resolve this struggle with Stalin's campaign of genocide against his own people. For Babel there was no severing of his roots without merging with the agency of his earlier oppression. Whatever we make of the complex ground of his pacifism, his rifle remained forever "useless," his flight from his origins an eager and outgoing interest in the world anchored in love for his spiritual kin.

Babel's stories of his Odessa childhood trace the trajectory of this flight, but only to anticipate the return of a "repressed" reservoir of Jewish humanity that made his vision of reality whole. In "In the Basement" the boy, solitary, bookish, and hyper-imaginative, courts with mendacities the friendship of a wealthy schoolmate, whose mansion fills him with visions of an exotic Western world. But when the visit is returned, his *masquerading self* ("nothing I had told him about really existed. What did exist was different, and much more surprising than anything I had invented, but at the age of twelve I had no idea how things stood with me and reality") is exploded by an invasion of his eccentric, drunken relatives—leaving the boy "dead" and shouting Mark Antony's ironic funeral oration as his guest takes flight. Later his inept, mock-heroic attempt at suicide by drowning himself in the water barrel only generates epiphany ("I opened my eyes and saw on the bottom of the barrel the swollen tail of my shirt and two feet pressed against one another") and provokes his grandfather to remark scornfully on his gesture of defeat: "Grandson, I am going to take a dose of castor oil, so as to have something to lay on your grave."

Such a tribal injunction to endure with an abiding joy in sheer existence would not be lost on the mature artist. Yet early on, Babel's need to escape the stunted aspects of his Jewish uprising steered him toward the voyaging invisibility of exile. This is exposed in "Awakening" as the young boy, burdened by his father's displaced ambitions, escapes Zagursky's violin school, "a factory of Jewish dwarfs in lace collars and patent-leather pumps," for the more manly pursuits of Odessa harbor. Here he learns to admire the crafted pipes ("in each one of them thought was invested, a drop of eternity") of an old English sailor. Here he battles the heavy sea waves that "swept me further and further away from our house, impregnated with the smell of leaks and Jewish destiny." Here his literary genius is recognized by Nikitich Smolich, a proofreader of the *Odessa News,* who replaces his father's passion of fame and "protested bills of exchange" with a love of the physical universe: "I came to love that man, with the love that only a lad suffering from hysteria and headaches can feel for a real man." Yet the boy can't conquer the hydrophobia of his ancestors, and once his truancy is discovered, he is pressed to take refuge from his raging father in a locked privy.

"I was thinking of running away." So Babel concludes this story, and, when he did, it was into Bohemian poverty in war-depressed Petrograd in 1916. Now his patron saint became Maksim Gorky, who, recognizing both his precocity as a writer and his lack of experience, advised that he abandon literature and go among the people. This was Gorky on the eve of the Revolution, before his conversion to Party rectitude—a voice already warning against Bolshevik abuse of power and labeling Lenin a "cold-blooded trickster who spares neither the honor nor the lives of the proletariet" (*You Must Know Everything*; all further references to this text will be abbreviated as *YMKE*). Under his auspices, then, Babel served on the Rumanian front in World War One and with the northern army against Yudenich in 1918. He returned to savor the dominant mood of elation in the Revolution's wake. And yet Babel's early journalistic pieces from this period, appearing in Gorky's *New Life*, focus upon subjects that forecast his later work of moral espionage: the wretched Bolshevik homes for juveniles and orphans, the neglect and abuse of blinded war veterans, the cruel dislocations and death visited upon the peasantry by enforced economic "evacuations," the emaciation of wet-nurses caused by corruption in the State nurseries. Too often these investigations led Babel to police stations and morgues. Out of his indignation grew a standard by which he would measure the achievements of the new era: "We must see to it that children are born properly. This is real revolution—of this I am quite sure" (*YMKE*).

Babel's early stories from this time appeared in the short-lived *Lava* and marked the beginning of his observations on war. With subject matter borrowed from books written by French officers who saw action in World War One, they reveal his bent for impersonation and his voyeuristic loss of self into others. "On the Field of Honor" tells of a shell-shocked village idiot in uniform who, caught masturbating in a crater, refuses a punitive order to go over the top. His captain urinates in his face, driving him in despair into no man's land where he is killed by fire both from the Germans and the officer. "The Deserter" focuses upon a young French soldier, tired of the carnage and ready to surrender, who is executed by his commanding officer when he refuses the "honorable" option of suicide. In "Old Marescot's Family" a French *père* wanders into a graveyard under bombardment with the bodies of his family in a sack, searching for his burial vault until he finds himself standing in it. In each case Babel strips away the vainglorious and jingoistic flourishes of the original, so that his dry, matter-of-fact narrative generates compassion for the common soldier—who emerges as a camouflaged alter ego. ("A soldier has no time for mysticism. A field of skulls has been churned up into trenches. That's war" [*YMKE*].) As exercises in compression, these stories bespeak the grainy, tight-lipped silence of the fallen dead. Already they forecast the moral issue of *Red Cavalry*, which, as Lionel Trilling has observed, is not whether the author-protagonist can endure violence and death with honor, but whether he can endure killing his fellow man.

The *Lava* stories were the last Babel published before he joined Budenny's First Cavalry for the Polish campaign of 1920. Afterward, no longer needing the recollections of others, he set to work creating his unmistakable literary identity. "It was only in 1923," he said, "that I learned to express my ideas clearly and at not too great length." These ideas fostered concrete images that speak for themselves. His aesthetic of compression was a kind of asthma before what W. B. Yeats called in "Easter 1916" the "terrible beauty" of the new century. While the Revolution during the 1920s went about its leisurely "revaluation of values," Babel excruciatingly revised his art by paring away all ideological prophylactics, leaving only flashlike seizures of a passionate moment. His irony, based on the naked juxtaposition of opposite modes of being, canceled out nothing. His own captivation by the will to violence floats like a psychological mote in the rays of a higher vision. By such techniques, he preserves what Nadezhda Mandelstam felt his artistic contemporaries had lost to the Revolution, "the feeling that every second of time is, in its fullness and destiny, the equal of eternity itself" (*Hope Against Hope,* trans. Max Hayward). Quite rightly his literary credo, embedded in "Guy de Maupassant," is couched in military terms, for, minus any intervening intellect, his art is calculated to penetrate consciousness like a bullet: "I began to speak of style, of the army of words, of the army in which all kinds of weapons may come into play. No iron can stab the breast with such force as a period put at the right place." With a limitless respect for the reader, Babel draws no conclusions, makes no value judgments. The right or wrong of what is witnessed is either self-evident or lost. There is an awesome aspect to this art, for its use of epiphany moves beyond morality only to recover its intuitive presence in the primitive joy of the sensuous universe.

II

For Babel, then, the only legitimate form of violence was pure perception. "There is no greater joy for me," he said, "than to follow impassively the play of passions on human faces" (in *Isaac Babel: Russian Master of the Short Story,* by James E. Falen). The only exception to this ethic is in the wholly imagined world of *Tales of Odessa.* These stories were composed concurrently with *Red Cavalry,* mischievously linked with that work, but clearly anterior in inspiration. For here Babel elaborates a jaunty, erotic dream of what legitimate violence might be like in the Jewish ghetto of Odessa, the Moldavanka, still laboring under czarist Russia of the 1890s. His single hero, Benya Krik, is a richly brocaded anti-self, a mask of physical potency and moral authority, a gangster who prevails because he "was passionate, and passion rules the universe" ("The King"). Placed in a frame of age addressing youth, *Tales of Odessa* insinuates the form of a Jewish wisdom book—but the law is revised to meet the exigencies and lawlessness of the Great Pale. Benya Krik is an heir to messianic echoes now turned ironic in an age of unbelief. At every stage, Babel's virtuoso narrative techniques both proclaim his "unreality" and elevate him to personal fable. Again the irony cancels out nothing. Benya is meant to be his creator's own dream of compensation and also, as John Berryman has observed, "the King that history had denied the exiled, dispossessed, persecuted, and suffering Jews" (*The Freedom of the Poet*).

Babel displays his own lavish poetic distortions and then collapses them in "The King." Here Benya, who reigns by turning a rabid Jewish business ethic into straightforward extortion in the service of the community, presides over his sister's wedding in the uterine folds of the Moldavanka. But his spies learn of a police raid timed to interrupt this most venerable of Jewish ceremonies. In clipped gangster lingo that mimics Homeric dialogue, Benya accepts the danger with stylish sang-froid in a pose of clairvoyance. A flashback to how he tamed the avaricious Eichbaum establishes the basis of this confidence. His extortion letters getting no response, Benya raided the old man's farm, his men putting a dairy herd to the knife and firing shots in the air—for as the narrator interjects: "If you don't fire in the air you may kill someone." Yet one glimpse of Eichbaum's beautiful daughter and Benya is "defeated"; he returns a day later and asks for her hand. Violence in *this* world only begets sons-in-law, not corpses. Now we are swept back to the wedding, with Benya's mafiosa in attendance ("aristocrats of the Moldavanka") and his sister ("a virgin of forty summers who suffered from goiter") hungrily awaiting her miserable, purchased bridegroom. This ironic touch suggests that *some* Jewish suffering is rooted in the mere depth of things. But the threat of the police raid remains. Reversing Jewish history, Benya's men strike first. Soon pogromlike flames have the police station "blazing like a house on fire" with the officers "rushing up smoky staircases and hurling boxes out of windows, while prisoners, unguarded, were making the most of their chance." Having staged this burlesque of revolution, Benya ambles up to the police captain to remark upon what has been ordained by the daring narrative design: "What do you say to this stroke of bad luck? A regular act of God!"

The secret of Benya's rise to power is narrated by the elder Arye-Leib in "How It Was Done in Odessa." In a self-referential aside Babel has the elder exhort his young listener on a cemetery wall to "quit playing rowdy at your desk" and to imagine a "rowdy in public places" who started his climb by overthrowing the legacy of a brutish father: "What would you have done in Benya Krik's place? You would have done nothing. But he did something. That's why he's the King, while you thumb your nose in the privy." What he does is put into action his creator's fantasies by challenging the reign of Tartakovsky, whose wealth and alliance with the anti-Semitic "Sloboda thugs" make him a prime target of the gangsters. "Jew-and-a-Half" has "the soul of a murderer" but "is our blood"—suggesting causes other than prejudice for the enslavement of the Moldavanka. This time Benya's extortion notes are lost in delivery, but the haphazard only produces the feeling of inevitability. In the ensuing raid on Tartakovsky's place, the tone turns dubious with an insistence on the theatrical: "Then . . . the curtain rose on a three act opera." First a clerk is *accidentally* shot, and Benya's ascendancy now lies in putting things right with justice. Next Tartakovsky is forced to pay compensation while Benya rationalizes the death to the clerk's aunt by associating himself with Jehovah: "A terrible mistake has been made, Aunt Pesya. But wasn't it a mistake on the part of God to settle Jews in Russia, for them to be tormented worse than in Hell?" But at the funeral Benya brings a new reign of protection ("on that day the cops wore cotton gloves,") and the community is united in earthly glory ("honorary dairymaids . . . wafted the odors of the sea and of milk") as Arye-Leib orates the proceedings like "the Lord God spoke on Mount Sinai from the Burning Bush." This parodic appropriation of the Law also extends to revolutionary socialism as Benya casts the clerk as a hero who "perished for the whole working class." This eclipse of every *ism* by the sheer force of personality earns Benya the title of "King" from the lisping lips of an onwatching gravedigger. Yet when Arye-Leib is done, the boy keeps silent, still with spectacles on his nose and autumn in his heart.

We must be wary, then, when Raymond Rosenthal calls Benya Krik a "Jewish Cossack." Structural ironies explode such a claim. Indeed in *Tales of Odessa* Babel reserves that title for a woman ("Lyubka the Cossack") who is then won over by the humanity of a wise old Jew. Again the issue is the proper raising of a child. Lyubka, in her various rowdy professions as innkeeper, winedealer, madam of a brothel, and dealer in smuggled goods, is a catalogue of her creator's own youthful enthusiasms. In real terms this amounts to neglecting her son. In her absence, Tsudechkis is detained in the inn due to unpaid bills. He likens his captivity to being "in the hands of Pharaoh" but trusts "in God, who will lead me out of here as he has led all Jews out—first from Egypt, and then from the wilderness." Once more Babel updates Jewish destiny, now with the Cossack ethos (internalized in Lyubka) assuming the role of traditional oppressor—and so projects (covertly) the resolution of his own split psyche upon the narrative fate of the child. Upon her return, Tsudechkis scolds the woman for having "ridden off for three years on business" and leaving him "at the mercy of a famished babe in arms." But despite Lyubka's barbs, he strikes a friendship by weaning her child. (Is the ironic message not that Babel recognized his own boyhood fantasies as vicarious breast-feeding?) This feat earns Tsudechkis a role as Lyubka's manager for fifteen years and, indeed, is a wry symbolic forecast of Babel's own "management" of the Cossack ethos that is the underlying dialectic of *Red Cavalry*.

III

Babel's masterpiece, based on his service as a transport officer with Budenny's First Cavalry in 1920, tells the saga of another kind of raid—a furious, endless campaign, spreading social justice through slaughter and trampling on horseback across a prostrate Poland. On this expanding edge of the Revolution, the law of "historical necessity" is reduced to a relentless pursuit of war and death. Babel, as Lyutov, is both cultural *naif* and urban *intelligent*, a stranger to the world he describes. This self is not impersonal, or primarily psychological, but effortlessly manifold, like the emotions and sensations of the campaign. Polished vignettes are framed in battlefield violence, yet etched in a remarkable calm. This "violence" between form and content generates a sense of wonder, a detachment of mood and time, "capturing" tableaux in a static tension of being. Silence acquires a maximum expressiveness. Babel used the traditional Russian *skaz* (written or spoken monologues of others) to deepen and to broaden the range of his witness. But either mode of narration is sounding the moral resonances of his own double allegiance to the cause of the Revolution and to the eternal suffering of its victims.

This tension is struck immediately in "Crossing into Poland." As the Red cavalry gallops across the Zbruch River, only the pure, neutral physical universe is expressive of the violation of a territory: "The orange sun rolled down the sky like a lopped-off head, and mild light glowed in the cloud gorges." In Novograd Lyutov billets in the ransacked home of three Jews, who, when ordered to clean up the filth, "skipped about noiselessly, monkey-fashion, like Japs in a circus act." But playing the invader is a kind of sacrilege, and, as Lyutov beds down on a disemboweled mattress, "the moon, clasping in her blue hands her round, bright, carefree face, wandered like a vagrant outside the window." That night in a dream Lyutov sees Savitsky shoot the eyes out of a retreating brigade commander. When the pregnant Jew awakens him from his nightmare with fingers groping his *own eyes,* we recognize the link between the Brigade Commander and his inner situation. Indeed Lyutov's bedfellow, upon inspection, is the woman's father, slain by the retreating Poles: "His throat had been torn out and his face cleft in two; in his beard blue blood was clotted like a lump of lead." Now she has the last word, a cry of "terrible violence," a lament of irremediable loss that rises unanswered above the bloody work of revolution. "And now I wish to know where in the whole world you could find another father like my father?"

This cry, in endless variations, invades Lyutov's consciousness via troubled dreams that universalize his sympathies. Adrift in the wilderness of war, the "chronicle of our workaday offenses oppressed me without respite, like an ailing heart" ("The Road to Brody"). And for moral ballast, despite himself, he starts to drift toward the peacemakers. In Novograd he meets a wandering Polish artist, a heretic and mystic whose "wise and beautiful life" ("Pan Apolek") intoxicates him and whose religious frescoes parallel Babel's own literary credo by raising the commonplace faces around him to sainthood: "I then made a vow to follow Pan Apolek's example. And the sweetness of meditated rancor, the bitter scorn I felt for the curs and swine of mankind, the fires of silent and intoxicating revenge—all this I sacrificed to my new vow." This vow of total acceptance unveils a multiplicity of worlds for the spy. At first repelled by the Polish Jews, by their poverty and warped physicality, Lyutov soon discovers "their capacity for suffering is full of a somber greatness, and their unvoiced contempt for the Polish gentry unbounded" ("Discourse on the *Tachanka*"). In Zhitomir, from their ranks, he meets old Gedali, the owner of a curio shop, who resumes for him on Sabbaths the lessons of "the rotten Talmuds of my childhood" ("Gedali"). Gedali welcomes the defeat of the Poles ("that is splendid, that is Revolution") but not the voice of the new regime: "You don' know what you are fond of, Gedali. I'll shoot you and then you'll know. I cannot do without shooting, because I am the Revolution." In reply all that Lyutov can do is repeat these words in a faint-hearted appeal to the laws of expediency. Then the elder replies:

> But the Poles, kind sir, shot because they were the Counter-Revolution. You shoot because you are the Revolution. But sure-

ly the Revolution means joy. And joy does not like orphans in the house. Good men do good deeds. The Revolution is the good deed of good men. But good men do not kill. So it is bad people that are making the Revolution. But the Poles are bad people, too. Then how is Gedali to tell which is Revolution and which is Counter-Revolution?"

Gedali's dream of an "International of good people" is dismissed by Lyutov as an impossibility—yet he is forced to admit with deepening disaffection that the real one is "eaten with gunpowder . . . and spiced with the best-quality blood."

This issue of violence is what checks Lyutov's desire, born of fancied inadequacies, to identify with the Cossacks. Joining the brigade in "My First Goose," he stands in voyeuristic awe of Savitsky, whose "long legs were like girls sheathed to the neck in shining riding boots." But he is snubbed and hazed by the men as a "brainy type," told to "go out and mess up a lady . . . and you'll have the boys patting you on the back." What Lyutov does to earn their homoerotic company is seize the goose of an imploring peasant woman and brutally kill it with a sword. That night he reads the *Red Trooper* aloud around the campfire and "rejoiced, spying out exultingly the secret curve of Lenin's straight line." But later: "I dreamed: and in my dreams saw women. But my heart, stained with bloodshed, grated and brimmed over." These rites of initiation involve a violation of the soul. That childhood trauma of having his own pigeon smashed against his face during a pogrom is both normative and ineradicable. Hence when the issue is killing humans, Lyutov turns stillborn. Accused by the epileptic Akinfiev of taking an unloaded revolver into battle, he drives his antagonist away, but that evening "I continued on my way, imploring fate to grant me the simplest of proficiencies—the ability to kill my fellow-men" ("After the Battle"). This incapacity operates beyond psychology, is an ontological grounding, and under some circumstances is recognized as a moral weakness. When Lyutov comes upon the wounded Dolgushov, who asks to be mercifully dispatched to escape Polish torture, he leaves the chore for Alfonka, to whom he explains ("with a wry smile"): "I couldn't, you see" ("The Death of Dolgushov"). This admits an element of squeamishness in Lyutov's abstention, as well as something else. "Get out of my sight," his friend mutters, "or I'll kill you. You guys in specs have about as much pity for chaps like us as a cat has for a mouse."

This charge is rebutted by the expansive pity shown for the plight of the Cossacks, but only to a degree. An element of exploitation remains. Good and evil interpenetrate in *Red Cavalry*, and Lyutov is no exception. Ultimately he must accept the charge of weakness leveled by those bloodied men "busy shelling and getting at the kernel for you" ("Evening"). *Red Cavalry* is utterly free of self-righteousness or hypocrisy on this matter. Any witness of stature knows he is as responsible for what he sees as for what he does. "What is our Cossack?" Babel wrote in his diary. "Layers of trashiness, daring, professionalism, revolutionary spirit, bestial cruelty." These realities are now what this spy knows, for our sake. By delivering in silence his dazzling images of the Cossacks, Babel runs the risk of becoming a scapegoat for their deeds. There is the professionalism of former Czarist "non-com" Budenny, who smiles and smokes behind the lines, ready to shoot anyone who turns back. Revolutionary spirit burns in the Kurdyukov brothers, "dull, broad-faced, goggle-eyed" giants who enter the stream of history by beating their father to death as a renegade White, and in Balmashev, who throws a peasant woman off a moving troop train for smuggling salt, then "took my faithful rifle off the wall and washed away that stain from the face of the workers' land and republic" ("Salt"). One recalls the trashiness of the Cossacks drunkenly plundering the Catholic church at Novograd. Or the bestial cruelty of Afonka Bida, who, losing his beloved horse in battle, searches for a new one in an endless, homicidal raid against the Polish countryside. The bellicose Pavlichenko, still smelling of the dairy herd, seeks out his former landlord and "trampled on him for an hour or maybe more. And in that time I got to know life through and through" ("The Life and Times of Matthew Pavlichenko").

As Lyutov, by proxy, also gets to know these things through and through, the tenor of *Red Cavalry* grows gradually more elegaic. And as he falls away from the cause of the Revolution, we watch the gradual expulsion of its forces from Poland itself. All this is telescoped with special horror in "Squad Commander Trunov." The story opens with Trunov, a "long corpse with its mouth stuffed full of broken teeth," being eulogized as a "world hero" by Pugachov. As a worshipper of heroes, Lyutov also pays his respects ("I would be the last of all to judge him"). But earlier that day the two of them had collided over the treatment of prisoners. Half-crazed by a head wound, Trunov had executed an old man, nearly shot a comrade over the corpse's trousers, then turned his rifle on another prisoner and "sent the Polish lad's skull flying, and bits of his brains dripped over my hands." Silence reigns. Enough time to recall (perhaps) an afternoon in Nikolayev long ago when his hands were covered with pigeon brains. In any case Lyutov thwarts Trunov by refusing to rub out this murdered prisoner from the official record. After this Trunov is strangely resigned to his own death and wanders off to a suicidal encounter with strafing American warplanes—

now just a heroic anachronism, both in the war and in Lyutov's expanding consciousness. Replacing him as an emerging authority is the white-clad Galician, a mysterious figure who wanders through the story radiating a Christ-like charity and humility, "his gibbet-like frame cleaving the burning brilliance of the skies."

Lyutov may have dismissed Gedali's "International of good people," then, but he is drawn as the campaign wears on to an informal one of his own composed of those, both Cossack and Pole, who are his secret selves. There is Khlebnikov, who, like himself, "looked on the world as a meadow in May—a meadow traversed by women and horses." Failing to reclaim his beloved stallion from Savitsky, he is at last, due to head wounds, declared unfit for service. There is Sandy the Christ, who, infected with syphilis through his brutish stepfather, remains a gentle peacemaker among the Cossacks. There are the voiceless dead. Lost on a night battlefield at Khotin with his own horse killed, Lyutov by accident spatters a Polish corpse with urine—"I wiped the skull of my unknown brother, and went on, bent beneath the weight of the saddle" ("Two Ivans"). And there is Elijah, the precocious son of the Polish rabbi of Zhitomir, whose wasted body Lyutov drags aboard a retreating Cossack troop train. His possessions objectify as well as anything the warring coordinates of the narrator's own psyche:

> His things were strewn about pell-mell—mandates of the propagandist and notebooks of the Jewish poet, the portraits of Lenin and Maimonides lay side by side, the knotted iron of Lenin's skull beside the dull silk of the portraits of Maimonides. A lock of woman's hair lay in a book, the Resolutions of the Party's Sixth Congress, and the margins of Communist leaflets were crowded with crooked lines of ancient Hebrew verse. They fell upon me in a mean and depressing rain—pages of the Song of Songs and revolver cartridges.
>
> ("The Rabbi's Son")

In his final breath, Elijah says that his loyalty to the feminine kept him from joining the Party, but now "when there's a revolution on, a mother's an episode." His death ("I was there beside my brother when he breathed his last") is the symbolic loss of Lyutov's hopes for himself and the Revolution. In its place is born a religion of universal brotherhood, washed in the compassion of old Gedali's vision:

> All is mortal. Only the Mother is destined to immortality. And when the mother is no longer among the living, she leaves a

memory which none yet has dared to sully. The memory of the mother nourishes in us a compassion that is like the ocean, and the measureless ocean feeds the rivers that dissect the universe.
("The Rabbi")

By the end of *Red Cavalry*, this compassion has been all but blotted out by the oozing red chloroform skies of the campaign. A brigade prostitute cries out after the slaughter at Chesniki, "Everything that's gone on today makes me want to go and hide my face" ("The Song"). As an historical experiment, the grafting of straight Party doctrine onto the primitive Cossacks has proven a failure. All that is "liberated" is an ideological paranoia ("Nowadays everybody judges everybody else" ["Two Ivans"]) and a license to conscience-free killing. Only the names of places retain a dignity—Brody, Berestechko, the cemetery at Kozin. Their "mummified passions" stand in eternal reproach to the campaign. Even the Cossacks have lost heart. Undersupplied, riddled with defections, demoralized by the futility of cavalry against trenches and automatic arms, they retreat into what forecasts the next stage of the Revolution: a suspicion of "winking" treason everywhere. A nameless Cossack, whose "savage bayonet" was turned by Lenin and Trotsky to "predestined guts and viscera" ("Treason"), informs the Party about slackness in a military hospital. He will eagerly embrace his next role as executioner of Russian dissidents. He does not know that the Cossacks, in their defiant ethnic identity, will themselves be liquidated by the Revolution in the next decade. We get a glimpse of the new breed of executioners, those of the revolutionary tribunals, with the sinister appearance of Baulin at the conclusion. Young, tough, stubborn, Baulin "had never known worry" ("Argamak"), and he assails Lyutov: "I see the whole of you. You're trying to live without enemies. That's all you think about, not having enemies." We accept the justice of this charge but now recognize it as a precious, vanishing virtue. There is dark menace and prophecy in his claim that "boredom comes of it." In the fading moments Lyutov fulfills his dream of riding a horse before the accepting eyes of the Cossacks, but ironically this feat has paled into invisibility before the advancing Revolution's new god of violence.

IV

"I'm pulling back now, but what does it matter," Babel wrote in his diary in the last month of the Russo-Polish campaign. "Others will make the Revolution . . . and once again I am thinking my own thoughts." No doubt these thoughts, private and disaffiliated, were keenly tuned to a changing political climate. Judging from Budenny's attack on *Red Cavalry*, and more generally from the eclipse of Trotsky and the expansion of state terror under Stalin, Babel had to recognize the risk in his continuing literary witness. A head-hunting mentality was taking root, a brand of "official" spying and "informing" that travestied the modus operandi of his own art. Still, Babel had gained an immense popularity and was under the protective sponsorship of Gorky. Most likely Soviet censors, blind to the very spirit they were trying to eradicate, were deaf to the subversive silences of his fiction. One imagines a margin of freedom here. Then why did Babel's productivity drop off sharply after 1925? We can dismiss the simple answer of fear. He might have escaped Russia several times, but he chose instead to be wrenched from his family (exiled in Paris) and to pursue his "hellish trade" on native soil. Nadezhda Mandelstam, in noting the silence of her husband (Osip), Pasternak, and Akhmatova in the late 1920s, speaks of "a hypnotic trance," the "onset of a kind of numbness, the first symptoms of lethargy," born of a pressure "to submit to historical inevitability.... another name for the dreams of all those who had ever fought for human happiness." But what if historical inevitability arrived as a bullet in the neck? Mandelstam speculates that writers, in order to find their voices again, "had first to determine their places in the new world being created before their eyes—and this they could only do by learning from experience how it affected everybody else." And yet Babel had been engaged in this work for a decade; he knew where he stood with his age: outside it. His declining productivity, then, his "early fading" had probably more to do with forging a new narrative art to speak to new realities. And with one other issue. Judging from his often-expressed dissatisfaction with *Red Cavalry*, it can be surmised he was chagrined by the prominence he had given to his own captivation by violence. What had become a monolithic tool of the Revolution was for him now an exploded romanticism.

At any rate, Babel's last stories reflect a new directness, a faith in psychological realism to explore the shaping influences of his childhood and the depredations of the Revolution. Two stories in particular measure his own development—the maturation of his curiosity from voyeurism to moral discovery. In "Through the Fanlight" the boy pays the madam of a brothel five roubles to spy from a bathroom window upon a young prostitute. All goes well until one day when, while she services a routinely disengaged client, he slips and is discovered hanging from the ledge. The prostitute arrives to scold him while comforting her client with kisses, and suddenly the boy wonders: "Why was she kissing him?" He had not been watching the real event. Now he rescales the ladder for ten roubles and witnesses the prostitute give herself "with the passion of one in love," while her protector "the lanky bloke wallowed in businesslike bliss." Out of a shallow interest in the prurient, the boy discovers a tragic incalculable of life. Love is the big surprise (from which there is no protection). The link between this epiphany and the Revolution is drawn in "With Old Man Makhno." Here Babel spies upon a Jewish maid the morning after her rape by six young Cossacks. Their underling, the retarded urchin Kikin, is protesting to her with aggrieved justice that he was not allowed his turn. The maid listens impassively ("of yesterday's virginity there remained only the cheeks, more than usually inflamed, and the eyes, thrust downward") as he elaborates upon the fame of the Makhno crowd: "but knock around with them for a while," he says, "and you'll soon find that each has a heart of stone." Kikin's inability to convert this truth into guilt, or into any compassionate solidarity with their victim, signals the moral myopia of his creator's early voyeuristic ties with the Revolution. All of this is rendered symbolically when suddenly "he pressed his palms to the floor, threw his legs in the air and, his protruding heels rigid, started walking quickly about on his hands."

More and more, then, Babel's witness returned a tragic sense of life. For instance, in the retrospective "The S.S. *Cow-Wheat*," set against the rich ethnic diversity of the Volga region during the Civil War, he measures the price of the Revolution's cold-blooded efficiency. The skipper of the *Cow-Wheat*, Korostelyov, a vodka-swilling mystic of pre-Revolutionary days, suspends his gunrunning duties for a secret night journey to procure liquor, only to be summarily executed by the Party official Makeyev upon his return: "It's all very well to be a fine fellow three times over, to have spent time in hermitages, to have sailed the White Sea, to be a desperate fellow generally; but please don't waste fuel . . ." The romantic gangster-world of the Moldavanka in *Tales of Odessa* is starkly changed in "The End of the Old Folks' Home," where Babel's former gallery of Jewish wise men (Arye-Lieb and others) is reduced to gravediggers pinched in poverty and persecuted by the Soviet authorities. In "Dante Street" his voyeuristic interest in the sexual exploits of a French friend issues in murder by a jealous lover, a deed subsumed into a tragic sense of French history reaching back to Danton. Early in his career, Babel had spoken of Russia's need for a "poet of the sun," even a "Literary Messiah," who will come "from the sunny steppes washed by the sea" (*YMKE*) to replenish the national literature. But by 1934, at the Soviet Writers' Congress, he declared that he was now "a master of the genre of silence." We might wonder whether, in addition to the obvious causes, Babel's silence wasn't part of the recognition that his own writing, with its truth-telling depths, could now only propagate despair.

This is suggested in "Guy de Maupassant," a brilliant summary of Babel's spiritual odyssey. Once again the place is Petrograd, 1916, with himself as a young Bohemian writer, spending his mornings "hanging around the morgues and police stations," his evenings dismissing Tolstoy's conversion to religion as "yellow.... all fear," abiding by the wisdom of his ancestors that "we are born to enjoy our work, our fights, and our love; we are born for that and for nothing else." Adrift in this callow buoyancy, Babel finds work in assisting the translations of Raisa, a handsome Jewess whose wizened husband has grown rich selling war materials to the army. Soon Raisa ravishes his dreams. He woos her with his mastery of Maupassant until one night, with both of them drunk, he reads aloud "L'Aveu," and their identities merge into their fictional counterparts: the lascivious Polyte and modestly submissive Celeste. After the seduction ("Of all the gods ever put on the crucifix, this was the most ravishing"), Babel feels intoxicated with life; yet returning to his digs he finds a biography of Maupassant and reads through the night:

> That night I learned from Edouard Maynial that Maupassant.... was twenty-five when he was first attacked by congenital syphilis. His productivity and *joie de vivre* withstood the onsets of the disease. At first he suffered from headaches and fits of hypochondria. Then the specter of blindness arose before him. His sight weakened. He became suspicious of everyone, unsociable and pettily quarrelsome. He struggled furiously, dashed about the Mediterranean in a yacht, fled to Tunis, Morocco, Central Africa ... and wrote ceaselessly. He attained fame, and at forty years of age cut his throat; lost a great deal of blood, yet lived through it. He was then put away in a madhouse. There he crawled about on his hands and knees, devouring his own excrement. The last line in his hospital report read: *Monsieur de Maupassant va s'animaliser.* He died at the age of forty-two, his mother surviving him.

Now Babel senses that although appropriating Maupassant's techniques of irony, he had missed his mentor's tragic sense, as he had Tolstoy's and Raisa's earlier. "The fog came close to the window, the world was hidden from me. My heart contracted as the foreboding of some essential truth touched me with light fingers." Fifteen years of experience had lifted the fog for the composer of these lines and confirmed their sense of personal foreboding. Like Maupassant, he would die of an "incurable ailment" in his early forties, his mother surviving him.

Babel's fate was most likely sealed with the death of Gorky in 1936. He continued to labor at writing but published little, turning for busy work to drama and film. "Daily I read idiotic screenplay manuscripts and revise them. I do anything—just in order not to write, let alone publish." There were rumors of a novel in progress. Babel also wrote a screenplay that contained a boldly derogatory portrait of Stalin—which most likely provoked his arrest in 1938. "They didn't give me enough time," he said when the KGB arrived. Still there was sufficient time to leave behind work of genius—fictionalized autobiography invaded by the nightmare energies of the early twentieth century yet curiously triumphant over them. In an era of mass cultural suicide, Babel's nascent sense of guilt as a survivor forged a bond of responsibility with his fallen brothers and so provided an etiological basis for morality once the Revolution had embarked on extirpating its memory through sheer violence. This was continuous with his aesthetics. The godlike concreteness of his prose links Babel with the poetic school of Acmeism, which Osip Mandelstam defined as "a nostalgia for world culture." Indeed this memory floats like a deep sea in the silences of his art. In these respects his stories are, as he said of Maupassant's, "the magnificent grave of a human heart," and it is consistent that his grave lay beside his unknown comrades in a Stalinist concentration camp. Yet his art also records a timeless present, piercing the heart with the depth and expansiveness of its vision. All of Babel's artistic "violences" are only meant to return us to the precious earth, so that we see, like the narrator of his final "Di Grasso," "for the first time the things surrounding me as they really were: frozen in silence and ineffably beautiful."

VICTOR ERLICH

Color and Line:
Notes on the Art of Isaac Babel

Western critics of Russian literature are fairly unanimous in hailing Isaac Babel as the finest early Soviet prose writer. Yet he remains to date one of the least deciphered modern Russian masters. His brilliantly idiosyncratic art eludes categories and subverts labels. Because of his proclivity for the hyperbole and his partiality for passion, he has been dubbed on occasion a romantic. Yet the stark and relentless naturalism of some of his scenes is not easily compatible with this designation. Even less illuminating, to be sure, is the "realistic" label pinned on Babel posthumously, in the process of his rehabilitation in the post-Stalin era, by Ilya Ehrenburg. This canny survivor knew only too well what he was doing: within the Soviet ambience to call a writer a realist is often simply an enabling act, a way of making him a safe topic of conversation or a legitimate subject of inquiry.

Clearly, in dealing with Babel "isms" will be of little avail. More helpful is the notion offered by some of the keenest commentators on Babel, notably that of contrast, incompatibility, incongruity as the distinguishing characteristic of the Babelian universe, as the organizing principle of his prose. N. Stepanov, an erstwhile fellow traveler of Russian Formalism, speaks of the "equalization of disparate and incommensurate entities." V. Shklovsky puts it more vividly: "Babel's principal device is to speak in the same tone of voice about the stars above and gonorrhea."

The tendency to bring together incompatibles, to juxtapose contraries, is a shaping force at all levels of Babel's art, from style through theme to narrative manner. First, there is a use of the starting epithet, a tension

© 1987 by Victor Erlich. Published for the first time in this volume.

between the adjective and the noun: in one of the key Odessa stories, "The King," we read: "During the raid on the dreadful night when cows bellowed as they were slaughtered and calves slipped and slithered in the blood of their dams, when the torch flames danced like the dark village maidens, and the farm women lunged back in horror from the muzzles of amiable revolvers." The sample principle is operative here on the thematic level: the chief protagonist of the Odessa cycle, built around the exploits of the legendary Benya Krik, is a Jewish gangster, or even more paradoxically, an engaging and generous bandit. Incongruity is built into the structure of *Red Cavalry*. One of the major themes of this masterful cycle is the plight of the narrator, Lyutov, a dreamy, ineffectual Jewish *intelligent* in specs among Cossack roughnecks, who comprise the division to which, like Babel, he is assigned as a war correspondent.

Possibly the most quintessential Babelian contrast is that between manner and matter. Note the narrator's unruffled, businesslike tone as he relates in one of the *Red Cavalry* stories, "Berestechko," the savage murder of an old Jew suspected of spying for the enemy: "Then Kudrya of the machine gun squad took a hold of his head and tucked it under his arm. The Jew stopped screaming and straddled his legs. Kudrya drew out his dagger with his right hand and carefully, without splashing himself, cut the old man's throat.

It would be naive and hopelessly literal-minded to construe the underlying authorial stance as actual detachment. In fact, there is good reason to view it not as absence of affect, but as flight from it, to posit a compelling need for "distancing" the nearly unbearable emotion, for keeping it at bay.

In her book *The Art of Isaac Babel*, Patricia Carden quotes a telling passage from a letter Babel wrote to his family from the Polish front in 1920: "I went through two weeks of utter despair here. That was because of the ferocious cruelty that never lets up for a moment, and because I clearly understand how unfit I am for the business of destruction, how difficult it is for me to break away from the past."

One of the strategies at Babel's disposal, serving to protect and conceal his emotional vulnerability, to distance his moral revulsion, is hiding behind the mask of a more or less crude rapporteur, clearly different from the primary narrator, be he a dull-clod Kurdyukov, who, in "A Letter," relates stolidly and clumsily the murder by his brother of their Czarist policeman father, or—a somewhat more complex case!—a Bolshevik Cossack, Balmashev, not devoid of moral sensitivity and poetic flair, but all too ready to use his trusty rifle in order to rub off an "enemy of the people."

Where the voice of a Babel-like figure is unmistakably heard, the underlying disarray is often muted or deflected through a significant shift of emphasis or a displacement. An interesting case in point is provided by the double transformation in the *Red Cavalry* cycle of a 1923 reportage, "And Then They Were None," which has never been published in the original. (its English translation appears in the volume edited by Nathalie Babel, *You Must Know Everything*.) I do not mean to suggest that the relationship between the sketch, a polished and well-rounded piece of writing, and the *Red Cavalry* stories is simply one between *Wahrheit* and *Dichtung*. But "And Then They Were None" seems to hew closer to Babel's actual experience as it is directly related to two August 1920 entries in his Polish campaign diary. The central event, in both the diary entries and the sketch, is a summary execution of nine prisoners of war, an execution which the narrator is powerless to prevent. The wanton savagery of this illegal act weighs heavily upon the speaker: "The prisoners are dead, all nine of them; I feel it in my bones." The one *Red Cavalry* story which bears visible resemblance to "And Then They Were None," "The Squadron Commander Trunov," features a conflict between the narrator and Trunov over the handling of prisoners. Yet as the story progresses, Lyutov's rage over this wanton murder yields to the theme of the selfless heroism of Trunov's death. Interestingly enough, the rhythms of the speaker's anguish heard in "And Then They Were None" are echoed, though in a quite different context, in another *Red Cavalry* tale, "The Road to Brody": "I felt sorry about the bees. The fighting armies treated them most brutally. There were no bees left in Volhynia." It is a curious and significant fact that in *Red Cavalry* the only explicit acknowledgment on the speaker's part of his guilt over what is being done to the ravaged, brutalized countryside, the only direct and personal statement about the "ferocious cruelty" of it all, is concerned with defiling the beehives, rather than destroying human lives.

It is at least arguable that these techniques of displacing and distancing affect, more broadly, this contrast between tone and subject bears some relation to what a number of Babel watchers assume to be a profound inner split in the author of *Red Cavalry*. Critics—both friendly and hostile—expatiated upon Babel's oscillation between two codes—the code of the humane old Jewish shopkeeper, Gedali, who dreams about the "International of good people," and that of the "soldier of the revolution," Balmashev. No less important, to my mind, is the hovering between the world which gave birth to Babel, the world he never fully repudiated or abandoned, one of dignified ritual, cozy family warmth, of strict discipline and sense of duty, and the lure of the disheveled, the unknown, the exotic, the forbidden, indeed, the hostile. In an interesting essay on Babel as a Russian-

Jewish writer, Simon Markish states Babel's central dilemma and major aspiration perceptively and eloquently: "Not to reject tradition, not to turn away from one's own history, but instead to leap into freedom, into open space, to burst free from one's chains, to know the taste, color, scent, texture of everything denied by the ghetto wall . . . And to find harmony in dichotomy."

To find harmony in dichotomy, to reconcile the unreconcilables, to square the circle, here is a paradoxical and gloriously unrealistic project. Markish is right in believing that Babel did crave "harmony in dichotomy" even as he must have felt in his bones that he would never achieve it. No wonder that in the story which concludes the first edition of *Red Cavalry*, "The Rabbi's Son," the narrator's heart goes out to the Jewish outcast hero, Elijah Braclavskij, a "Jewish prince" and intrepid soldier of the revolution. Elijah Braclavskij, who served the cause until his dying breath, who incurs a fatal wound in trying to hold the enemy at bay in the face of a powerful Polish offensive, represents a triumph over incongruity, a successful, indeed a heroic synthesis of polarities: "His things were strewn about him pell mell—anecdotes of the propagandists and notebooks of the Jewish poet, the portraits of Lenin and Maimonides lay side-by-side, the knotted iron of Lenin's skull beside the dull silk of the portraits of Maimonides."

Lyutov's "spiritual brother" appears to have achieved what Markish has called harmony in dichotomy by forcing the disparate and seemingly incompatible beliefs and values into a life of total commitment, a life where the Bolshevik chieftain and the Jewish moralist merge in the consuming fire of passionate action.

It is fair to assume that for Babel, not unlike the narrator of *Red Cavalry*, "who can scarcely contain the tempests of his imagination within his age-old body," the conflict between Lenin and Maimonides remains unsolved. Not for the first time and not for the last time, what appears to have been in the writer's life a source of anguish or of a stalemate served to enrich and brilliantly complicate his art, to enhance the uniqueness and the keenness of his perception of the world.

II

Babel's *oeuvre* contains several remarkable narratives bearing directly on his concept of art and the artist, most notably, "Guy de Maupassant," "Di Grasso," and, in part, "In the Basement." "Line and Color" (1923) lacks their power and poignancy, yet it can be seen as a telling commentary on the texture of Babel's imagination. This slender story is built around an encounter between the narrator and a man who was soon to become head of the ill-fated Provisional Government, A. F. Kerensky. The setting is provided by a Finnish sanitarium which bears the lilting name Olila; the time is December 1916. After a lyrical invocation of "Helsingfors, dream of my heart," and an olfactory recreation of the Olila dining room, which "smelled of pine trees, of the Countess Tyszkiewicz's fresh shoulders, and of the English officer's silk underwear," the narrator recounts a walk in the woods with the voluble, and, as it turns out, nearsighted luminary. As the evidence of Kerensky's myopia mounts—he is unable to recognize a single person he meets en route—the following exchange ensues:

> "Alexander Fyodorovich, you ought to wear glasses!"
> "Never!"
> Then bubbling over like a mere boy, I said to him: "Just think, you're not merely blind, you're practically dead. Line, . . . mistress of the world, eternally escapes you. Here we are, you and I, walking about in this magic garden, this Finnish forest that almost baffles description. All our lives we shall never see anything more beautiful. And you can't see the pink edges of the frozen waterfall over there by the stream! You're blind to the Japanese chiseling of the weeping willow leaning over the waterfall . . . The snow, shapeless when it fell, has draped itself along the branches lying under surfaces that undulate like a line drawn by Leonardo . . . And think what you'd have to say about Fröken Kirsti's silk stockings, about the line of her leg, that lovely line! I beseech you, Alexander Fyodorovich, buy a pair of glasses!"
> "My child," he replied, "don't waste your time. Forty kopecks for spectacles of only forty kopecks I've no wish to squander. I don't need your line, vulgar as the truth is vulgar. You live your life as though you were a teacher of trigonometry, while I for my part live in the world of miracles . . . What do I need Fröken Firsti's freckles for, if even when I can scarcely make her out, I can see in her all I wish to see? . . . What do I need line for when I have color? To me a whole universe is a gigantic theater and I am the only member of the audience who hasn't glued opera glasses to his eyes. The orchestra is playing the overture to the third act; the stage is far away, just as in a dream. My heart swells with ecstasy. I see Juliet's purple velvet, Romeo's lilac silk, and not a single false beard. And you want me to blind myself with the forty kopek spectacles."

When Kerensky reappears in the finale, he is at the peak of his short-lived power. This time he is cast in the role of a grandiloquent and somewhat maudlin orator, exhorting his audience to persevere in defending mother Russia against the German armies, and seemingly oblivious to the mounting hostility of the crowd:

> Six months later I saw Alexander Fyodorovich one more: it was June, 1917, and he was now supreme god of our army and arbiter of our destiny.... A rally had been called at a House of the People, and there Alexander Fyodorovich made a speech about Russia—Russia, mystic mother and spouse. The animal passion of the crowd stifled him. Could he, the only member of the audience without opera glasses, see how their hackles were rising? I don't know. But after him, Trotsky climbed to the rostrum, twisted his mouth and in an implacable voice began: "Comrades!" [Not surprisingly, the last words of the story as it appears in the 1966 Soviet edition of Babel's selected writings are "I don't know."]

Let us retrace our steps. One of the salient aspects of the dialogue quoted above is that the sense of color, which is, after all, a visual phenomenon, seems less affected by myopia, or near blindness, than that of the line, of the contours of reality. The narrator doesn't question, or to be exact, is not offered an opportunity to question, Kerensky's gesture of consigning color to the realm of imagination, the dreamer's "gigantic theater of the mind." I cannot help but be reminded of Babel's own use of color—of the extravagant, "theatrical" color themes of the *Tales of Odessa*: "Aristocrats of Moldavanka, they [the bandits] were tightly encased in raspberry waistcoats. Russet jackets clasped their shoulders and on their fleshy feet the sky-blue leather cracked." Parenthetically, it is imagery such as this that moved V. Shklovsky to insist in his already quoted essay that Babel was good for Russian literature: "[Today's] Russian literature is as grey as a siskin: it needs crimson riding breeches and boots of sky-blue leather."

To be sure, one does not need to be Isaac Babel to appreciate the "Japanese chiseling of the frozen waterfall," or, for that matter, the line of *Fröken* Firsti's leg, more broadly, to insist that it is impossible to do justice to the world's beauty without being fully responsive to both the line and the color and the intricate interplay between them. Yet there is something unmistakably Babelian about making a myopic dreamer who is also a political sentimentalist and a rhetorician better attuned to the sound of his own voice than to the menacing growls of the people "out there," an impassioned champion of color, while exalting the "line," at once the principle of control, the form-giving, limit-setting artistic discipline, and the inexorable thrust of what Freud called "the reality principle." For the dichotomy which shapes the story can be shown to be operative on two distinct, but criss-crossing planes. In one sense "Color and Line" is a metaphor for Babel's own art, where the "orgy of color," the "tempests of the imagination," the richness and exuberance of imagery are disciplined, hemmed in, held in check by the "line," streamlined into unsurpassed concision and brevity. (Is there another prose writer within the Western tradition who makes one think at once of Nikolay Gogol and Guy de Maupassant?) Yet in a different context the metapoetic dialogue which ushers in the Kerensky–Trotsky antithesis may well suggest the conflict within the Babelian persona between daydreaming, which comes naturally to him, and the determination to face reality whatever the cost—especially if it means working against the grain—to confront the "implacable" exigencies of the life of action.

Through the 1930s Babel seems to have been oscillating between increasing dismay over the bleakness and sterility of accredited Soviet writing and, hoping against hope, between disenchantment and fierce loyalty to the revolutionary myth. Yet whatever his extraliterary delusions or confusions may have been, he never faltered in his commitment to what was for him the central and the least questionable value—exacting craftsmanship. It is this commitment which made it virtually impossible for him to produce dutiful socialist-realist fiction. It is said that when he was arrested in 1939, he was overheard by a witness to mutter "They didn't let me finish." Was he talking about the collectivization novel which he had been forcing himself to write for years or some other unfinished or unfinishable business? We may never know. What we have the right to assume is that when his turn came, the reality principle obtruded itself upon the stalemated master not in the guise of an implacable orator, but that of a silent executioner.

Chronology

1894	Isaak Emmanuilovich Babel born into a middle-class Jewish family in Odessa on July 13.
1895	Babel's family moves to nearby port, Nikolaev.
1899	Meril, Babel's only sister, born.
1905	Pogroms in Southern Russia. Family returns to Odessa. Babel enters Nikolai I Commercial School.
1911	Babel sent to Kiev to continue education at the Institute of Financial and Business Studies.
1913	Publishes first story, "Old Shloyme." Theme is anti-Semitism. Meets future wife Evgenia (Zhenya) Gronfein.
1914	War breaks out. Kiev Institute moves to Saratov.
1915	Writes "Childhood II: At Grandmother's." Graduates from Institute at Saratov. Returns to Kiev, then moves to Petrograd (now Leningrad), where he lives without a residence permit until the Revolution.
1916	Meets Maksim Gorky. Publishes, "Mama, Rimma and Alla" and "Il'ya Isaakovich and Margarita Prokofyevna" in Gorky's journal *Letopis'*. Czarist critics prepare charges of pornography. Babel publishes five new stories, grouped together as *Leaves from My Notebook*.
1917	Bolsheviks seize power. Babel volunteers for the new regime on the Rumanian front.
1918	Contracts malaria. Returns to Petrograd and works for the Cheka, the Bolshevik secret police. Requisitions grain on the Volga.

1919	Works for the People's Commissariat for Education. Returns to Odessa and marries Zhenya Gronfein.
1920	During the summer, serves in the Polish campaign as war correspondent for ROSTA, the Soviet news agency. Is attached to Budenny's First Cavalry Army, composed primarily of Cossacks. At the end of the year, returns to Odessa.
1921	Meets Konstantin Paustovsky. Publishes "The King," the first of the *Tales of Odessa* centered around the Jewish gangster, Benya Krik.
1922	Travels to the Caucasus to improve his health. Begins work on *Red Cavalry*.
1923	His father, Emanuel, dies. Stories from *Red Cavalry* begin to appear, along with "Line and Color" and new Odessa tales.
1924	Moves to Moscow. Continues to publish a wide variety of stories.
1925	Babel's sister goes to live in Brussels. His wife emigrates to Paris. He publishes "The Story of My Dovecot" and "First Love," and new stories from *Red Cavalry*.
1926	Babel's mother emigrates. First publication of separate edition of *Red Cavalry*.
1927	Travels to Europe to visit relatives and salvage his marriage. Refuses to join emigrés in Paris. *Tales of Odessa* published as a book.
1928	Returns to Russia. Publishes first play, *Sunset*.
1929	Babel's daughter, Nathalie, is born in Paris. First Five Year Plan. Babel is accused of giving a defammatory interview in Europe.
1930	Cleared of charges. Tours the countryside for material on collectivization.
1931	Four new stories appear, including "In the Basement" and "Awakening."
1932	Publishes "Karl-Yankel," "The End of the Poorhouse," and other stories. Meets producer Georgy Munblit. Visits relatives in Europe.

1933	Visits Gorky in Serento, then returns to Moscow. Expurgation of Babel's work begins.
1934	Defends himself at First Congress of Soviet Writers.
1935	Publishes second play, *Maria*. Leaves for Paris as a delegate to The Congress for the Defense of Peace and Culture.
1936	Maksim Gorky dies. Babel declares himself master of the genre of silence.
1937	Actress Antonina Pirozhkova gives birth to Babel's second daughter. Babel publishes "The Kiss," "The Inquiry," and "Di Grasso."
1938	Babel's last known story, "The Trial," appears.
1939	On May 10 Babel sends his last letter to his mother and sister. On May 15 he is arrested and his manuscripts confiscated.
1940	Babel is tried and sentenced by a military court. Charges unclear.
1941	Babel dies in captivity, causes unknown. Official date of death given as March 17.
1956	Babel is posthumously cleared of charges against him, his confiscated manuscripts officially declared lost.

Contributors

HAROLD BLOOM, Sterling Professor of the Humanities at Yale University, is the author of *The Anxiety of Influence, Poetry and Repression,* and many other volumes of literary criticism. His forthcoming study, *Freud: Transference and Authority,* attempts a full-scale reading of all of Freud's major writings. A MacArthur Prize Fellow, he is general editor of five series of literary criticism published by Chelsea House. During 1987–88, he was appointed Charles Eliot Norton Professor of Poetry at Harvard University.

VIKTOR SHKLOVSKY is a major Soviet literary scholar and a founder of the Russian Formalist school of literary criticism. His most important critical writings include *The Resurrection of the Word, Art as Device, On the Theory of Prose,* and *On Mayakovsky.*

RAYMOND ROSENTHAL has worked as a translator, writer, and critic, collaborating with Maria Ginzburg on the only English translation of Babel's play *Sunset.*

LIONEL TRILLING, former Professor of English at Columbia University, led a critical generation with such works as *The Liberal Imagination, Freud and the Crisis of Our Culture,* and *Beyond Culture: Essays on Learning and Literature.*

IRVING HOWE is an American author, historian, and Distinguished Professor of English at The City University of New York at Hunter College. His major works are *The Decline of the New, The Critical Point,* and *Word of Our Fathers.*

RENATO POGGIOLI, American scholar, critic, and translator, was Curt Hugo Reisinger Professor of Slavic and Comparative Literature at Harvard University. Mr. Poggioli's principal critical works are *The Phoenix and the Spider, The Poets of Russia, 1890–1930, Rozanov,* and *The Theory of the Avant-garde.*

FRANK O'CONNOR, born in Cork, Ireland, is a master of the modern short story. His best known collections of stories are *Crab Apple Jelly, Guests of the Nation, Bones of Contention, The Common Chord,* and *Domestic Relations.*

ILYA EHRENBURG, Soviet Russian writer and journalist, was one of the few prominent Jews to survive Stalin's purges. In 1952 he received the Stalin prize. His most successful work was his first novel, *The Extraordinary Adventures of Julio Jurenito.*

EDWARD J. BROWN, Emeritus Professor of Slavic Languages and Literatures at Stanford University, has written extensively on Soviet Literature. His major works are *The Proletarian Episode in Russian Literature, Russian Literature Since the Revolution,* and *Mayakovsky: A Poet in Revolution.*

ANDREY SINYAVSKY (pseudonym Abram Tertz) is an imaginative postwar Soviet writer who now lives in Paris. In addition to his fiction, his critical writings include *The Poetry of the Revolutionary Era, Strolling with Pushkin,* and *In the Shadow of Gogol.*

VICTOR TERRAS is Professor of Slavic Languages and Literatures at Brown University. Among his most notable writings are *The Young Dostoevsky 1846–49: A Critical Study, Belinsky and Russian Literary Criticism,* and *A Karamazov Companion: Commentary on the Genesis, Language and Style of Dostoevsky's Novel.*

KONSTANTIN PAUSTOVSKY, Soviet writer and art critic, was instrumental both in Isaac Babel's early success and in his later rehabilitation. His main work, *The Tale of a Life,* is in several volumes.

PATRICIA CARDEN is Professor of Russian Literature at Cornell University and author of one of the first monographs on Babel.

RICHARD W. HALLET is the author of a monograph on Babel's life and work and a lecturer in Russian language and literature at the University of Aberdeen. His play, *The Love Child,* was broadcast on BBC radio in 1972.

JAMES FALEN is Professor of Russian language and literature at the University of Tennesse, Knoxville. His book, from which the essay included in this volume is drawn, *Isaac Babel: Russian Master of the Short Story,* is perhaps the most illuminating single study of Babel.

SIMON MARKISH, a classical philologist by training, teaches at the University of Geneva, Switzerland. In addition to numerous translations of classical authors, his works include *Erasmus and the Jews* and a study of Russian-Jewish literature before 1917.

MAURICE FRIEDBERG is Professor of Russian Literature and Head of the Department of Slavic Languages and Literatures at the University of Illinois, Urbana. He is a coeditor of the *Encyclopaedia Judaica,* and his works include *The Part of the Poet in the U.S.S.R., The Jews in Post-Stalin Soviet Literature* and *A Decade of Euphoria: Western Literature in Post-Stalin Russia, 1954–64.*

GREGORY FREIDIN is Assistant Professor of Russian literature in the Department of Slavic Languages and Literatures at Stanford University. Mr. Freidin is the author of several studies on the work of Osip Mandelstam in addition to the essay here reprinted on Babel.

EFRAIM SICHER is Director of Russian Studies at the Ben Gurion University of the Negev, Beer-Shiva, Israel. He is the author of several essays on Babel in addition to the one reprinted here.

PETER STINE is Lecturer in the Department of English Language and Literature at the University of Michigan, Ann Arbor.

VICTOR ERLICH is Emeritus Professor of Slavic Languages and Literatures at Yale University and editor of *Twentieth-Century Russian Criticism* and of *Boris Pasternak: Twentieth-Century Views.* His most important works include the seminal study, *Russian Formalism: History, Doctrine, The Double Image: Concepts of the Poet in Slavic Literature,* and *Gogol.*

Bibliography

Andrew, Joseph. "Structure and Style in the Short Story: Babel's 'My First Goose.'" *The Modern Language Review* 70 (1975): 366–79.
Babel, Isaac. *You Must Know Everything Stories: 1915–37*. Edited by Nathalie Babel, translated by Max Hayward. New York: Farrar, Straus & Giroux, 1969.
Isaac Babel: The Lonely Years 1925–1939, Unpublished Stories and Private Correspondence. Translated by Andrew MacAndrew and Max Hayward, edited with an introduction by Nathalie Babel. New York: Farrar, Straus & Giroux, 1964.
Blake, Patricia, and Max Hayward, eds. *Dissonant Voices in Soviet Literature*. New York: Pantheon, 1962.
Brodal, Jan. "Fathers and Sons: Isaac Babel and the Generation Conflict." *Scando-Slavica* 17 (1971): 27–43.
Brown, Nathalie Babel. "Isaac Babel, Screen Writer." *Ulbandus Review: A Journal of Slavic Languages and Literatures* 1, no. 2 (Spring 1978): 86–98.
Brown, Edward J., ed. *Major Soviet Writers: Essays in Criticism*. New York: Oxford University Press, 1973.
Clyman, Toby. "Babel as Colorist." *Slavic and East European Journal* 21, no. 3 (1977): 332–43.
Cukierman, Walenty. "The Odessan Myth and Idiom in Some Early Works of the Odessa Writers." *Canadian-American Slavic Studies* 14, no. 1 (1980): 36–51.
Davies, Norman. "Izaak Babel's 'Konarmija' Stories and the Polish-Soviet War." *The Modern Language Review* 67 (1972): 845–57.
Ehre, Milton. "Babel's *Red Cavalry*: Epic and Pathos, History and Culture." *Slavic Review* 40 (1981): 228–40.
Ehrenburg, Ilya. *People and Life: Memoirs of 1891–1921*. Translated by Anna Bostock and Yvonne Knapp. London: MacGibbon & Kee, 1961.
Falchikov, Michael. "Conflict and Contrast in Isaak Babel's *Konarmiya*." *The Modern Language Review* 72 (1977): 125–33.
Fanger, Donald. *Dostoevsky and Romantic Realism*. Cambridge: Harvard University Press, 1965.
Gereben, Agnes. "Isaac Babel: Our Contemporary." *Acta Litteraria Academiae Scientiarum Hungaricae* 23, nos. 1–2 (1981): 1–26.
Grongaard, Ragna. *An Investigation of the Composition and Theme in Isaak Babel's Literary Cycle "Konarmija."* Aarhus, Denmark: Arkona, 1979.
Howe, Irving. "The Genius of Isaac Babel." *The New York Review of Books*, 20 August 1964, 14–15.

Hymen, Stanley E. "Identities of Isaac Babel." *The Hudson Review* 8 (1956): 620–27.
Klotz, Martin B. "Poetry of the Present: Isaac Babel's *Red Cavalry*." *The Slavic and East European Journal* 18 (1974): 160–69.
Lee, Alice. "Epiphany in Babel's *Red Cavalry*." *Russian Literature Triquarterly* 2 (1972): 249–60.
Leiter, Louis H. "A Reading of Isaac Babel's 'Crossing into Poland.'" *Studies in Short Fiction* 3 (1966): 199–206.
Lowe, David. "A Generic Approach to Babel's *Red Cavalry*." *Modern Fiction Studies* 28 (1982): 69–78.
Luplow, Carol G. *Isaac Babel's Red Cavalry*. Ann Arbor: Ardis, 1982.
Maguire, Robert A. *Red Virgin Soil: Soviet Literature in the 1920s*. Princeton: Princeton University Press, 1968.
Marcus, Steven. "The Stories of Isaac Babel." *Partisan Review* 22 (1955): 400–11.
Marder, Herbert. "The Revolutionary Art of Isaac Babel." *Novel A Forum on Fiction* 7 (1973): 54–61.
Matthewson, Rufus W., Jr. *The Positive Hero in Russian Literature*. Palo Alto: Stanford University Press, 1975.
Mendelson, Danuta. *Metaphor in Babel's Short Stories*. Ann Arbor: Ardis, 1982.
Munblit, Gregory. "Reminiscences of Babel." In *You Must Know Everything Stories: 1915–37*, by Isaac Babel, edited by Nathalie Babel, translated by Max Hayward, 259–73. New York: Farrar, Straus & Giroux, 1969.
Murphy, A. B. "The Style of Isaac Babel." *The Slavonic and East European Review* 64 (1966): 361–80.
Murphy, Brian. "An Introduction to the Stories of Isaak Babel." *Journal of Russian Studies* 47 (1984): 3–10.
Nilsson, Nils A. "Isaac Babel's Story 'Guy de Maupassant.'" In *Studies in Twentieth Century Russian Prose*, edited by Nils Ake Nilsson, 213–27. Stockholm: Almquist & Wiksell, 1982.
Paustovsky, Konstantin. "A Few Words About Babel." In *You Must Know Everything Stories: 1915–37*, by Isaac Babel, edited by Nathalie Babel, translated by Max Hayward, 275–83. New York: Farrar, Straus & Giroux, 1969.
Sicher, Efraim. "Art as Metaphor, Epiphany and Aesthetic Statement: The Short Stories of Isaac Babel." *The Modern Language Review* 77 (1982): 387–96.
Slonim, Marc. *Soviet Russian Literature: Writers and Problems, 1917–1953*. New York: Oxford University Press, 1977.
Stroud, Nicholas. "The Art of Mystification: The 'Prehistoric' Isaac Babel." *Russian Literature Triquarterly* 13 (1976): 591–93.
Struve, Gleb. *Russian Literature under Lenin and Stalin, 1917–1953*. Norman: University of Oklahoma Press, 1971.
Tertz, Abram [Sinyausky]. *On Socialist Realism*. Introduced by Czeslaw Milosz and translated by George Dennis. New York: Pantheon, 1960.
Williams, Gareth. "Two Leitmotifs in Babel's 'Konarmija.'" *Die Welt der Slaven* 17 (1972): 308–17.
Young, Richard. "Theme in Fictional Literature: A Way into Complexity." *Language and Style* 13 (1980): 61–71.
Zavalishin, Viacheslav. *Early Soviet Writers*. New York: Praeger, 1958.

Acknowledgments

"Isaac Babel: A Critical Romance" by Viktor Shklovsky from *Major Soviet Writers: Essays in Criticism,* edited by Edward J. Brown, © 1973 by Oxford University Press. Reprinted by permission.

"The Fate of Isaak Babel: A Child of the Russian Emancipation" by Raymond Rosenthal from *Commentary* 3 (January–June 1947), © 1947 by the American Jewish Committee. Reprinted by permission of the author and *Commentary.* All rights reserved.

"The Forbidden Dialectic: Introduction to *The Collected Stories*" (originally entitled "Introduction") by Lionel Trilling from *Isaac Babel: The Collected Stories,* edited and translated by Walter Morison, © 1955 by Criterion Books. Reprinted by permission.

"The Right to Write Badly" by Irving Howe from *The New Republic* 133, no. 27, 4 July 1955, © 1955 by The New Republic, Inc. Reprinted by permission of *The New Republic.*

"Isaak Babel in Retrospect" by Renato Poggioli from *The Phoenix and the Spider* by Renato Poggioli, © 1957 by the President and Fellows of Harvard College; © 1985 by Renato Poggioli. Reprinted by permission of Harvard University Press.

"The Romanticism of Violence" by Frank O'Connor from *The Lonely Voice: A Study of the Short Story* by Frank O'Connor, © 1962, 1963 by Frank O'Connor. Reprinted by permission.

"The Wise Rabbi (Memoirs)" (originally entitled "Memoirs: Chapter 15") by Ilya Ehrenburg from *Memoirs: 1921–41* by Ilya Ehrenburg, translated by Tatania Shebunina, in collaboration with Yvonne Kapp. © 1963 by MacGibbon & Kee Ltd. Reprinted by permission of Harper & Row Publishers and Granada Publishing Co.

"Isaac Babel: Horror in a Minor Key" by Edward J. Brown from *Russian Literature Since the Revolution* by Edward J. Brown, © 1963, 1969, 1982 by Edward J. Brown. Reprinted by permission of the author and Harvard University Press.

"Isaac Babel" by Andrey Sinyavsky from *Major Soviet Writers: Essays in Criticism,* edited by Edward J. Brown, © 1973 by Oxford University Press. Reprinted by permission.

"Line and Color: The Structure of Isaac Babel's Short Stories in *Red Cavalry*" by Victor Terras from *Studies in Short Fiction* 3, no. 2 (Winter 1966), © 1966 by Newberry College. Reprinted by permission.

"I Promise You Maupassant" by Konstantin Paustovsky from *The Story of a Life: Years of Hope* by Konstantin Paustovsky, © 1968 by Harvill Press and Pantheon Books, Inc. Reprinted by permission of Collins Publishers Ltd., and Pantheon Books, a Division of Random House, Inc.

"*Red Cavalry:* Art Renders Justice" by Patricia Carden from *The Art of Isaac Babel* by Patricia Carden, © 1972 by Cornell University. Reprinted by permission of Cornell University Press.

"Babel the Dramatist" by Richard W. Hallett from *Isaac Babel* by Richard W. Hallett, © 1972 by Richard W. Hallett. Reprinted by permission of the author and Basil Blackwell Publishers Ltd.

"*The Odessa Tales:* An Introduction" by James Falen from *Isaac Babel: Russian Master of the Short Story* by James Falen, © 1974 by the University of Tennessee Press. Reprinted by permission of the University of Tennessee Press.

"The Example of Isaac Babel" by Shimon Markish from *Commentary* 64, no. 5 (November 1977), © 1977 by the American Jewish Committee. Reprinted by permission of the author and *Commentary*. All rights reserved.

"Yiddish Folklore Motifs in Isaak Babel"s *Konarmija*" by Maurice Friedberg from *American Contributions to the Eighth International Congress of Slavists*, vol. 2, edited by Victor Terras, © 1978 by Slavica Publishers and Maurice Friedberg. Reprinted by permission of the author and Slavica Publishers.

"Fat Tuesday in Odessa: Isaac Babel's 'Di Grasso' as Testament and Manifesto" by Gregory Freidin from *The Russian Review: An American Quarterly Devoted to Russia Past and Present*, 40, no. 2 (April 1981), © 1980 the Russian Review, Inc. Reprinted by permission.

"Midrash and History: A Key to the Babelesque Imagination" (originally entitled "The Road to a Red Cavalry: Myth and Mythology in the Works of Isaak Babel of the 1920s") by Efraim Sicher from *The Slavonic and East European Review* 60, no. 4 (October 1982), © 1982 by the University of London (School of Slavonic and East European Studies). Reprinted by permission of the author, *The Slavonic and East European Review*, and their publisher, MHRA.

"Isaac Babel and Violence" by Peter Stine from *Modern Fiction Studies* 30, no. 2 (Summer 1984), © 1984 by the Purdue Research Foundation, West Lafayette, Indiana. Reprinted by permission.

"Color and Line: Notes on the Art of Isaac Babel" by Victor Erlich, © 1987 by Victor Erlich. Published in this volume for the first time. Printed by permission.

Index

Aesthetic sensibility, 27; moral sensibility through, 132
"Afonka Bida" (*Red Cavalry*), 132
"After the Battle" (*Red Cavalry*), 44, 100, 103, 105, 109, 110; Akinfiev in, 241; Liutov in, 110, 241
Aitmatov, Genghis, 174
Aizman, David, 173
Akhmatova, Anna, 245
Aleichem, Sholom, 17, 146, 151, 176, 187; influence of, on Babel, 45–46
Alienation, Babel and, 21, 48, 166
Anderson, Sherwood, 19
"And Then They Were None," 251
Apolek, 39, 124–27. *See also* "Pan Apolek"
Apollinaire, 218
"Argamab" (*Red Cavalry*), 101–2, 105; Baulin in, 244; Liutov in, 244
Art: Babel's Vision of, 123–33, 252–55
"At the Troitsa," 70
Auerbach, Erich, 125
"Autobiography," 79, 93–94, 176, 184, 187, 201, 215
"Awakening, The," 6, 17, 32, 189, 200; Nikitich Smolich in, 234; themes in, 202, 204

Babel, Isaac: aesthetic elements in fiction of, 27, 132; alienation and, 21, 48, 166; animal characteristics ascribed to humans by, 156–57; arrest, death, and rehabilitation of, 1, 16–17, 26, 42, 50, 58, 76, 85, 93, 248, 255; art as seen by, 71, 123–33, 252–55; artistic freedom and, 20–22; autobiographical writings of, 79, 93–94, 176, 184, 187, 201, 215; biographical data of, 17, 33, 41, 47–50, 69–76, 78, 135, 142, 143, 165, 175–76, 187, 215–16, 231–36, 257–59; Bolshevism of, 43; carnivalesque vision of, 199–214; Communist vs. Jewish culture in, 64–66; compared to Hemingway, 57–61; conflict and contrast (dramatism) in, 87–91, 100–103, 250; Cossacks and, 2–4, 12, 13, 14, 65, 73, 78, 80, 81, 82, 97–103, 146–47, 221–30, 233, 239, 242; daughter Natasha and, 177; death motif in fiction of, 100–101, 158–59; decapitation as theme in fiction of, 205–14; diary of, 70–71, 72, 80, 84–85, 222, 244, 251; displacement and distancing techniques in fiction of, 250–52; as dramatist, 135–42; eroticism in fiction of, 156–58; father (Emanuel) of, 31–32, 176, 234; father as theme in fiction of, 204–5; first published stories of, 215–16, 235–36; French influence on, 19, 27, 37, 48, 49, 55, 56, 58, 78, 114–15, 203, 235, 247–48; Gogel and, 13; Gorky and, 16, 33, 41, 42, 48, 69, 73, 74, 78, 91–92, 93–94, 115, 215, 216, 235, 245; grandmother of,

269

Babel, Isaac (*continued*)
178; the grotesque in fiction of, 130–33; happiness motif in fiction of, 46, 75, 194–95, 232; humor in fiction of, 92; ideals of writing of, 55, 147; irony in fiction of, 5–6, 26, 28, 38, 39, 79–81, 88, 101, 109–10, 167–68, 169, 217, 233–35, 247; Jesuits and, 62, 64; Jewish character of, 38–40, 48, 55, 82–83, 172–73; Jewish education of, 31–32; as Jewish writer, 4–8; journalistic pieces for *New Life* of, 235; on Kipling, 114; last stories of, 245–48; legend motif in fiction of, 99; "line" and "color" motifs in fiction of, 102, 106–11; literary place of, in Soviet era, 15–16, 171–89; on *Maria*, 142; on Maupassant's stories, 56; military experience of, 41, 49, 79, 143–44, 179, 235–36, 239; myth and mythology in fiction of, 215–30; narrative technique in fiction of, 152–53, 237, 245; natural history and, 32, 48, 75; nightmare genre in fiction of, 103; novella genre and, 104, 105, 107, 108; Odessa heritage of, 113–22, 149–55, 175–76, 177; parody in, 167; physical appearance of, 9, 29–30, 68–69; plot in fiction of, 104–5; poetical qualities of, 71; Polish Jews and, 44; popularity of, among foreign writers, 73; on *Red Cavalry*, 72–73, 245; religious traditions and, 176–77; "ride" and "end-of-ride" as themes in fiction of, 98–99; right to write badly concept of, 42; place of, in Russian-Jewish literature, 45, 48, 171–89, 251–52; self-criticism of, 73; as short-story writer, 1, 6; significant themes in fiction of, 94–95, 103–4, 106–11, 215–30; silence genre in fiction of, 25–26, 42, 74, 85, 87, 189, 215, 216, 217, 239, 245, 246, 248, 255; *skaz* (monologues) in, 97, 103, 104, 106, 109, 227, 239; Socialist Realism and, 142; social satire in fiction of, 101–3; speech at Congress for Defence of Culture (Paris, 1935) of, 75; speech at First Soviet Writers Congress (1934) of, 25, 42, 49, 176, 227, 246; spirituality of, 39–40, 247–48; stream-of-consciousness style of, 104; structural composition in, 107–11; style in, 18, 45–46, 58, 83–84, 88, 91, 94, 97, 104, 110, 169, 188, 236; three curses in life of (Poggioli), 48; tragic sense of life in fiction of, 246–48; truth vs. fiction in, 94–95; underworld (gangsterism) motif in fiction of, 59–60, 64, 85, 147, 149–50, 155, 158, 161–62, 163, 171, 184; violence in fiction of, 26–27, 28, 33–40, 43, 141, 142, 144–47, 165, 168–70, 231–48; wife of, 16–17, 70, 75; Yiddish influence in fiction of, 45–46, 48, 55, 176, 191–98, 216. *See also individual works.*

Babel, Nathalie, ed., *You Must Know Everything*, 235, 246, 251
Bagritsky, Edward, 69, 76, 148, 177
Bakhtin, Mikhail, 204; on Babel's carnivalesque vision, 199, 203
"Barat-Ogly and the Eyes of His Bull," 208
Barbusse, Henri, 73, 75; *The Fire*, 115
Begin, Menachem, 2
"Beginning, The," 68
Bely, Andrey, 67, 73
Benya Krik (film scenario), 93, 229
Berestechko, Volhynia, 39, 244
"Berestechko" (*Red Cavalry*), 84, 103, 206; Kudrya in, 4, 250; Countess Raciborska in, 105; Count Raciborski in, 111
Bergelson, David, 176
Bergson, Henri, *The Creative Mind*, 21
Berryman, John: on Babel's style, 45; *The Freedom of the Poet*, 237
"Betrayal" (*Red Cavalry*), 182
Bezymenskii, Alexander, 174
Bialik, Chaim, 2, 30, 31, 216
Blok, Alexander, 18, 114; "The Twelve," 81, 115, 227
Boccaccio, 104, 114

Borisovna, Yevgenia, 75
Brecht, Bertolt, 73; "To Posterity," 43
Breugel, Peter, the Elder, 199
"Brigade Commander, The" (*Red Cavalry*), 100, 108; Kolesnikov in, 35
Brighton Beach, New York, as "Little Odessa," 2
Buber, Martin, 193
Budenny, General Semën, 4, 18, 28, 30, 33, 41, 49, 50, 62, 63, 78, 79, 80, 97, 100, 115, 117, 143, 217, 229, 236, 239, 242, 245
Bunin, Ivan A., 67
Bykov, Vasil, 174

Callot, Jacques, 55
Carden, Patricia, *The Art of Isaac Babel*, 250
"Cemetery at Kozin, The" (*Red Cavalry*), 103, 105, 110, 223
Černobyl', Ukraine, Hasidic dynasty of, 192, 223
Chagall, Marc, 108
Chekov, Anton, 45, 48, 61, 73; "Mire," 55; *Three Sisters*, 191
"Chesniki" (*Red Cavalry*), 100, 108, 244; Pavlichenko in, 182
"Childhood II: At Grandmother's," 178, 216
Chronicle, 9, 48, 78, 91
Chronos myth, 203–4
"Church at Novograd, The" (*Red Cavalry*), 99; Christian myth in, 226, 229; Pan Romuald in, 105, 127, 206, 219
Civil War, Russian, 15, 18–20, 41, 57, 70, 83, 140, 165, 221; as literary theme, 77–78, 171. *See also* October Revolution; Polish campaign; Russian Revolution
Collected Stories, The, 149
Color: use of, in Babel's fiction, 153–55, 158–62
"Color" and "line," as literary motifs, 102, 106–111, 252–55
Compression, aesthetic of, 236
"Concert in Katerinenstadt, A," 218
Congress for Defence of Culture (Paris, 1935), 75

Congress of Soviet Writers, First. *See* Soviet Writers Congress, First
Cossacks, 19, 20, 47; Babel's view of, 2–4, 12, 13, 14, 65, 73, 78, 80, 81, 82, 97–103, 146–47, 221–30, 233, 239, 242; Jews and, 24, 28–30, 33–40, 52–53. *See also* "Ljubka the Cossack"; *Red Cavalry*
Crane, Stephen, 27, 33; Babel's stylistic similarities to, 45
"Crossing into Poland." *See* "Crossing the Zbruch"
"Crossing the Zbruch" (*Red Cavalry*), 98, 104, 106, 108, 224, 230, 239; Liutov in, 205, 207, 239–40; Savitsky in, 205, 207, 240

"Dante Street," 187, 246
Death motif, 232–33
"Death of Dolgushov, The" (*Red Cavalry*), 38, 44, 64, 82, 105, 108, 110; Liutov in, 241
Decapitation motif, 205–14
"Demidovka," 222
"Deserter, The," 235
Diary, of Babel, 70–71, 72, 80, 84–85, 222, 244, 251
"Di Grasso," 6, 37, 40, 73, 135, 252; attitude toward art in, 71; Carnival vs. Lent motif in, 199–214; di Grasso in, 201–2, 203, 205; Giovanni in, 201, 203, 205, 213; Kolia Schwartz in, 201–2, 203, 204; Mme Schwartz in, 202, 203, 204; narrator in, 201–2, 203, 248
"Discourse on the *Tachanka*" (*Red Cavalry*), 103, 180, 186, 240
"Doroga." *See* "Journey"

Ehrenburg, Ilya: on Babel, 80, 111, 249; *People, Years, Life*, 84; *The Second Day*, 73–74
Eisenstein, Sergei, 22, 27
"End of Saint Hypatius, The," 60
"End of the Old Folks Home, The" (*Tales of Odessa*), 6–7, 66, 185, 228, 246; Broidin in, 61–62; Lugovoy in, 7

Epiphany theory, aesthetic of, 27–28
Eroticism, in Babel's fiction, 156–58
Escape concept, in Babel's fiction, 17–18, 234–35
"Evening" (*Red Cavalry*), 102, 105, 182–83; Liutov in, 242

Fadeyev, Alexander: *The Nineteen*, 70; *The Rout*, 171
Falen, James E., *Isaac Babel: Russian Master of the Short Story*, 236
"Father, The" (*Tales of Odessa*), 157, 160; Basja in, 147, 155–56; Capon in, 156, 161, 162; Grach in, 185; Benya Krik in, 185; Mendel Krik in, 158–59, 185; Levka in, 185
"First Love," 6, 34, 47, 184, 200; narrator in, 210–13; Galina Rubstova in, 210–13, 233; theme in, 210–13
Five Roubles, 121–22
Flaubert, Gustave, 11, 19; influence of, on Babel, 27, 48, 55, 58
Fleer, Gedaliah, 193, 195
Flight. *See* Escape concept
Folklore: Yiddish/Jewish, 145–46, 191–98, 216. *See also* Myth and mythology
Forster, E. M., *Where Angels Fear to Tread*, 35
French influence, in Babel, 19, 27, 37, 48, 49, 55, 56, 58, 78, 114–15, 203, 235, 247–48
Freud, Sigmund, 29, 31, 46, 255
"Froim Grach." *See* "Line and Color"
Frug, Semyon, 173
Furmanov, Dmitri, 73, 81; *Chapeyev*, 171

"Gapa Guzhva," 188
"Gedali" (*Red Cavalry*), 40, 44, 72, 83, 99, 103, 105, 108, 109, 179, 181, 240–41; Hasidic motif in, 191–98; meaning of *Gedali*, 198
Goethe, J. W., *Italian Journey*, 204
Gogol, Nikolay, 1, 13, 200, 255; "The Overcoat," 73; *Taras Bulba*, 73
Gold, Mike, 68

Gorky, Maksim, 10, 24, 63, 67, 143; death of, 248; influence of, on Babel, 16, 33, 41, 42, 48, 69, 73, 74, 78, 91–92, 93–94, 115, 215, 216, 235, 245; on *Maria*, 188; "revolutionary romanticism" formula of fiction of, 49; "Two Souls," 9
Goya, Francisco, 54
Grotesque, use of, in Babel, 130–33
Gukovsky, G. A., 135, 136
"Guy de Maupassant," 6, 19, 20, 21, 73, 187, 217, 226, 252; Babel's literary credo in, 236; mature talent of Babel in, 55–56; Raisa (translator) and, 208–9, 247; as summary of Babel's spiritual journey, 247–48; themes in, 202, 208–10

Happiness. *See* Joy motif
Hasidism, 18, 19, 22, 65, 80, 83, 99; Braclav sect of, 192–93; "Černobyl' dynasty" of, 192, 223; as motif in "Gedali," "Rabbi," "Rabbi's Son," 191–98, 221, 223; origins of, 191
Haskalah (Jewish Enlightenment), 173
Hazlitt, William, 37, 39, 58
Hecht, S. G., 70
Hemingway, Ernest, 27, 33, 67; Babel compared to, 57–61
Historical action, as literary problem, 42–43
Hogarth, William, 55
"How It Was Done in Odessa" (*Tales of Odessa*), 157, 161; Ar'ye-Leyb in, 138, 159, 162, 163, 183, 193, 224, 238; Savka Butsis in, 3, 163; Froim Grach in, 150, 156, 164; Benya Krik in, 1, 2, 3, 150–51, 159, 162–63, 224, 225, 238; Muginstein in, 3, 151, 156, 159, 163; Aunt Pesya in, 1, 8, 238; Tartakovsky in, 151, 183, 238

Ilf, and Petrov, 148
"Ilia Isaakovich and Margarita Prokofievna," 179
Inber, Vera, 148

"In St. Valentine's Church" (*Red Cavalry*), 99, 127–33, 221; Apolek in, 129–33; Afonka Bida in, 129, 132–33; Pan Ludomirski in, 130–33; narrator in, 128–33; Sasha in, 128; themes in, 205–6; Tuzinkiewicz in, 127–28, 133
"In the Basement," 6, 46, 61, 189, 200, 202, 213, 227–28, 234, 252
Irony: in Babel, 5–6, 12, 14, 26, 28, 38, 39, 79–81, 88, 101, 109–10, 167–68, 169, 217, 247; as reflection of divided psyche, 233–35
Isaac Babel: The Lonely Years (Babel's letters), 176
Iskander, Faizul, 174
"Italian Sunshine" (*Red Cavalry*), 103; Sidorov in, 105, 108
Iushkevich, Semyon, 173
Ivanov, Vsevolod, 171, 179

Jabotinsky, Vladimir, 2
Jesuits, in Babel's fiction, 62, 64
"Jewess, The," 229
Jewish-Russian literature, 171–89
"Journey, The," 217
Joyce, James, 19, 67; *The Dubliners*, 27; meaning of epiphany in, 27
Joy vs. sadness motifs, 46, 75, 194–95, 232
"Justice in Parentheses," 217

"Karl-Yankel," 46, 61, 75, 76, 223–24; Ovsei Belotserkovskii in, 187; Naftula Gerchikan in, 188
Karpovich, Ivan, 75
Kataev, Valentin, 148
Kaverin, Benjamin, 174
Kaverin, V., *The End of Khaza*, 171
Kazakevich, Emmanuel, 175
Kerensky, A., 37, 208, 253–54, 255
Khava, Aunt, 113; Babel's recollections of, 117–22
Khlebnikov, 75
Kiev, 32, 70
"King, The" (*Tales of Odessa*), 14, 113–14, 153, 155, 156–57, 160, 161, 162, 217; Dvoyra in, 152, 156, 226; Eichbaum in, 2–3, 147, 149, 152, 237; Benya Krik in, 2–3, 47, 51, 54–55, 147, 149–50, 152, 164, 237–38, 250; Manja in, 150; Tartakovsky in, 147, 163, 164, 166
Kipling, Rudyard, 114
Kniga, 4
Kolesnikov, 107
"Kolyvushka," 188
Konarmiya. *See Red Cavalry*
"Konkin's Prisoner" (*Red Cavalry*), 100, 105, 110
"Kontsert v Katerinenshtadte." *See* "Concert in Katerinenstadt"
"Korol." *See* "King"
Kozin, 244. *See also* "Cemetery at Kozin"
Kronos myth, 203–4, 205

Lawrence, D. H., 35
Lenin, V. I., 61, 195, 196, 235, 241, 244, 252
Leonov, Leonid, *The Thief*, 171
Letopis. *See Chronicle*
"Letter, A" (*Red Cavalry*), 14, 103, 104, 182; Kurdyukov in, 250
Letters, of Babel, 176
Lezhnyov, I., 142
"Life and Adventures of Matthew Pavlichenko, The" (*Red Cavalry*), 4, 35–36, 50, 98, 105, 182, 227, 242; Nikitinsky in, 3, 98; Nadezhda Vasilyevna in, 3
Lifshitz (Livshitz), Izya L., 70, 114, 115
"Line and Color" (*Red Cavalry*), 12, 37, 60, 102, 187, 228, 252–55
"Line" and "color" literary motifs, 102, 106–11, 252–55
Literature, Russian-Jewish, 171–89
"Ljubka the Cossack" (*Tales of Odessa*), 147, 156, 157, 160, 162, 228, 238–39; Tsudechkis in, 239

Magdalene, Mary, 125, 219
Maimonides, 195, 252; *Guide of the Perplexed*, 196
Malraux, André, 43
"Mama, Rimma, and Alla," 179

Mandelstam, Nadezhda, 245; *Hope Against Hope*, 236
Mandelstamm, Osip, 111, 245, 248
Mann, Heinrich, 67, 75
Mann, Thomas, 67, 73
Marcus, Steven, 168
Mardi Gras. *See* "Di Grasso"
Maria, 140–42, 188, 225; Dymshits in, 140, 141; Golitsyn in, 140, 141; General Mukovnin in, 141; Lyudmila Mukovnin in, 140, 141; Maria Mukovnin in, 140–41; Viskovsky in, 141
Markov, P., 140
Marseilles, France, 69, 70
Martin du Gard, Roger, 73
Marx, Karl, 224
Maupassant, Guy de, 61, 114, 200, 255; influence of, on Babel, 1, 11, 18, 19, 21, 27, 48, 56, 104, 247–48
Mayakovsky, Vladimir, 69, 73, 215
Mendelssohn, Moses, 173
Mokher-Sforim, Mendele, 216
Moldavanka, 30–31, 54, 113, 117, 118, 119, 120, 136, 139, 141, 237, 246; underworld of, 147, 155, 158, 161–62, 163
Moral sensibility, through aesthetic sensibility, 132
Moscow Art Theatre, 136, 140
Mussolini, Benito, 69
"My First Goose," 33–34; Liutov in, 207, 241; Savitsky in, 35, 39, 105, 109, 182, 207, 241
"My First Honorarium," 69, 94, 208; theme in, 202
Myth and mythology, 215–30. *See also* Folklore

Nabokov, Vladimir (Sirin), 69
Nahman ben Simhah of Braclav, Reb, 192–98
Na pole chesti. *See* "On the Field of Honor"
Narrative technique, in Babel, 152–53, 237, 245
Nathan of Nemirov, Rabbi, 194
Natural history, Babel and, 32, 48, 75, 156–57
"New Day, The," 10

Nicholas I (Tsar), 106
Nicholas II (Tsar), 30, 211
Nietzsche, Friedrich, 206, 212; *The Birth of Tragedy*, 200, 214
Nikolaev, 47, 232, 242
Nikolayevna, Antonia, 70
Novitskii, Pavel, 172
Novograd, Ukraine, 80, 98, 105, 123, 126, 191, 229, 239, 240, 242. *See also* "Church at Novograd"
Novy Mir, 73

October Revolution, 15, 16, 20, 216; Babel's attraction to, 231. *See also* Civil War; Russian Revolution
Odessa, 1, 2, 3, 20, 21, 48, 136; Babel and, 16, 17, 47, 76, 92–93, 113–22; as characterized in "Di Grasso," 202–3; Jewish community in, 2–3, 21, 30–31, 183; as moral center of Zionism, 48. *See also* Moldavanka; *Tales of Odessa*
"Odessa" (*Tales of Odessa*), 216; aesthetic principles in, 92
Oforty, 216
"Oil," 69, 73
"Old Marescot's Family," 235
"Old Shloyme," 216
"On the Field of Honor," 216, 235

"Pan Apolek" (*Red Cavalry*), 50, 105, 109, 111, 200, 240; Apolek as Babel's double in, 99; Gottfried in, 218; Sashka Konyayev in, 226–27; real vs. mythical persons in, 126–27, 218–20, 226–27, 228; Romauld in, 206, 210; Tarakanych in, 227; themes in, 202, 205–6, 218–20, 226–28; views of humankind in, 124–27; Yanek in, 126
Pasternak, Boris, 245
Peretz, I. L., 17
Perry gonorar. *See* "My First Honorarium"
Petersburg 1918, 216
Petrograd. *See* St. Petersburg
Pilnyak, Boris, 18

Plato, violence and intellect in, 36
Platonov, Andrei, 171
Pogroms (1905), 34, 47, 60, 78
Polish campaign (1921), 19, 49, 80, 84, 88, 236, 239–44, 250, 251
"Prishchepa's Vengeance," 64, 72, 98
Prokofiev, Alexander, 172
Proust, Marcel, 69

"Rabbi (Rebbe), The" (*Red Cavalry*), 6, 99, 108, 109; Il'ja (Elijah) Bratslavsky in, 5, 104–5, 192, 195–96, 243; Motele Bratslavsky in, 180, 183, 192, 195, 197; Gedali in, 5, 197; Hasidic motif in, 191–98; Hershele in, 195; Reb Mordecai in, 5, 192; themes in, 202
"Rabbi's (Rebbe's) Son, The" (*Red Cavalry*), 6, 9, 99, 104, 105, 110, 111, 180; Il'ja (Elijah) Bratslavsky in, 5, 110, 192, 195–96, 221–22, 228, 243, 252; Motele Bratslavsky in, 5, 192, 195; Gedali in, 5; Hasidic motif in, 191–98
Rabelais, Francois, 200, 204; influence of, on Babel, 48
Radziwill, Janusz, 229
Raisa (translator), 208–9, 247
Red Cavalry, 2, 4, 6, 13, 24, 33, 39, 41, 45, 58, 62, 68, 74, 178, 201, 212, 215, 233, 237; Ivan Akinfier in, 110; Babel on, 72–73, 245; Balmasher in, 250, 251; Baulin in, 102; Afonka Bida in, 50, 82, 88, 99, 105, 107, 242; Il'ya (Elijah) Bratsklavsky in, 22, 99, 225; Motele Bratslavsky in, 22; coherence of stories in, 28; compassion in, 244; contrast and paradox in, 97; Cossack motif in, 24, 41, 42, 43–44, 50, 51–53, 233; cyclic elements in, 97; Dyakov in, 50; Elka in, 126; Galin in, 102; Gedali in, 50, 223, 243, 251; Gottfried in, 50, 127; Irina in, 102; Jewish themes in, 83; Khlebnikov in, 243; Kolesnikov in, 50, 100; Konkin in, 50; Benya Krik in, 65; Kirill Vasilievich Liutov in, 2, 124–33, 179–82, 187, 205–8, 217, 239–44, 250, 252; main themes in, 98, 106–11, 123, 164, 171, 179; moral issue in, 236; Pavlichenko in, 50, 98; publication of, 49, 71; real vs. mythical persons in, 126–27; revolutionary character of, 43; Sandy in, 243; Sasha in, 100; Savitsky in, 4, 5, 50, 89, 243; Shaveliov in, 100–101; Sidorov in, 103; Tikhomolov in, 101–2; time element in, 108; Trunov in, 89–90; underlying dialectic of, 239; Vasily in, 102; violence in, 144, 239–44; Voroshilov in, 100; Andrey Vosmiletov in, 90; Yiddish folklore motifs in, 191–98. *See also individual stories*
"Remount Officer, The," 103; Dyakov in, 71–72
Renard, Jules, 87
"Reply to an Inquiry, A," 208
"Road to Brody, The" (*Red Cavalry*), 98–99, 103, 108, 110, 240, 251; Afonka Bida in, 226
Rolland, Romain, 73, 74
Roman Catholicism, 99
Rousseau, Jean-Jacques, 20
Rubens, Peter Paul, 228
Runyon, Damon, 60, 61, 163
Russian Association of Proletarian Writers, 24–25
Russian-Jewish literature, 171–89
Russian language, Jewish Diaspora and, 173
Russian Revolution, 23–24, 26, 33, 37, 41, 42, 48, 78, 188, 195, 196, 197; Babel's attraction to, 231, 233–34, 239; Russian culture and, 174, 179. *See also* Civil War; October Revolution; Polish campaign

"Šabos-naxmu," 145; Hershele in, 145
Sacrilege, nature of, in Babel's fiction, 132
Sadness vs. joy motif, 194–95, 232

St. Petersburg, Russia, 48, 55, 73, 78, 91, 215, 216, 235, 247; Babel in, 10–11, 32–33; as scene of *Maria*, 140, 141
"Salt" (*Red Cavalry*), 6, 103, 104, 182; Balmashev in, 242; Kurdyukov brothers in, 242
Samuel, Maurice, *The World of Sholom Aleichem*, 32
"Sandy the Christ" (*Red Cavalry*), 99, 107, 109, 110, 243
Sapieha, Eustachy, 229
Sapieha, Lew, 229
Saturnalia, 204
"Scissors" symbolism, 70
Seaman, The, 113, 114
Serov, A., *Judith*, 209
Sforim, Mendele Mocher, 2
"Shabbes Nakhamu," 183; Hershele in, 183
Sholokhov, Mikhail, *And Quiet Flows the Don*, 171
Silence, as literary genre, 25–56, 42, 74, 85, 87, 189, 215, 216, 217, 239, 245, 246, 248, 255
Silone, Ignazio, 43
Simon Lop-Ear, 120–22
"Sin of Jesus, The," 226, 227
Skaz (monologues), 97, 103, 104, 106, 109, 227, 239
Smolich, Yefim Nikitich, 32
"Song, The" (*Red Cavalry*), 103, 110, 244
Soviet Writers Congress, First (1934), 25, 42, 49, 74, 85, 95, 176, 246
Spinoza, Baruch, 195, 228
Spirituality, in Babel, 39–40, 247–48
"Squadron Commander Trunov" (*Red Cavalry*), 100, 105, 107, 108, 109, 180; Communist vs. Jewish culture in, 65; Liutov in, 242–43, 251; Pugachov in, 242
"S.S. *Cow-Wheat*, The": Korostelyov in, 246; Makeyev in, 61, 246
Staiger, Emil, 98
Stalin, Josef, 7, 25, 41, 50, 66, 136, 171, 175, 188, 245, 248
Stora-Sandor, Judith, 176; on Babel's "Jewishness," 172
"Story of a Horse, The" (*Red Cavalry*), 105, 189; Khlebnikov in, 98; Savitsky in, 98

"Story of a Horse, Continued, The" (*Red Cavalry*), 103
"Story of My Dovecot," 6, 34, 55, 69, 74, 82, 94, 136, 184, 200, 210, 216; themes in, 204; victims of violence in, 232–33
Struve, Gleb, on Babel, 97, 102
Style, in Babel, 18, 45–46, 55–56, 58, 83–84, 88, 91, 94, 97, 104, 110, 169, 188, 236
Succoth, 28
Suleimenov, Oljas, 174
Sunset, 21, 49, 74, 93, 135–40, 141, 142, 184–86; Ar'ye-Leyb in, 138, 139, 186; Boyarsky in, 137; Dvoyra in, 137, 138; Benya Krik in, 137–39, 140, 204, 224, 225; Mendel Krik in, 137, 138–39, 186, 189, 204, 224–25; Lyovka in, 137, 138; Marusya in, 137–38, 139, 204, 225–26; performances of, in Russia, 136; underworld depicted in, 171; Ben Zkhar'ya in, 139
"Sunset," 140, 204
Sunset symbolism, 225

Tabidze, Titian, 172
"Tale About a Woman," 226
Tales of Odessa, 6, 13, 45, 74, 178, 187, 201, 215, 236, 254; aesthetic principles in, 92; Levka Byk in, 72, 156; carnivalesque motif in, 200; Eichbaum in, 169; essential Babel in, 58; gangsterism motif in, 59–60, 85, 149–50, 171, 184, 246; Froim Grach in, 169; Benya Krik in, 14, 20, 31, 147, 156, 163, 166–68; Mendel Krik in, 31; publication of, 49; violence in, 144–47. *See also individual stories*.
Talmud, Gedali's acquaintance with, 197–98
Tchernovitz, Chaim, 31
"Three O'Clock in the Afternoon," 178
"Through the Fanlight," 245–46
Time, mythic concept of, 203–4
Tolstoy, Lev, 2, 29, 44, 48, 247; *The Cossacks*, 52–53; *Hadji Murad*,

52–53; influence of, on Babel, 55–56; *What is Art?*, 55–56
"Treason" (*Red Cavalry*), 103, 104, 244
"Trial, The," 73
Trilling, Lionel, on Babel, 1, 2, 42, 43, 45, 52, 53, 55, 58, 59, 62, 64, 97, 236
Trotsky, Leon, 24, 37, 244, 245, 254, 255; "fellow traveler" terminology of, 49
Tsires, 113; Babel's recollections of, 117–22
Turgenev, Ivan S., 61
Tuzinkiewicz, 72
"Two Ivans" (*Red Cavalry*), 244; Liutov in, 243
Tynyanov, Yury, 12

Vilna, Lithuania, 48
Violence: in Babel's fiction, 26–27, 28, 33–40, 43, 141, 142, 144–47, 165, 168–70, 213–48; content vs. form of, 239–44; and intellect, 36; legitimate form of, 236–37; representations of, 2–4; romanticism of, 57–66

"Widow, The" (*Red Cavalry*), 100
Wiesel, Elie, 193–94, 196
"With Old Man Makhno," Kikin in, 60, 246
Yagoda, 26
Yakovlev, Kondrat, 11
Yaponchik, Mishka, 68
Yeats, William Butler, 35; "Easter 1916," 236
Yiddish folklore, 145–46; in *Red Cavalry*, 191–98, 216
"You Were Too Trusting, Captain," 60
Yudenich, Nikolai, 33

Zakat. See Sunset
"Zamoste" (*Red Cavalry*), 103
Zamyatin, *My* (*We*), 225
Zeus, 203, 204, 205
Žitomir (Zhitomir), 83, 191–92, 197, 240, 243

Boston Public Library

COPLEY S
GENERAL L

PG3476
.B2Z715
1987

87032033-02

The Date Due Card in the pocket indicates the date on or before which this book should be returned to the Library.

Please do not remove cards from this pocket.